SHELLEY'S EYE

Shelley's Eye
Travel Writing and Aesthetic Vision

BENJAMIN COLBERT

LONDON AND NEW YORK

First published 2005 by Ashgate Publishing

Published 2016 by Routledge
2 Park Square, Milton Park, Abingdon, Oxon OX14 4RN
711 Third Avenue, New York, NY 10017, USA

Routledge is an imprint of the Taylor & Francis Group, an informa business

Copyright © Benjamin Colbert 2005

Benjamin Colbert has asserted his moral right under the Copyright, Designs and Patents Act, 1988, to be identified as the author of this work.

All rights reserved. No part of this book may be reprinted or reproduced or utilised in any form or by any electronic, mechanical, or other means, now known or hereafter invented, including photocopying and recording, or in any information storage or retrieval system, without permission in writing from the publishers.

Notice:
Product or corporate names may be trademarks or registered trademarks, and are used only for identification and explanation without intent to infringe.

British Library Cataloguing in Publication Data
Colbert, Benjamin
    Shelley's eye : travel writing and aesthetic vision. – (The nineteenth century series)
    1.Shelley, Percy Bysshe, 1792-1822 – Knowledge – Europe 2.Shelley, Percy Bysshe, 1792-1822 – Travel – Europe 3.Shelley, Percy Bysshe, 1792-1822 – Aesthetics 4.Travelers' writings, English – History and criticism 5.English literature – 19th century – History and criticism 6.Travelers – Europe – History – 19th century 7.British – Europe – History – 19th century 8.English poetry – European influences 9.Aesthetics, British – 19th century 10.Europe – Description and travel
    I.Title
    821.7

Library of Congress Cataloging-in-Publication Data
Colbert, Benjamin, 1961-
    Shelley's eye : travel writing and aesthetic vision / Benjamin Colbert.
      p. cm.—(The nineteenth century series)
    Includes bibliographical references and index.
    ISBN 0-7546-0485-3 (alk. paper)
    1. Shelley, Percy Bysshe, 1792-1822—Knowledge—Europe. 2. Shelley, Percy Bysshe, 1792-1822—Travel—Europe. 3. Travelers' writings, English—History and criticism. 4. Shelley, Percy Bysshe, 1792-1822—Aesthetics. 5. Travelers—Europe—History—19th century. 6. British—Europe—History—19th century. 7. English poetry—European influences. 8. Aesthetics, British—19th century. 9. Europe—Description and travel. 10. Europe—In literature. I. Title. II. Series: Nineteenth century (Aldershot, England).

PR5442.E85C65 2004
821'.7—dc22

2004013563

ISBN 13: 978-0-7546-0485-3 (hbk)

Contents

List of Illustrations		*vi*
General Editors' Preface		*vii*
Acknowledgements		*viii*
List of Abbreviations		*ix*

Introduction		1
1	'The Sun Rises over France': Post-Napoleonic Travellers' Europe	11
2	'Citizens of the World': Dislocated Vision in *Alastor*	44
3	'The Raptures of Travellers': Writing Mont Blanc	81
4	'Relics of Antiquity': Shelley's Classical Tour through Italy	116
5	'The Emblem of Italy': Two-Fold Vision in *Prometheus Unbound*	185
6	'Empire o'er the Unborn World': Shelley's *Hellas*	205
Bibliography		237
Index		250

List of Illustrations

Fig. 1 Detail from *Julian and Maddalo* MS.
MS. Shelley Adds. e. 11, p. 65.   9

Fig. 2 'Cascade of Terni': plate 16 and facing page from
Select Views in Italy . . . by John Smith, 1816.
Reference (shelfmark) 20503 d. 55.   167

Fig. 3 'Cascade of Terni': plate 7 and facing page from
A Picturesque Tour of Italy, from Drawings by J. Hakewill, 1820.
Reference (shelfmark) 20503 d. 44.   168

Fig. 4 Frontispiece from *Description of the Camera Lucida . . . by G. Dolland, 1830.*
Reference (shelfmark) G. Pamph. 2312 (5).   170

Fig. 5 Fold-out map from *An Explanation of the View of Rome . . . by R. R. Reinagle, 1817.*
Reference (shelfmark) 17006 d. 235 (4).   175

All reproductions have been supplied with kind permission from The Bodleian Library, University of Oxford.

The Nineteenth Century Series
General Editors' Preface

The aim of the series is to reflect, develop and extend the great burgeoning of interest in the nineteenth century that has been an inevitable feature of recent years, as that former epoch has come more sharply into focus as a locus for our understanding not only of the past but of the contours of our modernity. It centres primarily upon major authors and subjects within Romantic and Victorian literature. It also includes studies of other British writers and issues, where these are matters of current debate: for example, biography and autobiography, journalism, periodical literature, travel writing, book production, gender, non-canonical writing. We are dedicated principally to publishing original monographs and symposia; our policy is to embrace a broad scope in chronology, approach and range of concern, and both to recognize and cut innovatively across such parameters as those suggested by the designations 'Romantic' and 'Victorian'. We welcome new ideas and theories, while valuing traditional scholarship. It is hoped that the world which predates yet so forcibly predicts and engages our own will emerge in parts, in the wider sweep, and in the lively streams of disputation and change that are so manifest an aspect of its intellectual, artistic and social landscape.

Vincent Newey
Joanne Shattock

University of Leicester

Acknowledgements

This book would not and could not have been written but for the encouragement, support, and advice of my family, friends, and colleagues over what now must be many years. I am extremely grateful to Frederick Burwick for supervising the doctoral dissertation that spanned continents and became, through mysterious byways, the map for this book. Those who helped me see ways forward (and may not always recall having done so) include Charles L. Batten, Bruce Barker-Benfield, Betty T. Bennett, Jan Borm, Sarah Capitanio, Urszula Clark, Josie Dixon, Glyn Hambrook, Betty Hagglund, Gary Harrison, Jill Heydt-Stevenson, Nicholas A. Joukovsky, Rosie Miles, Jeanne Moskal, Graham Rees, John Strachan, Hilary Weeks, Frank Wilson, and Duncan Wu.

I would particularly like to thank Nora Crook, whose comments and criticisms on Chapter 4 helped make this a better and more accurate book, and Keith Crook for sharing with me his great knowledge of Joseph Forsyth and the Byron-Shelley circle. I am also grateful to my anonymous reader at Ashgate for generous and helpful suggestions; also to Vincent Newey, co-editor of the Series, for reading a late draft of the *Alastor* chapter. All errors and infelicities, of course, belong solely to myself.

Shelley's Eye was planned during a timely sabbatical awarded by the University of Wolverhampton, School of Humanities, Languages and Social Sciences, and supported for several years thereafter in smaller but no less important ways. Most of my research was conducted at The Bodleian Library, Oxford, and I would like to thank the staff of the Upper Reading Room and Duke Humphries Room for their courteous assistance. Similarly, I am grateful to those who have assisted me at the British Library and the Bibliothèque National de France. Finally, I am especially grateful to the Arts and Humanities Research Board for the Research Leave Award that allowed me to finish this book.

Some material on Arthur Young and the picturesque from Chapter 1 has previously been published in *European Romantic Review*, 13.1 (2002), 23-34. Similarly, a version of the opening section on the *History of a Six Weeks' Tour*'s reception in Chapter 3 first appeared in *Keats-Shelley Journal*, 48 (1999), 22-9. I would like to thank these journals and their editors for permission to reuse these materials here. I would also like to thank Oxford University Press for permission to include generous quotations from Shelley's travel letters in *The Letters of Percy Bysshe Shelley*, ed. Frederick L. Jones, 2 vols (Oxford: Clarendon Press, 1964).

List of Abbreviations

Byron LJ *Byron's Letters and Journals*, ed. Leslie A. Marchand, 13 vols (London: John Murray, 1973-94).

Byron PW Lord Byron, *Complete Poetical Works*, ed. Jerome McGann, 7 vols (Oxford: Clarendon Press, 1980-93).

CCJ *The Journals of Claire Clairmont*, ed. Marion Kingston Stocking, with the assistance of David Mackenzie Stocking (Cambridge, MA: Harvard University Press, 1968).

CT John Chetwode Eustace, *A Classical Tour through Italy*, 3rd edn, revised and enlarged, 4 vols (London: Printed for J. Mawman, 1815).

Excursion William Wordsworth, *The Excursion, Being a Portion of The Recluse, a Poem* (London: Printed for Longman, Hurst, Rees, Orme, and Brown, 1814). *Excursion* is followed by the book and page number. Line numbers in brackets refer to *The Poetical Works of William Wordsworth*, eds E. de Selincourt and Helen Darbishire, vol. 5 (Oxford: Clarendon Press, 1949).

HSWT Mary Shelley and Percy Bysshe Shelley, *History of a Six Weeks' Tour through a Part of France, Switzerland, Germany, and Holland: with Letters Descriptive of a Sail round the Lake of Geneva, and of the Glaciers of Chamouni* (London: Published by T. Hookham, Jun.; and C. and J. Ollier, 1817).

L *The Letters of Percy Bysshe Shelley*, ed. Frederick L. Jones, 2 vols (Oxford: Clarendon Press, 1964).

LSND Mary Wollstonecraft, *Letters Written during a Short Residence in Sweden, Norway, and Denmark* (London: Printed for J. Johnson, 1796).

LTLP *The Letters of Thomas Love Peacock*, ed. Nicholas A. Joukovsky, 2 vols (Oxford: Clarendon Press, 2001).

MWSJ	*The Journals of Mary Shelley*, ed. Paula R. Feldman and Diana Scott-Kilvert (Baltimore and London: Johns Hopkins University Press, 1995).
MWSL	*The Letters of Mary Wollstonecraft Shelley*, ed. Betty T. Bennett, 3 vols (Baltimore and London: Johns Hopkins University Press, 1980-88).
MSW	*The Novels and Selected Works of Mary Shelley*, gen. ed. Nora Crook, 8 vols (London: William Pickering, 1996).
Prose	*Shelley's Prose or the Trumpet of a Prophecy*, ed. David Lee Clark (London: Fourth Estate, 1988).
PS1	*The Poems of Shelley*, ed. Geoffrey Matthews and Kelvin Everest, vol. 1: 1804-1817 (London and New York: Longman, 1989).
PS2	*The Poems of Shelley*, ed. Kelvin Everest and Geoffrey Matthews, vol. 2: 1817-1819 (Harlow: Longman, 2000).
PW	*Shelley: Poetical Works*, ed. Thomas Hutchinson, corr. G. M. Matthews (Oxford: Oxford University Press, 1970).
SC	*Shelley and His Circle 1773-1822*, ed. K. N. Cameron, vols 1-4 (Cambridge, MA: Harvard University Press, 1961-70), ed. Donald H. Reiman, vols 5-8 (Cambridge, MA: Harvard University Press 1973-86), ed. Donald H. Reiman and Doucet Devin Fischer, vols 9-10 (Cambridge, MA: Harvard University Press, 2002). *SC* followed by a number = Pforzheimer's classification of a manuscript in its collection.
SPP	*Shelley's Poetry and Prose*, 2nd edn, ed. Donald H. Reiman and Neil Fraistat (New York and London: W. W. Norton & Company, 2002).
WTLP	*The Halliford Edition of the Works of Thomas Love Peacock*, eds H. F. B. Brett-Smith and C. E. Jones, 10 vols (London: Constable & Co., Ltd; New York: Gabriel Wells, 1924-34).

WW Prose	*The Prose Works of William Wordsworth*, eds W. J. B. Owen and Jane Worthington Smyser, 3 vols (Oxford: Clarendon Press, 1974).

Introduction

When continental Europe reopened to British travellers in 1814 and 1815, Sir Richard Colt Hoare anticipated a renewal of modes of travel he had known some twenty-five years previously. To 'smooth the way' for the 'inexperienced tourist', he quickly published a 'retrospective' guidebook, *Hints to Travellers in Italy* (1815), that unflinchingly recommends outdated books and maps, most published before 1786, and recounts his own youthful experiences in organising transportation, letters of credit, and passports, as if nothing essential had changed. In Hoare's view, young tourists of any era resemble each other; they travel with fresh eyes, unencumbered by nostalgia for what might no longer be seen on the beaten track. Two decades of revolutionary upheaval, the removal or destruction of art and antiquities by Napoleon's conquering armies, the redrawing of political boundaries, all are as nothing to the excitement of first impressions, and the seasoned traveller need only recall his own first steps abroad to sympathise. Yet Hoare also acts the part of fireside tutor, chiding inexperienced travellers lest they display the wrong kinds of excitement: 'I should entertain but a mean opinion either of the taste or enthusiasm of any young man, who, on the morning subsequent to his arrival at Rome, did not . . . hurry to see the Coliseum'. *Hints to Travellers* thus becomes a synopsis of the goals and values of 'what has generally been denominated the GRAND TOUR OF THE CONTINENT', refashioned for a new generation.[1]

Six years later, after thousands had made their European tours and hundreds had published accounts of them, one reviewer complained:

> It is certainly somewhat extraordinary, that of the great number of travellers sent forth by the peace from this country, with the design of recording their adventures, so few should have deviated from the most frequented routes. We hardly, indeed, can recollect above two or three who have written upon any thing beyond the limits of the *Grand Tour*.[2]

Although this was something of an exaggeration, the Grand Tour had left a legacy of well-developed tourist infrastructures, including posting routes, accommodations, and destinations.[3] Of course, there were novel variations and developments: the French wars added battlefields, especially Waterloo, to the

---

[1] Sir Richard Colt Hoare, *Hints to Travellers in Italy* (London, 1815), pp. 27; 74.
[2] Review of *A Tour through the Southern Provinces of the Kingdom of Naples*, by the Hon. Richard Keppel Craven. *Edinburgh Review*, 36 (Oct. 1821), pp. 153-4.
[3] For a statistical analysis of tourist destinations and objects of attention during the era of the Grand Tour, see John Towner, *An Historical Geography of Recreation and Tourism in the Western World, 1540-1940* (Chichester: John Wiley & Sons, 1996), pp. 96-138.

sightseeing itinerary; new fashions for picturesque tourism increased traffic to the Swiss Alps and on the Rhine; excavations at Pompeii and in the Roman Forum uncovered fresh attractions in Italy. Nevertheless, the British predilection for European cultural centres – Paris, Geneva, Rome, Naples – was as vigorous as ever and the 'tourist circuit' remained largely intact. Even trends towards greater class diversity among travellers did not entirely disturb such cultural imperatives. While affluence of would-be Grand Tourists lessened, as the post-war disparity between home and continental prices increased in Britain's favour, the rising middle classes regarded the European tour as a means of 'cultural accreditation'.[4] Gentlemen travellers, meanwhile, fought a rearguard action to uphold their privileges as cosmopolites by producing and buying expensive quarto editions of travel writing interlarded with classical quotations in Greek and Latin, or by forming cliques at home, such as the Traveller's Club (1819).

Nevertheless, several recent scholars have emphasised ways in which the formal patterns of Grand Tourism cannot conceal real changes in its substance, and have pronounced the post-Napoleonic Grand Tour dead on arrival. Brian Dolan argues that the war years shifted attention to Europe's peripheries, introducing a comparative method into cultural inquiry that forever changed the forms of European self-consciousness at heart of the Grand Tour.[5] Katherine Turner holds that the Tour was always something of a fiction, since its spokespersons, even in its heyday, tended to emerge from the middling ranks of society; if gentlemen paid for their sons' tours, it was their 'bearleaders', or tutors, many of them clergymen, who published the accounts.[6] Though there is a great deal of truth in these observations, I would like to suggest that in the years following 1815 the ideology of the Grand Tour held a new attraction, as re-experiencing 'old' Europe became integral to updating or redefining the traveller's new sense of national identity in the aftermath of the French Revolution. The war years had forced would-be tourists to look internally. William Gilpin and Thomas West, for example, helped popularise Lake District tourism as an alternative to Alpine adventures, and new tastes for the picturesque and the 'primitive' led travellers in increasing numbers to Scotland, Ireland, and Wales.[7] Robin Jarvis and Ann Wallace have discussed how in these years pedestrian tourism received new impetus, as the domestic subject measured out his or her relationship with the environment, stride by stride. As Jarvis puts it, the pedestrian subject, increasingly from the professional class, used

---

[4] James Buzard, *The Beaten Track: European Tourism, Literature, and the Ways to Culture, 1800-1918* (Oxford: Clarendon Press, 1993), p. 110. Buzard argues, however, that Romantic travel writers sought new forms of 'accreditation' that would free them from feelings of 'belatedness'.

[5] Brian Dolan, *Exploring European Frontiers: British Travellers in the Age of Enlightenment* (London: Macmillan, 2000), pp. 1-24 *passim*.

[6] Katherine Turner, *British Travel Writers in Europe, 1750-1800: Authorship, Gender and National Identity* (Aldershot: Ashgate, 2001), pp. 56-8.

[7] See, for example, Malcolm Andrews, *The Search for the Picturesque: Landscape Aesthetics and Tourism in Britain, 1760-1800* (Stanford: Stanford University Press, 1989), and John Glendening, *The High Road: Romantic Tourism, Scotland and Literature, 1720-1820* (Basingstoke: Macmillan, 1997).

walking as 'a radical assertion of autonomy'.[8] In post-war Europe, however, travellers and travel writers balanced, like Sir Richard Colt Hoare, between the impulse to see everything afresh, and the desire to reoccupy known haunts. In most of the post-war travel accounts considered in this study, a new and urgent emphasis is placed on time-honoured characteristics of travel and travel writing: observation, description, and interpretation. Travel writers asserted their authority as on-the-spot cultural commentators, recording phenomena, anatomising the national subjects they encounter, and sculpting a world view in which European cultural values were resuscitated and redefined to fit new political and economic circumstances.

The years 1814-22 were crucial, as Paul Johnson has argued, for 'the birth of the modern' after its revolutionary gestation.[9] However, modernity emerges not so much as a set of ideas or ideals reified in Romantic literature, but as a practice of seeing and writing about the world, and travel writing records this parturition better than any other discourse. Travellers turned their invigorated gazes first upon Waterloo and France, with a deluge of poems and travel accounts that transformed, in Philip Shaw's words, 'images of pain and suffering . . . into a site of individual and national resubstantiation'.[10] The Parisian capital offered what the journalist John Scott referred to as 'a glass beehive' in which scrutiny of the French empowered the British tourist to moralise on the extent to which government shapes character and to which character is political destiny.[11] The picturesque eye, trained by domestic tourism, was now at home in Switzerland, and travel writers fell to Alpine landscape description with new gusto. By 1818, travellers increasingly turned their attention to the Italian sites of the Grand Tour, once again interrogating how classicism might be incorporated into a modern British cultural consciousness.

Troublingly to contemporary moralists, this new orientation emerges under the sign of mass travel and mass culture. Three years into the continental scrum, the Reverend J. W. Cunningham published an anxious response to this state of affairs, *Cautions to Continental Travellers* (1818). Cunningham plays up the Malthusian explosion of tourism, estimating that '90,000 persons had embarked, in little more than two years, from one port alone', many lured by shallow, albeit fashionable motives: 'restlessness', 'ill-defined curiosity', 'ennui', 'love of dissipation', the 'spirit of wandering', 'a fancied regard to works of art', 'love of novelty', 'superabundance of money', and the 'consideration that "every body travels"'.[12]

---

[8] Robin Jarvis, *Romantic Writing and Pedestrian Travel* (Basingstoke: Macmillan, 1997), p. 29. See also, Anne D. Wallace, *Walking, Literature, and English Culture: The Origins and the Uses of Peripatetic in the Nineteenth Century* (Oxford: Clarendon Press, 1993).
[9] See Paul Johnson, *The Birth of the Modern: World Society, 1815-1830* (London: Weidenfeld and Nicolson, 1991), p. xvii: 'the actual birth, delayed by the long, destructive gestation period formed by the Napoleonic Wars, could begin in full measure only when the peace came'.
[10] Philip Shaw, *Waterloo and the Romantic Imagination* (London: Palgrave, 2002), p. 74.
[11] John Scott, *A Visit to Paris in 1814* (London, 1815), p. 53.
[12] J. W. Cunningham, *Cautions to Continental Travellers* (London, 1818), pp. 3; 9-10.

Swelling the numbers of this new breed of travellers, he laments, are those who are most impressionable: 'the young', 'females', and 'the subordinate classes of society'. Ill equipped to withstand the 'contagion' of foreign manners, these travellers threaten to enervate the British national character by weakening domestic and commercial foundations. While the gentlemen of the Grand Tour might be dismissed as macaronis or idle fops, Cunningham fears that the 'middling classes will transplant to the desk and the counting-house the habits of those . . . whose empty heads, and hollow hearts, and sceptical opinions, have assisted to hurry on the storm by which anarchy and irreligion have been conspiring to desolate some of the fairest portions of the globe'.[13] The previous year, William Jerdan's *Six Weeks in Paris; or, A Cure for the Gallomania* (1817; 2nd edn, 1818) portrayed the French capital as a world of mass tourist pleasure designed to break down an Englishman's moral fibre. Against this threat, Jerdan's 'Lord Beacon', a young gentleman fresh from Oxford, preserves the Grand Tourist ethos into modern times, lighting the way for others. His French guide, M. Fanfaron (a thinly veiled version of Napoleon's Minister of Police, Joseph Fouché), reveals a conspirator's Paris in which Napoleonic networks of internal espionage now function to keep tabs on tourists: hoteliers, guides, actresses, women of pleasure, and footpads all act their parts in a choreographed fleecing of the English. In Jerdan's satire, the *Palais Royal* forms a spectacle of interconnected pleasure and vice, gentility and vulgarity in French society, a vortex that would draw in the unwary traveller.

Others located the deleterious effects of mass travel culture closer to home. As Gillen D'Arcy Wood has recently argued in *The Shock of the Real: Romanticism and Visual Culture, 1760-1860* (2001), an array of cultural guardians including Royal Academicians and Romantic poets distrusted the mass appeal of popular visual entertainments that increasingly relied on travel verisimilitude for their effects.[14] The panorama was by far the most successful of these shows. For the admission price of a shilling, pedestrians left the bustling streets of London or Edinburgh and emerged as travellers to distant cities, picturesque viewpoints, and battlefields: 'The Storming of Seringapatam', 'The Battle of Trafalgar', 'Panorama of Paris, 'The View of Rome, Taken from the Tower of the Capitol'.[15] What Wood refers to as 'spectacular realism'[16] was created by Barker's realisation that new principles of perspective could be applied in the round; with advanced lighting techniques and a carefully positioned central viewing platform, a reality effect could be created without the discomforts and expense of actual travel. What then was the special value of travel? The answer to some, like Wordsworth and Coleridge, was that travel developed 'habits of mind' conducive to heightened

---

[13] Cunningham, *Cautions*, p. 19.
[14] Gillen D'Arcy Wood, *The Shock of the Real: Romanticism and Visual Culture, 1760-1860* (New York: Palgrave, 2001), pp. 6-14; 102-104.
[15] These are titles of various panoramas displayed in London and Edinburgh. See the exhibition catalogue by Ralph Hyde, *Panoramania! The Art and Entertainment of the 'All-Embracing' View* (London: Trefoil Publications, 1988), pp. 65-74. See also, Richard Altick, *The Shows of London* (Cambridge, MA: Harvard University Press, 1978), pp. 130-83.
[16] Wood, *Shock of the Real*, p. 101.

imaginative experience of the world rather than the static consumption of 'scenes', the immoveable and cheapened imagery of popular cultural accreditation.[17]

Shelley's life and work uniquely embody these post-Napoleonic tensions between Grand Tourism, modern travel, and mass culture. Shelley's father, a wealthy Sussex gentleman who had himself undertaken the Grand Tour, offered Shelley the chance of a voyage to Greece upon his expulsion from Oxford.[18] Instead, Shelley travelled widely in Britain, especially Wales, and formed lasting friendships with determined pedestrian tourists, including Thomas Jefferson Hogg, Thomas Love Peacock, and Walter Coulson.[19] Shelley, Mary Shelley, and Claire Clairmont were also among the first who ventured to the Continent during the period between Napoleon's first abdication and his return from Elba. Young, impoverished, irreligious, and motivated by prospects of freedom from paternal tyranny, they answered Cunningham's negative portrait of the mass traveller exactly. Closely shadowing subsequent tourist trends, the Shelleys returned to the Continent twice more, visiting Switzerland in 1816, and crossing the Alps to Italy in 1818. Thus, in little over a decade Shelley had wandered through England, Scotland, Wales, Ireland, France, Switzerland, Germany, The United Provinces, and Italy; his travel prose include travel diaries (1814, 1816), the collaborative *History of a Six Weeks' Tour* (1817), his fragmentary 'Notes on Sculptures in Rome and Florence' (1819), and a stunning but under-cited range of travel letters (1816, 1818-22, esp. 1818-19); his poetry foregrounds travelling protagonists and his subjects are entwined with foreign settings and landscapes.

Perhaps because Shelley's otherworldly or visionary ideals have deflected attention from visual culture, scholars have undertaken comparatively little study

---

[17] For Wordsworth's description of a panorama ('those mimic sights that ape / The absolute presence of reality'), see *The Prelude, 1799, 1805, 1850*, eds Jonathan Wordsworth, M. H. Abrams, and Stephen Gill (New York: Norton, 1979), 1805, VII, 248-64. Wordsworth concludes Book VII by celebrating the unifying 'spirit of Nature' that is 'present as a habit' to one who has experienced it in the field, and which countermands 'the press / Of self-destroying, transitory things' (ll. 714-41) (i.e. the shows of London).

[18] Thomas Medwin called Timothy Shelley 'one of those travellers, who, with so much waste of time, travel for the sake of saying they have travelled; and, after making the circuit of Europe, return home, knowing no more of the countries they have visited than the trunks attached to their carriages'. See *The Life of Percy Bysshe Shelley*, 2 vols (London: Thomas Cautley Newby, 1847), 1: 10. For the Grecian voyage (and Timothy's medical rationale in proposing it), see Roger Ingpen, *Shelley in England: New Facts and Letters from the Shelley-Whitton Papers* (London: Kegan Paul, Trench, Trubner & Co. Ltd, 1917), pp. 241-3: Timothy's letter to William Whitton reflected that 'Travelling would of course dispel the gloomy ideas which he [Shelley] has too long fix'd on objects, tending to produce Temporary Insanity, it would have rais'd his depress'd spirits to a proper height of vivacity, and by placing him constantly in the presence of real dignity, bring him naturally to reflect on his *own*'. This letter is also quoted by Edmund Blunden, *Shelley: A Life Story* (London: Collins, 1946), p. 62.

[19] See *LTLP*, 1: 116, where Peacock writes to Hogg, 'a due mixture of tea, Greek & pedestrianism constitute the summa bonum'. After Shelley's departure for Italy in 1818, Hogg, Peacock, Coulson, and James Mill 'formed a Sunday walking circle' (Winifred Scott, *Jefferson Hogg*, London: Jonathan Cape, 1951, p. 122).

of his travel experiences, travel readings, travel writings, or the wider contexts in which these are situated.[20] Shelley's many biographers and biographical critics have not failed to reconstruct his travel itineraries and consequent creative output,[21] while Shelley's Italian years have contributed to a significant body of social-historical criticism, detailing Italy's appeal to British writers, and source criticism.[22] These studies tend to assume with Herbert Barrows that Shelley's travel observations are 'broadly conventional', without realising that travel conventions themselves are under new but often subtle pressures in the twilight of the Grand Tour.[23] Frederick Colwell alone has situated Shelley's responses to painting and sculpture in contemporary aesthetic debates that involve travel writers as well as artists, although his illuminating references to travel literature are still incidental.[24] Even Alan Weinburg's *Shelley's Italian Experience* (1991) all but elides the travel literature that mediated most tourist experience. Here and elsewhere in Shelley criticism, Shelley's relationship to travel writings like John Chetwode Eustace's popular *Classical Tour through Italy* (3rd edn, 1815), which accompanied him on his 1818 progress to Rome, is deemed incidental to more 'literary' influences. Weinburg's book, therefore, has quite a different emphasis from this one, although I share his interest in the intertextuality of 'experience'.

That Shelley's politics and poetics are experiential rather than metaphysical, however, has been an important strain of Shelley criticism since the 1980s. Earl Wasserman's 'philosopher' Shelley gave way to a more fluid, anti-foundationalist thinker, who responds to and anxiously struggles against the linguistic indeterminacy of his medium, the tensions in his own eclectic philosophical-

---

[20] Stuart Curran remarked on the dearth of work on Shelley's 'extensive travels' as early as 1985, but the intervening years have seen few attempts to rectify this. See *The English Romantic Poets: A Review of Research and Criticism*, ed. Frank Jordan (New York: The Modern Language Association of America, 1985), p. 637.

[21] Despite a promising title, Charles I. Elton's *An Account of Shelley's Visits to France, Switzerland, and Savoy, in the Years 1814 and 1816* (London, 1894) merely re-narrates the *History of a Six Weeks' Tour*, with little more to add than is already provided in that text and relevant letters. For reconstructions of Shelley's itineraries during his continental tours, see *SC* 264, 3: 357-70 (the 1814 elopement tour); *SC*, 4: 690-702 (England to Geneva in 1816); *SC* 469, 6: 526-30, and *SC* 472, 6: 543-8 (Italian excursions in 1818-19).

[22] The best of these remains C. P. Brand, *Italy and the English Romantics: The Italianate Fashion in Early Nineteenth-Century England* (Cambridge: Cambridge University Press, 1957). See also Roderick Marshall, *Italy in English Literature, 1755-1815: Origins of the English Romantic Interest in Italy* (New York: Columbia University Press, 1934) and Kenneth Churchill, *Italy and English Literature, 1764-1930* (London: Macmillan, 1980). Representative examples of source criticism include Geoffrey Matthews, 'A Volcano's Voice in Shelley', *English Literary History*, 24.3 (1957), pp. 191-228; Donald Reiman, 'Roman Scenes in *Prometheus Unbound*', *Philological Quarterly*, 46 (1967), pp. 69-78; and Frederick S. Colwell, 'Figures in a Promethean Landscape', *Keats-Shelley Journal*, 45 (1996), pp. 118-31.

[23] Herbert Barrows, 'Convention and Novelty in the Romantic Generation's Experience of Italy', *Bulletin of the New York Public Library*, 67 (June 1963), pp. 360-75.

[24] See Colwell, 'Shelley and Italian Painting', *Keats-Shelley Journal*, 29 (1980), pp. 43-66.

political alliances, and the theory-resistant nature of change and experience.[25] However, Ronald Tetreault augured a new phase in Shelley studies by shifting focus from Shelley's agency within language to his experience of language and 'the *mutual* implication of reader and author in the experience of the text'.[26] From these beginnings, a debate has begun to emerge concerned with the cultural terrain of this meeting place in Shelley's work, and this, principally, is the context for *Shelley's Eye*. Important studies which embark, as mine does, on a radical rereading of Shelley's aesthetic *praxis* include William Ulmer, *Shelleyan Eros: The Rhetoric of Romantic Love* (1990), Nigel Leask, *British Romantic Writers and the East* (1992) and Jennifer Wallace, *Shelley and Greece: Rethinking Romantic Hellenism* (1997). With a different emphasis, mine joins with these in furthering the debate about how we read Shelley contextually and whether discursive contexts of Shelley's idealising politics compromise their radicalism.[27] Whereas Leask and Wallace imply that Shelleyan geography is an over-determined textual space, blind to the hierarchical violence of its own occupation of that space, my study investigates the instabilities already apparent in the observing 'eye' of travel writing.

This study is particularly concerned with the problem of the observer in poetry and travel writing. In Jonathan Crary's formulation, an observer is 'one who sees within a prescribed set of possibilities, one who is embedded in a system of conventions and limitations'.[28] In travel writing, the observer is always present in the narrative voice, but is often objectified in the figure of the eye under such variations as 'the travellers' eye', 'the picturesque eye', or 'the eye of taste'. In each of these figures, the 'eye' represents some form of motivated perception, in which aesthetic, moral, or political judgements are brought to bear on the observation of buildings, scenery, peoples, or complex tableaux containing multiple referents. In the early nineteenth century, according to J. Mordaunt Crook, the eye became richly associative, once Archibald Alison's theories were taken up

---

[25] See Earl R. Wasserman, *Shelley: A Critical Reading* (Baltimore and London: Johns Hopkins University Press, 1971). Among anti-foundationalist studies, see in particular Jean Hall, *The Transforming Image: A Study of Shelley's Major Poetry* (Urbana: University of Illinois Press, 1980); Angela Leighton, *Shelley and the Sublime: An Interpretation of the Major Poems* (Cambridge: Cambridge University Press, 1984); and Jerrold Hogle, *Shelley's Process: Radical Transference and the Development of His Major Works* (Oxford: Oxford University Press, 1988).

[26] Ronald Tetreault, *The Poetry of Life: Shelley and Literary Form* (Toronto: University of Toronto Press, 1987), p. 7; see also, Stephen C. Behrendt, *Shelley and His Audiences* (Lincoln and London: University of Nebraska Press, 1989), who argues for the 'multistability' of Shelleyan language, that is, its ability to be read in different ways by different audiences.

[27] See also James Chandler, *England in 1819: The Politics of Literary Culture and the Case of Romantic Historicism* (Chicago and London: University of Chicago Press, 1998).

[28] Jonathan Crary, *Techniques of the Observer: On Vision and Modernity in the Nineteenth Century* (Cambridge, MA: MIT Press, 2001), p. 6.

and disseminated by such organs as the *Edinburgh Review*.[29] As Richard Payne Knight writes, paraphrasing the essence of Alison, 'the spectator, having his mind enriched with the embellishments of the painter and the poet, . . . [acquires] beauties, which are not felt by the organic sense of vision; but by the intellect and imagination through that sense'.[30] The 'mind richly stored', I argue, becomes fundamental to period travel writings that ascribe a Grand Tourist accreditation to observers who demonstrate their command of culture by heightening description or, in Shelley's words, seeing 'beyond the present & tangible object' (*L*, 2: 47). In a similar way, the Romantic imagination becomes a technique of the observer, encoding within it a rejection of simple objectivity, fancy, or shallow perception.

Shelley's attempt to define, practise, and idealise 'authentic' observation takes a particularly self-reflexive form that might be emblematised by another figure of the eye, one that appears frequently among the doodles in Shelley's notebooks. The eyes in fig. 1 are embedded in an Italian landscape featuring trees and a pyramid, images of picturesque nature and classical culture. The sketch appears beneath a manuscript page from *Julian and Maddalo* that includes lines that 'interchange architectural and natural images'.[31] The embedded eyes, however, suggest that perception is always self-reflection; as the traveller looks at a landscape, he or she is always looking at him or herself looking as well. Aware that 'neither the eye nor the mind can see itself, unless reflected upon that which it resembles' (*SPP*, p. 520), Shelley continually rewrites situations where the eye does see itself, even when that vision is occluded or self-critical. This is a double gesture frequently repeated in the travel writings and poetry treated in this study, as when the *Alastor* narrator constructs a travel narrative out of the wanderings of his alter ego, or when Shelley responds to the overwhelming vision of Mont Blanc during his Swiss tour of 1816: 'All was as much our own as if we had been the creators of such impressions in the minds of others, as now occupied our own' (*L*, 1: 497).[32] Yet if 'Shelley's eye' calls attention to this reflexivity, his travel writings and poetry as a whole problematise it by considering the ways in which perception and expression are implicated in the cultural conditioning of the age as well as the ways in which a truly authentic and revolutionary aesthetic might be forged to fit the needs of post-revolutionary Europe. In these contexts, Shelley's marginal 'eye' signifies a new kind of observing subject emerging from travel discourse. 'Aesthetic Vision' in this book then is not one thing, but consists of any culturally located act of observation. For Shelley, however, it is also about the political, and

---

[29] J. Mordaunt Crook, *The Dilemma of Style: Architectural Ideas from the Picturesque to the Post-Modern* (London: John Murray, 1989), p. 18.
[30] Richard Payne Knight, *An Analytic Enquiry into the Principles of Taste* (London, 1805), pp. 150-51; also quoted in Crook, *Dilemma*, p. 20.
[31] Nancy Moore Goslee, 'Shelley at Play: A Study of Sketch and Text in His Prometheus Notebooks', *Huntington Library Quarterly*, 48.3 (Summer 1985), p. 226.
[32] For another figure of the reflexive eye, see Shelley's preface to *Laon and Cythna* where he describes the 'education peculiarly fitted for a Poet' in terms of travel and habits of observation: 'I have trodden the glaciers of the Alps, and lived under the eye of Mont Blanc' (*PS2*, pp. 39-40).

Introduction

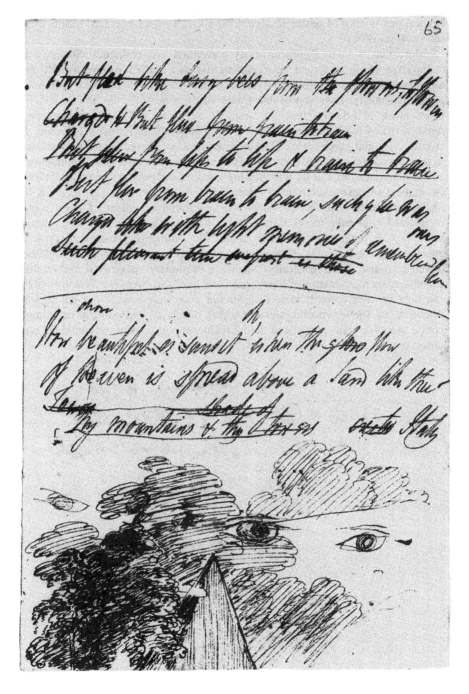

Fig. 1. Detail from *Julian and Maddalo* MS. MS. Shelley Adds. e. 11, p. 65.

cultural positioning of aesthetic argument, about how art interacts within society for social good or ill.

More than a mere argument about perception and aesthetics, *Shelley's Eye* demonstrates how the Grand Tour remains vital as a cultural metaphor in the early nineteenth century, a cluster of values under pressure from mass culture and political idealism. Post-Napoleonic travel writings demonstrate how older class-based ideals of liberal classicism, aesthetic authority, and national manners are remotivated as fundamental precepts of a modern British tourist subjectivity that crosses class and gender lines. Shelley's writings on foreign encounter participate in this renovation of subjectivity by valorising European travel as a foundation for the poet's education and by historicising earlier debates over cosmopolitanism in the context of post-revolutionary reform politics. At the same time, I show how Shelley distrusts what he considers the superficial populism of mass tourism propagated by popular travel writing and 'virtual' tourism. His own travel writings negotiate an alternative cultural space for authentic aesthetic vision by interrogating the language of travellers and the motives of perception underlying travel discourse more generally. Shelley's 'visionary' poetry of meta-cultural encounter, such as *Alastor*, *Prometheus Unbound*, and even *The Triumph of Life*, can now be seen to participate in a similar contestation with and within travel discourse, as Shelley reconfigures the social, historical, and political meanings of public spaces or signs in terms of the individuated consciousness of an ideal tourist observer.

Chapter 1

'The Sun Rises over France': Post-Napoleonic Travellers' Europe

> The morning broke, the lightning died away, the violence of the wind abated. We arrived at Calais whilst Mary still slept. We drove upon the sands. Suddenly the broad sun rose over France.
> France ~~Tuesday~~ Friday. 29
> I said — Mary look. the sun rises over France.
>
> (Shelley's entry, 28-29 July 1814, *MWSJ*, p. 7)

The French Revolution may have interrupted Continental travel, but it also increased readers' appetites for the latest accounts of itineraries already covered by eighteenth-century Grand Tourists. In the early 1790s, Edmund Burke's and Thomas Paine's theoretical debate on the effects of the Revolution was balanced against numerous 'on the spot' travel journals covering events in Paris, the French provinces, and beyond. During and immediately after the Peace of Amiens, the presses groaned with travellers' assessments of the changes between pre- and post-revolutionary manners throughout the theatre of war, and the exercise was repeated in 1814 and 1815 after Napoleon's defeats.[1] In the decade after the Revolution, travel literature maps out the new Europe and bears witness to rising nationalist movements in Spain, Italy, Greece, and Germany.

During the years of hostilities, travellers who could not penetrate France or French-occupied countries reported on Sweden, Denmark, and Russia in the North, or Spain, Sicily, and Greece in the South. Translations of French and German travel books were published almost simultaneously with the originals.[2] Reprints of

---

[1] See my article, 'New Pictures of Paris: British Travellers' Views of the French Metropolis, 1814-1816', in *Seuils & Traverses: Enjeux de l'écriture du voyage*, eds Jean-Yves Le Disez and Jan Borm, 2 vols (Brest: Centre de Recherche Bretonne et Celtique, Université de Bretagne Occidentale, 2002), 1: 45-54.

[2] Cf. Review of *Travels from Berlin through Switzerland to Paris in the Year 1804*. By August Von Kotzebue, in *Edinburgh Review*, 5 (Oct. 1804), p. 78: 'About the beginning of the present year, M. Kotzebue sets out upon his travels. He performs a long tour through four different countries . . . concocts a narrative with a few quires of tender effusion and rambling reflection. – He returns. – In three months . . . his article is ready for the market – it is sold – translated into English in a few weeks – read in this country, and, before much more than half a year is expired from the commencement of the tour, we are now engaged in reviewing it'.

eighteenth-century travel classics, or pre-war journals newly worked up into editions appeared, as well as multi-volume collections with generous sections on Europe, such as John Pinkerton's *General Collection of the Best and Most Interesting Voyages and Travels in All Parts of the World* (1808-14).[3] The displacement of the Grand Tour breathed life and variety into travel literature, even as new modes of travel gained popularity: the pedestrian tour, the agricultural tour, the picturesque tour, the scientific tour. Domestic travel benefited too, as the discovery of picturesque spots and curiosities within the borders of Great Britain became a kind of national passion among the leisured classes.

This unlikely renaissance of travel writing fostered a new wave of tourists. Mary Wollstonecraft, Helen Maria Williams, Lady Morgan, and Mary Shelley are perhaps the best-known women Romantic travellers, but they were succeeded throughout the century by increasing numbers of women reporting from the continent and throughout the world.[4] Improvements in transportation and tourist infrastructures helped increase the numbers of English tourists exponentially, and they went armed with increasingly reliable guidebooks such as Murray's and later Baedeker's.[5] With this spate of tourism came a greater diversity in class: the working men's tour dates from 1841 when Thomas Cook organised the first railway junket under the auspices of the Temperance Society, and by the 1850s Cook had instituted a network that extended the Grand Tourist 'experience' to the professional classes.[6] Though the vast majority of accounts published during Shelley's lifetime were still by those who could afford comforts and privileges, there was a new perspective abroad that the heyday of the gentlemanly Grand Tour was over; witness the Shelleys' *History of a Six Weeks' Tour*, which valorises thrifty pedestrianism. As the *Monthly Review* summed up, 'The dashing *milords* of the last age are now succeeded by a host of *roturiers*, who expatriate themselves for the sake of economy; or by a migratory tribe who are accused of never being satisfied with the spot on which they happen to reside'.[7]

---

[3] Other collections include the first modern edition of Richard Hakluyt's *Principal Navigations* in five volumes (1809-12), Robert Kerr's *A General History and Collection of Voyages and Travels* (18 vols, Edinburgh, 1811-24), and Sir Richard Phillips's *A Collection of Modern and Contemporary Voyages and Travels* (11 vols, 1805-10). For a full discussion of these and others of similar extent, see Edward Lynam, ed., *Richard Hakluyt & His Successors* (London: The Hakluyt Society, 1946), pp. 78-140. See also, Jennifer Speake, 'Collections of Literature of Travel and Exploration, Anthologies', *Literature of Travel and Exploration: An Encyclopedia*, ed. Jennifer Speake, 3 vols (New York and London: Fitzroy Dearborn, 2003), 1: 263-6.
[4] See Brian Dolan, *Ladies of the Grand Tour* (London: Flamingo, 2001); Shirley Foster, *Across New Worlds: Nineteenth-Century Women Travellers and Their Writings* (London: Harvester Wheatsheaf, 1990).
[5] See John Edmund Vaughan, *The English Guide Book, c.1780-1870; An Illustrated History* (Newton Abbot; North Pomfret, VT: David & Charles, 1974).
[6] See Edmund Swinglehurst, *Cook's Tours: The Story of Popular Travel* (Poole: Blandford Press, 1982).
[7] Review of *History of a Six Weeks' Tour*, [by Mary Shelley and Percy Bysshe Shelley], *Monthly Review*, 88 (Jan. 1819), p. 97.

There can be no mistake about the connotation of this reviewer's French. 'Roturiers', the common or humble people, are deemed un-English insofar as they travel out of dissatisfaction rather than to test the foreign against their own established virtues (one ostensible value of the Grand Tour). The French word gestures at those influences of the French Revolution that the battlefield victories of the allies could not suppress, those recrudescences of republicanism in the habits of the middle and lower classes, the reification of Jacobin tendencies among the new 'citizens of the world'.[8] Lord Castlereagh offered a counter weight to roturier culture when he proposed the Travellers' Club in 1814, an institution akin to the well-established Society of Dilettanti, although less concerned with antiquarianism as reinforcing taste in contemporary Europe through genteel tourism.[9] In the event, the club was not founded until 1819, the year ironically enough of great social unrest at home. Even as Shelley, in 'The Mask of Anarchy', wrote of the voice from over the sea that awakens him to his encounter with Castlereagh's likeness in the public way ('I met Murder on the way– / He had a mask like Castlereagh'; *SPP*, ll. 5-6), Castlereagh's brainchild, the Travellers' Club was receiving its first envoys from the continent.

The Travellers' Club and *Monthly Review* may have been nostalgic for a golden age when continental travel had clear patriotic overtones, but the French Revolution had disrupted the Grand Tour and its conventions. Jeremy Black writes that with the outbreak of war in 1793, 'Europe became less accessible, less comprehensive, and hostile, and the old-fashioned Grand Tour was a victim of that change. Tourism continued, but it followed a different course'.[10] For a while, travellers literally changed course, steering clear of established itineraries that would have led through military zones. Between 1795 and the Peace of Amiens, very few British accounts of travels in France were published. In 1804, after the Peace, Napoleon ordered the detention of all British subjects, thus ending even the pretence of an open-borders policy. One thinks of Coleridge's difficulties in finding an overland route back from Malta in 1806.[11] After fleeing from Rome and the ever-widening circle of French power in Italy, Coleridge posed as a neutral American for the sea passage out of Leghorn. He later claimed that subterfuge was necessitated because of Napoleon's blacklisting him for anti-Jacobin articles published in *The Morning Post*. Whether this be mere bravado or not, the

---

[8] Lady Morgan notes that post-revolutionary royalists snubbed their noses at Napoleon's '*roturier* origins' when discussing his use of the familiar 'tu-toyer' towards Maria Louisa. See *France* (London, 1817), 1: 73.

[9] See Sir Almeric Fitzroy, *History of the Travellers' Club* ([London]: George Allen & Unwin, 1927). Fitroy describes the Club as 'the offspring of the return to the peaceable organization of society . . . following upon the years of conflict and confusion wherewith the nineteenth century opened' (p. 9).

[10] Jeremy Black, *The British and the Grand Tour* (London: Croom Helm, 1985), p. 96.

[11] See Alethea Hayter, *A Voyage in Vain: Coleridge's Journey to Malta in 1804* (London: Robin Clark, 1993).

precedent of travellers detained at Verdun in 1804-5 would have been enough to dissuade any Englishman from risking discovery on French-held territory, particularly a civil servant.[12]

After Napoleon's first abdication and, more decisively, after Waterloo, travellers flocked to the continent, some like Byron and Southey to reflect on famous battlefields, most to follow beaten tracks. It was in some respects natural that large numbers of tourists should traverse routes that offered them accommodation, and which had even been improved, as in the Alpine passes, by Napoleon's road-building efforts.[13] But travellers were also drawn to routes that would offer comparisons between pre- and post-revolutionary Europe. It was for some a salvage effort to determine how much of the Grand Tour could be reclaimed, but the fact remained that the events begun in 1793 influenced not only itineraries but also responses. Travel writing had been affected as much as travelling itself.

Travel writing, as Charles L. Batten argues, was already showing signs of change as the eighteenth century drew to a close. The genre which almost 'uniformly aimed at blending pleasure with useful instruction' increasingly emphasised the pleasures of travel: after decades of exhaustive Grand Tourism, writers had ransacked Europe for useful information regarding over-described itineraries and their cultural 'stations'.[14] This trend included, first, a movement away from objective reporting towards more subjective accounts, with the observer as a character at the centre of his or her own narrative. Second, more travel writings focused on 'ornamental subjects that demanded increasingly more difficult descriptive techniques'.[15] Most notably, William Gilpin's picturesque tours of the 1780s and 1790s helped popularise a mode of tourism, and what is more, literary landscape description, which had become standard fare for readers of travel books by Shelley's time. By debating the application of aesthetic terminology to the description of landscape, Gilpin and his followers developed a seemingly limitless source of novelty and variation for travel writers and readers

---

[12] One of the few travel-related books on France published between 1811 and 1814 was an account of a Briton's escape from the French detention centre, Verdun, where British subjects not actually incarcerated were forced to report to officials twice daily. See *Escape from France: A Narrative of the Hardships and Sufferings of Several British Subjects Who Effected Their Escape from Verdun. With an Appendix, Containing Observations on the Policy and Conduct of Buonaparte towards British Subjects* (London: Vernor, Hood, and Sharpe, 1811). For an earlier account of the effects of the Napoleonic decree, see James Forbes, *Letters from France, Written in the Years 1803 & 1804. Including a Particular Account of Verdun, and the Situation of the British Captives in that City*, 2 vols (London: Printed for J. White, 1806).

[13] Claire Clairmont records in her journal for 8 April 1818: 'We dine on the top of Cenis & bless Napoleon for the passage must have been dreadful before the new Road was made' (*CCJ*, pp. 88-9).

[14] Charles L. Batten, *Pleasurable Instruction: Form and Convention in Eighteenth-Century Travel Literature* (Berkeley: University of California Press, 1978), p. 110.

[15] Batten, *Pleasurable Instruction*, p. 109; see also pp. 106-110 *passim*.

alike. Increasingly, useful information for travellers was relegated to specialised guidebooks, the progenitors of the Murrays and the Baedekers.

Though this may be a faithful portrait of general trends, some qualifications should be noted. First, both entertainment and instruction continue to be expected by reviewers and offered by travel writers well into the nineteenth century, though the pleasures of travel writing were often implicated in 'the picture which [travel books] exhibit of the traveller's mind'.[16] Second, 'useful information' such as exchange conversions, customs rules, or posting routes, may have increasingly become the domain of guidebooks, but this did not stop the travel writer from offering other kinds of instruction on, for example, the moral, political, and social state of a country, or where to stand in order to obtain a sublime or picturesque view. Third, and more to my present concerns, during the revolutionary years many travel writers, particularly on French-held territories, focused their attention on useful political or sociological information at the expense of ornamental or landscape description; even after the revolutionary years, travellers in France reported largely on Paris as the centre of cultural changes. But where trends towards subjectivity and aesthetic description may, as Batten asserts, break down or 'blur' the genre's 'distinction between "objective" observations and "subjective" reflections',[17] a space remains in the emerging narrative structures for ideological debate; there is no such thing as an innocent eye.

In this way, the French Revolution at once reopened the mine of materials for useful instruction, but also highlighted new ways that narrative could be influenced by political activity. For travel writers, political events challenged the travel book's traditional role as 'pleasurable instruction' by preventing a naive recounting of well-annotated landscapes, famous artefacts, manners, and customs. More and more, landscapes were celebrated or mourned as scenes of martial power or in their relation to revolutionary figures, most notably Rousseau and Napoleon. Even potentially stock picturesque landscape descriptions after 1789 often have political resonances; feudal piles, the rural poor, and land use make up both the painterly subjects of the picturesque and the subjects of revolutionary political and economic debate. By 1802, Napoleon's victorious forces had carted Europe's most valued paintings and sculpture to the Louvre, and in an age of paternal regard for cultural riches, more than one traveller glorified this concentration, or at least played down the First Consul's rapacity.[18] Even those artefacts that remained in their historical

---

[16] Review of *Travels through Sweden, Finland, and Lapland, to the Northern Cape*, By Joseph Acerbi. *Edinburgh Review*, 1 (Oct. 1802), p. 163.

[17] Batten, *Pleasurable Instruction*, pp. 112-13.

[18] Many travellers were particularly impressed by the new French policy of making the Louvre, and thus the treasures of European culture, accessible to the general public. Francis William Blagdon, the author of *Paris As It Was and As It Is; or A Sketch of the French Capital, Illustrative of the Effects of the Revolution* (London: C. and R. Baldwin, 1803), not only catalogues displays of art and antiquities, but applauds Napoleon's regal promotion and popularisation of the arts and sciences. Sir John Carr, however, in his *The Stranger in*

locations might be said to be woven by travellers into larger narratives of cultural appropriation, the travel books themselves. Manners, meanwhile, the outgrowth of the Grand Tourists' preoccupation with national character, became the key term in a wider political discussion as to the effects of revolutionary social policy on the labouring classes in particular and the economic health of nations as a whole. Though travel writers supplied a marketplace especially eager to trace these changes in France, they also turned to peripheral or neutral countries from Sweden to Switzerland in order to compare and contrast the revolutionary situation; the establishment of the Helvetian Republic in Switzerland after the French invasion of 1798, for example, provided a context for the radical Helen Maria Williams's *A Tour in Switzerland*, in which she reports on the positive influence of French systems of governing outside France itself.[19] Correspondingly, Swiss glaciers and Neapolitan volcanoes simultaneously served as sublime tableaux and metaphors for revolutionary change.

This new reportage on a Europe in which social, political, and cultural norms were under pressure often appears unruly, decentred, disorganised, partly in reflection of what Lady Morgan refers to as the 'fermentation' of the times, and partly again because of the travel genre. Travel writing, usually presented as a series of letters or journal entries, tends to follow the itinerary and eye of the observer and records a sometimes bewildering hodgepodge of detail: landscape description, personal anecdote, theatre and art criticism, festivals, agricultural notes, and much more.[20] Travellers themselves recognised their difficulties and some justified their method as a cumulative attempt to satisfy readers' long-starved curiosity. Others attempted to organise their observations under headings, although any departure from the verisimilitude of the observer's gaze could lead to that bugbear, charges of plagiarism or outright fabrication.[21] Still others, like Arthur Young or the Shelleys, tried to have it both ways, deploying different narrative

---

France (London: J. Johnson, 1807) qualifies his praise insofar as he believes that the availability of Christian art to the atheistical populace will instil humanising principles that run counter to the France in which they live. Travellers more partial to Italy, such as Richard Duppa, deplored the ransacking of Rome in the first place, much as Byron condemned Lord Elgin's nearly contemporaneous depredations at Athens. See Duppa's *A Journal of the Most Remarkable Occurences that Took Place in Rome: upon the Subversion of the Ecclesiastical Government, in 1798* (London: Printed for G. G. and J. Robinson, 1799).

[19] Helen Maria Williams, *A Tour in Switzerland; or, A View of the Present State of the Government and Manners of the Cantons: With Comparative Sketches of the Present State of Paris* (London: Printed for G. G. and J. Robinson, 1798).

[20] Making a virtue out of necessity, *Paris As It Was and As It Is* (1803) explains: 'To banish uniformity in my description of that metropolis, I have, as much as possible, varied my subjects. Fashions, sciences, absurdities, anecdotes, education, fêtes, useful arts, places of amusement, music, learned and scientific institutions, inventions, public buildings, industry, agriculture, &c. &c. &c. being all jumbled together in my brain, I have thence drawn them, like tickets from a lottery . . . .' (p. xx).

[21] Batten, *Pleasureable Instruction*, pp. 19-24.

strategies in a single travel book.[22] All, however, relied on and posited a reader capable of synthesising the materials, though not without some strong hints how to do so suggested by the experienced author's own interpretations of key moments in the narrative. All, more or less self-consciously, wrote towards defining the Europeanness of which they and their readers partook in an age in which nationalist was replacing dynastic Europe.

At stake was the value and kind of cultural currency suitable for a new world order whose boundaries, real and figurative, were in flux. It was precisely this period when the term 'culture' itself began to take on its modern sociological meaning, as opposed to the older agricultural sense of 'cultivated nature'. If culture, as Raymond Williams observes, emerges as 'a special kind of map' in which 'new kinds of personal and social relationship' are delineated, then travel writers bear a distinct responsibility for tracing its outlines as they explore in person the new geo-political situation in Europe and beyond.[23] The traveller does this by describing and participating in everyday European life, both as representative of a member state, and as an individual, deploying, re-evaluating, or revalidating customary responses to landscapes, artefacts, social institutions, men, and women. Travel writing, like journalism or what has now become known as 'foreign correspondence', earns its status as cultural arbiter by appropriating its objects through discourse. Landscapes are reviewed in terms of aesthetic categories like the sublime, the beautiful, and the picturesque, as are buildings, ruins, and other historical sites. Objects of art are described in terms of their value to 'civilisation', as points on a timeline of social advancement, or cultural evolution towards the very Europeanness for which they are used as evidence.[24] In other words, travel writing becomes the site of cultural production, the place where cultural unity-in-diversity is posited, planned, or promoted. It is what Simon Gikandi calls, in a related context, a 'mechanism of totalization'.[25]

Travel accounts of Europe in the period work out the kind of international identity at the heart of nineteenth-century imperial expansionism, and without which the rigid dialectic between a hazily defined European imperial centre and the empire itself of some influential post-colonial theory, becomes at best an

---

[22] See my account of Young's 'multimedia' experiments with the travel book format, in 'Aesthetics of Enclosure: Agricultural Tourism and the Place of the Picturesque', *European Romantic Review*, 13.1 (Mar. 2002), pp. 28-30.

[23] Raymond Williams, *Culture & Society: 1780-1950* (New York: Columbia University Press, 1983), pp. xvi-xviii.

[24] According to Johannes Fabian, 'the *topos of travel*' in the late eighteenth century has a crucial role in shaping an idea of time as a 'superior knowledge' with which to understand, judge, and intervene in human affairs. See *Time and the Other: How Anthropology Makes Its Object* (New York: Columbia University Press, 1983), pp. 6-11.

[25] Simon Gikandi, 'Englishness, Travel, and Theory: Writing the West Indies in the Nineteenth Century', *Nineteenth-Century Contexts: An Interdisciplinary Journal*, vol. 18, no. 1 (1994), p. 50.

oversimplification.[26] In a market flooded with extra-European travels to Africa, Asia, and America, the European travel account creates and validates, or alternatively questions and problematises the centrality of a European cultural identity. It does so even as some of these extra-European travels document the cultural resistance at the edges of empire (China, Afghanistan, Africa, revolutionary South America) which in turn relativise any sense of a European centre for world power, conquest, or cultural superiority. In this way, the European travel text may be seen to negotiate between myths of centrality, unity, or civilisation, and the unruly forces, both natural and social, that threaten these with fragmentation or meaninglessness.

One of the most compelling ideas of Europe and myths of golden age European unity at the beginning of this transitional period, for both contemporary travel writers and subsequent historians, was that of Edmund Burke. Even before his *Reflections on the Revolution in France* (1790), Burke understood the events in France in the largest of contexts. To Earl Fitzwilliam in November 1789, Burke wrote, 'I think I see many inconveniences not only to Europe, but to this Country in particular from the total political extinction of a great civilised Nation situated in the heart of this our Western System'.[27] Though Burke shows himself a conscientious politician in placing his country's self-interest foremost, his internationalist terms of reference are borne out not only in this letter, but also in all of his public writings of the 1790s. Europe and, in its imperial guise, the Western System, depend upon an 'equipoise', the term with which the *Reflections* closes, between constituent states. This equipoise in turn depends on the internal social and political structures of those states (Great Britain, France, Austria, Prussia, and Russia). His use of the term 'civilized', however, warns us against regarding these structures as discrete concerns of individual states. Instead, Burke prescribes a hierarchical system of relations between the nobility, the clergy, and the other propertied classes as the hallmark of a civilised nation. To tamper with these in one country may weaken them in another and threaten the system as a whole. Burke's Europe was not a conflict-free Europe, but it was one in which foreign wars threatened only administrations rather than the fabric of government itself. It was the Europe of, and validated by, the Grand Tour.

In a telling phrase at the end of one of the most famous sections of the *Reflections*, Burke identifies a central difference between his idea of Europe and that inaugurated by the French Revolution:

---

[26] Edward Said's *Orientalism* (1978) and *Culture and Imperialism* (1993) have been criticised for their unquestioning formulation of a cohesive 'imperial centre' responsible for colonialist oppression. See Ernest Gellner, 'The Mightier Pen? Edward Said and the Double Standards of Inside-Outside Colonialism', *The Times Literary Supplement*, (19 Feb. 1993), pp. 3-4, and John M. Mackenzie, 'Edward Said and the Historians', *Nineteenth-Century Contexts*, 18.1 (1994), pp. 9-25.

[27] *The Correspondence of Edmund Burke*, vol. 6, eds Alfred Cobban and Robert A. Smith (London: Cambridge University Press, 1967), p. 36.

> Excuse me, therefore, if I have dwelt too long on the atrocious spectacle of the 6th of October, 1789, or have given too much scope to the reflections which have arisen in my mind on occasion of the most important of all revolutions, which may be dated from that day—I mean a revolution in sentiments, manners, and moral opinions.[28]

The 'spectacle' is that of the fall of Marie Antoinette, and Burke's 'reflections' include those on the extinguished 'glory of Europe'. His emphasis on a 'revolution in sentiments, manners, and moral opinions' must not be dismissed as a final rhetorical flourish in a passage of remarkable prose, which it is as well. In addition to appealing to his readers' emotions, Burke places emotion centre stage along with conduct and morality as principles related to individuals, but which bind them to larger communities: the family, state, Europe, and civilisation. He also gives these principles a historical pedigree; derived from medieval codes of chivalry, they are imported from France to Great Britain and the other European powers. Disregarding Burke's subsequent appeals to nature and the natural, this is what we might now call a carefully crafted cultural argument.[29]

In attacking traditional structures of European unity, the French Revolutionaries were questioning the idea of Europe itself. For Burke, this would have global repercussions. In his own words, the destruction of the structures of European unity rooted in chivalry and embodied in sentiment, manners, and opinions, would result in the extinction of everything that distinguished Europe 'to its advantage, from the states of Asia and possibly from those states which flourished in the most brilliant periods of the antique world'.[30] For Burke, pre-revolutionary Europe had achieved the heights of civilisation and the Revolution threatened to shake it to its foundations.

Of the triumvirate, 'sentiments, manners, and moral opinions', the most versatile principle is 'manners', a word Burke repeats eleven times in four pages, sometimes emphasising its emotive basis and sometimes its moral attributes. Contemporary usage varied from the more modern sense of politeness ('table manners') to the sociological senses that seem to be the stock in trade of much of the period's travel literature: the term 'manners' appears time and time again in travel titles along with similar social key words, such as laws, institutions, customs, character, society, religion, politics, and amusements.[31] Burke's predominant usage coincides with the travel literature, and may be broadly summed up with reference to manners as 'conduct in its moral aspect' and 'the modes of life, customary rules of behaviour, conditions of society, prevailing in a

---

[28] Edmund Burke, *Reflections on the Revolution in France*, ed. J. G. A. Pocock (Indianapolis: Hackett Publishing Company, 1987), p. 70.
[29] For Burke 'nature' and 'culture' are interchangeable; there is never a sense in the *Reflections* of an appeal to a Rousseauian 'state of nature' as an *a priori* condition of egalitarian culture.
[30] Burke, *Reflections*, p. 67.
[31] Cf. Batten, *Pleasureable Instruction*, pp. 96-7.

people' (*OED*). While travellers measure manners on a sliding scale between the civilised and the primitive depending on how far from the centres of power they go, Burke's discussion emphasises the ideal commonalty of European life so crucial to his polemic.[32] In doing so, he enters a wider ethnological discussion that privileges genteel, literate, acculturated behaviour as the universal basis for social and political life. Even those subsequent travellers and intellectuals – Arthur Young, Mary Wollstonecraft, and Shelley included – who took issue with Burke's rhetoric and underlying political philosophy in *Reflections* are often to be found deploying similar biases. Shelley, not often compared to Burke, offers such sentiments after touring Ireland in 1811 and France in 1814, both times witnessing first-hand what he regarded as the filth and degradation of the non-propertied classes to whom his philosophy was devoted in the abstract. In 1812, he wrote to Hogg,

> Perhaps you will say that my republicanism is proud. it [sic] certainly is far removed from pothouse democracy . . . . My republicanism it is true would bear with an aristocracy of chivalry, & refinement, before an aristocracy of commerce & vulgarity, not however from pride but because the one I consider as approaching most nearly to what man ought to be. (*L*, 1: 352)[33]

True to his own social background in ways that may well have made him uncomfortable, Shelley fashions his internationalist political agenda out of a code of moral conduct, or manners, to which the term 'chivalry' is not anathema. To bring all men to 'what man ought to be' involves lifting the lower classes to the level of refinement and education that Shelley shared with his own class. This is not to say that more radical visions of alternative societies were not available during the progress or aftermath of the French Revolution; the Spenceans, for example, called for the complete abolition of private property and the cultivation of all 'waste' lands devoted to privileged leisure.[34] But it is to suggest that the universalist class biases encoded in that much-discussed concept of 'manners' had an extraordinary currency across a broad political spectrum.

---

[32] Travellers like Hester Lynch Piozzi, however, were ready with Burke to discard the scales when comparing Europe to non-Europe: 'But what is our difference of manners, compared to that prodigious effect produced by the much shorter passage from Spain to Africa; where an hour's time, and sixteen miles space only, carries you from Europe, from civilization, from Christianity' (*Observations Made in the Course of a Journey through France, Italy, and Germany [1789]*, ed. Herbert Barrows, Ann Arbor, University of Michigan Press, 1967, p. 5).

[33] See also *MWSJ*, pp. 63-4, where Shelley has this to say about his conversations in February 1815 with the radical printer, George Cannon: 'it is disgusting to hear such a beast speak of philosophy & republicanism. — Let refinement & benevolence convey these ideas'.

[34] See David Worrall, 'Agrarians against the Picturesque: Ultra-Radicalism and the Revolutionary Politics of Land', *The Politics of the Picturesque: Literature, Landscape and Aesthetics since 1770*, eds Stephen Copley and Peter Garside (Cambridge: Cambridge University Press, 1994), pp. 240-43.

Shelley's comment about 'commerce & vulgarity' recalls another of Burke's uses of 'manners' in *Reflections*. 'Even commerce and trade and manufacture', he writes, 'the gods of our economical politicians . . . are themselves but effects which, as first causes, we choose to worship'. Burke criticises a *laissez faire* economics that he associates with French republican principles by suggesting that the French (and the followers of Adam Smith at home by implication) have been dissociated from their 'natural protecting principles', 'ancient manners'.[35] Equally important, 'ancient manners' are also the protecting progenitors of the arts. The result is a family tree that emphasises the kinship of economics and the arts in the organic European society that Burke promotes. To Burke, this means that economic life should resemble art as a model and transmitter of moral conduct. Both the arts and economic transactions carry the message of civilisation to the ends of empire, quite literally in their tandem employment in the marketplace of representation; art, art criticism, manufactures, and educational syllabi are among the exports from imperial centres to their international clients.[36]

To look at this from another angle, which Burke does, art also models how politics should operate, both on the national and multinational level. Quoting from Horace's *Ars Poetica*, Burke concludes that 'the construction of poems is equally true as to states:–*Non satis est pulchra esse poemata, dulcia sunto*'.[37] Once again, the parent of arts, economics, and now it appears, politics turns out to be 'manners' and Burke says as much in what follows: 'There ought to be a system of manners in every nation which a well-informed mind would be disposed to relish. To make us love our country, our country ought to be lovely'.[38] It is perhaps a sleight of hand that so binds aesthetics with moral conduct and the composition of the state, but it is one with profound importance for the history of Romantic aesthetics, not to mention the various attempts by Romantic writers of various political stripes to link the production of art with amelioration in political life. As a 'mechanism for totalization' Burke's approach to politics successfully and masterfully intertwines a theory of the balance of power between European states with aesthetic absolutes, as in his defence of the *ancien régime*:

> In your old states . . . you had all that combination and all that opposition of interests; you had that action and counteraction which, in the natural and in the political world, from the reciprocal struggle of discordant powers, draws out the harmony of the universe.[39]

---

[35] Burke, *Reflections*, p. 69.
[36] See Gauri Viswanathan, *Masks of Conquest: Literary Study and British Rule in India* (New York: Columbia University Press, 1989).
[37] Burke, *Reflections*, p. 68. The line from Horace, *Ars Poetica*, l. 99, is translated by Pococke: 'It is not enough that poems be beautiful; they must also be tender' (p. 223, n. liii).
[38] Burke, *Reflections*, p. 68.
[39] Burke, *Reflections*, p. 31.

Better than anyone, Coleridge has shown the adaptability of this formulation to the language of the Romantic imagination in a passage from *Biographia Literaria* that must have Burke behind it:

> This power [the imagination] . . . reveals itself in the balance or reconciliation of opposite or discordant qualities . . . and while it blends and harmonizes the natural and the artificial, still subordinates art to nature . . . .[40]

In Coleridge's syntax, imagination stands in for Burke's 'harmony of the universe' – an apt substitution given Coleridge's claims for the primary imagination as 'a repetition in the finite mind of the eternal act of creation in the infinite I AM'.[41] Nevertheless, Coleridge and Burke privilege the dialectic of discordant qualities or powers in the most universalised terms that religion, politics, and aesthetics offer.

In his *Defence of Poetry* (1821), Shelley too makes a case for the imagination as the supreme intellectual and political power, and dwells like Burke and Coleridge on the metaphor of 'harmony' for describing the ways that art and the imagination link the individual to nature and society, in the present and throughout history.[42] Like Burke's *Reflections*, Shelley's essay has a polemical flavour, for both function as replies to antagonists and elaborations on their themes: Burke had his Price, and Shelley his Peacock. But Shelley's serious answer to Peacock's playful charges against poetry as an ineffectual pursuit, degenerating from age to age, leads him to make claims that resemble those of Burke on, in Shelley's words this time, the correlations between poetry and 'the history of manners' (*SPP*, p. 519). In an important digression on the drama, Shelley writes:

> The connexion of scenic exhibitions with the improvement or corruption of the manners of men, has been universally recognized: in other words, the presence or absence of poetry in its most perfect and universal form has been found to be connected with good and evil in conduct and habit. (*SPP*, p. 519)

This passage could fittingly gloss Burke's claims in *Reflections* that art should instruct life, or his many references to the events of 1789 as 'spectacle'. Burke not only renders tableaux like that of Marie Antoinette with all the trappings of a contemporary stage set, he also argues that the drama elicits authentic human emotions from spectators through scenes that in actual life should do the same: 'Indeed, the theatre is a better school of moral sentiments than churches [i.e. Richard Price's congregation], where the feelings of humanity are thus outraged. Poets . . . must apply themselves to the moral constitution of the heart . . . '.[43] In a

---

[40] Samuel Taylor Coleridge, *Biographia Literaria*, 2 vols in 1, eds James Engel and W. Jackson Bate (Princeton: Princeton University Press, 1983), 2: 16-17.
[41] Coleridge, *Biographia*, 1: 304.
[42] For an earlier statement on the interrelatedness between the imagination and civilisation, see Shelley's discussion of benevolence in the fragmentary 'Treatise on Morals' (*Prose*, pp. 188-9).
[43] Burke, *Reflections*, p. 71.

passage that bears several striking resemblances to Burke's paragraph, Shelley similarly writes that 'the connexion of poetry and social good is more observable in the drama than in whatever other form' (*SPP*, p. 521).[44] Both essentialise art and human emotion as universal standards by which political life can be measured. Both contextualise these standards in a discussion of the history of European manners and culture, though Shelley extends his gaze beyond medieval chivalry to ancient Greece for his ultimate model.

Shelley's use of such arguments for his conclusion that 'Poets are the unacknowledged legislators of the World' (*SPP*, p. 535) reminds us to what extent that legislation has its basis in European leisure class culture. The proximity of his discourse to that of Burke, moreover, suggests that Burke, or other conservatives, do not hold a monopoly on the Euro-centric viewpoint of home and imperial affairs. In fact, the global consciousness of almost every English traveller, or reader of travel literature, or thinker on the global situation, reflected this same tendency. Though Burke offended proponents of the Revolution by linking modern European civilisation to medieval historical imperatives, or by clouding arguments with appeals to prejudice, he shared with his critics a view that Europeanness contained the essence of world legislation. He also shared with them a discourse on the cultural basis of this concept of legislation, most notably worked out with reference to the 'history of manners'.

Burke's Europe was a powerful example of an ideology of cultural imperialism that would underlie even radical accounts of Europe in histories, political polemics, and travel literature. But if Shelley's relation to this discourse seems tangential with reference to Burke alone, it may be well at this point to cite other pictures of Europe to which Shelley would have had greater affinity. Edward Gibbon ('without whose work no library is complete'; *L*, 2: 142) offers one of these. Gibbon, whose *Decline and Fall of the Roman Empire* Marilyn Butler says 'potentially seems so subversive of [the era's] institutions',[45] may be usefully compared to Burke in his support of the imperial myth of European unity, not least because the Enlightenment formulations of his historiography retained their potency in the coming age. Referring to 'the great republic of Europe', Gibbon

---

[44] Burke makes slighting reference to the 'Machiavellian policy' of the French revolutionaries who cannot follow their 'natural' or dramatic impulses. Shelley, however, writes that 'as Machiavelli says of political institutions, that life may be preserved and renewed, if men should arise capable of bringing back the drama to its principles' (*SPP*, p. 521). As a friend of reform, Shelley distinguishes himself from Burke by considering Machiavelli as an Italian patriot, at a time when the Neapolitan rebellion appeared to give hopes to Machiavelli's dream of an independent Italy. Though it cannot be positively said that Shelley had Burke in mind in the *Defence* the proximity of the two discussions at the very least indicates the degree to which they share a common discourse.

[45] Marilyn Butler, *Romantics, Rebels and Reactionaries: English Literature and Its Background, 1760-1830* (Oxford: Oxford University Press, 1981), p. 25.

parallels Burke in looking beyond the self-interest of individual states and ascribing to civilised manners the glue that holds Europe together:

> It is the duty of a patriot to prefer and promote the exclusive interest and glory of his native country: but a philosopher may be permitted . . . to consider Europe as one great republic, whose various inhabitants have attained almost the same level of politeness and cultivation. The balance of power will continue to fluctuate, and the prosperity of our own or the neighbouring kingdoms may be alternately exalted or depressed; but these partial events cannot essentially injure our general state of happiness, the system of arts, and laws, and manners, which so advantageously distinguish, above the rest of mankind, the Europeans and their colonies. The savage nations of the globe are the common enemies of civilized society.[46]

Gibbon's 'one great nation' and Burke's glorious Europe are cast in the same mould. Even as Gibbon deems 'the savage nations' enemies of civilisation, Burke vilifies French Revolutionaries as 'cannibals', 'American savages', and oriental despots. As yet unaware of the threat of savagery from within – as Burke saw the unleashing of the 'swinish multitude' by the French Revolution – Gibbon writes with the confidence that Europe had escaped the fate of the Roman Empire, destroyed at last by Celtic invaders. He instead argues that the gulf between civilised Europeans and 'savage' peoples of Asia, Africa, and America is too great for Europe to slip low enough, or the others to rise high enough to threaten the European concentration of military, cultural, and political power. 'Europe is secure from any future irruption of barbarians', he writes, 'since, before they can conquer, they must cease to be barbarous'.[47] Even if such an 'irruption' did come about, he reasons, 'ten thousand vessels would transport beyond their pursuit the remains of civilised society; and Europe would revive and flourish in the American world, which is already filled with her colonies and institutions'.[48]

Gibbon himself saw no discrepancy between his views and the institutions of his age, despite the retrospectives of subsequent historians and literary critics. On the contrary, when he witnessed the early stages of the French Revolution and its threats to those institutions, Gibbon very naturally threw in his lot with his old friend Burke. In his *Memoirs*, which Shelley read in 1815, he wrote: 'I beg leave to subscribe my assent to Mr. Burke's creed on the revolution of France. I admire his eloquence, I approve his politics, I adore his chivalry, and I can almost excuse his reverence for church establishments'.[49] Any subversion to which Gibbon contributed was due to the notorious fifteenth and sixteenth chapters of his *Decline and Fall*, which called into question ahistorical reverence for church establishments, most notably the use of miracles as a basis for dogma. It is this

---

[46] Edward Gibbon, *The Decline and Fall of the Roman Empire*, 3 vols (New York: The Modern Library, [n.d.]), 2: 439-40.
[47] Gibbon, *Decline and Fall*, 2: 442.
[48] Gibbon, *Decline and Fall*, 2: 441.
[49] *The Miscellaneous Works of Edward Gibbon, Esq. with Memoirs of his Life and Writings*, 5 vols, ed. John, Lord Sheffield (London: John Murray, 1814), 1: 269.

aspect of Gibbon's work that raised the hackles of Christian apologists in his own time, and it is this that Shelley particularly appreciated. But like Burke, Gibbon offered successive generations an appealing myth of European cultural hegemony supported by some of the most painstaking historical scholarship ever undertaken.

Gibbon's pre-revolutionary European empires occupy, assimilate, and consolidate the space of the Roman Empire. The Revolution itself, however, opened up the possibility of another world view unavailable to Gibbon. For Shelley, this new picture found a partisan in Constantine Volney, traveller, visionary, and member of the French National Assembly.[50] Unlike Gibbon's *Decline and Fall*, Volney's *Ruins* (1791) does not neatly reconstruct empire within the civilised network of modern European manners. Instead Volney attacks any nation where political or cultural authority has its basis in institutions of inequality. In his comparative gaze over cultures, races, religions, and political institutions, Volney finds few models for future regeneration in either the present or the past, and turns instead to the origins of society for his pathology of inequality and the remedies. Like Rousseau before him, Volney traces human evolution from the state of nature to organised political society, and locates the source of inequality in man's mistaking or breaking 'the laws of nature, as they related to the connexion between him and exterior objects'.[51] Though Volney emphasises what Marilyn Butler has called a 'proto-Foucaultian critique of discourse . . . as power',[52] rather than ownership of property as the initial manifestation of inequality, the result is the same: political-economic oppression and institutionalised religion are built on perverse fictions (particularly the 'right' of the few to appropriate the labour or authority of the many). It is this critique that Shelley uses to effect in his own world surveys in *Queen Mab* (1813), and later in *A Philosophical View of Reform* (1819-20).

Despite his levelling syncretism, Volney's vision of the future embodies a very French Revolutionary optimism in the worldwide applicability of that secular slogan, 'Liberty, Equality, and Fraternity'. His survey of the present, however, leaves little quarter for the kernel of these ideas, except maybe in France:

> All Asia is buried in the most profound darkness. The Chinese, subjected to an insolent despotism . . . offer to my view an abortive civilization and a race of automatons. The

---

[50] Volney's *Ruins* appears on the monster's reading list in Mary Shelley's *Frankenstein*, and it is likely that Shelley knew it as well as he did the other books on that list, though there is no direct reference to Volney in Shelley's own work. Kenneth Neill Cameron, however, argues for the importance of *Ruins* to Shelley in 'A Major Source of *The Revolt of Islam*', *PMLA*, 56 (1941), pp. 175-206.

[51] C. F. Volney, *The Ruins, or, A Survey of the Revolutions of Empires*, trans. [James Marshall], 5th edn (London, 1807), p. 37.

[52] Marilyn Butler, 'Shelley and the Empire in the East', *Shelley: Poet and Legislator of the World*, eds Betty T. Bennett and Stuart Curran (Baltimore and London: Johns Hopkins University Press, 1996), p. 160.

Indian . . . vegetates in an incurable apathy. The Tartar . . . lives in the barbarity of his ancestors. The Arab, endowed with a happy genius, loses its force and the fruit of his labour in the anarchy of his tribes, and the jealousy of his families. The African . . . seems irremediably devoted to servitude. In the North I see nothing but serfs, reduced to the level of cattle, the live stock of the estate upon which they live.[53]

Sure enough, only in parts of Europe 'reason begins to expand its wings', inverting the emphasis of Burke's rhetoric, which attributes the decline of civilised morality and 'pleasing illusions' to the 'new conquering empire of light and reason'.[54] Like Burke's, Volney's partisanship reveals a common enemy in the non-European, but emphasises that only in a Europe which has succumbed to French Revolutionary principles can a system of world legislation be propagated. The Assembly of Nations, with which the vision ends, seems to be no more than an extrapolation of the National Assembly.

Mary Wollstonecraft's *An Historical and Moral View of the Origin and Progress of the French Revolution and the Effect It Has Produced in Europe* (1794), published three years after Volney's vision, also posits a historiography culminating in a new dawn of civilisation in Europe, yet begins to take into account the limitations of a single cataclysmic event like revolution for achieving this end – a Godwinian position as amenable to Shelley as Volney's. Wollstonecraft had been present in Paris during the trial and execution of Louis XVI, the destruction of the Girondin Party, and the Terror. She had avoided imprisonment along with other English expatriates only by virtue of her having been registered as the wife of an American, Gilbert Imlay. Though her book deals with events preceding her residence in France – the weeks before and immediately succeeding the storming of the Bastille – it is coloured by the urgency of her own experiences of the daily round of revolutionary hopes among the literati contrasted with the equally common spectacles of rioting, arrests, and political demagoguery. Wollstonecraft can be polemical in her support for the radical cause, but it also becomes clear that she distances that cause from the scenes that transpired among the populace and in the National Assembly. *An Historical and Moral View* is an apology for the gradual improvement of civilisation towards political justice, not for the Revolution itself.

In fact, Wollstonecraft can be as critical of the National Assembly – its pusillanimous political decisions in times of crisis or the licentiousness of its members – as of the King and his intrigues against the cause of reform. Painting with the large brush strokes of the Grand Tourist, Wollstonecraft argues that the French were defeated by their own national character – vain, sanguinary, enthusiastic, and egotistical – exacerbated in turn by the corruptions of a too highly refined code of manners. Despite this conscious refutation of Burke, Wollstonecraft shares with that antagonist a distrust of modern economics, though, to be sure, for reasons differing from as much as they resemble Burke's. Her

---

[53] Volney, *The Ruins*, pp. 94-5.
[54] Volney, *The Ruins*, p. 95; Burke, *Reflections*, p. 67.

closing chapter thus indicts commerce, 'the aristocracy of wealth',[55] and its baneful effects on labour. She argues that commerce forces workers into exacting manufacturing roles and destroys their opportunity for independence of character through education and leisure. Though Claire Tomalin has stated that this makes Wollstonecraft sound 'something like a founding mother of utopian socialism', it also firmly places Wollstonecraft in the tradition of a discourse of manners.[56] Like Shelley, who esteems 'an aristocracy of chivalry, & refinement' over one of 'commerce & vulgarity' as 'approaching most nearly to what man ought to be' (*L*, 1: 352), Wollstonecraft draws her models for the future from European leisure class culture.[57]

Unlike Shelley, Wollstonecraft was not ready to rehabilitate Burke's 'chivalry' in any form, and her historiography of manners privileges 'improvements in reason and experience and moral philosophy'[58] over aesthetic refinement – in the *Defence*, Shelley overlooks the evil produced by 'the Christian and Chivalric systems' and emphasises their essential poetry, the 'forms of opinion and action never before conceived' (*SPP*, p. 523) that they introduce. Wollstonecraft argues that 'the civilization of the world, hitherto, has consisted rather in cultivating the taste, than in exercising the understanding'. The ancient world developed taste and the arts, but without improving political science. The modern world, benefited by the manners instilled by the arts, has yet to escape the inequality encoded in them. The chivalry of the crusades may have introduced 'the character of a *gentleman*, held ever since so dear in France', but Wollstonecraft condemns this as a 'bastard morality' that 'kept those men within bounds, who obeyed no other law'.[59] The modern French national character becomes a reflection of this old morality during a transition from the barbaric to the civilised world. The Revolution would have been successful if the French had not been so caught between two widely separate ages.

Wollstonecraft poses the problem that if 'the degrading distinctions of rank born in barbarism, and nourished by chivalry' are being gradually eradicated in the modern world and 'the complexion of manners in Europe be completely changed from what it was half a century ago', then revolution may be counterproductive; 'the tumult of internal commotion and civil discord'[60] replaces the slow advance of

---

[55] Mary Wollstonecraft, *An Historical and Moral View of the Origin and Progress of the French Revolution and the Effect It Has Produced in Europe*, 2nd edn, 1795 (Delmar, NY: Scholars' Facsimiles and Reprints, 1975), p. 518.

[56] Claire Tomalin, *The Life and Death of Mary Wollstonecraft* (New York: New American Library, 1974), p. 166.

[57] Cf. Wollstonecraft, *Historical and Moral View*, p. 311: 'It is . . . in a state of comparative idleness – pursuing employments not absolutely necessary to support life, that the finest polish is given to the mind'.

[58] Wollstonecraft, *Historical and Moral View*, p. 3.

[59] Wollstonecraft, *Historical and Moral View*, pp. 2; 22.

[60] Wollstonecraft, *Historical and Moral View*, p. 69.

reason. But the tyranny of the rich over the poor may be so well entrenched that only revolt can begin to redress the imbalance, a similar view of the horns of the dilemma that Shelley would later deal with, particularly in his Irish crusade. Like Shelley and later radicals forced to reconcile revolutionary excesses with their confidence in the necessity of reform, Wollstonecraft takes the long-term view that her historiography of manners accommodates:

> Europe will probably be, for some years to come, in a state of anarchy; till a change of sentiments, gradually undermining the strongholds of custom, alters the manners, without rousing the little passions of men.... [61]

Wollstonecraft's Europe is a concept largely yet to be achieved, one whose glory is far from extinguished, but only beginning to glimmer. From her vantage as an expatriate in a Paris already showing the most ill side of revolutionary progress, she managed yet to confirm the hopes of reformers within a discourse shaped as much by Burke as his opponents.

The overlap between Burke's powerful defence of *ancien régime* Europe and Volney's radical refiguration of European cultural hegemony, helps define the perimeters of a cultural discourse, within which Wollstonecraft writes her history. But even as Wollstonecraft's own residence in Paris informs the tone of her history, an important opportunity remained for English travellers to fill in the middle ground of this discourse with on the spot accounts of the progress and aftermath of the French Revolutionary experiment. This is not to minimise the importance of other contributors to the Revolution debate. Paine, Godwin, Mackintosh, and many others, attacked Burke's formulations with criticism of his language, historiography, and political philosophy. Hannah More, Richard Watson, and others, countered with similar appeals.[62] But travellers could claim the privilege of first-hand evidence as to the manner in which new political theories were introduced by the chief participants in the drama unfolding in the National Assembly, and what is more, the effects on the citizenry, both in Paris and in the French nation as a whole. It was only against the backdrop of this kind of journalism that the more theoretical polemics on the Revolution controversy could gain ground with moderates, over whose political souls much of the battle was fought.

This is not to say that travellers were never quite capable of the outpourings of enthusiasm that characterised revolutionary clubbists at home. 'Bliss was it in that dawn to be alive', Wordsworth famously exclaims in *The Prelude*, remembering his elation as a traveller in France during the early days of the Revolution. Though he did not write up his travels then, Helen Maria Williams did (the Shelleys eagerly sought out Williams when visiting Paris in 1814). Williams arrived in Paris

---

[61] Wollstonecraft, *Historical and Moral View*, pp. 71-2.
[62] See *Burke, Paine, Godwin, and the Revolution Controversy*, ed. Marilyn Butler (Cambridge: Cambridge University Press, 1984), for a representative selection of these writings.

on 13 July 1790, the same day as Wordsworth's arrival at Calais.[63] Williams's account, *Letters Written in France* (1790), paints an almost flawless picture of joyful liberty that not even the sight of 'la Lantern' can disturb for long. The evidence of her book would suggest that Williams had a limited understanding of the Revolution debates in the National Assembly (unlike her contemporaries Arthur Young, John Moore, and Mary Wollstonecraft) yet she skilfully renders the symbolic dimensions of the times and recounts history as if it were romance: the memoirs of 'Mons. and Madame du F—' that occupy nearly a third of the narrative follow the persecution of a Frenchman who marries below his station. The tale indicts not only the cruelty of a monstrous father but also the patriarchal *ancien régime* that he represents. The father dies, the *ancien régime* is overthrown, and Mons. du F— simultaneously regains his estate, becoming for the people the model he never had in a parent: 'His tenants consider him as a father, and, "when the eye sees him it blesses him"'.[64]

The Williams that Shelley would have found in 1814 (had she been at home) would have espoused radical views, though tempered more in line with Wollstonecraft's in *An Historical and Moral View*,[65] and Shelley may well have known this if he had encountered any of Williams's subsequent travel books on France or Switzerland.[66] Even if Shelley had been looking for the author of *Letters from France*, any enthusiasm he may have retained for the early days of the Revolution would have been challenged by its aftermath. His itinerary included many of the principle seats of the late war, and he encountered little to remind him of the promise of liberty that the Revolution seemed to herald. When Shelley returned from this first continental tour in September 1814, he began to take stock of the changes that had occurred in Europe since 1789. He turned to writers who had struggled to affirm the value of revolution towards a European renaissance, and it was then that he read Mary Wollstonecraft's *An Historical and Moral View* and reread parts of Godwin's *Political Justice* and Paine's *Rights of Man*. Between 1814 and 1817, Shelley perused numerous histories, biographies, and memoirs, largely in French, on the events and characters of 1790s France: Augustin Barruel's *Mémoires pour servir à l'histoire du Jacobinisme* (1797), Jean-Baptiste Louvet's *Quelque notices pour l'histoire et le récit de mes perils depuis le 31 Mai*

---

[63] See Jonathan Wordsworth's useful introduction to Williams's *Letters Written in France, 1790* (Oxford: Woodstock Books, 1989).

[64] Williams, *Letters*, p. 192.

[65] Helen Williams had in fact struck up a friendship with Wollstonecraft during the years that produced that book, and Williams had suffered imprisonment along with the other English expatriates during the Terror.

[66] Williams published an expanded edition of *Letters* (1790) as *Letters Written in France in 1790, 1793, and 1794, to a Friend in England, Containing Anecdotes Relative to the French Revolution; Concerning Important Events, Particularly Relating to the Campaign of 1792; A Sketch of the Politics of France during 1793-4, and Scenes in the Prisons of Paris*, 7 vols in 3 (London, 1793-96), as well as *New Travels in Switzerland, Containing a Picture of the Country, the Manners and the Actual Government*, 2 vols (London, 1796).

1793 (1793), John Adolphus's *Biographical Memoirs of the French Revolution*, Louis-Marie Prudhomme's *Histoire générale et impartiale des erreurs, des fautes et des crimes commis pendant la révolution française* (1797), and others. While Wollstonecraft, Godwin, and Paine are Shelley's guiding lights for his larger historical perspective, these other works indicate Shelley's hunger for details from a variety of perspectives, from the 'expatriated Jesuit' (*Prose*, p. 67) Barruel's conspiracy theories to Prudhomme's less than impartial history of royal imposture. The readings indicate both Shelley's attempt to consolidate a vision of reform, such as that propounded in his preface to *The Revolt of Islam*, and his desire for precise on the spot details from which to build that vision.

Of the English travel writers who reported on the early stages of the Revolution, Shelley is known to have read Dr John Moore's *A Journal during a Residence in France* (1793) in December 1814. Moore studies events succeeding those of which Wollstonecraft treats, particularly the attack on the royal palace of the Tuileries of 10 August 1792 and its aftermath, up to the eve of Louis XVI's execution. Shelley, who had studied 'the rhetoric of tyranny' in *Queen Mab* (1813), would have been interested in Moore's frequent notes on the semiotics of revolutionary change: the replacement of statues of kings with those of Liberty, the effacement of 'every word, emblem, or sign' that referred to royalty from 'every shop, magazine, auberge, or hotel', the transformation of the theatre, pantomimes, and puppet-shows to reflect the new political ideology.[67] Equally as appealing would have been Moore's generous liberalism and balanced assessment of political events, their causes and effects. Convinced throughout that the *ancien régime* was an insupportable tyranny, Moore nevertheless documents the excesses that new-found liberty seems to provoke in the streets of Paris and in the National Assembly itself. He does this not only as a historian of recent events, as does Wollstonecraft, but also as a journalist, weighing carefully what he regards as the benefits and ills of the day. One of Moore's conclusions anticipates what Shelley later referred to as the 'age of despair' (*PS2*, p. 35) following the Revolution: 'Of all the evils which have attended this extraordinary Revolution, the most important to mankind in general, perhaps, is, that it weakens the indignation which every liberal mind naturally feels for despotism, and inclines them to submit to the awful tranquillity of methodised oppression'.[68]

Moore's journal is also a measured, old Whig response to Burke's alarmism; while giving Burke his due as a powerful rhetorician and even as a penetrating philosopher of the human heart, Moore nevertheless uses his privilege as an on the spot observer of events that Burke could only sketchily anticipate to challenge Burke's overly conservative philosophy of manners. Physically closer to the events

---

[67] John Moore, *A Journal During a Residence in France, from the Beginning of August, to the Middle of December, 1792*, 2 vols (London: Printed for G. G. J. and J. Robinson, 1793), 1: 85. See also 1: 123: 'One fellow, on a kind of stage, had a monkey who played a thousand tricks. When the man called him aristocrate, the monkey flew at his throat with every mark of rage; but when he called him un bon patriote, the monkey expressed satisfaction, and caressed his master'.

[68] Moore, *Journal*, 2: 450-51.

of 10 August 1792 than Burke was to those of 6 October 1789, Moore at first uses his position to validate some of Burke's impressions of the Queen. While Burke stylises the Queen's 'almost naked' flight from her pursuers to the 'feet of a king and husband' on 6 October, Moore relies on first-hand reports of the Queen's behaviour. He is 'assured that she behaved with great firmness' and 'spoke in an encouraging manner to the guards' during her later ordeal on 10 August 1792.[69] Moore uses this as a basis for his validation of Burke's fetishism regarding the effects of suffering royalty on human sympathies. We are more affected by the misfortunes of the great than those of more common people, Moore asserts with something of a backhanded scepticism at Burke's less than philosophical rhetoric: 'Without disputing about what ought to be, but avowing honestly what is, the human heart, faithful to its first impressions, or prejudices if you please, will answer – I take a stronger interest in the distresses of the Queen'.[70] Towards the conclusion of his narrative, Moore returns to Burke's account of 6 October 1789 more directly in order to counter the wider applications of this kind of sympathy. In the 'glory of Europe' passage, Burke finishes his portrait of Marie Antoinette with a nostalgia for an age in which 'vice itself lost half its evil, by losing all its grossness'. Referring to this line in particular, Moore responds like Shelley by affirming the superiority of cultivation over savagery while recognising new ways in which savagery might be masked by cultivation: 'All the refinements of Courts cannot alter the nature of falsehood, ingratitude, or treachery; nor can all the perfumes of the East sweeten the corruption of vice'. Several pages later, Moore argues with Wollstonecraft that new manners suitable to a republic have yet to evolve, and that the suddenness of the change from the *ancien régime* would hinder the permanence of such a change.[71]

Moore's journal would have complemented Shelley's thinking on the discourse of manners and the idea of Europe, already discussed with reference to Burke, Gibbon, Volney, and Wollstonecraft, and would have helped locate these concerns in a specific geographical-political moment: revolutionary Paris in the autumn of 1793. The extent to which Shelley turned to travel literature to help bring these ideas up to date, however, is difficult to determine. It is tempting to imagine him reading Thomas Holcroft's *Travels from Hamburg . . . to Paris* (1804) alongside Mary Shelley in October 1816 (*MWSJ*, p. 141), for Holcroft had joined the throng of English tourists taking advantage of the Peace of Amiens for a trip to Paris. Holcroft prefaces his account as a series of notes, albeit sentimental ones, towards 'a universal and permanent code of ethics' and he goes on to affirm the value of travel observations to this effect: 'By habits, manners, and customs, the history of Man is most clearly and emphatically written; and this history is the book of knowledge, in which must be read all the grand and useful lessons the experiences

---

[69] Moore, *Journal*, 1: 164.
[70] Moore, *Journal*, 1: 166.
[71] Moore, *Journal*, 2: 425-6; 432.

of ages has taught'.[72] We do know, however, that in December 1817 Shelley studied Lady Morgan's *France* (1817). Published soon after Shelley completed his own mythic refiguration of Europe, the French Revolution, and the evolution of manners in *Laon and Cythna: Or, A Vision of the Nineteenth Century* (1817), Morgan's book would have offered Shelley favourable grounds for comparison between what he envisioned and what she purported to be the effects of the French Revolution on the progress of society.

Already a champion of the Irish cause Shelley had defended, Morgan perceived in the example of post-revolutionary France an image of social amelioration among the agrarian peasantry that contrasted sharply with her native Ireland. In *France* she set out to describe this transformation and to give credit where she thought it due, namely, to reforms instituted by the French Revolution and by Napoleon. Referring frequently to Arthur Young's travels in France in the late 1780s, Morgan paints a bleak picture of pre-revolutionary France, and like Young attributes this to government: 'This frightful picture of national poverty is corroborated by Mr. Young . . . who observes that the original sin of its institutions struck at the root of national prosperity, and produced a poverty, that "reminded him of Ireland"'.[73] By contrast, Morgan's idyllic description of post-revolutionary manners reveals a more cheerful, moral, sober, and prosperous peasantry. While Morgan gives numerous on the spot vignettes to support her more general observations, there is often something of golden age pastoralism in her phrases, as in this deistic euphemism for agriculture: 'it is impossible not to envy a country whose population is invited, by a bounteous and prodigal soil, to devote its energies to the service of nature'.[74]

Morgan's political rivals took her enthusiasm to task: John Wilson Croker in the *Quarterly Review*[75] and William Playfair in *France As It Is: Not Lady Morgan's France* (1819).[76] Nevertheless, her defence in principle of gradual improvement through revolutionary change made her travel book a powerful ally

---

[72] Thomas Holcroft, *Travels from Hamburgh, through Westphalia, Holland, and the Netherlands, to Paris*, 2 vols (London: Printed for Richard Phillips, 1804), 1: v, vi.

[73] Sidney Owenson, Lady Morgan, *France*, 2 vols (London: Printed for Henry Colburn, 1817), 1: 121.

[74] Morgan, *France*, 1: 42.

[75] See Review of *France*, by Lady Morgan, *Quarterly Review*, vol. 17, no. 33 (April 1817), pp. 260-86.

[76] William Playfair, *France As It Is: Not Lady Morgan's France*, 2 vols, [London, 1819], gives Morgan a sharp lecture on the Gilpinian picturesque for aestheticising the peasantry:

> Before *we* begin to give any account of France, it may not be amiss to make a few observations concerning the descriptive. Most of our readers no doubt have heard of the picturesque. . . . If not, let them begin by the study of Mr. Gilpin's tour, written 35 years ago.
>
> . . . There is nothing of the picturesque in an English post chaise and four with two postilions . . . sweeping along a fine road; but there is a great deal of it in a French diligence . . . with half-starved horses, and passengers with their heads all wrapped up, as if they were returning wounded from the battle of Waterloo. (1: 5-6)

of Old Whigs and new radicals again agitating for parliamentary reform at home and disheartened by the Congress of Vienna's endorsement of the pre-revolutionary status quo in Europe. Like Shelley in the preface to *Laon and Cythna*, Morgan wrote with a consciousness that her book would enter a marketplace polarised along party lines, and she appealed for her readers to think for themselves. While Shelley castigates anonymous critics in his preface with an analogy between them and the 'hired sophists' upholding state power in ancient Rome (*PS2*, p. 44), Morgan prefaces her account with a more direct condemnation of the *Quarterly* critics who had previously accused her of 'licentiousness, profligacy, irreverence, blasphemy, libertinism, disloyalty, and atheism'[77] – in short, the epithets with which Shelley too was branded at various points in his career.

This public posturing stamps Shelley's and Morgan's contributions to the debate over post-revolutionary France as contemporaneous and related discussions. Shelley's *Laon and Cythna* proves to be very much about learning to read the larger shape of historical progression, and the poem begins with a visionary led to a precipice in despair over the fallen hopes of France. Here he must learn to find hope and to reread the visionary scene that unfolds before him, reassigning proper values to the eagle and serpent 'wreathed in fight' (*PS2*, I, l. 193), the latter more representing the spirit of good than its usual Judeo-Christian symbolic value. Morgan's book begins with a very similar vision of revolutionary change along with an appeal for a hermeneutics untainted by party politics:

> When the burning floods and frightful explosions of Vesuvius poured ruin and desolation on every object within the sphere of its convulsed action, the elder Pliny was seen exposing himself to its varied forms of danger, in the cause of knowledge, and for the benefit of his species: his spirit soaring in sublimity above the wreck of matter, as nature, with all her awful secrets, stood revealed before him. But to the greatest political explosion that time has ever witnessed, or history recorded; to the revolution of France few philosophical Plinys have brought their cool and unbiased scrutiny.[78]

Shelley's Canto 1 could have taken its cue from such a passage, with the Visionary standing in for Pliny and the revolutionary tempest for the 'wreck of matter'. Shelley's Visionary, however, is an underdeveloped Pliny, neither cool nor unbiased at first; he sees nature's 'awful secrets', misinterprets them, and must be taught to see better. In the end, he is more like Milton's Adam receiving visionary instruction from the Archangel Michael.

That Shelley's vision may have been in some part a response to Morgan's *France*, however, as Gerald McNiece implies, appears highly unlikely, unless it could be shown that Shelley had Morgan in mind when revising the proofs of the

---

[77] Morgan, *France*, 1: viii.
[78] Morgan, *France*, 1: 4-5.

original poem into *The Revolt of Islam* (1818).[79] But McNiece quite rightly wonders at the disparity between Shelley's creative versions of the Revolution and his 'full and factual' sources, more plausibly concluding that Shelley 'created his own revolutionary events, purged of the dross of actuality and factional corruption'.[80] From this point of view, *Laon and Cythna* pits the tyrant Othman against the eponymous hero and heroine, the eagle principle of evil against the serpent principle of good. Though Shelley delineates the shades between the poles where, for example, the essentially good Laon participates in the asocial thoughtlessness of his oppressors, and suffers madness as a consequence, there are no overt correspondences or references to the complex nets of political intrigue that Wollstonecraft, Moore, or Morgan describe. While the events of 1790s Paris that Shelley read so much about ring true as footnotes to his sentiments in the Preface and to the revolutionary and counter-revolutionary stages of the epic, they are unacknowledged, silent presences.[81]

The intersection between the poem, political debate, and travel literature instead works on the level of what Holcroft calls 'habits, manners, and customs', and which this chapter has traced in some detail. In *Laon and Cythna* the story of failed revolution nevertheless outlines the successful amelioration of habits of thought and conduct, not only by the example of Laon, whose education includes, besides madness, old books and new love, but also by the example of the Visionary himself whose despair and subsequent misreadings of the eagle, serpent, and mysterious woman in Canto 1 sets all in motion. By implication, Shelley's reader stands in relation to the poem as does the Visionary to Laon's embedded narrative, except that Shelley's reader sees his own maps of misreading enacted by the Visionary – an example of Shelley's dictum in the *Defence* that 'neither the eye nor the mind can see itself, unless reflected upon that which it resembles' (*SPP*, p. 520). In this way, Shelley's poem enacts the historiographical optimism on the evolution or improvement of manners that informs the hermeneutics in much of his readings.

I would like to conclude by considering a travel book of the 1790s that Shelley may not have read: Arthur Young's *Travels in France* (1792). For during the years of Shelley's greatest interest in and contact with France, 1814-17, he was not only formulating a theory of cultural progress but he was also learning to observe and describe the events and places which are the particulars of historical perspective: hence the journal he shared with Mary Shelley which recorded their first impressions of the continent in 1814, the Geneva Journal of 1816 with Shelley's account of their return through Paris, the letters to Peacock from Switzerland in 1816, and the *History of a Six Weeks' Tour* (1817) in which all these materials were collated. While Moore, Holcroft, and Lady Morgan are important for the evidence they offer towards the meta-narratives that Burke, Wollstonecraft, and

---

[79] Gerald McNiece, *Shelley and the Revolutionary Idea* (Cambridge, MA: Harvard University Press, 1969), p. 19.

[80] McNiece, *Shelley and the Revolutionary Ideal*, p. 20.

[81] See *L*, 1: 430: 'In considering the political events of the day I endeavour to divest my mind of temporary sensations, to consider them as already historical'.

Volney endorse, a traveller like Young, whose interests take him beyond Paris, reveals how observation and description in a travel narrative can be structured in terms of these larger discourses.

Young's *Travels* was among the most celebrated responses to Burke and the French Revolution.[82] Its arguments strongly influenced public perceptions, and were still the subject of much post-revolutionary debate on the state of rural France, including Morris Birkbeck's *Notes on a Journey through France* (1814) and Lady Morgan's *France* (1817). Several aspects of Young's approach to travel and travel writing provide a basis of comparison with later writers, including Shelley, who are concerned as much with nature, cultivated and uncultivated, as with metropolitan culture. Though Young does not shy away from serious political and economic analysis of the present state of France and its recent past under the *ancien régime*, he structures his book as an empirical diary integrated with descriptive passages on sublime and picturesque landscapes which subtly encode his political and economic ideals, themselves relegated to factual essays appearing at the end of the volume. In the journal section, Young also enthusiastically claims for his readership several landmarks of European culture associated with Rousseau and Petrarch at Ermenonville, Chambéry, and Avignon in a way that also begs political interpretation, and anticipates Shelley's homage to Rousseau around Lake Geneva in 1816. Finally, throughout the journal section, Young appears in the first person, a character and presence in his own narrative, embodying observations and reflections in a way that signals his departure from the less personalised narratives of the Grand Tourists.

In his political critique, Young balances his distrust of revolution against his practical belief in the morbidity of the *ancien régime* in terms of France's and Europe's future economic health. In a manner that endeared him to apologists for the Revolution like Birkbeck and Morgan, Young attributes the root cause of poverty and social misery to government, but his indictment of the *ancien régime* works equally well as a warning to the National Assembly to institute agrarian reform, without which, he argues, no nation can prosper. Contra Burke, he holds that property does not make wealth, nor do manufactures and commerce. Instead there must be a national effort to make land fertile, and to encourage an economic infrastructure that takes every particular of this goal into account. Consequently, Young condemns the system of rents widely employed in France and Italy, and argues for enclosure; the best way to improve the standard of living is to free people from subsistence farming and the burden of credit.[83] With enclosure,

---

[82] First published at Bury St Edwards in 1792, *Travels* was reprinted in Dublin the following year. A second edition appeared in 1794, followed by numerous expensive editions, and the text was reprinted in John Pinkerton's *A General Collection of the Best and Most Interesting Voyages and Travels in All Parts of the World*, 17 vols (London, 1808-14).

[83] Cf. Ann Bermingham, *Landscape and Ideology: The English Rustic Tradition, 1740-1860* (Berkeley: University of California Press, 1986), p. 77. Bermingham's picture of Young, drawn from essays of the 1790s in the Board of Agriculture's *Annals of Agriculture*,

displaced freeholders and tenants become farm workers or migrate to urban centres, where they become consumers of agricultural products; a more efficient agriculture propagates the manufacturing industries that employ this newly formed labouring class. In no way do these principles constitute an uncritical defence of the Revolution, since Young holds the new government to the same standards and finds it wanting in many of its initial reforms. Young merely details the ways in which the regime that Burke defends on almost mystical grounds has failed in its practical public duties.

When Young turns from agricultural and political observations to landscape description, the transitions can seem abrupt. His eye, wandering from cultivated to uncultivated ground, seems to rest on the latter for pleasant excursion, an escape from more weighty matter. Yet, as I have argued elsewhere, the valuable aesthetic view for Young becomes that which synecdochically anticipates the success of his economic policy; his aesthetic prospects become in a very important sense 'prospective' and encode a futurist logic.[84] If enclosure refashions labourers into urban consumers, as Young predicted, then rural regions would be increasingly gentrified. As signs of poverty recede, the rural scene would become more like its picturesque rendering – a harmony of enclosures and nature, where enclosures are naturalised and nature is enclosed. Young thus aims to abolish 'the contradiction between the social reality of the countryside and its idealised aesthetic'; his picturesque views are characterised less by what Ann Bermingham has called 'aesthetic idealization' as by aesthetic realisation.[85]

Young's principal arguments for the advantages of enclosure emerge from both the diary sections of his text and the discursive essays summarising his conclusions. Nevertheless, in his 'Note upon Methods of Writing Books of Travel', Young harbours no illusions as to which section would attract most readers. The journal form establishes the reader's trust in the traveller, and offers data in the raw, mixed with aesthetic, political, and economic impressions, observations, appreciations, or disgust. Avoiding the single-mindedness of the picturesque tour, Young's journal offers a discursive panorama in which the eye wanders between cultivated and uncultivated ground, as in this description above the village of Argenton:

> It is a delicious scene. A natural ledge of perpendicular rock pushes forward abruptly over the vale . . . at one end closed by hills, and at the other filled by the town with vineyards rising above it; the surrounding scene that hems in the vale is high enough for

---

suggests a man much less comfortable with the details of enclosure as they affected poor relief. Young's proposals for a minimum wage aspired, in Bermingham's view, 'to re-create the living conditions of the rural poor before enclosure'. Bermingham goes on to assert that 'such solutions borrowed on nostalgia for the old order to maintain the new'. In the earlier *Travels*, however, Young still maintained the efficacy of displacing farmers without rights of common to the urban centres.

[84] The arguments here are developed more fully in my article, 'Aesthetics of Enclosure', pp. 23-34.
[85] Bermingham, *Landscape and Ideology*, p. 11.

relief; vineyards, rocks or hills covered with wood. The vale cut into inclosures of a lovely verdure, and a fine river winds through it, with an outline that leaves nothing to wish. The venerable fragments of a castle's ruins, near the point of view . . . awaken reflections on the triumph of the arts of peace over the barbarous ravages of the feudal ages, when every class of society was involved in commotion, and the lower ranks were worse slaves than at present.[86]

Castle, vale, and hills form a series of horizontal planes that, along with the bird's-eye viewpoint, comprise a descriptive composition. But this is also a miniature of the economic life that Young argues for throughout his book. The vale's 'lovely verdure' is causally related to its enclosure, while the river provides the irrigation and circulation of traffic upon which economic life depends. While it may appear that distance elides these relations, the contexts provided by the book as a whole more than compensate for any 'acts of exclusion', as Marjorie Levinson calls them, in the scene itself.[87] Young's point of view provides distance and consequently harmony, while his closer itinerant observations of shoeless peasants, wretched inns, and potholed roads satisfy his scientific enquiry into the incapacitated relation between infrastructures and social justice.[88] More explicitly, however, the tableau enacts an aesthetics of enclosure in which a sense of completion is predominant. Far from encoding a 'structure of desire' that 'escapes the materiality of beautiful objects', as John Whale, Kim Ian Michasiw, and others have analysed in Gilpin's picturesque,[89] Young's sketch leaves 'nothing to wish' – it is first and foremost a structure of fulfilment. Nevertheless, this fulfilment operates within a larger structure of desire that is contingent not on the escape from but on the application of the material relations epitomised in the scene. The associative castle, symbolically placed in the viewer's plane, at once complements the tableau and awakens reflections beyond it, reminding the traveller that the one thing truly to be wished is the realisation of the economic argument in the nation as a whole.

---

[86] Arthur Young, *Travels during the Years 1787, 1788, and 1789 . . . with a View of Ascertaining the Cultivation, Wealth, Resources, and National Prosperity of the Kingdom of France* (1792), reprinted in Pinkerton, ed., *General Collection*, 4: 89.
[87] Marjorie Levinson, *Wordsworth's Great Period Poems: Four Essays* (Cambridge: Cambridge University Press, 1986), pp. 14-57 *passim*. Of Tintern Abbey, Levinson concludes: 'whatever interpretation we choose, we are bound to see that Wordsworth's pastoral prospect is a fragile affair, artfully assembled by acts of exclusion' (p. 32).
[88] Cf. John Barrell, *The Idea of Landscape and the Sense of Place, 1730-1840* (Cambridge: Cambridge University Press, 1972), pp. 81-4. Barrell's argument that Young's descriptions betray his 'guilt at having a taste for the sublime' misses the way in which the picturesque can reinforce rather than undermine Young's preference for cultivated landscape.
[89] John Whale, 'Romantics, Explorers and Picturesque Travellers', *The Politics of the Picturesque*, p. 178. See also, Kim Ian Michasiw, 'Nine Revisionist Theses on the Picturesque', *Representations*, 38 (Spring 1992), pp. 76-100.

Young's picturesque, as in the example of Argenton, keeps nature closely contiguous to agriculture, anticipating popular notions of picturesque beauty that run counter to William Gilpin's famous dictum, '[the picturesque] has nothing to do with the affairs of the plough and the spade'.[90] While Gilpin's followers studiously implemented his restriction, many travel writers like Shelley celebrated 'the union of culture & the untameable profusion & loveliness of nature' (*L*, 2: 7). Young's sublime is also exemplary of wider trends. As he moves in his text into the cultivated valley and up the slopes of the surrounding mountains to the regions where the picturesque shades into the sublime, he appears very reluctant to relinquish that human hold over the landscape. Rapturous without being overwhelmed, he continually gestures towards the resistance of human endeavour to greater powers, as in this passage concerning his ascent from the valley of Larbousse to Montaubin in the Pyrenees (near present day Bagneres de-Luchon):

> The range which closes in the valley to the east is of a character different from the others; it has more variety, more cultivation, villages, forests, glens, and cascades. That of Gouzat, which turns a mill as soon as it falls from the mountain, is romantic, with every accompaniment necessary to give a high degree of picturesque beauty. There are features in that of Montauban, which Claude Loraine would not have failed transfusing on his canvass; and the view of the vale from the chesnut rock is gay and animated. The termination of our valley to the south is striking; the river Neste pours in incessant cascades over rocks that seem an eternal resistance. The eminence in the centre of a small vale, on which is an old tower, is *a wild and romantic spot; the roar of the waters beneath unites in effect with the mountains, whose towering forests, finishing in snow, give an awful grandeur, a gloomy greatness to the scene; and seem to raise a barrier of separation between two kingdoms, too formidable even for armies to pass*. But what are rocks, and mountains, and snow, when opposed to human ambition? – *In the recesses of the pendent woods, the bears find their habitation, and on the rocks above, the eagles have their nests. All around is great; the sublime of nature, with imposing majesty, impresses awe upon the mind*; attention is rivetted to the spot; and imagination, with all its excursive powers, seeks not to wander beyond the scene.
>
> > Deepens the murmurs of the falling floods,
> > And breathes a browner horror o'er the woods.[91]

I have italicised the places where Young seems most to describe the scenes and effects of sublimity, where strategies of containment are in less evidence, in order to draw attention to his dependence on these strategies in the passage as a whole. Even the highlighted passages allude to human powers that give them meaning. The 'towering forests' merely amplify the effect of the 'old tower' that stands

---

[90] William Gilpin, *Remarks on Forest Scenery, and Other Woodland Views (Relative Chiefly to Picturesque Beauty) Illustrated by the Scenes of the New-Forest in Hampshire*, 2 vols (London: R. Blamire, 1791), 1: 298.
[91] Young, *Travels*, 4: 100; my italics.

above the waters whose roar 'unites in effect with the mountains', while the derelict tower itself recalls the working mill at the beginning of the passage. In a similar manner, the 'imposing majesty' of the second highlighted passage seems to follow on from Young's reflections on the kingdoms of France and Spain, and human ambition.

Young's carefully regulated sublime, like his picturesque, does not annihilate human concerns and culture, but intensifies them. He has no doubt that the picturesque features of Montaubin worth observing would have been successfully transcribed by Claude Lorrain, and Young attempts to do the same in language. Similarly, the couplet from Pope's *Eloise to Abelard* that Young reapplies, asserts the painterly limitations of the imagination itself, for the imagination superadds tints and colour when most in awe. Young's question, 'What are rocks, and mountains, and snow, when opposed to human ambition?', at such a moment, anticipates a similar gesture towards human power in Shelley's 'Mont Blanc': 'And what were thou and Earth and Stars and Sea / If to the human mind's imaginings / Silence and solitude were vacancy?' (*PS1*, B Text, ll. 144-5). Like Shelley, Young celebrates man's power ('ambition') to overcome and transform a scene that seems to present a great and eternal obstacle in its very sublime detachment. But for Young, ambition replaces imagination (and farming is ultimately more important for him than art) as the power to do this. Imagination is relegated to the scene itself despite its excursive powers. Shelley, I believe, gives greater scope to the creative imagination, but like Young emphasises it as a power that embosses culture on landscape.

Young's landscape descriptions point to a truism about tourism with an important bearing on my discussion of Shelley: tourists describe what others report to have seen or in the way others see. They continually traverse a textual landscape and implicitly compare notes against other travellers, painters, and poets, sometimes revising and sometimes revalidating their forerunners. Landscape, like urban manners, gains value by virtue of its cultural currency as much if not more than its otherness from human concerns. In these terms, what I have called strategies of containment are not merely conscious plans for bringing a recalcitrant nature into the fold of culture, but the assumptions underlying descriptive technique, and perhaps writing itself if representation may be said to always render the phenomenal cultural.

For Young, and other travellers, there are also places where landscape mediated by human interest is positively celebrated and the value of landscape as a cultural semiotic stated in no uncertain terms. His reference to Claude in the Montaubin passage is one example. Another occurs during the 1789 tour when Young goes on a kind of pilgrimage in the environs of Lille to the fountain of Vaucluse:

> On the summit of a rock above the village, but much below the mountain, is a ruin, called, by the poor people here, the chateau of Petrarch – who tell you it was inhabited by Mons. Petrarch and Madame Laura. The scene is sublime; but what renders it truly

interesting to our feelings, is the celebrity which great talents have given it. The power of rocks, and water, and mountains, even in their boldest features, to arrest attention, and fill the bosom with sensations that banish the insipid feelings of common life – holds not of inanimate nature. To give energy to such sensations, it must receive animation from the creative touch of a vivid fancy: described by the poet, or connected with the residence, actions, pursuits, or passions of great geniuses; it lives, as it were, personified by talents, and commands the interest that breathes around whatever is consecrated by fame.[92]

Later travellers like William Shepherd, Shelley, and Byron would also deploy arguments for the animating touch of genius. But Young represents an early recognition of the aesthetic grounds of heightened empirical sensation; not only does poetry and art structure the way we see or write, but poets and artists personify places by their former presence in them. It is as if nature cannot resist culture, but must always be transformed by it. Or to put this in Romantic terms, the human mind always structures the object world through the medium of aesthetic idealisation. Describing nature, becomes a way of describing desire, a utopian gesture with a humanist core of being (what Young calls the 'passions common to the human race'[93]) located in a particular place and drawing on a particular historiographical vision of culture.[94]

Like Young's other sublime and picturesque tableaux, the visit to Vaucluse takes on a political resonance in the context of the larger 1789 narrative where such idealisations are shattered by daily acts of violence. The day after recording the above passage, Young adds a subtext, quite likely to have been left out of his description for genre reasons: 'I forgot to observe that, for a few days past, I have been pestered with all the mob of the country shooting: one would think that every rusty gun in Provence is at work, killing all sorts of birds' (the National Assembly, he informs us, had relaxed the game laws).[95] The entry reminds us of the differential between what ought to be and what is, and reinforces Young's larger tenet that only particularised observation and policy action can effect the changes towards the society reflected in his landscape aesthetic.

The politicisation of genius in the landscape would come home to Young in his fetishising of Rousseau. There was nothing unusual about his pilgrimage to Ermenonville in 1787 to view the tomb of Rousseau and the ornamental grounds of the Marquis of Girardon laid out in tribute to Rousseau. In fact, Young decides not to describe all this in detail precisely because previous travellers had already done

---

[92] Young, *Travels*, 4: 222.
[93] Young, *Travels*, 4: 221
[94] Young seeks the universal in the particular, traces of common humanity in the objects of his gaze. Wordsworth and Shelley, likewise, empower the poet, whose eye looks steadily on his object, with a similar idealising perspective. See Wordsworth's 'Preface' to *Lyrical Ballads*: 'the Poet binds together by passion and knowledge the vast empire of human society, as it is spread over the whole earth, and over all time' (*WW Prose*, 1: 141, ll. 448-50).
[95] Young, *Travels*, 4: 222-3.

so.[96] Moreover, before the French Revolution there would have been nothing particularly remarkable about Young's adulation of a revolution in French manners 'assisted by the magic of Rousseau's writings'.[97] But in the 1789 tour, Young's 24 December visit to the home of Madam Warens near Chambéry elicits that combination of picturesque landscape description, invocations to genius, and reflections on revolutionary change that characterise the description of Petrarch's Vaucluse mentioned above, but which also begin to suggest the way in which Rousseau's name could never be used innocently by travellers like Shelley after the failure of the French Revolution.

The Chambéry entry begins with remarks on improvements in cultivation and the welcome presence of country houses. On seeing a 'seigneural standard', Young indulges in tragic reflections on stubborn aristocratic arrogance and the need for violence to redress the feudal poor: 'Will nothing but revolutions, which cause their *chateaux* to be burnt, induce them to give to reason and humanity, what will be extorted by violence and commotion?'. What follows answers the rhetorical question; in noting the Court's refusal to allow a touring company of comedians to visit the region out of fear of 'importing among the rough mountaineers the present spirit of French liberty', Young acknowledges the power of art over human consciousness and action. When he then turns to the places 'described by the inimitable pencil of Rousseau' ('objects to me more interesting'), it is not without a sense that he is now talking about a higher art that can achieve the ends of humanity through pacification rather than provocation.[98] Rousseau's descriptions utterly transform 'the leafless melancholy of December' and Young returns 'to Chambéry, with my heart full of Madame de Warens'. Even the rough mountaineers are rendered sympathetic; in the 25 December entry, Young writes, 'Rousseau gives a good character of the people, and I wished to know them better'. His vision of the landscape towards the end of this entry, likewise, echoes the effects of Rousseau's softening influence: 'All hill and dale, tossed about with so much wildness, that the features are bold enough for the irregularity of a forest scene; and yet withal, softened and melted down by culture and habitation, to be eminently beautiful'.[99] Significantly, after receiving in later years an anonymous letter that criticised this celebration of an atheist republican, Young recanted the

---

[96] See *A Tour through Part of France, Containing a Description of Paris, Cherbourg, and Ermenonville, with A Rhapsody, Composed at the Tomb of Rousseau* (London: Printed for T. Cadell, 1789), based on a 1788 tour. In addition to the Rhapsody itself, the author celebrates Rousseau's sensibility with a detailed description of the grounds of Girardon's estate, and by reporting his fetishistic conversation about Rousseau's shoes with an old man, resident in the house in which Rousseau died.
[97] Young, *Travels*, 4: 133.
[98] Young, *Travels*, 4: 284.
[99] Young, *Travels*, 4: 285.

passage.[100] By the late 1790s to imbue landscape with the lessons of Rousseau could be seen as an anti-religious, pro-revolutionary gesture.

If Young's strategies of containment and mediation over nature complement a liberal Whig optimism towards the early stages of the French Revolution, later travellers reflected the changing mood in England. William Clubbe's *Three Days Tour into France* (1798), although based on a much earlier tour, presses all the old Grand Tour descriptive buttons, but contains a startling tableau of gibbeted pirates that must have impressed readers with a horror against the multitudinous underclass, especially in the context of the Nore and Hermione mutinies.[101] Similarly, Sir John Carr's popular travel books in the next decade, including his *Stranger in France* (1807), are replete with sentimental portraits of suffering *émigrés* that in turn colour his linkages between 'picturesque beauty and national glory'.[102] After the war, with the return of 'milords' and 'roturiers' to France the explosion of travelogues reveal the entire gamut of aesthetic argument, from the Lady Morgan / William Playfair dispute over the politics of the picturesque already mentioned, to William Hazlitt's later complex anatomy of the 'uneasy' imagination, deploying its powers from a defective core of self-love.[103]

Like Hazlitt's, Shelley's travel prose explores the imagination's purchase on the object world, even as his poetry and philosophical writings develop the connections between the imagination and the progressive historiography of manners. Shelley is also similar to Hazlitt in his attitude towards France as the site of such inquiry. Both partisans of the French Revolution as master theme at once recognised the centrality of France and England as counterpoints in any national or imperial discourse, and yet both give France relatively short shrift as a subject for travel writing, preferring to set their imaginations free in and beyond the Alps.[104] Hazlitt, to be sure, does treat Napoleonic France generously in his own *Notes of a Journey* (1826), but his essay 'Travelling Abroad' (1828) sums up his earlier argument by locating a politically enlightening escape from self-love in the 'waking dream' of Mont Blanc, or in Italy, 'the home of early imagination', while 'in France I am always an Englishman'.[105] Shelley's first impressions of France in 1814 evince a generosity towards Napoleon, whom liberals like Morris Birkbeck, Lady Morgan, and later Hazlitt considered the 'creator of Paris' rather than the despoiler of Europe. In this vein, the Shelleys' *History of a Six Weeks' Tour* notes

---

[100] Entry on Arthur Young, *Dictionary of National Biography* on CD-ROM (Oxford: Oxford University Press, 1995).

[101] William Clubbe, *The Omnium: Containing the Journal of a Late Three Days Tour to France* (Ipswich, 1798), p. 14.

[102] Sir John Carr, *The Stranger in France*, 2nd edn (London: Printed for J. Johnson, 1807), p. 1.

[103] William Hazlitt, *Notes of a Journey Through France and Italy* (1826), in *The Complete Works of William Hazlitt*, ed. P. P. Howe, vol. 17 (London: Dent, 1933). Cf. 302-3: 'Not only can we not attach the same meaning to words, but we cannot see objects with the same eyes .... The pictures that most delighted me in Italy were those I had before seen in the Louvre "with the eyes of youth"'.

[104] See *L*, 2: 221, where Shelley tells Keats that 'France is not worth seeing'.

[105] Hazlitt, *Notes of a Journey*, 17: 343-4.

the 'Gothic barbarism' of the allied conquerors who pull down the monuments of Napoleon's almost 'Roman greatness' (*HSWT*, p. 12). But the *History of a Six Weeks' Tour* narrative strains forwards until it moves into the Alps, and the 1816 portion deals almost exclusively with the environs of Mont Blanc. With *Alastor*, composed between the 1814 and 1816 tours, Shelley firmly dislocates French themes into a travelogue from the margins of power. For Hazlitt, such dislocation means an escape from post-revolutionary disillusionment and disappointment into an identitylessness that seems to be a romantic gloss of Shelley and Keats:

> I was not displeased to have got so far south as to have worn out the traces of my personal identity . . . . Anything to leave the sense of self behind us, and not to aggravate it by foreign travel and national antipathies! It is well to be a citizen of the world, to fall in, as nearly as we can, with the ways and feelings of others, and make one's self at home wherever one comes: or it is better still to live in an *ideal* world . . . that no accident of time or place, irritation or disappointment can assail . . .; not to be calm in solitude and agitated in the assemblies of men, but in the midst of a great city to retain possession of one's faculties as in a perfect solitude, and in a wilderness to be surrounded with the gorgeousness of art . . . .[106]

Shelley's work after 1814 also begins to remotivate Goldsmith's phrase, 'citizen of the world', to explore the internationalist subjectivity opened up by a historiography of manners, but for Shelley, writing over a decade before Hazlitt, the ideal was still tied up in real debates and attitudes encompassed by travellers' interpretations of post-revolutionary Europe.

---

[106] Hazlitt, *Notes of a Journey*, 17: 344.

Chapter 2

'Citizens of the World': Dislocated Vision in *Alastor*

> Ah! what avails Imagination high
> Or Question deep? what profits all that Earth,
> Or Heaven's blue Vault, is suffered to put forth
> Of impulse or allurement, for the Soul
> To quit the beaten track of life, and soar
> Far as she finds a yielding element
> In past or future; as far as she can go
> Through time or space; if neither in the one
> Nor in the other region, nor in aught
> That Fancy, dreaming o'er the map of things,
> Hath placed beyond these penetrable bounds,
> Words of assurance can be heard; if no where
> A habitation, for consummate good,
> Or for progressive virtue, by the search
> Can be attained, a better sanctuary
> From doubt and sorrow, than the senseless grave?
>
> (Wordsworth, *The Excursion*, Book III, 1814)

They who, deluded by no generous error, instigated by no sacred thirst for doubtful knowledge, duped by no illustrious superstition, loving nothing on this earth, and cherishing no hopes beyond, yet keep aloof from sympathies with their kind, rejoicing neither in human joy nor mourning with human grief; these, and such as they, have their apportioned curse. They languish, because none feel with them their common nature. They are morally dead. They are neither friends, nor lovers, nor fathers, nor citizens of the world, nor benefactors of their country.

(Shelley, Preface to *Alastor*, 1816)

The day after the Shelley party returned from the Continent in September 1814, Mary Shelley recorded in her journal that Shelley 'calls on Hookham and brings home Wordsworths [sic] Excursion of which we read a part – much disappointed — He is a slave — ' (*MWSJ*, p. 25). The next day, 15 September, she continued reading aloud 'the history of Margeret' (*MWSJ*, p. 26) from Book I. Claire

Clairmont, very likely articulating the impressions of all three, wrote in her journal for the day, 'Read in the Excursion – the Story of Margaret very beautiful' (*CCJ*, p. 43). This mixture of disappointment and admiration resurfaces in Shelley's *Alastor* volume published early in 1816. Here first appeared the startling elegiac sonnet 'To Wordsworth' along with the title poem, for which Paul Mueschke and Earl L. Griggs first catalogued numerous allusions to Wordsworth's poetry, especially *The Excursion* and the Intimations Ode. Mueschke and Griggs argue that Wordsworth was 'the prototype of the poet in *Alastor*' which was concerned with Wordsworth's 'declining poetic power'.[1] For Shelley, this falling off was directly related to Wordsworth's inability to maintain his earliest ideological commitments in the post-Napoleonic era. As Shelley writes unambiguously in 'To Wordsworth': 'In honoured poverty thy voice did weave / Songs consecrate to truth and liberty, – / Deserting these, thou leavest me to grieve' (*PS1*, ll. 11-12).

Since Mueschke and Griggs's article, the voluminous critical debate over *Alastor* has centred on the nature of Shelley's critique of Wordsworth, and to a lesser extent Coleridge.[2] Earl Wasserman's influential *Shelley: A Critical Reading* (1971) focused attention on the poem's narrative ambiguities, distinguishing the fictional Narrator from his subject, the 'Visionary', and both from 'Shelley', who speaks in the poem's preface.[3] For Wasserman, the action of the poem is dialogic, modulating 'the Narrator (poet of the natural world) and his subject (poet of the ideal)' against each other, an ironic interplay that produces a metaphysical scepticism related to the near contemporaneous *A Refutation of Deism* (1814).[4] Subsequent criticism has developed, modified, or contested Wasserman's position on the poem's metaphysics by exploring the extent to which Wordsworth can be identified with the Narrator or the Poet, and how such identifications either stabilise or obscure Shelley's epistemology. This criticism has been well-rehearsed elsewhere, most fully by Christopher Heppner, who himself exemplifies the poem's slipperiness with an *almost* persuasive argument that the opening invocation, commonly attributed to a Wordsworthian Narrator, actually belongs to the Poet himself.[5] Donna Richardson has brought out the consanguinity between Wasserman's 'sceptical idealist' interpretation of the poem and post-structuralist readings. In her view, both Wasserman and Jerrold Hogle respond to the

---

[1] Paul Mueschke and Earl L. Griggs, 'Wordsworth as the Prototype of the Poet in Shelley's *Alastor*', *PMLA*, 49 (1934), pp. 229-30.

[2] For Coleridgean arguments, see Joseph Raban, 'Coleridge as the Prototype of the Poet in Shelley's *Alastor*', *Review of English Studies*, n.s., 17 (1966), pp. 278-92, and Edward Strickland, 'Transfigured Night: The Visionary Inversions of *Alastor*', *Keats-Shelley Journal*, 33 (1984), pp. 148-60. Both Raban and Strickland argue that *Alastor*, with 'The Ancient Mariner' or 'Kubla Khan', is preoccupied with visionary or 'mental' landscapes.

[3] In the discussion that follows, I adopt the more usual practice of referring to the 'Visionary' as the 'Poet'.

[4] Earl R. Wasserman, *Shelley: A Critical Reading* (Baltimore: Johns Hopkins University Press, 1971), pp. 11; 34.

[5] Christopher Heppner, 'Alastor: The Poet and the Narrator Reconsidered', *Keats-Shelley Journal*, 37 (1988), pp. 91-109. For Heppner's review of *Alastor* criticism, see pp. 91-4.

'indeterminacy of phenomenal nature' in *Alastor*, 'denying significant human relation to nature'.[6] Richardson believes that the poem 'explicitly rejects the assertion in Wordsworth's *The Excursion* that mind and nature are so "fitted" to each other they can experience a "wedded" union', but that it does recommend a 'partnership' without the epistemological certainties implied by the spousal metaphor.[7]

More recent critics have seen the poem's metaphysical problems wedded to politics and culture. The fact that Shelley's dialogue with Wordsworth over the correspondences between mind and nature, knowledge and the object world, takes place within what Stuart Curran has called a 'grand tour of the orient'[8] indicates the importance of discourses of travel and colonial encounter in shaping the poem. The most thorough study of this kind, Nigel Leask's *British Romantic Writers and the East* (1992), explores Shelley's orient as a dislocated topos for revolutionary change that nevertheless exposes him as a 'confirmed orientalist and liberal imperialist'.[9] Leask roots Shelley's political idealism in utopian discourses surrounding the French Revolution, but questions his awareness of the actual mechanisms of British colonial rule in India, a 'reality . . . which returned to undermine the coherence and the totalizing aspirations of his poetry and politics'.[10] In response to Edward Said's over-determined sense of Western orientalist hegemony, Leask acknowledges the presence of a telltale 'anxiety' in Shelley's work, or, as Michael Rossington more generously puts it, a 'diversity of impulses in Shelley's attitude to the East'.[11] Leask and Rossington both follow post-colonial paths laid by such writers as Homi Bhabha and Robert Young, recognising that European articulations of the orient are far more ambivalent than Said's binary theory seems to allow, and both find that Shelley's scepticism towards sources of power and authority positions him precariously between exposure and participation in orientalist discourses.[12]

---

[6] Donna Richardson, 'An Anatomy of Solitude: Shelley's Response to Radical Scepticism in *Alastor*', *Studies in Romanticism*, 31 (Summer 1992), pp. 172-3, n. 4; 174.
[7] Richardson, 'Anatomy of Solitude', pp. 173; 175-7.
[8] Stuart Curran, *Shelley's Annus Mirabilis* (San Marino, CA: Huntington Library, 1975), p. 64.
[9] Nigel Leask, *British Romantic Writers and the East* (Cambridge: Cambridge University Press, 1992), p. 70. See also Michael Rossington, 'Shelley and the Orient', *Keats-Shelley Review*, 6 (Autumn 1991), pp. 18-36, and Nicholas Birns, 'Secrets of the Birth of Time: The Rhetoric of Cultural Origins in *Alastor* and "Mont Blanc"', *Studies in Romanticism*, 32 (Fall 1993), pp. 339-65.
[10] Leask, *British Romantic Writers*, p. 6.
[11] Rossington, 'Shelley and the Orient', p. 20.
[12] See Homi Bhabha, 'Signs Taken for Wonders: Questions of Ambivalence and Authority under a Tree Outside Delhi, May 1817', in *Europe and Its Others*, 2 vols, ed. Francis Barker, et al. (Colchester: University of Essex, 1985), 1: 89-106; Robert Young, *White Mythologies: Writing History and the West* (London: Routledge, 1990), esp. Ch. 7, 'Disorientating Orientalism', pp. 119-40.

My primary concern here is with Shelley's constitution of self and social being in the discourse of European travel and *its* figuring of cultural hegemony. If, as Brian Dolan has recently argued, 'the level of concern to define "the European" seems to be proportionate to the degree of political power emanating from central Europe', then the post-Napoleonic shift of power to the victorious allies, chiefly Britain, created new and urgent conditions for a reassessment of the boundaries between self and 'other', national and cosmopolitan subjectivity.[13] For Dolan, Europe's own frontiers, those peripheral destinations beyond the usual itineraries of the eighteenth-century Grand Tour, become the spaces out of which travel writing asserts and modifies its discourse of empowered subjectivity, and in which a dialectical interplay between alterity and familiarity becomes more telling than in more exotic travels, where the self is defined in stark contrast to the savage 'other'. Shelley's Continental travels in 1814, I will argue, become a crucial experience and source of imagery for his reflections on this problematic. Insofar as the 1814 tour functions as a compressed Grand Tour under extreme conditions, it collapses Shelley's sense of periphery and centre, opening up a syncretic space for imagining peripheries in a purposely vague orientalist landscape; as the *Alastor* poet leaves the familiarity of historical objects he traverses an increasingly symbolic Asia emptied of signs of its historicism. As Robert Young has remarked, 'the creation of the Orient, if it does not really represent the East, signifies the West's own dislocation from itself, something inside that is presented, narrativized, as being outside'.[14] Instead of contextualising Shelley's orient in terms of British imperial aspirations and institutions in India, therefore, I will consider the discursive strategies of travel writing as it rewrites or recomposes a disrupted European centre.

By these terms, my approach complements the Wordsworthian focus of *Alastor* scholarship. *The Excursion* becomes an argument not only for an authentic imaginative or religious reorientation of the post-revolutionary character (negatively represented by the Solitary and positively by the Wanderer), but also for an Anglo-centric Europe, backed up by the symbolic strategies of containment enacted in domestic tourist literature such as William Gilpin's or Thomas West's Lake District guides. Katherine Turner has recently discussed the turn to travelogues with British itineraries in the 1790s as part of a 'pervasive discourse of conservative insularity', citing Thomas Macdonald's outcry in *Thoughts on the Public Duties of Private Life* (1795) against a '"general philanthropy" which would maintain that "the heart is a citizen of the world"'.[15] Macdonald promotes instead a new reliance upon British national values as protection against an insidious Jacobin

---

[13] Brian Dolan, *Exploring European Frontiers: British Travellers in the Age of Enlightenment* (London: Macmillan, 2000), p. 4. Dolan is concerned with travel writing up to 1815 and sees the French Revolution as the landmark from which to date the reorientation of European subjectivity.

[14] Young, *White Mythologies*, p. 139.

[15] Katherine Turner, *British Travel Writers in Europe, 1750-1800: Authorship, Gender and National Identity* (Aldershot: Ashgate, 2001), p. 206.

universalism, an exportation of revolution that must be resisted by all means. With *Alastor*, Shelley resuscitates this 'citizen of the world' debate and applies it to a post-Napoleonic internationalist perspective; the 'cold fireside and alienated home' of England is presented as the site of a post-revolutionary alienation that must be reintegrated into the world. To be the 'benefactor of [one's] country', as Shelley's syntax in the preface suggests, one must first become a 'citizen of the world' (*PS1*, p. 463).[16] Like Wordsworth, however, Shelley figures reintegration as an excursion to sites of cultural achievement through tracts of 'unappropriated' nature and he deploys a symbolic geography that overlaps and alludes to *The Excursion*. The very proximity of these geographies to each other, and to those of European travel books generally, forms another kind of dialogue that has received very little attention. If Shelley 'corrects Wordsworth', as Yvonne Carothers fittingly puts it, the context is in a literature that endeavoured to establish universal cultural values in restoration Europe.[17]

Alastor and the Six Weeks' Tour

The relevance of post-revolutionary travel for *Alastor* is strongly suggested by the contiguity of the problem of Wordsworth with Shelley's own travels in 1814. After his pivotal reading of *The Excursion* within a day of his return from the Continent, Shelley was haunted by Wordsworth's apostasy as the continental political situation deteriorated in liberals' eyes; Napoleon's 'Hundred Days' ended at Waterloo and the ultra-royalist backlash against republicans in France (the 'White Terror') was more severe than anything travellers of the previous summer could have foreseen. Mary Shelley's 1839 note to *Alastor*, however, downplays post-revolutionary European politics, highlighting instead the benign interplay between Shelley's travels and poetic composition:

> As soon as the Peace of 1814 had opened the Continent, [Shelley] went abroad. He visited some of the more magnificent scenes of Switzerland, and returned to England from Lucerne, by the Reuss and the Rhine. This river navigation enchanted him. In his favourite poem of "Thalaba," his imagination had been excited by a description of such a voyage. In the summer of 1815, after a tour along the southern coast of Devonshire and a visit to Clifton, he rented a house on Bishopgate Heath, on the borders of Windsor Forest, where he enjoyed several months of comparative health and tranquil happiness. The later summer months were warm and dry. Accompanied by a few friends, he visited the source of the Thames, making the voyage in a wherry from Windsor to Crichlade...

---

[16] Despite the verbal parallels between Shelley's preface here and Mcdonald's *Thoughts on the Public Duties of Private Life* (1815), there is no evidence of Shelley having read this book. As I argue below, Mary Wollstonecraft is the more likely source of Shelley's reflections on this 1790s political dialogue.

[17] See Yvonne M. Carothers, '*Alastor*: Shelley Corrects Wordsworth', *Modern Language Quarterly*, 42 (1981), pp. 21-47.

. "Alastor" was composed on his return. He spent his days under the oak shades of Windsor Great Park; and the magnificent woodland was a fitting study to inspire the various descriptions of forest scenery we find in the poem. (*MSW*, 2: 267-8)

In emphasising the 'Spirit of Solitude' that inspires the poem, this history re-enacts the poem's own 'argument'. Accordingly, Mary Shelley elides her own presence on the Rhine voyage, and safely locates the tour during 'the Peace', detached from the turbulent strife of the times. She does not mention their travels through war-torn France, instead representing the sublime solitudes of Switzerland and the Rhine. Subsequent tour and river voyage sources are recounted, and she ends with an almost Gilpinesque suggestion that the poem contains domestic 'forest scenery'.[18] The passage not only fits Shelley to the tastes of his posthumous reading public – and worth noticing is how amenable *Alastor* is for this kind of appropriation – but it also presents tourism as a structure of leisure conducive to physical and imaginative health and productivity. The river voyages give Southey's oriental imaginations an increasingly localised life (Switzerland, Devonshire, Windsor Forest) and the substantial presences of 'magnificent scenes' are in turn re-appropriated by Shelley's own orientalist poem. While Mary Shelley does not foreground the political or imperial connotations of the poem's international sources, she identifies its syncretic provenance among such materials, even as she domesticates the foreign for her readers.[19]

The Shelleys' journals of their 1814 tour, and of the Rhine voyage in particular, strongly suggest that the poem's origins and some of its imagery lay in particular travel experiences.[20] Shelley recorded their departure from London on 28 July 1814

---

[18] See William Gilpin, *Remarks on Forest Scenery and Other Woodland Views, Relative Chiefly to Picturesque Beauty*, 2 vols (London, 1791).

[19] Mary Shelley's failure to mention *The Excursion* may also be accounted for by her unwillingness to politicise the provenance of *Alastor*. *The Excursion* more clearly than *Thalaba* addresses post-revolutionary political consciousness. *Thalaba*, however, may betray what Mary Shelley would conceal, if Marilyn Butler is correct in arguing that the spiritual 'quest' theme 'could equally well be read as a plot characteristically signifying revolution, its re-enactments, its threatened return. Southey's *Thalaba the Destroyer* . . . develops the narrative symbolic revolution, on such terms that it is no longer confined to France, or to Europe, or in the literal revolutions of the past'. See Butler's 'Repossessing the Past: The Case for an Open Literary History', *Rethinking Historicism* (Oxford: Blackwell, 1988), pp. 82-3.

[20] The term 'Alastor', which Peacock incorrectly glosses as Greek for 'evil genius', may owe something to Southey's 'God's Judgment on a Bishop' (1799), a poem treating the familiar Rhine legend of Hatto, Archbishop of Mainz. During a time of plague, Bishop Hatto absconds with his wealth to a tower mid-river only to be himself devoured by mice. Southey's poem begins by citing a version related in Thomas Coryate's *Crudities* (1611): 'God Almighty the just avenger of the poor folks Quarrel . . . sent [the mice] to persecute him as his furious Alastors, so that they afflicted him both day and night, and would not suffer him to take his rest in any place'. Southey first published the poem in the *Annual Anthology* (1799) and reprinted it in *Metrical Tales and Other Poems* (London, 1805). Shelley ordered *Metrical Tales* on 24 December 1812 (*L*, 1: 345).

and the journal continues in his hand until 11 August when Mary Shelley took over, after which their respective entries alternate at irregular intervals.[21] These notes are at times sparse or elliptical, often impressionistic, and rarely self-conscious of the momentous historical timing of the elopement tour. Nevertheless, instances of aesthetic vision can give impressions that anticipate *Alastor*. In an early entry, for example, Shelley comments on Mary Shelley's reading of Byron to him in Paris: 'I was not before so clearly aware [of] how much of the colouring our own feelings throw upon the liveliest delineations of other minds. Our own perceptions are the world to us' (*MWSJ*, p. 9). Here might be the kernel of the *Alastor* Narrator's situation as he emotionally reanimates the Poet's visions and wanderings. Here also might be a source for the sense in which the Narrator's world remains radically disjointed from the Poet's; the Narrator visualises geography as a whole as he writes the Poet's tour, while the Poet lives the tour, experiences its immanence, and sees secrets beneath surfaces until objectless love limits his gaze to self-seeking.

In a later entry, Shelley's musings on the 'romantic situations' occupied by 'little villages ruined by the war' recall Arthur Young's pre-war aesthetic idealisations of picturesque landscapes, existing beyond yet within the economic realities they punctuate. Yet Shelley's tableaux function more obviously as places of relief, even escape, from the marks of devastation in the French countryside:

> We rest at vandavres [sic] two hours. We walk in a wood belonging to a neighbouring chateau & sleep under its shade. The moss was so soft, the murmur of the wind in the leaves was sweeter than aeolian music.. we forgot that we were in France or in the world for a time. (*MWSJ*, p. 14)

In this instance, Shelley appropriates the property of a gentleman's estate for a vision of nature that surpasses, yet is seen in terms of cultural ideals (the 'aeolian music'). Any potential associations with *ancien régime* or post-Napoleonic inequities are overpowered by the tactile pleasures of cultivated nature and the wind in the wood, while the travellers' perceptions effectively displace nation, politics, and the world itself.[22] The dislocation of political realities into otherworldly geographies also characterises *Alastor*, where the Poet's eastern journey extends beyond cultural signifiers into a landscape where the Poet may relinquish his last ties in sleep or death. In *Alastor*, politics are foregrounded as principles (the veiled maid sings of 'divine liberty'; *PS1*, l. 159) but displaced as events.

This suggests the real possibility that *Alastor* achieves a level of political self-consciousness that eluded Shelley the hectic tourist, and that *Alastor* may be read in part as a self-critique of Shelley's own escapist tendencies in the journal, or at least

---

[21] Mary Shelley did add a few words to the 29 July entry on the arrival in Calais; after Shelley's 'Mary was there', she writes, 'S.helley [sic] was also with me' (*MWSJ*, p. 7).

[22] See also *MWSJ*, p. 16: 'At Noè, whilst our postillion waited, we walked into the forest of pines. It was a scene of enchantment where every sound & sight contributed to charm. One mossy seat in the deepest recesses of the wood was enclosed from the world by an impenetrable veil'.

as a refiguring of the journal's uneasy tension between aesthetic idealisation and post-Napoleonic political realities. As such, *Alastor* provides a bridge to the *History of a Six Weeks' Tour* (1817), which subjects the same journal materials to a new geographical hermeneutic, in which the ideal of liberty is relocated in the 'chainless winds' of Mont Blanc rather than in picturesque England or post-revolutionary France. Indeed, the *History* contains an increasingly Swiss orientation, with Shelley's letters from Switzerland and 'Mont Blanc' ending the collection. In this context, Vandeuvres comes to represent the last outpost of English sensibility before the increasingly sublime scenes of Alpine dislocation:

> Vandeuvres is a pleasant town, at which we rested during the hours of noon. We walked in the grounds of a nobleman, laid out in the English taste, and terminated in a pretty wood; it was a scene that reminded us of our native country. (*HSWT*, p. 28)

The scene that made them forget 'that we were in France or in the world for a time', as Shelley wrote on the spot in 1814, now reminds them 'of our native country' and 'terminates in a pretty wood', leaving open the possibility of a freedom that transcends the confines of national identity without escaping history. Though Shelley's original impulse recorded in the journal seems closer to the geographical sense developed in *Alastor*, all three of these works explore the space out of which the mind constructs or reconstructs cultural location. For its part, *Alastor* looks back at its own origins in a European sensibility from a position of exteriority, while the *History of a Six Weeks' Tour* finds a space for exteriority within the European theatre itself.

Highly suggestive evidence for an *Alastor* source in the elopement tour is also raised by the journal account of the Rhine voyage. The 'shallop' whose 'sides / Gaped wide with many a rift, and [whose] frail joints / Swayed with the undulations of the tide' (*PS1*, ll. 301-3) has its prototype as much in the river craft hired by the Shelleys on the Rhine as in a more literary source like Southey's *Thalaba*. On 29 August 1814, Shelley describes the boat that would convey them from Laufenburg to Mumpf as 'small & frail' and states that 'it requires much attention to prevent an overset' (*MWSJ*, p. 21). Mary Shelley's elaboration of these notes for *History of a Six Weeks' Tour* provides a realistic gloss to the *Alastor* boat's sea-worthiness, as well as to the death-defying impulse that urges the Poet to 'meet lone Death on the drear ocean's waste' (l. 305):

> Sleeping at Dettingen, we arrived the next morning at Loffenburgh, where we engaged a small canoe to convey us to Mumph. I give these boats this Indian appellation, as they were of the rudest construction – long, narrow, and flat-bottomed: they consisted merely of straight pieces of deal board, unpainted, and nailed together with so little care, that the water constantly poured in at the crevices, and the boat perpetually required emptying. The river was rapid, and sped swiftly, breaking as it passed on innumerable rocks just covered by the water: it was a sight of some dread to see our frail boat

winding among the eddies of the rocks, which it was death to touch, and when the slightest inclination on one side would instantly have overset it. (*HSWT*, pp. 57-8)

Of course, Mary Shelley may be remembering through the glass of Shelley's poem, recasting the Rhine experience as their path of departure from scenes of 'Vision and Love' (*PS1*, l. 366), the return to England, debt, and Godwin. Nevertheless, the primitivism of the experience (Mary Shelley's 'Indian appelation'), the proximity of life to death ('death to touch'), the frailty of the boat and rapidity of the voyage, each have their types in a poem very much concerned with the tenuous grasp of elemental humanity on the perceived certainties that bolster civilised consciousness.

Equally suggestive is Shelley's entry in the 1814 journal for 30 August, Mary Shelley's birthday:

The Rhine is violently rapid today . . . & although interrupted by no rocks is swoln with high waves. It is full of little islands green & beautiful. Before we arrived at Shaufhauc the river became suddenly narrow, & the boat dashed with inconcievable [sic] rapidity round the base of a rocky hill covered with pines. A ruined tower with its desolated windows stood on the summit of another hill that jutted into the river. [sic] beyond the sunset was . . . illumining the mountains & the clouds, & casting the reflection of its hues on the agitated river. The brilliance & contrasts of the shades & colourings on the circling whirl pools of the stream was an appearance entirely new & most beautiful[.]

(*MWSJ*, pp. 21-2)

This 'new' appearance seems to have begun its fermentation in the minds of the Shelley party immediately. Claire Clairmont records in her journal for the day that the 'effect [is] as if snakes were creeping perpetually onwards', and she associatively concludes that 'the descriptions contained in [Coleridge's 'Ancient Mariner'] are more copied from Nature than one is at first aware of' (*CCJ*, p. 34). If Edward Strickland is right in seeing Coleridge's poem more immediately behind the *Alastor* voyage than Wordsworth's *The Excursion*, perhaps Clairmont indicates how the poems need not depict 'radically anti-mimetic voyages'.[23] In any case, Shelley's depiction in *Alastor* of the whirlpool's calm centre 'reflecting, yet distorting every cloud' (*PS1*, l. 385), I would suggest, is another fruit of the Rhine voyage impression. In the *History of a Six Weeks' Tour* version of the slightly later Rhine experiences of 4 September, Mary Shelley draws on this description when describing the Rhine's 'rapid current', its 'desolate towers, and wooded islands', and the effect of ruins' reflections 'on the troubled waters, which *distorted without deforming them*' (*HSWT*, p. 69; my italics). In echoing, yet refining the meaning of the *Alastor* line, Mary Shelley at once implicitly acknowledges the poem's origin in the Rhine voyage, and at the same time reminds us how natural optics reduplicate epistemological problems – certainly a large part of the function of reflections and

---

[23] Strickland, 'Transfigured Night', p. 149.

Narcissism in *Alastor*.[24] In *Alastor*, both moments of the whirlpool voyage that describe distorted reflections (in the second, the yellow flowers' reflection is 'marred' by 'the boat's motion'; l. 408) emphasise natural conditions for the kind of vital metaphoricity that the Narrator's descriptions continuously enact. The Poet's desire for perfect reciprocity between subject and object, self and other, is 'marred' by the linguistic conditions of discovery; the traveller's very presence is like the temporal motion of the whirlpool that reflects, yet distorts the heavens.

If *Alastor*'s imagery and narrative reconfigure Shelley's own tours then we can see more clearly how his strange geographies might be constructed out of structures whose provenance the poem can never escape. Shelley's eastern geographical points of reference in North Africa, 'Arabie / And Persia' (ll. 140-41) are connected to the pedestrian tour book, in which descriptions of objects link the wider world aesthetically with a European authorising gaze based on taste and the structures of taste. This is of course basic to an 'orientalist' argument and Nicholas Birns has pointed out how the Poet's itinerary reflects contemporaneous European interest in the origins of European culture, relocated eastwards in the light of, among other things, Sir William Jones's discovery of a common Indo-European linguistic source.[25] Nevertheless, the focus of *Alastor* is on the Narrator's imaginative reconstruction of a geography over which he himself may not have travelled; certainly the latter part of the poem figures a landscape that the Poet alone is said to have traversed. Unlike the Poet's, the Narrator's eye, grounded allusively in a Wordsworthian perspective, can uncover no more secrets than those revealed in the phenomenal 'flow' of his own language, for like the travel writer, his narrative is controlled and adapted to movement through time and space. The Poet 'ever gazed / And gazed, till meaning on his vacant mind / Flashed like strong inspiration' (ll. 125-7), after which he loses interest in his surroundings; the Narrator, never so successful in his past 'obstinate questionings', can rarely pause for such concentrated inquiry, but must instead construct meaning as he constructs the journey itself. His loco-description is bound as much by his locomotion as location.

'Following the Footsteps of Matilda': Shelley and Wollstonecraft

Before considering how Shelley's debt to Wordsworth might be reconfigured in tourist discourse, I would like to entertain the possibility of another travel text behind Shelley's thinking: Mary Wollstonecraft's *Letters Written during a Short Residence in Sweden, Norway, and Denmark* (1796).[26] Shelley began reading

---

[24] See Susan Fischman, '"Like the Sound of His own Voice": Gender, Audition, and Echo in *Alastor*', *Keats-Shelley Journal*, 43 (1994), pp. 141-69.

[25] See Birns, 'Secrets', p. 348.

[26] For the continued importance of Wollstonecraft's travel writings to Mary Shelley, see Esther H. Schor, 'Mary Shelley in Transit', *The Other Mary Shelley: Beyond Frankenstein*,

Wollstonecraft's *Short Residence* aloud during the Rhine voyage; Claire Clairmont's record of Shelley taking up the book immediately precedes her comments on the river reflections, and draws an analogy between book and river: 'This is one of my very favorite Books – The *language is so very flowing & Eloquent* & it is altogether a beautiful Poem' (*CCJ*, p. 33; my italics).[27] Shelley likely shared Claire's sentiments towards Wollstonecraft's *Short Residence*, and its textual mediation of the scenes over which the Shelley party travelled might help us understand Shelley's own sense of landscape in *Alastor*. Anticipating Shelley, Wollstonecraft's *Short Residence* recasts her own progressivist historiography of manners in *An Historical and Moral View of the . . . French Revolution* (1794) as a solitary travelogue over strange lands, both in, yet outside of a European, French-dominated centre of cultural reference.[28]

Reading *Alastor* with Wollstonecraft in mind, one is struck by the lines Shelley uses to conclude his preface, drawn from Book I of *The Excursion*: 'The good die first, / And those whose hearts are dry as summer dust, / Burn to the socket!' (*PS1*, p. 463). Shelley discovers in Wordsworth's tragic story of Margaret a fitting epitaph for that class which the preface deems 'the unforeseeing multitudes' who are 'morally dead' (*PS1*, p. 463); Margaret's death, like the *Alastor* Poet's, follows a long wasting illness as she fruitlessly waits for the return of her husband, Robert, from the battlefields. But Shelley may also have remembered another instance of injustice. In her *Short Residence*, Wollstonecraft deplores the fate of Caroline Matilda, the adulterous queen of Christian VII and sister to George III. Wollstonecraft respects Matilda as a revolutionary feminist suffering 'an error common to innovators, in wishing to do immediately what can only be done by time' (*LSND*, p. 204), and rejects imputations against the late Queen's maternal character as well as charges that she and her lover, Struensee, kept Christian VII in thrall with drugs.[29] Instead, Wollstonecraft resuscitates them as enlightened usurpers attempting to better the lot of a people suffering the effects of monarchical misrule. The sight of the imbecilic Christian VII manipulated like a 'machine of state' by his ministers leads her to exclaim, 'What a farce is life! This effigy of majesty is allowed to burn down to the socket, whilst the hapless Matilda was hurried into an untimely grave' (*LSND*, p. 206). It is unlikely Shelley would have missed Wordsworth's allusion, particularly as he echoes Wollstonecraft's phrasing

---

eds Audrey A. Fisch, Anne K. Mellor, and Esther H. Schor (New York and Oxford: Oxford University Press, 1993), pp. 235-57.

[27] The readings continued from Mary Shelley's birthday through 1 September (*CCJ*, p. 34).

[28] Wollstonecraft's narrative is a 'solitary travelogue' only insofar as Wollstonecraft rarely alludes to her infant daughter and the nurse who accompanied her. Wollstonecraft's prose, so occupied with her own impressions of nature and manners, makes it easy to forget her companions.

[29] Turner considers Wollstonecraft's Matilda as an 'emblem of radical femininity', especially when juxtaposed against Nathaniel Wraxall's version of the '*passive* queen' in his *Cursory Remarks Made in a Tour through Some of the Northern Parts of Europe, Particularly Copenhagen, Stockholm, and Petersburgh* (1775). See *British Travel Writers*, p. 231.

elsewhere in the preface; the *Alastor* Poet too suffers from the discrepancy between his ideals and his ability to maintain them, and like Matilda 'descends to an untimely grave'.[30] In reading Wordsworth's similar phrasing in *The Excursion*, Shelley would have remembered these lines, and his own epigraph triangulates his argument in the preface alongside both Wordsworth and Wollstonecraft.[31] Though the same degree of allusive texture cannot be found in *Alastor* for Wollstonecraft's text as for Wordsworth's, the former shares with Shelley's poem a geographical excursus that spatialises a historiography of revolutionary progress at the margins of European culture. If *Alastor* responds to the vision of Europe encoded in Wordsworth's poem, Wollstonecraft's own solitary travels in the revolutionary years may well inform Shelley's geographical imagination.

Near the end of the *Short Residence*, the letter in which Wollstonecraft voices her sympathy for Matilda is the only one headed with a place name, Copenhagen, the metropolitan centre of Scandinavian culture that is the journey's anticlimactic bourn. Though Wollstonecraft obviously relishes the sublime and picturesque scenery of Sweden's and Norway's wilder regions, she argues elsewhere that it is 'the good and evil flowing from the capitals of states' that '. . . give the tone to the national sentiments and taste'.[32] If Wollstonecraft locates the unorganised elements of manners at the circumference of Europe, Copenhagen should occupy a middle state where manners have gradually though inexorably been updated in light of modern, largely French influences, which radiate centrifugally from the Parisian centre. But Copenhagen disappoints; the devastation of the 1795 fire that destroyed much of the city leaves little 'to allure the imagination into soothing melancholy reveries; nothing to attract the eye of taste' (*LSND*, p. 198) and becomes an ever-present symbol of the inhabitants' 'sluggish concentration in themselves' (*LSND*, p. 201). For Wollstonecraft, the positive influence of Paris lay in its revolutionary promise to lift common people towards a level of refinement hitherto reserved for the bourgeoisie and aristocracy. Copenhagen forces her to conclude that 'the danes are the people who have made the fewest sacrifices to the graces' (*LSND*, p. 202).

A political preoccupation with cultural progress informs Wollstonecraft's travel narrative at every point, but is thus diverted into a backward-glancing melancholy in the Copenhagen letters, a gesture that I believe illuminates the crisis of the Poet, and of the Narrator who represents him, in *Alastor*. When Wollstonecraft visits the palace of Rosenborg, her reflections take a Volneyan historical tack, not unusual in

---

[30] Immediately after the lines here quoted, Wollstonecraft cites a couplet from *King Lear* (IV, i. 36-7). On 31 August 1814, Claire Clairmont records 'Read King Lear a second time' immediately after noting 'Shelley reads aloud Letters from Norway' (*CCJ*, p. 34).

[31] With reference to the possible allusion to Wollstonecraft, Duncan Wu raises the interesting question of whether Wordsworth's story of Margaret might have owed something to Wollstonecraft's text. See Wu, *Wordsworth's Reading, 1770-1799* (Cambridge: Cambridge University Press, 1993), pp. 152-3.

[32] Wollstonecraft, *An Historical and Moral View of the Origin and Progress of the French Revolution and the Effect it has Produced in Europe*, 2nd edn [1795] (Delmar, NY: Scholars' Facsimiles and Reprints, 1975), p. 224.

a genre accustomed to evaluating paintings, sculpture, and architecture in terms of the level of cultural refinement that produced them. 'Every object carried me back to past times', she reflects, 'and impressed the manners of the age forcibly on my mind' (*LSND*, p. 221). The sentiment and situation recall the *Alastor* Poet, who, '*Obedient* to high thoughts, has visited / The awful ruins of the days of old' (*PS1*, ll. 107-8; my italics); despite the Narrator's emotionally charged diction, there is something of the earnest tourist in the Poet, a sightseer who pays tribute to ruins by rote (even visiting them by fashionable moonlight).

Like the Poet, who interprets a language of objects, ciphers, and sculptures, Wollstonecraft reads a broken language suggested by the iconography that surrounds her, both in the palace and in the public library. The two locations suggest opposing values – monarchical privilege and republican dissemination respectively – but Wollstonecraft's progressivist historiography allows her to read didactic stories of greatness and misery in either place. 'The vacuum left by departed greatness was every where observable', she remarks in the palace:

> . . . . It seemed a vast tomb, full of the shadowy phantoms of those who had played or toiled their hour out, and sunk behind the tapestry, which celebrated the conquests of love or war. Could they be no more – to whom my imagination thus gave life? Could the thoughts, of which there remained so many vestiges, have vanished quite away? And these beings, composed of such noble materials of thinking and feeling, have they only melted into the elements to keep in motion the grand mass of life? It cannot be!
>
> (*LSND*, pp. 221-2)

In the library, Icelandic runes impress her '. . . by shewing what immense labour men will submit to, in order to transmit their ideas to posterity':

> I have sometimes thought it a great misfortune for individuals to acquire a certain delicacy of sentiment, which often makes them weary of the common occurrences of life; yet it is this very delicacy of feeling and thinking which probably has produced most of the performances that have benefited mankind. It might with propriety, perhaps, be termed the malady of genius . . . . (*LSND*, pp. 223-4)

From the first passage, Shelley might have conceived not only the Poet's exclamations on the loss of the veiled maid, but even more so the Narrator's on the loss of the Poet, that 'surpassing Spirit' (l. 714) – not to mention the poem's own tenuous affirmations that such absolute loss 'cannot be!'. From the library sketch Shelley might have drawn the Poet's plight – that over-refined delicacy weary of the common – while the 'malady of genius' captures the Narrator's sense of waste for one who, despite his 'delicacy of sentiment,' has left behind no great work behind, but only a pregnant and awful silence. Again, I am not arguing that this is the principal source for the personae of Shelley's poem, but that the structures of perception that he creates around his characters inform conventional historical attitudes in travel writings such as Wollstonecraft's *Short Residence*.

According to Wollstonecraft, the path from nature to culture, from the frontiers to Copenhagen, should be traversed by a 'contemplative man, or poet', for only the poet 'feels and sees what would escape vulgar eyes' (*LSND*, p. 47), confirming the superiority of cultural advancement over 'Rousseau's golden age of stupidity' (*LSND*, p. 116). This seems at odds with the trajectory in *Alastor*, which proceeds beyond cultural landmarks. But the Narrator's elegiac tone sufficiently indicates his dismay at the loss of cultural *loci*, while his desire to build a word monument confirms culture's inexorable momentum, despite the resistances of the effacing wilderness and the Poet's own otherness. While the Narrator calls for 'Medea's wondrous alchemy' (l. 672) near the end of the poem, there is an ironic sense in which his own language performatively achieves the sublimation he desires. Wollstonecraft more confidently gives Matilda the Medean power of transforming nature into representations and confirmations of progressive manners. In a digression on the Hirsholm gardens (between her palace and library reflections), Wollstonecraft muses: 'as they are in the modern and english style, I thought I was following the footsteps of Matilda, who wished to multiply around her the images of her beloved country' (*LSND*, p. 223). We might again recall the Narrator following the dying Poet's footsteps in *Alastor*: 'so from his steps / Bright flowers departed, and the beautiful shade / Of the green groves' (ll. 536-8). The Narrator's grief at the Poet's shrinking faculties registered metaphorically in an ageing, shrinking landscape (ll. 532-6) has its inverse counterpart in Wollstonecraft's celebration of the dead Matilda's fruitfulness. The first expresses a nature emptied of connection, the second a nature heightened by taste.

Wollstonecraft's meditation on Matilda's imperial influence on the landscape might be contrasted with her earlier observation on the Norwegian town of Portoer, isolated by mountains and sea: 'Talk not of bastilles! To be born here, was to be bastilled by nature – shut out from all that opens the understanding, or enlarges the heart' (*LSND*, p. 133). The metaphor is exact, for if unimproved and unmediated nature reminds Wollstonecraft of *ancien régime* tyranny, liberty becomes aligned with cultivation and, almost ironically, aesthetic control. But liberty is not 'unbridled license',[33] and depends on raising the individual to a communally shared level of cultural apperception. Wollstonecraft envisions a revolutionary culture dependant upon the cultivation of taste, which in turn requires free circulation of cultural progress among European states and all economic classes. Europe's manifest destiny was to extend taste to all its subjects and to subject nature to the eye of taste, and Wollstonecraft herself becomes this representative 'eye', as in her account of a visit to a villa and English garden outside Christiana:

> To a norwegian both might have been objects of curiosity, and of use, by exciting to the comparison which leads to improvement. But whilst I gazed, I was employed in restoring the place to nature, or taste, by giving it the character of the surrounding scene. Serpentine walks, and flowering shrubs, looked trifling in a grand recess of the rocks,

---

[33] Jean-Jacques Rousseau, 'Discourse on the Origin of Inequality', in *Basic Political Writings*, trans. and ed. Donald A. Cress (Indianapolis: Hackett, 1987), p. 27.

> shaded by towering pines. Groves of lesser trees might have been sheltered under them, which would have melted into the landscape, displaying only the art which ought to point out the vicinity of a human abode, furnished with some elegance. (*LSND*, pp. 162-3)

The pun on 'improvement' relates cultural progress to landscape design, while Wollstonecraft distinguishes between three levels of refinement. Though closest to nature, the Norwegians are least susceptible to apprehending landscape aesthetics and most likely to be affected by the stark contrast between dwelling and garden. At the next level, the colonial 'English' eye has imposed an outmoded vision of utility on the landscape that still subordinates nature to art in the manner of Capability Brown (e.g. the serpentine walks).[34] Finally, Wollstonecraft aligns herself with the modern Whig tastes of Uvedale Price and Richard Payne Knight,[35] one-upping both Norwegian peasants and proprietors by demonstrating an empowered perception that constructs as it gazes upon the object world, restoring art to nature and nature to art. This is not mere connoisseurship, as Wollstonecraft's utilitarian language always suggests, but a virtuoso performance of the principles that guide her evaluations of men, manners, and cultural production.

Wollstonecraft's corrected scene in which art melds with landscape to 'point out the vicinity of a human abode' anticipates the *Alastor* Narrator's desperate attempt to prevent nature from effacing the Poet, and resembles his rhetorical transference of monumental architecture from human to natural agency:

> There was a Poet whose untimely tomb
> No human hands with pious reverence reared,
> But the charmed eddies of autumnal winds
> Built o'er his mouldering bones a pyramid
> Of mouldering leaves . . . . (*PS1*, ll. 50-54)

Though nature imitates art, nature cannot resist time in the same way as art aspires to do (with limited success, as Shelley's 'Ozymandias' pointedly remarks). The 'pyramid' consists not of stone but 'mouldering leaves' that will not outlast the

---

[34] See *LSND*, pp. 34-6 and p. 34 n. Here Wollstonecraft argues against 'improvements' of picturesque landscape unless accompanied by 'uncommon taste'. In the note, Wollstonecraft rails against 'serpentine walks, the rage for the line of beauty', and concludes, 'When the weather is fine, the meadows offer winding paths, far superior to the formal turnings that interrupt reflection, without amusing the fancy'.

[35] As Alan Liu argues, Price and Knight politicised the picturesque from a Foxite Whig perspective, registering in their specialised vocabularies the liberal tolerance of Jacobinism in France as the counterpart to British liberty (*Wordsworth: The Sense of History*, Stanford, CA, Stanford University Press, 1989, ch. 3, 'The Politics of the Picturesque', esp. pp. 106-15). For Wollstonecraft's rejection of 'the erotics of Picturesque texts', however, see Vivien Jones, 'Politics and the Picturesque in Women's Fiction', in *The Politics of the Picturesque: Literature, Landscape and Aesthetics since 1770*, eds Stephen Copley and Peter Garside (Cambridge: Cambridge University Press, 1994), pp. 127-9.

'mouldering bones'. Instead, the Narrator attempts to construct a more lasting memorial in elegiac verse, giving life where nature promises only oblivion. By Wollstonecraft's terms, the Narrator too becomes the liberal eye of taste, and we see that much of his anxiety comes to the fore over his fear that that eye has a blind spot.

For Wollstonecraft that blind spot lay in unmediated nature's power to 'bastille' the solitary mind, cutting it off from the lifeblood of social intercourse. Approaching the formidable coast of Sweden, she observes:

> . . . a solemn silence in this scene, which made itself be felt. The sun-beams that played on the ocean, scarcely ruffled by the lightest breeze, contrasted with the huge, dark rocks, that looked like the rude materials of creation forming the barrier of unwrought space, forcibly struck me. (*LSND*, p. 5)

Her prose syntactically privileges light over dark, the playful over the rude, and this in turn reinforces a moral contrast between Parisian refinement, or 'the art of living', and 'the sluggish inhabitants' (*LSND*, p. 6) living 'so near the brute creation' (*LSND*, p. 5). Vision comes athwart the 'unwrought', the 'rude materials' not of nature but creation; for the constructive imagination resists a nature not 'made' in its image, neither ordered nor preordained. Later, as Wollstonecraft travels again towards the seacoast, she re-emphasises this discrepancy: 'Approaching the frontiers, consequently the sea, nature resumed an aspect ruder and ruder, or rather seemed the bones of the world waiting to be clothed with every thing necessary to give life and beauty' (*LSND*, p. 49). At this extreme point in human cartography, Wollstonecraft would agree with Burke that a 'wardrobe of a moral imagination' is a necessity for life, though she would clearly select rather different, less alluring garments in dressing 'naked, shivering nature'.[36]

It remains the ideal *Alastor* Poet's province to experience the gaze that allows 'the secrets of the birth of time' to be 'flashed like strong inspiration' upon his non-transforming retina. While travellers spread a veil of language between themselves and the scenes that 'remind [them] of the creation of things' (*LSND*, p. 47), the Poet pulls back this veil of signifiers. Prepared for this by the languagelessness of his surroundings – the 'mute thoughts on the mute walls', the 'speechless shapes' (ll. 120; 123) – the Poet's gaze prepares for reception by dispensing with intervening words and metaphors. The Narrator's simile, 'like strong inspiration', underscores its own status as linguistic mediation by inadequately conceptualising the Poet's experience. In spite of the Narrator's intervention, we must conclude that for the Poet meaning *flashes*, and he *sees* the secrets, directly.

The Narrator's mediation here is best understood in terms of travellers' descriptions of their 'raptures'. When confronting awe-inspiring landscapes, travel writers attempt to describe what they would have us believe is ineffable, but very often such scenes confirm or give rise to mental activity, as in Shelley's accounts of

---

[36] Burke, *Reflections*, p. 67.

Mont Blanc. Wollstonecraft's meditation on the hills above Tonsberg relates another such moment:

> With what ineffable pleasure have I not gazed – and gazed again, losing my breath through my eyes – my very soul diffused itself in the scene – and, seeming to become all senses, glided in the scarcely-agitated waves, melted in the freshening breeze, or, taking its flight with fairy wing, to the misty mountains which bounded the prospect, fancy tript over new lawns, more beautiful even than the lovely slopes on the winding shore before me. – I pause, again breathless, to trace, with renewed delight, sentiments which entranced me, when, turning my humid eyes from the expanse below to the vault above, my sight pierced the fleecy clouds that softened the azure brightness; and, imperceptibly recalling the reveries of childhood, I bowed before the awful throne of my Creator, whilst I rested on its footstool. (*LSND*, p. 94)

Like the Poet's, Wollstonecraft's experience is 'ineffable', and she too claims a heightened state for her senses, particularly sight. In a nice contrast to the Narrator's 'inspiration' simile, Wollstonecraft *loses* her breath through her eyes. But like the Narrator (and unlike the Poet), Wollstonecraft mediates her experience; seeming, fancy, and reverie lead the ideal senses on excursions through time and space; mental activity rather than any transcendental passivity of the senses characterises the moment.[37] Wollstonecraft's ability to duplicate the experience of travel through writing travel – 'I pause, again breathless, to trace . . .' – indicates another way in which the Narrator's role as mediating scribe can be empowering, restocking lived experience with new associations.

While Wollstonecraft and Shelley's Narrator resist the perceived Bastille of Nature, the Poet's early history and initial travels depict a man who courts rather than seeks to transform unmediated nature:

> Nature's most secret steps
> He like her shadow has pursued, where'er
> The red volcano overcanopies
> Its fields of snow and pinnacles of ice . . . . (*PS1*, ll. 81-4)

His geological tourism recalls Wollstonecraft's confrontation with the 'rude materials of creation' (*LSND*, p. 5),[38] yet the Poet does not acknowledge any

---

[37] Cf. Sara Mills, 'Written on the Landscape: Mary Wollstonecraft's *Letters Written During a Short Residence in Sweden, Norway and Denmark*', *Romantic Geographies: Discourses of Travel, 1775-1844*, ed. Amanda Gilroy (Manchester: Manchester University Press, 2000), pp. 29-31. Mills argues that Wollstonecraft's sublime tableau seems 'more concerned with negotiating with the visual stimulations and her emotions than controlling them' (p. 29).

[38] More immediately, the passage recalls Patrick Brydone's view of Mount Aetna, though there is no evidence that Shelley had read *A Tour through Sicily and Malta* (1774) before 1820. Brydone observes: 'But our astonishment still increases, on casting our eyes on the higher regions of the mountain. There we behold, in perpetual union, the two elements that

barrier; he pursues his inquiry into caverns, while back in the light of day, he makes 'the wild his home' (ll. 87-94; 99). The Poet's cultural journey, described in lines 106-28, depicts one intent not on building up culture, but breaking it down; he seeks 'a past deliberately disconnected from any contemporary European present',[39] and only the Narrator's rhetorical structures of narration re-establish connection after the fact. The Poet's pursuit of lowest common denominators leads him 'in joy and exultation' (l. 144) on his wider oriental travels even to the Vale of Cashmere, itself the symbolic denominator of nature and culture.[40] But if the Poet refuses to acknowledge any Bastille in nature, the result of his peregrinations may be said to confirm Wollstonecraft's conclusions; though the visionary maid speaks of 'divine liberty', she proves a tyrant phantom, rising up between the Poet and his last social ties.[41] After the vision, the Poet not only does not mediate nature, he is largely unconscious of it. He pursues 'Vision and Love' (l. 366), and sees by 'the light / That shone within his soul' (ll. 492-3); what objects he does notice, like the swan (ll. 275-90) or the stream (ll. 502-14), he regards as allegorical images of his own situation. He wanders on to the only truly 'undiscovered lands' in the poem, but by then he is all but unaware of the 'strange truths' that might be found there. Instead, the Poet who had once sought a domestic economy in nature, sharing his 'bloodless food' (l. 101) with animals, goes back to unwrought nature, wasting his 'bloodless limbs . . . / I' the passing wind!' (ll. 513-14).

The *Alastor* preface advertises the poet and his like as 'luminaries' blasted by 'self-centred seclusion' (*PS1*, p. 463). This 'malady of genius', to borrow Wollstonecraft's formulation, opens a space for political responsibility which geniuses themselves are unable to exploit. If Shelley figures this space in unmediated nature, it is not because he recommends a retreat into Rousseau's state of nature, which the Poet's journey in many ways resembles. As Shelley writes in the *Essay on Christianity*, 'Nothing is more obviously false than that the remedy of inequality among men consists in their return to the condition of savages and beasts' (*Prose*, p. 210). Instead, Shelley recognises with Rousseau that the state of nature is not a social state, but the condition out of which society can be generated; it is a sublime fiction that can provide models of simplicity with which to augment cultural advances. For the 'natural man', it is a condition of some peril. Shelley's

---

are at perpetual war; and immense gulph of fire, for ever existing in the midst of shows which it has not power to melt; and immense fields of snow and ice for ever surrounding this gulph of fire, which they have not power to extinguish' (p. 187).

[39] Birns, 'Secrets', p. 344.

[40] Stuart Curran discusses the significance of the Vale of Cashmere in terms of its location beneath the Indian Caucasus, 'a landscape of fertile suggestiveness . . . unsurpassed until the present century' as a 'focus of history and myth' (*Shelley's Annus Mirabilis*, pp. 61-4). Nigel Leask notes that Cashmere was 'the birthplace of Hinduism, Zoroastrianism and religious mysticism' (*British Romantic Writers*, p. 122).

[41] Note also the proximity of the Veiled Maid episode to Wollstonecraft's reflections on 'the origin of many poetical fictions' in Letter IX of *Short Residence*: 'In solitude, the imagination bodies forth its conceptions unrestrained, and stops enraptured to adore the beings of its own creation' (*LSND*, p. 110).

pathology of the origins of inequality in *Queen Mab* indicts the self-reflexivity of original attempts to encode hierarchical power relations in the institutions of property, religion, and language itself. As Neil Freistat points out, *Alastor*'s companion poem 'Superstition' (excerpted from *Queen Mab*) further indicts 'the fallen mind of man for accepting its own enslavement'.[42]

Both Rousseau and Shelley use fiction to explore the relationship between the 'state of nature' and 'civilised' consciousness. The *Discourse on Inequality* nevertheless gestures towards travel writing as a necessary supplement. In an important note, Rousseau posits travel as the means of gathering information from existing cultural resources that could provide materials for, as Edward Duffy writes, an 'effective critical technique of cultural primitivism'[43]:

> Let us suppose a Montesquieu, a Buffon, a Diderot, a Duclos, a d'Alembert, a Condillac, or men of that ilk traveling in order to inform their compatriots, observing and describing as they know how to do, Turkey, Egypt, Barbary, the empire of Morocco, Guinea, the land of the Bantus, the interior of Africa and its eastern coastlines, the Malabars, Mogul, the banks of the Ganges . . . finally the Caribbean Islands, Florida, and all the savage countries–the most important voyage of all and the one that should be embarked upon with the greatest care.[44]

Alastor explores this same enlightenment topos for the critique by positing the Poet's travels in and beyond the 'savage' countries, but it also re-enacts the original mythopoeic impulse from which equality or inequality might be produced; the Poet as modern cultural primitivist unwittingly becomes the subject of his own study. He journeys to discover a free space out of which 'divine liberty' might emerge as a social condition, yet leaves the vantage of social being necessary for its articulation.

As a whole, *Alastor* exploits the space between Poet's primitivism and Wollstonecraft's constructivism, each of which pull on the Narrator. This is the space in which Rousseau's politics of nature shade into the politics of mediated nature, whose representative discourse in Shelley's time was that of the picturesque. Stephen Copley has argued that picturesque tours 'invite readings which see them as symbolic journeys through landscapes inscribed with overdetermined moral values. As such, they construct their own symbolic geography of

---

[42] Neil Freistat, 'Poetic Quests and Questioning in Shelley's *Alastor* collection', *Keats-Shelley Journal*, 33 (1984), p. 172.

[43] Edward Duffy, *Rousseau in England: The Context for Shelley's Critique of the Enlightenment* (Berkeley: University of California Press, 1979), p. 92.

[44] Rousseau, 'Discourse on the Origin of Inequality', p. 100. While this essay is not among any of the reading lists ordered by Shelley or noted by Mary Shelley, Shelley seems to have known it well and cites one of its footnotes in his own note to the fifth canto of *Queen Mab* (*PS1*, p. 365). Peacock quotes the passage cited in my text in a note to *Melincourt* (1817). See *WTLP*, 2: 71-2 n.

the country'.[45] Movements through landscape highlight the ways in which symbolic geographies appropriate the unmediated, Rousseauian topos of natural space for rather different ends:

> the tourist visibly – if temporarily – renounces city luxury and domestic security for rural simplicity, and beyond that, for exposure to, and confrontation with, an imagined Other, the natural, outside the realms of the social and the economic.[46]

In other words, picturesque tourists conduct their own kind of ethnological travel without having to leave the beaten track. Yet such tourists renounce in order to reaffirm the values of metropolitan culture. Their aesthetic operates by appropriating the anti-aesthetic of a more 'natural' state. The picturesque becomes the aesthetic idealisation of property: to see is to possess, to aestheticise is to cultivate. While Wollstonecraft remains unwilling or unable to anticipate the political consequences this appropriation might entail, Shelley begins to realise the ways in which Wollstonecraft's discourse too easily shades into that of Knight and Price; how in a post-revolutionary context terms can so easily gravitate towards a more intricate form of aesthetic nationalism. What for Wollstonecraft, Knight, and Price might have been a tug of war between radical and liberal interpretations of an aesthetic, becomes for Shelley and Wordsworth one between liberal and Tory.[47]

---

[45] Stephen Copley, 'William Gilpin and the Black-lead Mine', in *The Politics of the Picturesque*, p. 50.

[46] Copley, 'William Gilpin', p. 50. As a gloss to movements in *Alastor* this seems quite exact. The Poet leaves his 'cold fireside and alienated home / To seek strange truths in undiscovered lands' (ll. 76-7), a journey that leads him increasingly away from civilisation and even the ruins of past civilisations towards a region untrodden except by 'one human step alone' (l. 589), the Poet's own. The Poet's movement beyond society and beyond economy is also marked. Dispensing with the cash nexus, the Poet makes his way in 'primitive' society through non-utilitarian forms of exchange, perhaps bartering bard-like his song for supper: 'he has bought / With his sweet voice and eyes, from savage men, / His rest and food' (ll. 79-81). After imagining his own Other, the veiled maid, the Poet slips beyond exchange altogether; his last contacts are 'the cottagers, / Who ministered with human *charity* / His human wants' (ll. 254-6, my italics). While cottagers arguably have attained a more 'advanced' economic level than 'savage men', the Poet's 'wild eyes' (l. 264) and indifference to family life indicate that he is already beyond the pale of social being.

[47] See Liu, *Wordsworth's Sense*, p. 113: 'The picturesque, in sum, was a political platform whose declaration of British constitutional freedom gravitated increasingly leftward in the period that most concerns us toward an idea of revolution cognate with the American or very early French Revolution. The lasting effect of such politicisation, no matter a writer's final stance after the French Revolution, was that picturesque landscape became an almost automatic second language of politics. Indeed, efforts to rehabilitate the post-Waterloo landscape simply turned the vocabulary of Whiggish landscape to new purposes'.

'Beyond these Penetrable Bounds': Shelley and Wordsworth

When we turn from Wollstonecraft's *Short Residence* to Wordsworth's *Excursion* in our discussion of *Alastor*, we must do so from this vantage. Wordsworth's own tourist literature – his *Guide to the Lakes*, and 'An Unpublished Tour', both of which, in their original forms, predate the publication of *The Excursion*[48] – argues for a structure of picturesque taste that can sound very much like that of Knight, Price, Wollstonecraft, or more likely, Gilpin. Wordsworth argues for natural variety of landscape characterised by gradations in form, colour, and texture – nature observed by the organising eye of taste, but itself unimproved as much as possible. In *The Excursion*, successive editions of the *Guide*, and such works as his *Address to the Freeholders of Westmoreland* (1818), Wordsworth's aesthetic becomes increasingly associated with his defence and celebration of British national and moral self-sufficiency, as Wordsworth transforms the liberal celebration of liberty in the landscape into a mandate for righteous exportation of cultural values. *The Excursion* itself, as Laura Dabundo contends, becomes both a 'document of . . . English national identity' and an argument that 'England alone can and must save' the post-Waterloo world.[49] The Wanderer and Pastor become 'vehicle[s] for official comment' who 'validate a priesthood of the imagination' represented by the Poet-narrator,[50] while the despondent Solitary highlights the failure of liberal and radical revolutionary values. The landscapes of the Lake District wherein their conversation takes place validate the entire undertaking, particularly as they recommend an ideal observer, one who 'no longer read[s] / The forms of things with an unworthy eye' (*Excursion*, I, 47 [939-40]). The worthy eye, by contrast, sees, evaluates, and values things; nature becomes landscape, the imaginary property that makes up a nation and validates its imperial claims.

Neither Wollstonecraft nor Shelley would object to an imperial taste represented by the English eye. But both would rather its genealogy be in a liberal discourse that does not privilege English religious or political institutions, these being in their view holdovers from a less progressive state of society. Wollstonecraft and Shelley conspicuously construct English taste from a position of exteriority; to be a 'citizen of the world' (a phrase both use) must be a condition in their construction of Englishness. Wollstonecraft recasts the Grand Tour, that enlightenment repository of 'world' cultural value so integral to the making of a gentleman, as a bourgeois ethnological exploration of cultural peripheries rather than a mad dash for cultural centres or pre-established stations for the appreciation of landscape:

---

[48] *Guide to the Lakes* was first published as the introduction to Joseph Wilkinson's *Select Views in Cumberland, Westmoreland, and Lancashire* (London, 1810). [An Unpublished Tour] 'Upon the Best Approach to the Lakes' and a related essay, 'The Sublime and the Beautiful', date from around 1811-12. See *WW Prose*, 2: 123-35.

[49] Laura Dabundo, 'The Extrospective Vision: *The Excursion* as Transitional in Wordsworth's Poetry and Age', *Wordsworth Circle*, 19.1 (Winter 1988), pp. 8; 12.

[50] Dabundo, 'Extrospective Vision', p. 10.

If travelling, as the completion of a liberal education, were to be adopted on rational grounds, the northern states ought to be visited before the more polished parts of Europe, to serve as the elements even of the knowledge of manners, only to be acquired by tracing the various shades in different countries. (*LSND*, p. 217)

As I have suggested above, Shelley follows in *Alastor* by re-enacting a complicated version of Rousseau's idea of ethnological travel in order to recommend an aesthetic centre offered to an English readership, but dislocated from it. By contrast, Wordsworth retrenches from any openly avowed internationalism in the wake of the post-war settlement, and emphasises a conservative 'anti-tourism', affirming not only the value of unimproved nature to the eye of taste, but relocating European and world 'centres' in a self-sufficient English Lake District.[51] Citing Thomas West's best-selling *A Guide to the Lakes* as itself a kind of national monument, Wordsworth quotes a passage in later editions of his own *Guide* that refigures the Grand Tour in a characteristic manner:

"They who intend to make the continental tour should begin here; as it will give, in miniature, an idea of what they are to meet with there, in traversing the Alps and Appenines; to which our northern mountains are not inferior in beauty of line, or variety of summit, number of lakes, and transparency of water; not in colouring of rock, or softness of turf; but in height and extent only. The mountains here are all accessible to the summit, and furnish prospects no less surprising, and with more variety, than the Alps themselves. The tops of the highest Alps are inaccessible, being covered with everlasting snow, which commencing at regular heights above the cultivated tracts, or wooded and verdant sides, form indeed the highest contrast in nature. For there may be seen all the variety of climate in one view. To this, however, we oppose the sight of the ocean, from the summits of all the higher mountains, as it appears intersected with promontories, decorated with islands, and animated with navigation" – West's *Guide*, p. 5.

(*WW Prose*, 2: 239)

This conscious dislocation of the European Grand Tourist cultural experience onto English landscapes is quite a contrary impulse to that of Wollstonecraft or Shelley, but one that lay behind the geography of *The Excursion*, where Wordsworth pays 'tribute to a spot that seemed / Like the fixed centre of a troubled World' (*Excursion*, V, 202 [15-16]). This impulse is integral to understanding Shelley's rejection of Wordsworth's picturesque nationalism in 1815.

The dialogue between *Alastor* and *The Excursion* has been customarily pursued in terms of parallels between their respective protagonists. While Mueschke and

---

[51] See Buzard, *Beaten Track*, pp. 27-31. See also Kim Ian Michisaw, 'Nine Revisionist Theses on the Picturesque', *Representations*, 38 (Spring 1992), p. 84. Michisaw argues that Gilpin's picturesque program was designed to replace the Grand Tour by keeping 'the young man within Great Britain, hence away from foreign contaminants'.

Griggs see the *Alastor* Poet as a type of Wordsworth himself, others have suggested Wordsworth's Wanderer or Solitary (or some combined persona) as more likely candidates, while Wasserman has identified Margaret.[52] The *Alastor* Poet shares with the Wanderer a childhood nursed by nature and great books, after which their careers diverge: the Poet pursues a solitary self-idolatry, while the Wanderer embraces a 'quasi-orthodox faith' and a comfortable communion with nature.[53] The Poet's self-destructive solitude more resembles that of Wordsworth's Solitary. Both experience the loss of real human contact and ideal social vision. The Poet leaves his 'cold fireside and alienated home' (*PS1*, l. 76), yet spurns further human relationships (such as the 'Arab maiden'). Instead, he envisions a lover who embodies his ideals of 'divine liberty' (l. 159), but who 'fold[s] his frame in her dissolving arms' (l. 187) and disappears. The Solitary experiences the same disillusionment with political ideals, though Wordsworth provides a more coherent psychological explanation. 'Nor wishing aught / Beyond the allowance of [his] own fire-side' (*Excursion*, III, 122 [587-8]), the Solitary first suffers the tragic loss of wife and children to disease; his wife, he laments, 'melted from my arms; / And left me, on this earth, disconsolate' (*Excursion*, III, 126 [678-9]). In his pain, he transfers familial love to society; his 'soul diffused itself in wide embrace / Of institutions, and the forms of things' and 'Society became [his] glittering Bride' (*Excursion*, III, 128 [735]). Unfortunately, the failure of the French Revolution to actualise his newly adopted social ideals leaves him again disconsolate, this time seeking a spot of 'unappropriated earth' (*Excursion*, III, 137 [939]) in the wilds of America.

While the case for the Solitary as the Poet's prototype is particularly strong, Carothers follows Edward E. Bostetter's belief that the Wanderer and Solitary 'embody the "two consciousnesses" of the "psychomachia" that is *The Excursion*', and that 'Shelley's Narrator and Poet are aspects of a single consciousness'.[54] Without following the psychoanalytical argument further, I would concur that one-to-one correspondences between the two texts are to be avoided; Shelley responds as much to the politics of Wordsworth's aesthetic as to any single embodiment of it. When we consider the confusing range of allusions in *Alastor* to *The Excursion*, the fact of their general provenance in Book III-IV is as important as how cross-

---

[52] Wasserman, *Shelley*, p. 20. Several critics emphasise Shelley's composite handling of Wordsworthian models and highlight the complexity of Shelley's response to Wordsworth: part admiration, part critique. Vincent Newey, in 'Shelley's "Dream of Youth": *Alastor*, "Selving" and the Psychic Realm', *Percy Bysshe Shelley: Bicentenary Essays* (Cambridge: D. S. Brewer, 1992), argues that Shelley found a model for the development of the Poet in the biography of Wordsworth's Wanderer, but uses this to subvert and reject the Wanderer's Wordsworthian equanimity. Donna Richardson believes Shelley's Poet 'occupies the rhetorical position of the Solitary', but that 'the Poet is primarily compared and contrasted with the Wanderer' (Richardson, 'Anatomy of Solitude', p. 175, n. 8).

[53] Carothers, '*Alastor*: Shelley Corrects Wordsworth', p. 26.

[54] Carothers, '*Alastor*: Shelley Corrects Wordsworth', pp. 26-7. See also, Edward E. Bostetter, *The Romantic Ventriloquists: Wordsworth, Coleridge, Keats, Shelley, Byron* (Seattle: University of Washington Press, 1963), p. 68, the source of Carothers's quotations.

character comparisons work. These books are crucial to Wordsworth's 'high argument' on the moral fitness of the human mind to nature, and the Solitary's autobiography is there related in intimate counterpoint to the poem's Lake District topography. At the same time, the Wanderer's vision of the landscape (and the Pastor's in Book X) complements his Christian consolations, reproving and succouring the misguided Solitary, disillusioned by foreign revolutionary quarrels. Against this ideologically loaded dialogue over landscape, Shelley registers what he believes to be a more politically authentic epistemology by rendering his own characters' interpretations of nature and landscape productively ambiguous.

Both poems locate the fulcrum for narrative in what Wordsworth's narrator calls in Book III 'a nook for self-examination framed, / Or, for confession, in the sinner's need, / Hidden from all Men's view' (*Excursion*, III, 116-17 [471-4]). With its 'moist precipice', its 'shining Holly' that 'had found / A hospitable chink', and its 'white-robed Waterfall', the Solitary's nook answers closely to the 'grey precipice and solemn pine / And torrent' of the 'silent nook' (l. 572) in which the *Alastor* Poet ends his existence (and in which the Narrator struggles to locate some ultimate meaning in dissolution and death).[55] In *The Excursion*, the Solitary leads his guests by way of a 'Streamlet' until their passage is barred by 'an ample Crag', forming the nook (*Excursion*, III, 96-7). From this vantage, the Solitary and Wanderer trade interpretations of surrounding objects, readings of landscape, before the Solitary confesses his life's history. The Wanderer recognises in the landscape signs of a natural theology, an argument by design for a transcendent narrative order that accommodates human activity:

> Among these Rocks and Stones, methinks, I see
> More than the heedless impress that belongs
> To lonely Nature's casual work: they bear
> A semblance strange of power intelligent,
> And of design not wholly worn away.
> . . . .
> I cannot but incline to a belief
> That in these shows a chronicle survives
> Of purposes akin to those of Man . . . .
>
> (*Excursion*, III, 99 [80-84, 87-90])

For the Solitary, the same scene gives rise to opposite impressions:

---

[55] Shelley's Narrator remarks that the nook 'seemed to smile / Even in the lap of horror'. As Geoffrey Matthews and Kelvin Everest note, this is 'a phrase coined, according to William Gilpin (*Observation, Relatively Chiefly to Picturesque Beauty, Made in the Year 1772 [on Several Parts of England; Particularly the Mountains, and Lakes of Cumberland, and Westmoreland]*, 1786 edn, i 183), by one Mr Avison to describe Derwentwater' (*PS1*, 577-8 n.). If Shelley did know the Gilpin source, the allusion may be another way of acknowledging the Wordsworthian origins of the 'nook'.

> ... The shapes before our eyes,
> And their arrangement, doubtless must be deemed
> The sport of Nature, aided by blind Chance
> Rudely to mock the works of toiling Man.
>
> (*Excursion*, III, 101 [124-7])

That Wordsworth sides ultimately with the Wanderer's view comes as no surprise, especially when the Solitary's own emphasis on 'sport' and 'chance' are explained by his complicity in French Revolutionary atheism. Rather than inverting Wordsworth's message, however, Shelley explores the fractures that Wordsworth himself opens up in the character of the Wanderer, before embracing a modified version of the Solitary's scepticism. The *Alastor* Narrator thus *desires* to find 'purposes akin to those of Man' in the funeral nook, but cannot escape the possibility that nature mocks him.

What I have called a 'fracture' in the Wanderer's character may be elucidated when we consider tensions between his readings of nature in Book I and Book III. The Book I 'Story of Margaret' that so impressed the Shelleys in 1814 begins with another nook, a 'chearless spot' to Wordsworth's narrator and, to the Wanderer, a 'pensive sight / . . . recalling former days' (*Excursion*, I, 26).[56] The Wanderer's purpose in telling the story is to teach his interlocutor how to 'read / The forms of things' and trace the 'secret spirit of humanity / . . . mid the calm oblivious tendencies / Of Nature' (I, 47). Yet his initial reading is darker:

> ... we die, my Friend,
> Nor we alone, but that which each man loved
> And prized in his peculiar nook of earth
> Dies with him, or is changed; and very soon
> Even of the good is no memorial left. (*Excursion*, I, 26 [470-74])

The Wanderer's exordium ends in 'the good die first' (I, 27) passage that Shelley quotes in the *Alastor* preface, and the Wanderer's emphasis on effacement anticipates the *Alastor* Narrator's elegy for the Poet. Yet the Wanderer's vision of loss gives way to consolation. His Book III position establishes in pointed contrast a transcendental comfort in speaking nature, an ever-present 'chronicle' of absolute good that replaces mere human 'memorial'. I would like to suggest that Shelley seizes on the Wanderer's earlier celebration of elegiac 'invocations', 'the strong creative power / Of human passion' (*Excursion*, I, 27 [480-81]) that invests 'senseless rocks' with meaning. Expression of 'creative power' and 'human

---

[56] Much of Book I, including the story of Margaret, was composed in 1797 as part of 'The Pedlar' sequence, Wordsworth's pilot sketches for his never completed epic, *The Recluse*. The lines then became 'The Ruined Cottage'. Perhaps unbeknownst to Shelley, he most appreciated a part of *The Excursion* that was coeval with *Lyrical Ballads*, the period of (to Shelley) Wordsworth's 'honoured poverty'.

passion' become for Shelley ends in themselves, rather than immanent evidence of a transcendental order.

When separated from his later transcendental and nationalist consolations, the Wanderer's own passionate expression of waste in Book I bears more than a passing resemblance to the Solitary's Book III position. Instead of seeing a semblance of intelligence in the landscape, the Solitary argues that only the moods of the mind can put one there:

> And hence, this upright Shaft of unhewn stone,
> From Fancy, willing to set off her stores
> By sounding Titles, hath acquired the name
> Of Pompey's Pillar; that I gravely style
> My Theban Obelisk; and, there, behold
> A Druid Cromlech! – thus I entertain
> The antiquarian humour, and am pleased
> To skim along the surfaces of things,
> Beguiling harmlessly the listless hours.
> But, if the spirit be oppressed by sense
> Of instability, revolt, decay,
> And change, and emptiness, these freaks of Nature
> And her blind helper Chance, do *then* suffice
> To quicken, and to aggravate, to feed
> Pity and scorn, and melancholy pride,
> Not less than that huge Pile (from some abyss
> Of mortal power unquestionably sprung)
> Whose hoary Diadem of pendant rocks
> Confines the shrill-voiced whirlwind, round and round
> Eddying within its vast circumference,
> On Sarum's naked plain; – than Pyramid
> Of Egypt, unsubverted, undissolved;
> Or Syria's marble Ruins towering high
> Above the sandy Desart, in the light
> Of sun or moon. – Forgive me, if I say
> That an appearance, which hath raised your minds
> To an exalted pitch . . .
>   . . . is for me
> Fraught rather with depression than delight . . . .
>
> (*Excursion*, III, 101-2 [128-56])

Undeterred by the Wanderer's sublime example, the Solitary ends his argument by recommending the geologist's or botanist's eye, that pores over fragments rather than skimming 'along the surfaces of things'. Wordsworth would have us reject both of these partial (in both senses of the word) gazes, and the Wanderer later uses the Solitary's raptures at other landscapes as *prima facie* evidence of the Solitary's positive moral disposition. The passage, however, has another important resonance for the Shelleyan reader, as the Solitary's 'antiquarian humour' seems cousin to the *Alastor* Poet's antiquarian fervour. In imagining the ruins of civilisation figured in 'unhewn stone', the Solitary self-consciously privileges the imagination itself as the source of powerful feelings. At the same time, the Solitary's rhetoric suggests that natural forms are the primary stuff of the imagination, the building blocks of creation, out of which human power is crafted. Stonehenge becomes a 'hoary Diadem of pendant rocks' that 'confines' an eddying whirlwind, an apt emblem for culture's dependency on nature. This is a rather different perspective on the fitness of mind to nature, and vice versa, than that which Wordsworth celebrates in his 'spousal verse', and one that the Wanderer counters with his exhortations on balance in Book IV, 'Despondency Corrected'.[57]

For Wordsworth, the Solitary's aesthetic may have reflected pathology, but for Shelley it would have been more in line with his own philosophical scepticism.[58] Yet the Solitary's position out-Shelleys Shelley by leaving no place for 'doubtful knowledge' or 'illustrious superstition' (*PS1*, p. 463); nature becomes a mere register of a percipient's mood swings rather than a mirror for beautiful ideals. Wordsworth is keen that the Solitary not provide beau ideals, particularly for the French Revolution; Shelley, however, reworks Wordsworth's materials to strengthen the moral role of the imagination. Through the dialogics of *Alastor*, Shelley attempts to bridge the gap between the Solitary's hard and fast atheism and what the Wanderer refers to as 'the strong creative power of human passion'.

The travel theme with which Shelley works out his response to *The Excursion* may have been suggested by the Solitary, whose disillusionment induces a flight away from society towards the wilds of America in search of Rousseau's state of nature and 'Primeval Nature's Child' (*Excursion*, III, 137 [919]). Convinced that he will find minds that will project their own 'unshackled' liberty on the scenes that surround them, rather than freighting them with depression, the Solitary imagines the noble savage in a self-empowered prospect:

>   ... when having gained the top
> Of some commanding Eminence, which yet
> Intruder ne'er beheld, he thence surveys
> Regions of wood and wide Savannah, vast
> Expanse of unappropriated earth,
> With mind that sheds a light on what he sees[.]
>
>   (*Excursion*, III, 137 [935-40])

---

[57] See also *Excursion*, IV, 165 [531-2], where Wordsworth's Narrator seconds the Wanderer by exhorting the Solitary 'to roam / An *Equal* among the mightiest Energies' in nature (my italics).

[58] For the importance of David Hume's sceptical empiricism to Shelley's epistemology, see C. E. Pulos, *The Deep Truth: A Study of Shelley's Scepticism* (Lincoln: University of Nebraska Press, 1962).

By Rousseau's and Shelley's terms, as I have argued, the Solitary sets himself up for one final disappointment: 'But that pure Archetype of human greatness, / [He] found him not. There, in his stead, appeared / A Creature, squalid, vengeful, and impure' (*Excursion*, III, 138 [951-3]). The Solitary's mistake is ironically enough in leaving civilisation to find the pure appropriation of landscape by the mind. At an earlier point of his narrative, the Solitary himself provides the counter-description:

> — Wild were the walks upon those lonely Downs,
> Track leading into track, how marked, how worn
> Into bright verdure, among fern and gorse
> Winding away its never-ending line,
> On the smooth surface, evidence was none:
> But, there, lay open to our daily haunt,
> A range of unappropriated earth . . . .
>
> (*Excursion*, III, 119 [532-8])

This description appropriates the unappropriated by eliding the tracks of human art into the winding lines of the landscape. Wordsworth's point seems to be that the Solitary's error lay in seeking the unappropriated itself, in leaving the beaten track altogether, rather than seeking truth in the world of all of us where we find our happiness or not at all. Shelley, however, locates here a radical but subtle difference between himself and Wordsworth. For Shelley, the unappropriated must maintain a disconcerting presence by its very absence. In *Alastor*, the Poet opens the 'undiscovered' space of cultural primitivism and oriental cultural otherness over which the Narrator writes landscape description, and yet the Narrator never achieves the comfortable closure that allows Wordsworth to locate his 'deep abiding place' in appropriated nature. For Shelley, the Poet's travels and the Narrator's travel writings form a fulcrum around otherness and desire that should be fundamental to the 'citizens' and 'benefactors' that the preface celebrates.

The Solitary's experiences lead him to the question that I have used as an epigraph to this chapter:

> Ah! what avails Imagination high
> Or Question deep? what profits all that Earth,
> Or Heaven's blue Vault, is suffered to put forth
> Of impulse or allurement, for the Soul
> To quit the beaten track of life, and soar
> Far as she finds a yielding element
> In past or future; as far as she can go
> Through time or space; if neither in the one
> Nor in the other region, nor in aught
> That Fancy, dreaming o'er the map of things,
> Hath placed beyond these penetrable bounds,

> Words of assurance can be heard; if no where
> A habitation, for consummate good,
> Or for progressive virtue, by the search
> Can be attained, a better sanctuary
> From doubt and sorrow, than the senseless grave?
>
> (*Excursion*, III, 105 [209-24])

The Excursion makes clear that words of assurance may be found in duty, conscience, and Christian resignation. Moreover, the habitation for consummate good is the 'deep Abiding place' beneath the Solitary's feet – not in foreign or noumenal regions, but in English mountains, beside an English fire. *Alastor*, as Neil Freistat notes, may very well be considered as 'a not unsympathetic . . . meditation' on this 'objection to imaginative questing',[59] but the poem answers the Solitary's question rather differently. Assurances emerge from the elegiac space between the Narrator's appropriation of the luminary's story and that story itself, a presence charged with all the hopes latent in unappropriated nature, but always absent except as it can be recreated. While Shelley's Poet might accept the terms of the Solitary's question, Shelley himself rejects the *telos* of imaginative 'profit' or of the self-reinforcing 'habitation-sanctuary' that the Solitary seeks. For Shelley, nature's impulses and allurements, dreams over the map of things, and words can be enough.

Aesthetic Idealisation and the Limits of National Identity

In summary, neither the Narrator nor the Poet can be identified with Shelley's 'position', which emerges ironically from the disjunction between narrative rhetorical structure and the subject of narration – what I have referred to as the Narrator's travel writings and the Poet's travels.[60] The Narrator's aesthetic construction of the Poet's journey in search of 'unappropriated earth' is subject to the same epistemological failures as his vaunted attempts to penetrate into nature's 'inmost sanctuary' (*PS1*, l. 38), yet the Narrator gradually achieves a rhetorical confidence in describing the ineffable which foregrounds even as it denies the power of the cultural imagination to locate the metaphysical certainties that the Narrator, like the Poet, longs for. The Poet opens up spaces that prevent the Narrator from resting on the kinds of metaphysical, aesthetic, and political solutions recommended by Wordsworth's *The Excursion*, without revealing any

---

[59] Freistat, 'Poetic Quests', p. 180.

[60] Nor can the Narrator and Poet by themselves be associated with Wordsworth, despite the allusive texture that links them to Wordsworth's poetry. Instead, Shelley refigures the Wordsworthian subject position in *The Excursion* so as to undermine the kind of 'natural piety' recommended by the Wanderer and the Pastor in which the wedding of mind and nature become analogical arguments for religious orthodoxy, political conservatism, and the imperial export of counter-revolutionary values.

replacement certainties. These 'spaces', which include the place of cultural primitivism and 'undiscovered lands', dislocate the Narrator's initial desire for a simple pantheistic union with nature and in so doing exercise the Narrator's colonial imagination. The Narrator rebuilds the world out of his own thoughts around the Poet, in this way confirming both his own power over the object world and the inaccessibility of the object of his desire. This two-directional impulse duplicates the 'structure of desire' that John Whale and Alan Liu have associated with the picturesque, while privileging a consciousness that applies itself not merely to a British but an internationalist perspective.[61] To elucidate this reading, I would like to conclude by focusing on the Narrator's strategies of containment in coming to grips with the subject positions opened up to him by the Poet's oriental experiences. For the purposes of my discussion, I follow Mueschke and Griggs, and most commentators, in dividing the poem into three parts: the Narrator's introductory invocation (ll. 1-49), the narrative of the Poet's journeys (ll. 50-671), and the Narrator's concluding eulogy for the Poet (ll. 672-720).

The Narrator's invocation establishes the absence in any tangible sense of that which he invokes: a pantheistic connection between himself and nature. While in his prospectus for *The Recluse* Wordsworth can confidently anticipate 'words / Which speak of nothing more than what we are' (*Excursion*, Preface, xii [58-9]), the Narrator's attempt to 'render up the tale / Of what we are' (*PS1*, ll. 28-9) is continually thwarted. He ransacks language for tropes that posit the connections they cannot establish, opening his invocation by imagining a 'brotherhood' between 'earth, ocean, air' and himself, and extending the metaphor to include a maternal presiding presence, the 'Mother of this unfathomable world' (l. 18). The personifications of sunset, midnight, and the seasons continue the strategy of claiming connection by finding it already imaged in nature, but the cumulative force of these tropes cannot overcome the unease encoded in the if-clauses that make up the 'boast'. The Narrator is an adopted brother, dependent on the 'favour' of his siblings, and the order of this 'brethren' seems less familial than monastic, while the Narrator's 'natural piety' seems rather a desperate faith (not unlike that of the alchemist with whom he compares himself). The Narrator's self-image of the 'long-forgotten lyre / Suspended in the solitary dome / Of some mysterious and deserted fane' (ll. 42-4), with which the first part ends, plangently captures the uncertainty of this faith whose followers have largely deserted it, while his concluding invocation to the 'Great Parent' forcefully reiterates his familial longings. Whether the Narrator's words, his 'strain', will modulate with nature, remains palpably uncertain – Shelley's scepticism barely concealed by the Narrator's metaphoricity reminds us that this is not Tintern Abbey despite the Wordsworthian overtones.[62]

---

[61] John Whale, 'Romantics, Explorers and Picturesque Travellers', in *The Politics of the Picturesque*, p. 178; Liu, *Wordsworth's Sense*, pp. 61-3.

[62] William Keach has recognised that the Narrator's is a 'troubled' or 'insecure' Wordsworthianism, and 'never the simple pantheistic nature-worship invoked by

Though the Narrator claims to 'wait thy breath, Great Parent' (l. 45) to set his lyre to work, this is not what happens. Instead, his efforts to trace the history of the Poet are decidedly self-instigated and self-sustained. The extreme otherness of the Poet's journey and insights provokes a music far different than that for which the Narrator hopes; rather than 'modulating' his strain to 'murmurs of the air', the journey calls into question art's ability to represent phenomena as well as noumena, and certainly undermines the familial union posited by the invocation. Thus, the unfolding story's tangential relationships with the Narrator's own structures of feeling both elucidate and problematise his nature-worship. The Poet's solitude, for example, calls attention to the Narrator's own. The Poet's radical human disconnection from 'mourning maiden[s]' (l. 55), the 'Arab maiden' (l. 129) and 'youthful maidens' (l. 266) reflects the Narrator's insistence on his own sexual 'innocence' in the invocation, while the Poet's erotic dream of the 'veiled maid' reconstitutes the Narrator's sublimated eroticism. Despite the Narrator's assurances to his 'Mother' over the exclusivity of his love, this appears not to be the case. His 'innocent love' with whom he mixes 'awful talk and asking looks' along with 'breathless kisses' can hardly refer to the 'Mother' he has never seen, and though he uses the epithet 'innocent', the moment echoes the sublimated eroticism of his earlier personification: 'spring's voluptuous pantings when she breathes / Her first sweet kisses' (ll. 11-12). The Poet's impossible projection of the veiled maid calls attention to the elusiveness of the Narrator's own, partly by drawing attention to the strands of sexual desire that have become confused or interwoven with desire for the 'prototype of [a] conception' (*PS1*, pp. 462-3). The inaccessibility of a fulfilled passion, likewise, is figured in the oriental otherness of femininity throughout the Poet's journey.[63]

I want to pass over the Poet's outward journey in search of 'the secrets of the birth of time', which I have treated in connection with Wollstonecraft's frontier journeys, and trace the narrative after the vision of the veiled maid. At this point the Poet reverses his direction and follows a meandering course from the Vale of Cashmere to the Georgian Caucuses, voyaging across the intervening Caspian Sea. The westward trajectory brings the Poet no closer to civilisation, since his final resting place is an undiscovered space. But the new occidental orientation does highlight the strategies of appropriation that the Narrator employs in relating the journey. If, as Nicholas Birns asserts, 'Shelley's itinerary has taken him away from any region with a particular connotative heft in Western cultural hermeneutics',[64] the reason is because he now relies on his Narrator to construct a cultural hermeneutic upon disembodied signifiers: Aornos, Petra, Balk, and where 'Parthian kings scatter to every wind / Their wasting dust' (ll. 243-4). This is of course no easy task, and the Narrator is ever conscious of his potential failure; indeed, upon such a note the poem ends. Moreover, it is no coincidence that the phrase

---

Wasserman'. See his essay, 'Obstinate Questionings: The Immortality Ode and *Alastor*', *Wordsworth Circle*, 12 (Winter 1981), pp. 37; 41.
[63] Cf. Fischman, 'Gender, Audition, and Echo', pp. 154-5.
[64] Birns, 'Secrets', p. 354.

describing the Parthian kings is recycled several times to express the physical and cultural disembodying of the Poet, whose existence the Narrator reconstructs out of the memorial of verse: we learn from the Poet's 'voice' that his 'bloodless limbs shall waste / I' the passing wind' (ll. 513-14); and later how a 'broad river' joins the 'homeless streams' by 'scattering its waters in the passing winds' (l. 570); and finally, the full disjointing force of the analogy now apparent to the Narrator, how the Poet's voice shall 'render up its *majesty*, / Scatter its music on the unfeeling storm' (ll. 596-7; my italics). The waste places in nature are thus related to the wasting away of the body, and the waste of value inherent in the cultural embodiments of power or art.[65]

Natural description begins to figure more in the Narrator's discourse, sometimes as a contrast with the Poet's self-imposed disconnection – 'Red morning dawned upon his flight / Shedding the mockery of its vital hues / Upon his cheek of death' (ll. 237-9) – but with increasing specificity of detail. As cultural *loci* diminish in importance, the Narrator's descriptions themselves appropriate the unappropriated, but, unlike Wordsworth's more equanimous aesthetic, they are increasingly self-conscious of the indeterminacy of the reality that all art reflects, the distortion-in-reflection which I have earlier discussed with reference to the Poet's boat journey. That journey itself forms a kind of bridge or transition into the more mediated and meditative conclusion. The sublime danger of the sea and leaky shallop combined with the preternatural motion that hurries the action forward creates a tension of 'mutual incomprehension'[66] between Narrator and Poet, and the fulcrum out of which the more carefully constructive descriptions emerge. The Narrator's attempts to mythologise the elements (e.g. 'Night followed, clad with stars'; l. 340) seem feeble gestures punctuated by references to 'fearful war', 'mutual war', and sudden death. The turning point comes with the calm, the 'wandering stream of wind, / Breathed from the west' (ll. 397-8) which saves the shallop from the reflux of the whirlpool.

It is tempting to interpret that wandering wind as an emblem of Western revolutionary values, the last draughts of the wild west wind that Shelley would later mythologise in his famous ode. But the wind does augur the reflux of the Narrator's own attempts to locate the dislocated cultural loci in a self-constructed bower; to enclose the space of incomprehension opened by the Poet's career. The

---

[65] Cf. Shelley's use of the metaphor in *Julian and Maddalo* (1819):

> I love all waste
> And solitary places; where we taste
> The pleasure of believing what we see
> Is boundless, as we wish our souls to be[.](*PS2*, ll. 14-17)

For Shelley, believing what we see is a pleasure not related to structures of taste in sublime and picturesque landscape description, and yet there is no soul-ratifying certainty in the love, pleasure, or wish. 'Wastes' in *Alastor* are similar spaces out of which wishes may be constructed but which in themselves prevent these structures from ossifying into dogma.

[66] Birns, 'Secrets', p. 357.

long verse paragraph following the boat passage finds the Narrator's gaze leaving the Poet for the first time, as he constructs the landscape around him. The Poet is 'placed' in a landscape rather than constructed simultaneously with it:

> The noonday sun
> Now shone upon the forest, one vast mass
> Of mingling shade, whose brown magnificence
> A narrow vale embosoms. There, huge caves,
> Scooped in the dark base of their aëry rocks
> Mocking its moans, respond and roar for ever.
> The meeting boughs and implicated leaves
> Wove twilight o'er the Poet's path, as led
> By love, or dream, or god, or mightier Death,
> He sought in Nature's dearest haunt, some bank,
> Her cradle, and his sepulchre. More dark
> And dark the shades accumulate. (ll. 420-31)

If the Poet is 'obedient to the light / That shone within his soul' (ll. 492-93), the Narrator shows himself obedient to an external light source, like a painter. Having established this, he proceeds to sketch the rest of the scene. The 'brown magnificence' of the 'mingling shade' recalls Pope's *Eloisa to Abelard*, in which imagination 'breathes a browner horror on the woods'.[67] The 'narrow vale' too seems apropos and the verb 'embosoms' captures both the Narrator's earlier sense of the maternal properties of nature, along with the self-containment fostered by the picturesque. The 'huge caves' and 'aëry rocks' recall that this is a landscape more likely to be painted by Salvator Rosa than Nicholas Poussin, where the picturesque modulates with, or may be said to be contained within the sublime. The caves are 'scooped' out of the unknowable space the Poet seeks and form an immediate contrast with maternal nature. They 'mock' the moans of the forest and remind us that the embosoming vale is a metaphor for the hues of the scene and not its sounds. The full sensuous experience contains the disharmony that the visual scene belies.

The Narrator continues to focus: in the lines following those quoted above, the 'meeting boughs and implicated leaves' (l. 426) of the forest canopy are distinguished by species; the oak, beech, and cedar lead the eye to smaller undergrowth, the ash, acacia, and colourful parasites. By line 448 the eye has been led to the lowest point, the 'mossy lawns', the 'perfumed herbs . . . eyed with blooms / Minute yet beautiful' (ll. 448; 450-51). This last qualification works as a kind of apology for the introduction of minutiae normally disregarded by the picturesque eye, intent instead on variation and unity of composition. The Narrator does emphasise the unity with a Darwinian diction that stresses 'the loves of the

---

[67] *The Twickenham Edition of the Poems of Alexander Pope*, vol. 2, ed. Geoffrey Tillotsen (London: Methuen & Co., Ltd; New Haven: Yale University Press, 1966), p. 333, l. 170.

plants' as the oak 'embraces' the beech, the parasites 'flow around' the tree trunks and 'twine their tendrils with the wedded boughs / Uniting their close union' (ll. 433; 440; 444-5). The landscape not only embodies the fruits of desire that elude the Poet, but reconstitutes the fundamental structures of oriental architecture that he seeks out in his early journeys: 'The *pyramids* / Of the tall cedar over*arch*ing, frame / Most solemn *domes* within' (ll. 433-5; my italics). Despite the flowing movements of the vegetation that carry the eye in intricate paths, the Narrator constructs a series of frames around increasingly self-contained, harmonious natural scenes. These express aesthetic ideals of natural culture, religion, and human relationship without going so far as to image any 'wedded' union of mind and nature. It is not surprising to find the larger passage ending in the account of the 'darkest glen' (the light has been steadily dimming) where is found a central well that sends the eye back where it came from. The well,

> Dark, gleaming, and of most translucent wave,
> Images all the woven boughs above,
> And each depending leaf, and every speck
> Of azure sky, darting between their chasms[.] (ll. 458-61)

This final frame becomes a mirror that completes the scene by turning the eye to the minutiae of the sky, up becomes structured like down. But for the caves that mock the larger scene, the tableau is complete in itself, appropriating all that desire could want to complete itself.

The reintroduction of the Poet into this scene is predictably anti-climactic: 'Hither the Poet came. His eyes beheld / Their own wan light through the reflected lines / Of his thin hair . . .' (ll. 469-70). But the Narrator's previous aesthetic idealisation of nature has its fruit in his palpable distrust of the Poet's vision; what the Poet sees we are told is his 'own treacherous likeness' (l. 474) and the Spirit that seems to communicate with him becomes a distortion of the scene itself. The 'gloom of thought' (l. 490) where the 'starry eyes' appear is a function of the 'evening gloom' (l. 485) while the starry eyes themselves have been anticipated by the specks of azure sky reflected in the pool – the Poet mistakes the fretwork light for a numinous being, and the Narrator drives home the point by echoing the language of the previous passage (i.e. the 'serene and azure smiles' of the eyes reconstitute the 'specks of azure sky' reflected in the pool before the Poet arrives on the scene). In the next verse paragraph, the Narrator recounts the Poet's invocation to the stream – 'Thou imagest my life' (l. 505). By this point nature has become art, both for the Poet and the Narrator, mimetically reflecting the perceptions of the beholder. The metaphysical connection between human agency and an agency in nature itself, however, continues to elude both Narrator and Poet.

The Narrator's subsequent landscape descriptions trace a pathway towards increasingly sublime regions. The self-contained glen tableau gradually opens out into the 'unimaginable forms' of a rocky vista that seems 'to overhang the world' (ll. 544; 553), reminiscent of the frontiers that impressed Wollstonecraft as 'the bones of the world waiting to be clothed' (*LSND*, p. 49). The Narrator's impulse to imagine the forms ('stony jaws'; l. 551) and to clothe the bones is similar to Wollstonecraft's, and even here, especially here, he attempts to carve out a space for the Poet that does not threaten the Poet with sublime dissolution:

> ... The near scene,
> In naked and severe simplicity,
> Made contrast with the universe. A pine,
> Rock-rooted, stretched athwart the vacancy
> Its swinging boughs, to each inconstant blast
> Yielding one only response .... (ll. 559-64)

The pine becomes emblematic of this resistance to the sublime – its roots are in the 'unimaginable forms' of the rocks, and it confronts vacancy and inconstancy by stubbornly making a unified response out of its unpredictable materials. Likewise, the nook which receives the Poet 'overlooked in its serenity / The dark earth' and 'was a tranquil spot, that seemed to smile / Even in the lap of horror' (ll. 575-8).

In the nook, the Poet attempts to reconstitute an aesthetically idealised scene such as that discussed above, but the proximity and threat of sublime dissolution continually encroaches on it, whereas in the previous scene it was kept safely in the outer frame (the mocking caves). The stakes however have changed in this final scene, for the Narrator more desperately explores the possibility of a meta-cultural being that can survive the inexorable temporality of an indifferent nature – a sort of last resort in face of our ultimate disconnection with the earth on which we live:

> ... One step,
> One human step alone, has ever broken
> The stillness of its solitude: – one voice
> Alone inspired its echoes; – even that voice
> Which hither came, floating among the winds,
> And led the loveliest among human forms
> To make their wild haunts the depository
> Of all the grace and beauty that endued
> Its motions, render up its majesty,
> Scatter its music on the unfeeling storm,
> And to the damp leaves and blue cavern mould,
> Nurses of rainbow flowers and branching moss,
> Commit the colours of that varying cheek,
> That snowy breast, those dark and drooping eyes. (ll. 588-601)

The possibility of a poet inspiring nature (rather than vice versa) establishes the beautiful ideal of a colonialist imagination that occupies without violence the vacuum of culture, inexorably and naturally. So tantalising a possibility is it that the Narrator seems to articulate the more likely scenario as a subtext; that is, the Poet has followed his own voice, disembodied as an echo, as if it were another's. At yet another level, the real irony is that the voice, which leads the Poet, is the Narrator's own as he constructs in 'high verse' the scenes into which the poet enters. The Narrator himself structures unappropriated earth as a 'repository' for music and painting.

In the death scene, the Narrator monumentalises the Poet as the meeting place of culture and nature, even as he continues metaphorically to explore the possibility of nature becoming such a site in its own right. The Poet 'resign[s] his high and holy soul / To images of the majestic past' (ll. 628-9) and 'surrender[s]' to the 'final impulses' (l. 638) of his natural surroundings; impulses from within the mind and from external objects feed 'the stream of thought' (l. 644) – a topography of perception and being that anticipates 'Mont Blanc'. The influx of imagery from within is compared with personified 'winds that bear sweet music, when they breathe / Through some dim latticed chamber' (ll. 631-2), picking up on numerous motifs that had gone into the Narrator's previous nature descriptions. But in the last part of the poem, the Narrator's coda, an implicit recognition of the failure of nature to appropriate culture and culture to appropriate nature is evident:

> ... Nor, when those hues
> Are gone, and those divinest lineaments,
> Worn by the senseless wind, shall live alone
> In the frail pauses of this simple strain,
> Let not high verse, mourning the memory
> Of that which is no more, or painting's woe
> Or sculpture, speak in feeble imagery
> Their own cold powers. Art and eloquence,
> And all the shows o' the world are frail and vain
> To weep a loss that turns their lights to shade. (ll. 703-12)

The Narrator has attempted what he decries: he has used the rhythms and imagery of high verse; he has employed picturesque discursive structures; he has figured his dying Poet in sculpturesque attitudes. But his recognition that the Poet can only survive in the 'pauses' opened by language is significant. Shelley seems to be saying that the 'frail pauses' of language not only construct meaning as much as the signifiers themselves, but that meaning must be generated out of a space of unmeaning. For the Narrator such recognition defies his longing for a higher pantheistic order, but seems a 'natural' outcome from his confrontation with the 'strange truths in undiscovered lands' raised by his unfathomable subject. In the Narrator's very sense of loss, Shelley locates a saving grace – it is precisely the metaphysical sense of loss that accompanies any reaching after certainties that complements the reaching itself. The Narrator's final recognition of 'Nature's vast frame, the web of human things, / Birth and the grave, that are not as they were' (ll. 719-20) contains a similar double meaning. The ineffable change that the Narrator laments also confirms the power of art and imagination to effect change. The

Narrator, who has continually imposed aesthetic frames on nature, now offers the image of nature itself as a frame, and culture ('human things') as a natural artifice or 'web' and yet between whose threads is the space out of which all meaning is generated.

Throughout this chapter I have been concerned with the aesthetic structures that Shelley employs when representing otherness in *Alastor*. While my conclusion concentrates on the Narrator's bid to acculturate a resistant nature, it does so without minimising the importance of the first half of my argument. In his exploration of aesthetic spaces in the poem, Shelley uses world geography in an integral way; there is nothing tangential or purely allegorical about the oriental geographies in *Alastor*, despite the trajectory of the poem towards issues in European aesthetics which were to figure in Shelley's subsequent work, his letters from Switzerland collected in *History of a Six Weeks' Tour* and 'Mont Blanc'. Instead, with *Alastor* Shelley holds a prism up to landscape aesthetics and studies the political, epistemological, and historical refractions, which I have attempted to elucidate with the help of Wordsworth's *Excursion* and Wollstonecraft's *Short Residence*. By 1816 when he again leaves England, Shelley is in a much better position to reflect on the language of travellers as it bears on the refiguring of a European cultural landscape.

Chapter 3

'The Raptures of Travellers': Writing Mont Blanc

> The immensity of these aerial summits excited, when they suddenly burst upon the sight, a sentiment of extatic wonder, not unallied to madness—And remember this was all one scene. It all pressed home to our regard & to our imagination.—Though it embraced a great number of miles the snowy pyramids which shot into the bright blue sky seemed to overhang our path—the ravine, clothed with gigantic pines and black with its depth below.—so deep that the very roaring of the untameable Arve which rolled through it could not be heard above—was close to our very footsteps. All was as much our own as if we had been the creators of such impressions in the minds of others, as now occupied our own.—Nature was the poet whose harmony held our spirits more breathless than that of the divinest.
>
> (Shelley, 'To Thomas Love Peacock', 22 July 1816; *L*, 1: 497)

In October 1817 notices began appearing for the imminent publication of the Shelleys' anonymous *History of a Six Weeks' Tour through a Part of France, Switzerland, Germany, and Holland: with Letters Descriptive of a Sail round the Lake of Geneva, and of the Glaciers of Chamouni*.[1] The volume that appeared in November consisted of a short preface followed by three sections, each headed by a separate title page.[2] The preface, written by Shelley, announces the

---

[1] E. B. Murray, ed., *The Prose Works of Percy Bysshe Shelley* (Oxford: Clarendon Press, 1993), I, 433-4, finds advertisements for the *History of a Six Weeks' Tour* in a copy of *Laon and Cythna* (Oct. 1817) as well as in the *Morning Chronicle* (30 Oct.), *The Times* (1 Nov., 12 Nov.), and the *Morning Chronicle* (13 Nov.). Charles E. Robinson, 'Percy Bysshe Shelley, Charles Ollier, and William Blackwood: the Contexts of Early Nineteenth-Century Publishing', in *Shelley Revalued: Essays from the Gregynog Conference*, ed. Kelvin Everest (Leicester University Press, 1983), pp. 218-19, n. 42, notes that 'eight more advertisements appeared in these two papers between 13 Dec. 1817 and 3 Sept. 1818'. In addition to these, I have located notices in: *Anti-Jacobin Review*, 53 (Oct. 1817), p. 160; *British Critic*, n.s., 8 (Oct. 1817), 444; *Quarterly Review*, 18 (Oct. 1817), p. 258; *Blackwood's Magazine*, 2 (Jan. 1818), p. 453; *Monthly Magazine*, 306 (1 Jan. 1818); *Edinburgh Review*, 29 (Feb. 1818), p. 517; and *Literary Panorama* (Feb. 1818), p. 612.

[2] For the date of publication, see *MSW*, 8: 6, n. 8, and Robinson, 'Percy Bysshe Shelley, Charles Ollier, and William Blackwood', pp. 218-19, n. 42. The *Morning Chronicle* (30 Oct. 1817) and *The Times* (1 Nov. 1817) both advertised a publication date of 6 Nov., though the *History* was not registered at Stationer's Hall (for T. Hookham) until 10 Dec.

'unpresuming' volume as 'the account of some desultory visits by a party of young people to scenes which are now so familiar to our countrymen' (*HSWT*, p. iii), locating the interest less in the scenes described as in the record of the perceptions of youth. The first section, 'History of a Six Weeks' Tour', presents a journal of the party's Continental excursions in the summer of 1814, including a return voyage along the Rhine. The second section, 'Letters' (expanded to 'Letters Written during a Residence of Three Months in the Environs of Geneva, in the Summer of the Year 1816' on the first page of text), contains two letters signed 'M'. followed by two more signed 'S'., generally attributable to Mary Shelley and Shelley respectively. The final section, 'Lines Written in the Vale of Chamouni', consists of the first and only publication in Shelley's lifetime of one of his most canonical poems, 'Mont Blanc'. The poem's placement as a section, rather than an appendix, would appear to support Donald Reiman's belief that the entire *History* was 'carefully constructed to culminate' in 'Mont Blanc', and that, accordingly, the poem 'should be studied . . . in terms of the ideas and attitudes that precede it' (*SC* 571, 7: 41).[3]

Robert Brinkley, one of the few scholars to take up Reiman's suggestion, has also shown how problematic the issue of precedence is. Brinkley's work on the Geneva notebook (Bodleian Shelley MS. adds. e. 16), which contains the earliest drafts of 'Mont Blanc', reveals that the poem itself represents a composite experience rather than a particular vision from 'a bridge over the Arve River' (*SPP*, p. 96). In its initial stages, the poem seems to have drawn its 'inspiration' from a number of stations along Shelley's route through the Valley of Chamounix and the surrounding glaciers, and, equally important, from impressions recorded in the travel letter to Peacock that Shelley was writing along the way.[4] But even as Brinkley traces in his earliest essay upon the subject, 'the process by which language from the letter was transferred to the poem', he also speculates on ways in which Shelley's first poetic impulses may have influenced the tone of subsequent letters.[5] If this is true, the 'unremitting interchange' of poem and prose might also suggest the problem with viewing the final drafts registered by the published *History* as a teleological arrangement. Even if Shelley or Mary Shelley revised the prose in 1817 to anticipate the poem, the poem and prose are profoundly of a piece, neither one nor the other the sole reason for the volume.

The teleological argument that interests those who come to the text through their interest in 'Mont Blanc' rather than their interest in travel literature would have been less obvious to the volume's immediate audience. Shelley's

---

[3] For a dissenting view on the intentionality of the poem's placement, see Jonathan Wordsworth's 'Introduction' to Mary Shelley and Percy Bysshe Shelley, *History of a Six Weeks' Tour 1817* (Otley: Woodstock Books, 2002), where he points out that 'Mont Blanc' appeared in smaller type and was not mentioned on the title page.
[4] Brinkley makes this point in 'Spaces Between Words: Writing Mont Blanc', in *Romantic Revisions*, eds Robert Brinkley and Keith Hanley (Cambridge: Cambridge University Press, 1992), pp. 243-5. See also his article, 'On the Composition of "Mont Blanc": Staging a Wordsworthian Scene', *English Language Notes*, 24.2 (Dec. 1986), pp. 50-53.
[5] Brinkley, 'On the Composition of "Mont Blanc"', pp. 50, n. 12; 53.

contemporaries, more accustomed to poetical effusions on Alpine scenes accompanying travel books or accompanied by travel description, may have been more inclined to view 'Mont Blanc' as an appendix to the sublimities of the Geneva letters.[6] A reading public already well accustomed to picturesque travel accounts of Alpine regions also might have found the 1814 journal comparatively more novel, by virtue of its air of juvenile innocence, than the later effusions in prose or poetry. Shelley's faithfulness to the picturesque travel genre in his contributions to the latter part of the volume suggests that his argument in 'Mont Blanc' more obviously takes place within, rather than tries to subvert, the genre of landscape description with which he engages.

Reiman's contrary suggestion that Shelley 'may purposely have constructed *History of a Six Weeks' Tour* in the hope that the sympathetic interest and involvement created by the portions signed "M" would win a fair hearing for what even he knew would, without such preparation, be rejected out of hand' (*SC* 571, 7: 45) is based on William Beckford's marginalia in a copy of the *History*, 'in the absence of other records of contemporary reaction' (*SC* 571, 7: 44). Beckford's otherwise unremarkable comments on the text give way to vitriolic criticism only in response to Shelley's final letter and poem: 'Your prose most pompously picturesque Sir is high flown enough God knows but your poetry! is overwhelming, an avalanche of nonsense' (*SC* 571, 7: 44). This kind of response recalls unfavourable reviews of Shelley's owned verse – what the *Monthly Review* labels Shelley's 'sublime obscurity' in a review of the *Alastor* volume[7] – but it would be misleading to see Beckford's comments outside the context Beckford himself establishes. Having identified the authors as 'picturesque Tourists' (*SC* 571, 7: 44), he objects to 'S' pandering to the mood of the marketplace for superlatives, rather than seeking truth in observation. This was a danger that Shelley himself was well aware of, as he makes clear in his letter to Peacock, reprinted as the beginning of 'Letter IV': 'To exhaust the epithets which express the astonishment and the admiration – . . . is this, to impress upon your mind the images which fill mine now even till it overflow? I too have read the raptures of travellers; I will be warned by their example' (*HSWT*, pp. 140-41).

In the presence of other contemporary reactions, Beckford's seems less idiosyncratic, and the place of the *History* among similar travel books highlights the Shelleys' engagement with discourses on and disputes over tourism, landscape description, and the state of post-revolutionary Europe. The fact is, not only was the *History* widely advertised, but it also received its fair share of reviews for such

---

[6] Two examples of Alpine poems in travel books are Helen Maria Williams's 'A Hymn Written among the Alps', in *A Tour In Switzerland*, vol. 2 (London: Printed for G. G. and J. Robinson, 1798), 16-19, and John Sheppard's 'To Mont Blanc', in *Letters, Descriptive of a Tour through some Parts of France, Italy, Switzerland, and Germany, in 1816* (Edinburgh: Printed for Oliphant, Waugh and Innes, 1817), pp. 209-13. See also *The Passage of the Mountain of Saint Gothard, a Poem*, by Georgiana, Duchess of Devonshire (London: For Prosper and Co., 1802), and its copious notes explaining passages with reference to the journey itself.

[7] See Theodore Redpath, *The Young Romantics and Critical Opinion, 1807-1824* (London: Harrap, 1973), p. 305.

a modest production. Marcel Kessel first noted the review that appeared in the July 1818 issue of *Blackwood's Edinburgh Magazine*, but the volume had already been reviewed in the May issue of *The Eclectic Review*, while the *Monthly Review* for January 1819 noticed it again in a series of brief reviews in its 'Monthly Catalogue'.[8] The most favourable of the three was that in *Blackwood's*, but even the animadversions of the others confirm the intersections between both Mary Shelley's and Shelley's contributions to the *History* with the field of continental travel literature then available.

The Eclectic Review considered the Shelleys' tour alongside their publisher Thomas Hookham's *A Walk through Switzerland in September 1816* (London: T. Hookham, Jun., and Baldwin, Cradock, and Joy, 1818), an anonymous account of a Swiss tour conducted in the month following the Shelleys' residence around Lake Geneva. Under the proprietorship of the evangelical Josiah Conder, the *Eclectic* was by this time establishing 'a reputation for liberal opinion',[9] but Hookham's obvious enthusiasm throughout his excursion for the character, writings, and beliefs of Rousseau, as well as associated landscapes, reveal that the review's liberalism did not extend to matters of religion. Confining its notice of the *Walk* to a mere paragraph, the review was uncompromising:

> The 'Walk' is the production of some gentleman exceedingly addicted to fine writing, and is the flimsiest and most unprofitable reading imaginable. His vocabulary has been ransacked for superlatives, and he betrays the most unequivocal sign of a cold imagination in his eternal extravagance of admiration and rapture. An adequate notion of his morality may be formed from his boundless idolatry of the *nastiest* of mortals – Rousseau, and of his religious creed ....[10]

What makes this response especially interesting is the fact that Shelley's text shares many of Hookham's enthusiasms, for fine landscapes and for Rousseau, but the reviewer largely passes them over. This is because Shelley tends to remain on safer ground; while he does trace the 'classic ground' (*HSWT*, p. v) associated with Rousseau around Lake Geneva, his apparent interest is in 'the divine beauty of Rousseau's imagination, *as it exhibits itself in Julie*' (*HSWT*, p. 107; my italics). Rousseau's *Julie, ou la nouvelle Héloïse* (1760) became enmeshed in a cult of sensibility that established Lake Geneva, the setting associated with the love affair

---

[8] Marcel Kessel, 'An Early Review of the Shelleys' "Six Weeks' Tour"', *Modern Language Notes*, 58 (Dec. 1943), p. 623. The *Eclectic* and *Monthly* reviews of the *History* first came to light in my article, 'Contemporary Notice of the Shelleys' *History of a Six Weeks' Tour*: Two New Early Reviews', *Keats-Shelley Journal*, 48 (1999), pp. 22-9. The three known reviews of the *History* are, in full: *Eclectic Review*, ser. 2, vol. 9 (May 1818), pp. 470-74; *Blackwood's Edinburgh Magazine*, 3.16 (July 1818), pp. 412-16; and *Monthly Review*, 88 (Jan. 1819), pp. 97-9.
[9] John O. Hayden, *The Romantic Reviewers* (Chicago: University of Chicago Press, 1968), p. 49.
[10] Review of *A Walk through Switzerland*, [by Thomas Hookham, Jun.], *Eclectic Review*, ser. 2, vol. 9 (May 1818), 473-4.

between Julie and St Preux, as a tourist destination. In his *Sketches of . . . Swisserland* (1779), William Coxe found the region 'faithfully delineated' by the novel, which he had checked out of a circulating library at Lausanne. Thereafter, as Katherine Turner observes, the 'affective responses' of travellers to scenes associated with Rousseau and his works 'are described with increasing frequency'.[11] By 1817, Shelley's descriptions would have seemed conventional, especially since the 'classic ground' around Lake Geneva supported a mini tourist industry, complete with plaques, ruins, and the best of guidebooks: the novel itself.[12] In the post-revolutionary period, as Edward Duffy asserts, sensibility might be said to be 'undergoing a negative appraisal' because of its associations with Rousseau's political doctrines and supposed Jacobin disciples, yet *Julie* could still receive praise from the Tory *Quarterly Review* for its eloquence and provide scenes of beauty or intrigue for tourists hungry for things to see and morals to savour, no longer hampered by imminent political threats.[13] One could condemn Rousseau's character while admiring his idealism, censor the effects of his writing while, as one reviewer puts it, 'follow[ing] his footsteps, and the vestiges and memorials even of his fictitious personages, with a spirit of devout observance'.[14]

Informed by a perspective conscious of travel conventions, the *Eclectic* reviewer questions the *History*'s authenticity: 'To us . . . the value of the book is considerably lessened by a strong suspicion that the *dramatis personae* are fictitious, and that the little adventures introduced for the purpose of giving life and interest to the narration, are the mere inventions of the Author'.[15] Shelley's sprained ankle reminds the reviewer of that which prevented Patrick Brydone from ascending Mount Aetna, while the Rhine voyage seems derivative of tours conducted by Ann Radcliffe in 1794 and Sir John Carr in 1806. The obvious reference to Byron in the Geneva letters, as well as the poem 'intended to pass for his Lordship's composition' ('Mont Blanc') all contribute to the reviewer's scepticism at the verisimilitude of the entire production. Though wrong in the main, the review does get the tradition right, for as Charles Batten has shown, Brydone's *Tour through Sicily and Malta* (1773) introduced the vogue for 'evocative description' that informed such works as Radcliffe's *Journey Made in*

---

[11] Katherine Turner, *British Travel Writers in Europe, 1750-1800: Authorship, Gender and National Identity* (Aldershot: Ashgate, 2001), pp. 33-4. Turner cites John Moore and James Edward Smith as other travellers who use the phrase 'classic ground' for sites associated with Rousseau.

[12] In his 1814 travel diary, Samuel Rogers notes how plaques for literati, such at those in Geneva for Rousseau and Charles Bonnet, are unknown in England: 'No such things with us. None on Dryden's House in Gerard St. None on Johnson's in Ball Court or Milton's in Jewin Street'. In the entry that follows he mentions visiting 'the Maison Rousseau now a heap of stones, supposed to be the scite [sic] of Julia's house' as well as another house intact 'in which Rousseau is said to have lived with Mme De Warens'. See *The Italian Journal of Samuel Rogers*, ed. J. R. Hale (London: Faber and Faber, 1956), pp. 142-3.

[13] See Edward Duffy, *Rousseau in England: The Context for Shelley's Critique of the Enlightenment* (Berkeley: University of California Press, 1979), p. 46.

[14] Review of *Switzerland*, by L. Simond, *Edinburgh Review*, 37 (Nov. 1822), p. 320.

[15] *Eclectic Review*, ser. 2, vol. 9 (May 1818), pp. 470-71.

the Summer of 1794 (1795).[16] Like Horace Bénedict de Saussure, whose *Voyage dans les Alpes* (1779) is another antecedent to the Shelleys' *History*, Brydone makes a neat leap from the scientific to the sublime, when passing from matter of fact travellers' chat to the wonder of scenes of 'awful horror'. Here is Brydone on Aetna:

> The scene enlarges, and the horizon seems to widen and expand itself on all sides; till the sun, like the great Creator, appears in the east, and with his plastic ray completes the mighty scene. – All appears enchantment; and it is with difficulty we can believe we are still on earth.[17]

Here is Saussure on the slopes of Mont Blanc:

> The repose and profound silence which reigned in this vast extent, still heightened by the imagination, inspired me with a sort of terror; it appeared to me as if I had outlived the universe, and that I saw its corpse at my feet.[18]

And here are Shelley's first impressions of the Alps in 1814, also cited in the *Eclectic* article:

> Their immensity staggers the imagination, and so far surpasses all conception, that it requires an effort of the understanding to believe that they indeed form a part of the earth. (*HSWT*, p. 44)

In Shelley's 1814 journal entry, which forms the basis for this description, he had written that 'it requ[i]res an effort of the understanding to believe that they are indeed mountains' (*MWSJ*, p. 17). The revision calibrates the earlier impression with Shelley's 1816 description of the mountains surrounding the glacier of Montanvert, which 'pierce the clouds like things not belonging to this earth' (*HSWT*, p. 166). But in the light of contexts suggested by the *Eclectic* article, this shows as much as anything the way Shelley made the description conventional. The other-worldliness of the sublime that has received so much attention with regards to the epistemological originality of Romantic artists, it must be remembered, was very much standard fare for readers and reviewers of travel literature.[19] The lines quoted above help us understand what Shelley was

---

[16] Charles L. Batten, *Pleasurable Instruction* (Berkeley: University of California Press, 1978), pp. 97-8; 97-107 *passim*.
[17] Patrick Brydone, *A Tour through Sicily and Malta. In a Series of Letters to William Beckford*, 3rd edn, 2 vols (London: Printed for W. Strahan; and T. Cadell, 1774), 1: 202.
[18] Horace Bénedict de Saussure, *An Account of the Attempts that Have Been Made to Attain the Summit of Mont Blanc*, in *A General Collection of the Best and Most Interesting Voyages and Travels in All Parts of the World*, ed. John Pinkerton, 17 vols (London, 1808-14), 4: 682.
[19] See Thomas Weiskel, *The Romantic Sublime: Studies in the Structure and Psychology of Transcendence* (Baltimore: Johns Hopkins University Press, 1976).

attempting within these conventions, and confirm the structures of perception that provided him with his vocabulary, idiom, and audience.

While the *Eclectic* may have missed the *History*'s anti-religious scepticism (particularly in 'Mont Blanc'), the 'ultra-Tory' *Blackwood's* seems to have been diverted from the book's liberal political sympathies.[20] Instead, the *Blackwood's* article, by far the most favourable notice, continually finds its bearings against travel writing conventions. What impresses the reviewer most is the 1814 journal; he finds novelty in its informality, its brevity of presentation, and its lack of stock description: 'the perusal of it rather produces the same effect as a smart walk before breakfast, in company with a lively friend who hates long stories'.[21] Fooled by the Shelleys' gloss over the elopement tour, the reviewer considers the author 'a sweet-blooded wedded wife' who 'prattles away very prettily in the true English idiom'[22] – a patronising assessment that allows the reviewer to overlook the author's liberal alliances (e.g. reading Wollstonecraft's *Short Residence* on the Rhine) and focus instead on her national character and picturesque representations. Indeed, the review consists largely of long extracts from the journal portion, accompanied by a brief, but sympathetic, commentary.

Following Reiman's hypothesis, one might expect the reviewer's patience to run out when moving from the journal materials to the more Shelleyan Geneva letters and 'Mont Blanc', as did Beckford's. On the contrary, this part is deemed 'lively and well-written' though 'the Swiss scenery is often therein described with something of a poetical fervour'. While Beckford may have regarded 'Mont Blanc' as 'an avalanche of nonsense', *Blackwood's* was again much more positive, seeing in Shelley's poem a 'too ambitious, and at times too close an imitation of Coleridge's sublime hymn on the vale of Chamouni', a poem which may have indeed influenced Shelley.[23] The review concludes with a generous extract from 'Mont Blanc' – in fact, the entire third part, which also contains the majority of allusions to the travel letters that precede it in the volume. Once again, what points Shelley seems to score with this reviewer are not based on his originality or the provocative implications of his descriptions, but on his approximation of a success already mapped out by other travel writers and poets.

The *Monthly Review* was less satisfied with the 'hurried journey' recounted by the 1814 journal, but considered 'the second tour less aukwardly [sic] managed'.[24] This last and shortest notice is of interest as much for the context of similar tours in the 'Monthly Catalogue' as for anything in the review itself. The review of Hookham's *Walk*, appearing immediately before that of the *History*, helps gloss the

---

[20] See Hayden, *Romantic Reviewers*, p. 62, for an account of *Blackwood's* political partisanship.

[21] *Blackwood's*, 3.16 (July 1818), p. 412.

[22] *Blackwood's*, 3.16 (July 1818), p. 412.

[23] *Blackwood's*, 3.16 (July 1818), p. 416. See Charles E. Robinson, *Shelley and Byron: The Snake and Eagle Wreathed in Fight* (Baltimore: Johns Hopkins University Press, 1976), p. 36, for Shelley's probable familiarity with Coleridge's periodical, *The Friend*, the eleventh number of which contains the 'Hymn Before Sunrise'.

[24] *Monthly Review*, 88 (Jan. 1819), p. 97.

Monthly's faint praise for the Shelleys' Swiss tour, for Hookham is taken to task for the same reasons the *Eclectic* had advanced earlier: Hookham's overambitious descriptions and his over-vehement admiration for Rousseau. Shelley's writing again escapes these charges, it would appear, because he has not impressed his reviewers with 'the reiterated introduction of exaggerated phrases' nor has he transgressed the code of sensibility with regards to Rousseau; that is, he has kept politics and religion out of the foreground.[25] But the *History* does not escape charges of mishandling the representation of national character, something that reviewing pundits were becoming increasingly touchy about in light of the opening up of the Grand Tour to all classes of pedestrians. While the *History* gives rise to the reviewer's lament about 'dashing *milords* of the last age' being superseded by 'a host of *roturiers*', the subsequent review in the 'Monthly Catalogue' of Thomas Raffles' *Letters during a Tour* pointedly praises Raffles for being

> a true Englishman, determined to give a resolute preference to the customs of his own country over those of our continental neighbours; and considering our inferiority in point of magnificent edifices and sublime scenery as more than compensated by our comforts, our regular habits, and, above all, our more serious impressions of religion.[26]

A peculiar irony unknown to the reviewer or to the general public was that 'the wretch' whom Raffles chastises in his book for 'having written over against his name in the Album at Montanvert, "*an atheist*"', had co-authored the tour reviewed immediately before Raffles' own.[27]

In Shelley's first letter to Peacock from Switzerland in 1816, he writes, 'I fear that it will be long before I shall play the tourist deftly' (*L*, 1: 475), but if the reviews of the *History* are anything to go by, it appears that Shelley would learn the lesson well. That the *History* could be reviewed alongside Raffles' *Letters* or that 'Mont Blanc' could be somewhat favourably compared with Coleridge's 'Hymn' in a Tory periodical ('Who *would* be, who *could* be an Atheist in this valley of wonders', writes Coleridge in a note to his poem)[28] shows that Shelley had succeeded in adapting his language to the language of travellers, in the process glossing over his own more fervent religious and political creed – against which 'Mont Blanc' has received most of its critical attention. This is not to say that the fault lines are not there in the *History* or the poem, opening up a more comprehensive polemical engagement with travel writers like Raffles or Coleridge, but that Shelley conducts his argument within a field common to writers on the meaning of landscape and travel.

---

[25] *Monthly Review*, 88 (Jan. 1819), p. 97.
[26] *Monthly Review*, 88 (Jan. 1819), p. 98.
[27] *Letters during a Tour through Some Parts of France, Savoy, Switzerland, Germany, and the Netherlands* (Liverpool, 1818), p. 208, as quoted in Gavin de Beer, 'An "Atheist" in the Alps', *Keats-Shelley Memorial Bulletin*, 9 (1958), p. 7.
[28] *Coleridge: Poetical Works*, ed. Ernest Hartley Coleridge (Oxford: Oxford University Press, 1969), p. 377.

When we do turn to Shelley's on the spot responses recorded in the letters and journals from the 1816 tour – the same materials that Mary Shelley revised in 1817 for the *History* – the fault lines appear closer to the surface. On the one hand, Shelley depends on established itineraries and tourist infrastructures; he follows Rousseau's footsteps around Lake Geneva, undertakes the excursion to Chamounix, hires a guide to approach the glaciers, visits cabinets of Natural History, and buys souvenirs. On the other hand, his disgust at the tourist industry indicates more than the conventional anti-tourist stance, assumed to privilege a particular traveller's cultural position and perceptions over those of the herd. Shelley also appears conscious of tourism as an industry with international implications, at best an economic and moral circulation of a cultural currency 'not understood by all', particularly its bearers and recipients, the tourists and hosts. At worst, tourism becomes a mutual imposition of 'large codes of fraud and woe' on native populations or unsuspecting travellers, as the following two examples will highlight, both drawn from Shelley's journal letter to Peacock from Chamounix. The first was omitted from the *History*:

> We met I lament to say some English people here. I will not detail to you the melancholy exhibitions of tourism which altho they emanate from the profusion & exigences of these vulgar great corrupt the manners of the people, & make this place another Keswick. But the inhabitants of Cumberland are not for a moment to be compared with these people, on whose stupidity, avarice & imposture engenders a mixture of vices truly horrible & disgusting.— (*L*, 1: 500-501)

The second, forming part of the conclusion to Shelley's journal letter, was retained for the *History*:

> We have bought some specimens of minerals & plants & two or three crystal seals at Mont Blanc, to preserve the remembrance of having approached it.—There is a Cabinet d'Histoire Naturelle at Chamouni, just as at Matlock & Keswick & Clifton; the proprietor of which is the very vilest specimen, of that vile species of quack that together with the whole army of aubergistes & guides & indeed the entire mass of the population subsist on the weakness & credulity of travellers as leeches subsist on the sick. (*L*, 1: 501)

Here the travellers and the Swiss, like the kings and subjects in *Queen Mab*, are 'mutual foes, [who] for ever play / A losing game into each other's hands, / Whose stakes are vice and misery' (*PS1*, III, 172-4). The reference to tourists as the 'vulgar great' echoes the anti-luxury arguments of *Queen Mab* where Shelley indicts commerce as 'the venal interchange / Of all that human art or nature yield' (V, 38-9), particularly gold 'before whose image bow the *vulgar great*, / . . . / The mob of peasants, nobles, priests, and kings' (V, 56-8; my italics). That continental tourists struck Shelley as another venal mob is clear from his recycled diction, and from his recollection of a similar concurrence of fashionable tourism with economic predation. Keswick, where *Queen Mab* was conceived, seemed to

Shelley in 1812 'more like a suburb of London than a village of Cumberland' (*L*, 1: 223), and Chamounix must have struck him, as it did other travellers, in a similar manner. The trouble in Keswick had been 'debauched servants of the great families who resort' (*L*, 1: 223) seducing female labourers already exploited by the manufacturing industries. 'Children are frequently found in the River which the unfortunate women . . . destroy' (*L*, 1: 223), Shelley concludes, having briefly sketched a chain of corruption and exploitation that transfers London's urban blight to a provincial beauty spot that he, like Wordsworth, had hoped would contain less complicated, more humane economic and social models.[29] In the environs of Chamounix, Shelley is less impressed with the intellectual stock of the often-idealised Swiss peasants, but certain of the no less disastrous effects on them of this worst of exports, the English tourist and his appetites. It is no wonder that in 'Mont Blanc', Shelley sublimates the base 'venal interchange' of mundane economics into the 'unremitting interchange' between the man of taste and 'the clear universe of things around' (*PS1*, B Text, ll. 39-40).

Against Shelley's more prosaic condemnation of a tourist economy, we might cite a less passionate response to the same scenes by John Sheppard in his *Letters, Descriptive of a Tour through Some Parts of France, Italy, Switzerland, and Germany, in 1816* (Edinburgh, 1817):

> Two English gentlemen . . . in the year 1741, were the first who traversed this wild region, contrary to the advice of friends, and attended by an armed escort to defend them against the fancied barbarism of its inhabitants. Seventy years have passed since their enterprise, which opened sources of high gratification to subsequent travellers, and carried civilization and prosperity into these solitudes. And the change is now complete: the peasants round Mont Blanc are found a civil and intelligent race; a generation of professed and well-qualified guides has arisen: all seems waiting for the stranger. There you are waylaid with milk or strawberries or crystals. In the village, you find regular cabinets of botany and minerology, and collections arranged for sale.[30]

Compared with Shelley's remarks about leeches subsisting on the sick, a more contrary account of the same objects observed can hardly be imagined. Where Shelley sees stupidity, Sheppard discovers intelligence; where Shelley rails against imposture, Sheppard commends a well-ordered and generous mercantilism. What for Shelley seems the export of vulgarity is for Sheppard the imperial imperative of civilisation, circulating from England's advanced economy to Europe's primitive interior. While Shelley condemns tourism, Sheppard sees it as the measure of progress; the accessibility of a region to English strangers and the hospitality they

---

[29] John Towner points out that Lake District visitors began commenting on the changes wrought by tourism on the local inhabitants from the late eighteenth century: 'Much of this . . . was based on a romantic ideal of rural innocence but, nevertheless, it does show that . . . tourism was seen as a powerful agent of social change' (*An Historical Geography of Recreation and Tourism in the Western World, 1540-1940*, Chichester, John Wiley & Sons, 1996, p. 152).

[30] Sheppard, *Letters*, pp. 196-7.

receive indicate the degree to which their wants and needs have been understood, anticipated, and internalised. Sheppard sketches a cultural geography that grants civilisation to the region only as it has accommodated itself to British interests. The English first 'opened' the region where they are now 'waylaid' not by banditti but with 'milk or strawberries' – the service economy of guides, *aubergistes*, and souvenir merchants signifies a prosperity that satisfies the self-congratulatory stranger.[31]

Shelley's argument with Sheppard might be said to be over the cultural location of Mont Blanc and surrounding regions within an Anglo-European consciousness. If Shelley dislocates the Swiss peasantry from any hegemonic map of European culture, he is also unable to take solace from traditional associations of sublime objects with the immanence of God. Turning from the otherness of inhabitants to the otherness of nature, he destabilises any certain subject position in face of Mont Blanc or other uninhabitable glacial scenes. Sheppard's more self-congratulatory response to man and nature not only fixes the inhabitants within an Anglo-European economy of cultural circulation but also locates in Mont Blanc an other-worldliness, transcendentally appropriated by Christian faith for moral purposes. As Sheppard puts this in his own poem, 'To Mont Blanc', included in *Letters*:

> . . . upon the eye
> Of earnest faith and full awakened hope
> Crowds the bright evidence of things unseen:
> In earth's low reckoning doubtful and remote;
> But to the gazer, close and palpable,
> Immense, unfolding, infinitely sure.[32]

For Shelley, the same scenes impress the gazer with a sense of 'Power', 'remote, serene, and inaccessible' (*PS1*, B Text, l. 97) – 'earth's low reckoning' to Sheppard, who resists the inaccessible by writing cultural and religious narratives in its place. Sheppard's confidence in an English cultural imperative exported by the leisure classes and confirmed by their experience runs askew Shelley's related confidence in a European imperative foreshadowed by the refinement of the leisure classes but not actualised in any existing political state (even if best *approximated* in England). Both Shelley and Sheppard use the travel narrative to show how the worldly mind figures or reconfigures the European landscape, but only Shelley values foreign regions for teasing the mind's certainties, stabilities, and

---

[31] Mary Shelley gives one of the best sociological accounts of this so-called prosperity in her journals: 'I talked with the guide about the manner of living in the country — the women do almost all the work such as reaping making hay &c – the men serve for guides in the summer which is lucrative as they are able sometimes to put bye about 20 louis for winter exigences — in the autumn they hunt the Chamois — an occupation they delight in . . . . In the winter many of the men go to Paris and hire themselves as porters at hotels &c – for the winter here is a starving kind of thing — they can gain little or no money during the whole course of it — ' (*MWSJ*, p. 120).

[32] Sheppard, *Letters*, p. 209.

confidences. Shelley explores how travel can change the traveller, how returning from travel augments the traveller's experience of his or her own country. Instead of measuring a region by its accessibility to a stranger, Shelley seems to unmeasure it in proportion to its resistance to the stranger, without arguing that the stranger is or must be overcome by that resistance – the victory of culture in 'Mont Blanc', after all, is the imagination's very trial against the unknowable.

Shelley's three Geneva letters to Peacock help elucidate a cultural geography underlying the *History of a Six Weeks' Tour* and 'Mont Blanc' in which England ('that most excellent of nations'; *SC* 571, 7: 26) maintains a relative superiority against France and Switzerland. The first of these letters (15 May 1816) sets the terms for this in England's political advantages over restoration France where Shelley reads a 'discontent & sullenness' in the minds of the people, 'less attractive' than what he had perceived during the 1814 tour when 'the lower orders' (*HSWT*, p. 9) displayed hints of the classless attitude remarked by other liberal travellers. To Peacock, Shelley makes the contrast plain: 'You live in a free country where you may act without restraint & posess [sic] that which you posess in security' (*L*, 1: 474). What follows, however, is a curious defence of England and an elaboration of the uses of foreign travel which has behind it the long debates over the value of the Grand Tour, and perhaps more immediately Byron's famous dismissal of the self-congratulatory values of the Grand Tourist in *Childe Harold* I and II, as proposed by its epigraph:

> L'univers est une espèce de livre, dont on n'a lu que la première page quand on n'a vu que son pays. J'en ai feuilleté un assez grand nombre, que j'ai trouvé également mauvaises. Cet examen ne m'a point été infructueux. Je haïssais ma patrie. Toutes les impertinences des peuples divers, parmi lesquels j'ai vécu, m'ont réconcilié avec elle. Quand je n'aurais tiré d'autre bénéfice de mes voyages que celui-là, je n'en regretterais ni les frais, ni les fatigues. (*Byron PW*, 2: [3])[33]

Shelley intervenes between the Grand Tourists' 'ideology of the tour's benefit for young men of property'[34] and Byron's more levelling impulse by setting his moral and political standards above that level achieved by England, while affirming the psychological ties that give meaning to the phrase, 'my country':

> ... so long as the name of *country* & the selfish conceptions which it includes shall subsist England I am persuaded, is the most free & the most refined.... But if I return & follow your example it will be no subject of regret to me that I have seen other things. Surely there is much of bad & much of good, there is much to disgust & much to elevate which he will never feel or know who has never passed the limits of his native land.

---

[33] According to McGann, 'these are the opening sentences of *Le Cosmopolite, ou le Citoyen du Monde* (1753), by Louise Charles Fougeret de Monbron' (*Byron PW*, 2: 271).

[34] James Buzard, *The Beaten Track: European Tourism, Literature, and the Ways to Culture, 1800-1918* (Oxford: Clarendon Press, 1993), p. 98.

So long as man is such as he now is, the experience of which I speak will never teach him to despise the country of his birth. Far otherwise,—like Wordsworth he will never know what love subsisted between himself & it, until absence shall have made its beauty heartfelt. (*L*, 1: 474-5)

In using Wordsworth to refute Byron, Shelley anticipates his dosing of Byron with Wordsworth at Lake Geneva, the fruits of which campaign were to appear in *Childe Harold* III. Like Wordsworth in 'I travelled among Unknown Men', Shelley argues for England as a 'state' of mind which lays foundations for the cultural apperception that travel entails; the standard of freedom and refinement at home allows the traveller abroad to be disgusted or elevated, and more importantly, aware of the (superior) grounds of his sensibility. Unlike Wordsworth, Shelley continually circles back to destabilise the position of England by making it the representative of consciousness-in-transition rather than an end in itself, an emphasis absent from Wordsworth's more equanimous and patriotic lyric.

In analysing 'country', Shelley arrives at a concept of property that haunts his negotiations with Peacock in subsequent letters for a real property, a 'perpetual resting place' (*SC* 571, 7: 26, l. 40) where Shelley might put down roots. Still uncertain that such were his intentions in the 15 May letter, Shelley nevertheless prepares the ground for his thinking by describing the benefits of what might be called intellectual property – the impulse to possession that the mind exercises on familiar surroundings, or by which the unfamiliar is familiarised. In the lines following his reflections on Wordsworth, quoted above, Shelley continues:

Our Poets & our Philosophers our mountains & our lakes, the rural lanes & fields which are ours so especially, are ties which unless I become utterly senseless can never be broken asunder. These & the memory of them if I never should return, these & the affections of the mind with which having once been united they are inseparably united, will make the name of England, my country dear to me forever, even if I should permanently return to it no more. Yes, they constitute my country, & in the general term under which all that is so dear to me in that thought must be vitally comprehended.

(*L*, 1: 475).

'England' and 'country' refer to emotional ties ('the affections') that the mind forms with cultural and natural objects (poetry, philosophy, scenery) that nurture it – what Wordsworth refers to as

> ... those first affections,
> Those shadowy recollections,
> Which, be they what they may,
> Are yet the fountain light of all our day,
> Are yet a master light of all our seeing[.][35]

---

[35] 'Ode', ll. 151-5, in William Wordsworth, *Poems in Two Volumes, and Other Poems, 1800-1807*, ed. Jared Curtis (Ithaca, NY: Cornell University Press, 1983), pp. 275-6.

As Shelley's string of possessive pronouns indicates, this also comprehends a psychology of appropriation; the process of inseparably uniting mind and object interposes private boundaries and, as the self becomes implicated in the collective, national geography. Private and national possessions, at least for the Englishman, are confirmed by relative political freedom, one's ability, as Shelley had initially told Peacock, 'to posess that which you posess in security'. Against or beyond this lay geography – physical, cultural, and political – where security seems absent. Shelley's first descriptions of the Alps that end the 15 May letter contain a barrage of epithets that destabilise the connections that characterise 'country': 'impenetrable', 'untrodden', 'inaccessible', 'incredibl[e]', 'desolate', 'uninhabited' (*L*, 1: 475-6). The traveller's apparent inability to occupy and possess these scenes effectively reinforces definitions of the self that depend on what he can possess. By the same token, this kind of dispossession opens the space for imagining property – aesthetically appropriating the unappropriated.

The three manuscript letters to Peacock[36] show how Shelley's musings on property and ownership give rise to such epistemological and psychological issues, culminating in an aesthetic of appropriation for sublime landscapes such as those anticipated by the 15 May epithets. In the 17 July letter, which recounts the tour around Lake Geneva, Shelley first broaches the idea of returning to England: 'My opinion of the necessity of turning to one spot of earth & calling it my home, & of the excellence & usefulness of the sentiments arising out of this attachment has at length produced in me the resolution of acquiring this posession' (*SC* 571, 7: 25-6). The resolution owes much to Shelley's recent visits to sites associated with Rousseau and Gibbon, for there he had been impressed with the manner in which actual scenes enhanced his appreciation of intellectual productions that took place in them or that invoked them. Of 'the excellence & usefulness of the sentiments arising out of this attachment', the example of the Empress Marie Louise roughing it at Mellerie 'from veneration to the recollections of Julie' (*SC* 571, 7: 32) might have been on Shelley's mind. In the *History*, Shelley calls this an instance of how '*the common sentiments of human nature can attach themselves* to those who are the most removed from its duties and its enjoyments, when Genius pleads for admission at the gate of Power' (*HSWT*, p. 118; my italics). In possessing 'one spot of earth', Shelley anticipates the possibility of attaching its landscape to associations generated from his art, his own voice becoming a future power like that of Rousseau's. By the terms of the 15 May letter, intellectual 'ownership' of the object world secures the usefulness of culture to the permanence of landscape.

Shelley's 22 July-2 August journal letter to Peacock, often taken as the most immediate source for 'Mont Blanc', brings Shelley's speculations on property to bear on a sublime aesthetic that resists appropriation, yet for which travel writers had already standardised an appropriative diction. Shelley specifically addresses this generic problem in his opener to Peacock:

---

[36] These are the letters of 15 May (discussed above), 17 July, and 22-5 July 1816. Because he did not have access to the MS and was working from previously published copy texts, Jones mistakenly prints 17 July as two separate letters (see *L*, 1: 480-88; 1: 488-91). In my discussion below, therefore, I use *SC* 571, which reproduces the original MS.

Whilst you are engaged in securing a home for us, we are wandering in search of recollections to embellish it. I do not err in conceiving that you are interested in details of all that is majestic or beautiful in nature—But how shall I describe to you the scenes by which I am now surrounded.—To exhaust epithets which express the astonishment & the admiration—the very excess of satisfied expectation, where expectation scarcely acknowledged any boundary—is this to impress upon your mind the images which fill mine now, even until it overflows? I too had read before now the raptures of travellers. I will be warned by their example. I will simply detail to you, all that I can relate, or all that if related I could enable you to conceive of what we have done or seen . . . .

(*L*, 1: 495)

The securing and security of a home that had preoccupied Shelley in previous letters here comes athwart the problem of language that cannot be secured. In taking heed of the 'raptures of travellers', Shelley most immediately gestures towards the hackneyed descriptive language that had drawn a good deal of critical censure and satire.[37] James Plumptre's comic operetta, *The Lakers* (1798), for example, is one early indicator of the reading public's over-saturation with what must have increasingly seemed like a stock descriptive vocabulary. Targeting the vogue for picturesque travel and travel writing, Plumptre has his heroine, Beccabunga Veronica, contemplate scenery and anticipate writing it up without Shelley's worry about exhaustive epithets: 'The amphitheatrical perspective of the long landscape; the peeping points of the many-coloured crags of the head-long mountains . . . the picturesque luxuriance of the bowery foliage . . .the horrific mountains, such scenes of ruin and privation!'. Reflecting on the objects represented by this interminable string of adjectives, some of which may be found in Shelley's own writing, Veronica concludes that they are 'so many circumstances of imagery, which all together combine a picture, which for its sentimental beauty and assemblages of sublimity, I never exceeded in the warmest glow of my fancied descriptions'.[38] As usual, comedy betrays serious criticisms. Plumptre shows Veronica all too eager to mediate her perceptions with language, or 'circumstances of imagery', rather than appreciating nature in itself; she attempts to write the landscape simultaneous to seeing it. Sublimity does not overwhelm this traveller, but is assembled by her. The irony here is that such 'assemblages' are qualitatively indistinguishable from 'fancied descriptions'. The sentimental and the marvellous,

---

[37] Shelley's attraction to sublime enthusiasm and scepticism over representing it to readers repeats a similar stylistic dilemma experienced by Patrick Brydone, who attempts to fuse the language of sentimental discourse with scientific accuracy: 'Few things I believe in writing being more difficult than thus "s'emparer de l'imagination," to seize, – to make ourselves masters of the reader's imagination, to carry it along with us through every scene, and make it in a manner congenial with our own' (cited in Turner, *British Travel Writers*, p. 116).

[38] James Plumptre, *The Lakers, 1798* (Oxford and New York: Woodstock Books, 1990), p. 19.

singled out by Plumptre in a later passage, become aesthetic diversions from a more authentic rapture and rapturous response to the landscape.[39]

Shelley handles the problem elucidated at the beginning of his journal letter precisely, though his continual proximity to the language of travellers very often conceals his manoeuvres – witness Beckford's sarcasm or *Blackwood's* comments on Shelley's 'poetical fervour'. With broad gestures at the debates over landscape description, to which Peacock was no stranger, Shelley rejects the language of gratuitous excess for a more empirical diction, without however denying the excess of sublime experience over language.[40] Wary of falling into the trap of unwittingly substituting diction for the experience itself, Shelley nevertheless seeks 'to impress upon your [Peacock's] mind the images which fill mine now', postulating in so doing a language empowered like nature itself to produce images that correspond to those impressed by nature, yet recognising that 'the images ... now' are already once removed from experience. Shelley also suggests that nature and language impress the mind with imagery in excess of that which corresponds to empirical reality; the mind is impressed both with its own boundaries, limitations, capacities, and the feeling that these have been exceeded.[41] The mind must acknowledge a boundary to expectation by the co-presence of satisfaction and a sense that there is

---

[39] The anonymous editor of Karl Philipp Moritz's *Travels, Chiefly on Foot, through Several Parts of England in 1782* (London, 1795), which was on Shelley's reading list for 1816, provides a similar insight into critical attitudes towards this kind of writing. In the preface, the editor writes: 'Our German does not deal in the marvelous; neither does he affect to be sentimental. On a fine prospect, it is to be owned, he loves to dwell, and describe, with some degree of rapture; but he does not bewilder either himself, or his readers in the fairey scenes of picturesque beauty'. See *Travels of Carl Philipp Moritz in England in 1782*, repr. English trans. of 1795 (London: Humphrey Milford, 1924), p. 8.

[40] Peacock may have recognised a larger context for Shelley's position in the criticism that Richard Payne Knight directs at Burke's use of *Paradise Lost* to illustrate obscurity in language. For Knight, *Paradise Lost* is sublime only insofar as it is *not* obscure. The seeming paradox is based on the following rationale: 'if obscurity means indistinctness, it is always imperfection. The more distinct a description; and the more clearly the qualities, properties, and energies, intended to be signified or expressed, are brought, as it were, before the eyes, the more effect it will have on the imagination and the passions: but then, it should be *distinct* without being *determinate*'. 'Critics', continues Knight a little further on, 'have been led into the notion that imagery is rendered sublime by being indistinct and obscure, by mistaking energies for images, and looking for *pictures* where *powers* only were meant to be expressed'. Applying an associationist philosophy, Knight argues that distinct yet indeterminate language in its 'enthusiastic and impassioned modes' communicates by conveying distinct impressions and exciting 'trains of many others'. See Knight's *An Analytic Inquiry into the Principles of Taste* (London, 1805), pp. 386; 387; 389-90.

[41] Cf. L. Simond, *Switzerland* (1822): 'The human mind thirsts after immensity and immutability, and duration without bounds; but it needs some tangible object from which to take its flight, – something present to lead to futurity, something bounded from whence to rise to the infinite' (as quoted in *Edinburgh Review*, 37 (Nov. 1822), p. 292). In the same review, Simond is praised for not sacrificing 'fidelity to effect': 'Though plainly a devoted, and even passionate admirer of natural beauty, his descriptions are never florid or rapturous' (p. 288).

something left over; the mind acknowledges its limited capacity by its overflowing. For Shelley, the language of travel must express the excess or supplement of experience without itself becoming part of that meta-empirical space. His solution is to select 'detail' rather than overdo 'description', and to develop a language answerable to aesthetic principles. Questions of language, however, are always bound up in Shelley's quest for poetic permanence in landscape, his desire to make landscape through poetry a force for renewal and hope. The problem with the rhetoric of rapture is that it becomes detached from landscape by its excess; clichés pall rather than refresh, and the imagination remains unprepared for positive and moral exertion. While I do not think Shelley is always successful in avoiding the raptures of travellers, I would like to suggest that his interest in discovering an authentic language of travel is one of the motivating forces behind the revised *History of a Six Weeks' Tour* and 'Mont Blanc'.

The description in the journal letter closest to the 'raptures of travellers' also comprises an aesthetic statement: Shelley's encounter with Mont Blanc itself. The passage, retained nearly intact in the *History*, falls neatly into two parts, a careful description of all that can be related, followed by a self-reflexive analysis of the conception:

> Mont Blanc was before us. The Alps with their innumerable glacie[r]s on high, all around; closing in the complicated windings of the single vale:—forests inexpressibly beautiful—but majestic in their beauty—interwoven beech & pine & oak overshadowed our road or receded whilst lawns of such verdure as I had never seen before, occupied these opening[s], & extending gradually becoming darker into their recesses.—Mont Blanc was before us but was covered with cloud, & its base furrowed with dreadful gaps was seen alone. Pinnacles of snow, intolerably bright, part of the chain connected with Mont Blanc shone thro the clouds at intervals on high. I never knew I never imagined what mountains were before. The immensity of these aerial summits excited, when they suddenly burst upon the sight, a sentiment of extatic wonder, not unallied to madness— And remember this was all one scene. It all pressed home to our regard & to our imagination.—Though it embraced a great number of miles the snowy pyramids which shot into the bright blue sky seemed to overhang our path—the ravine, clothed with gigantic pines and black with its depth below.—so deep that the very roaring of the untameable Arve which rolled through it could not be heard above—was close to our very footsteps. *All was as much our own as if we had been the creators of such impressions in the minds of others, as now occupied our own.*—Nature was the poet whose harmony held our spirits more breathless than that of the divinest. (*L*, 1: 496-7; my italics)

As Angela Leighton has noted, negative adjectives characterise Shelley's diction, yet Shelley exploits language's limits as much as he admits its failure before 'defeating and privative appearance[s]'.[42] '*Innumerable* glaciers', 'forests

---

[42] Angela Leighton, *Shelley and the Sublime* (Cambridge University Press, 1984), p. 37. See also Timothy Webb, 'The Unascended Heaven: Negatives in "Prometheus Unbound"', in

inexpressibly beautiful', 'snow *intolerably* bright': such negatives by themselves might indicate the defeat of language, but Shelley bolsters descriptions with a carefully qualified aesthetic organisation. Though innumerable, the glaciers have a clear position 'on high'; though inexpressibly beautiful, the forest can be accounted for by species of tree, and even its beauty graded in terms of accepted aesthetic categories; though intolerable, the snow's brightness is located in the chain and framed by the clouds. While Shelley directs Peacock's eye from the beautiful to the majestic to the sublime, his emphasis on the scene's aesthetic unity recalls William Gilpin's multifaceted notion of the picturesque. According to Gilpin, '*Sublimity alone* cannot make an object *picturesque*. However grand the mountain, or the rock may be, it has no claim to this epithet, unless it's [sic] form, it's colour, or it's accompaniments have *some degree of beauty*'.[43] Though Shelley does not use the epithet, picturesque, he carefully distinguishes the effects of magnitude associated with the sublime from other qualities inherent in the scene. 'It is not alone that these mountains are immense in size', he confirms in a letter to Byron of 22 July, ' . . . there is grandeur in the very shapes and colours which could not fail to impress, even on a smaller scale' (*L*, 1: 494).[44]

Kim Ian Michasiw's reading of Gilpin's sublime is equally applicable to Shelley's description as a whole: 'This element of the beautiful, hence the small, the dominable, allows both a degree of control and a locus for individual desire in the scene'.[45] To be sure, this is a degree of, not absolute control, but it is in keeping with Shelley's professed desire to 'impress upon your mind the images which fill mine now'. In building in a containing clause in his category of the sublime, Shelley is able to explore the boundaries of language where expression is both made possible by the aesthetic imagination's purchase on the object world, and denied by the presence of the unpresentable. It is in this sense that Shelley's sublime and beautiful oxymoron in his contemporaneous 'Hymn to Intellectual Beauty' ('O awful LOVELINESS'; *PS1*, B Text, 1. 71) maintains an aesthetic border position within discourses of the picturesque.

The second part of the passage, beginning 'I never knew I never imagined', emphasises a degree of control in its very negatives. If Shelley never knew or imagined, he does so now as a result of the unexpected overpowering of conception and imagination that is 'not unallied to madness'.[46] Moreover, the

---

Shelley Revalued, pp. 37-62, where Webb explores Shelley's 'predilection for the negative' in 'his most positive and enraptured moments' (p. 38): 'The *via negativa* is the road not of despair but of hope' (p. 57).

[43] William Gilpin, 'On Picturesque Travel', *Three Essays* (London: Printed for R. Blamire, 1792), p. 43.

[44] Cf. *HSWT*, p. 155: 'There is more in all these scenes than mere magnitude of proportion: there is a majesty of outline; there is an awful grace in the very colours which invest these wonderful shapes – a charm which is peculiar to them, quite distinct even from the reality of their unutterable greatness'.

[45] Kim Ian Michasiw, 'Nine Revisionist Theses on the Picturesque', *Representations*, 38 (Spring 1992), p. 86.

[46] Cf. Shelley's 'Speculations on Metaphysics': 'Thoughts, or ideas, or notions . . . differ from each other, not in kind, but in force. It has commonly been supposed that those distinct

passage ends with an assertion that echoes Shelley's opening intention to 'impress' Peacock's mind with images: 'All was as much our own as if we had been the creators of such impressions in the minds of others, as now occupied our own'. Despite the moment of madness, the suggestion is that understanding and imagination are up to the secondary task of containing the uncontainable. In describing the most sublime objects, Shelley's emphasis is on the delusion of their proximity: the snowy pyramids crowd over their path and the Ravine of Arve lay subdued and quiet at their feet. In claiming the scene as intellectual property – 'all was as much our own' – ratified by a creative Nature, Shelley asserts an almost essentialist aestheticism, as if the picturesque were not an imposition of 'the rules of art' onto an unorganised object world, but a mental reflex to an already immanent organisation. Yet Shelley's prose falters at the crucial juncture; the as- and if- clauses are too tenuous to support the implication. The measure of aesthetic ownership appears to be creative dispensation, giving to others what one has created. The scene may seem as if it were created, but there is no real justification for Shelley's playful attribution of creation to Nature ('Nature was the poet') rather than to the receiving mind itself.[47]

In figuring Nature as a poet, however, Shelley imposes a literary identity on the phenomenal object world, *as if* the object world *were* subject to the same limitations as the human mind's imaginings. By allowing Nature to stand in for the ideal poet (the 'divinest'), Shelley naturalises his aesthetic, thereby privileging the human mind's appropriation of the object world in all of its secondary capacities: observation, memory, and writing. His language calls particular attention to the temporality of creativity. What gives him a sense of 'ownership' is the scene's pastness – 'all *was* as much our own as if we *had been* the creators' (my italics) – signalled by the past perfect verb. Similarly Gilpin, towards the end of his essay 'On Picturesque Travel', suggests that the experience of landscape appreciation is heightened with increasing distance in time and space from the original picturesque moment:

> There may be more pleasure in recollecting, and recording, from a few transient lines, the scenes we have admired, than in the present enjoyment of them. If the scenes indeed have *peculiar greatness*, this secondary pleasure cannot be attended with those enthusiastic feelings, which accompanied the real exhibition. But, in general, tho it may be a calmer species of pleasure, it is more uniform, and uninterrupted. It flatters us too

---

thoughts ... which are called *real*, or *external objects*, are totally different in kind from ... hallucinations, dreams, and the ideas of madness. No essential distinction between any one of these ... is founded on a correct observation of the nature of things, but merely on a consideration of what thoughts are most invariably subservient to the security and happiness of life' (*Prose*, p. 183).

[47] See Frances Ferguson, 'Shelley's *Mont Blanc*: What the Mountain Said', in *Romanticism and Language*, ed. Arden Reed (London: Methuen, 1984), pp. 202-14. Ferguson asserts the 'confusion between activity and agency' does not support an argument by design but 'identifies the sublime as the aesthetic operation through which one makes an implicit argument for the transcendent existence of man' (p. 213).

with the idea of a sort of creation of our own; and it is unalloyed with that fatigue, which is often a considerable abatement to the pleasures of travelling the wild, and savage parts of nature.[48]

Gilpin concludes this essay with a celebration of the distanced and distancing imagination's increasing autonomy from any particular scene, once 'impressed with the most beautiful scenes, and chastened by the rules of art'.[49] But in increasing the stakes of landscape appreciation from mere amusement or pleasure, to a question of identity itself, Shelley endeavours to have the best of both worlds. He celebrates both the imagination's recreation of past experiences and its power to approximate 'enthusiastic feelings' in all their presentness (what Gilpin sees as a fair trade off for the former). In so doing, Shelley elides personal with national identity as a function of aesthetic 'ownership' while retaining a regulated instability at the moment of appropriation with which to suggest the transcendental instability of all identity.

Still, we cannot ignore that immediacy of perception that both Gilpin and Shelley recognise as a precondition for the kinds of temporal recreation that they describe. For Gilpin, the picturesque traveller's very movement through space establishes a tension between expectation and attainment that approximates the conditions of discovery: 'We suppose the country to have been unexplored'.[50] But Gilpin's metaphors belie a gentleman's sensibility, hedged by rules of art, as his explorer becomes a sportsman, delighting in 'the pleasures of the chase' as a holiday from other concerns: 'The plough, and the spade are deserted. Care is left behind; and every human faculty is dilated with joy'. The attainment of the object results in its objectification, as the mind delights in beholding the 'composition' of a scene. Nevertheless, Gilpin leaves open the possibility of a more direct experience of nature 'when a scene of grandeur bursts unexpectedly upon the eye'.[51] Anticipating the language of Wordsworthian vision, Gilpin broadens this kind of picturesque experience to include the kinds of noumenal climaxes that occur in 'Tintern Abbey':

> We are most delighted, when some grand scene, tho perhaps of incorrect composition, rising before the eye, strikes us beyond the power of thought – when the *vox faucibus haeret*; and every mental operation is suspended. In this pause of the intellect; this *deliquium* of the soul, an enthusiastic sensation of pleasure overspreads it, previous to any examination by the rules of art. The general idea of the scene makes an impression, before any appeal is made to the judgment. We rather feel, than survey it.[52]

---

[48] Gilpin, *Three Essays*, pp. 51-2.
[49] Gilpin, *Three Essays*, p. 52.
[50] Gilpin, *Three Essays*, p. 47.
[51] Gilpin, *Three Essays*, p. 44.
[52] Gilpin, *Three Essays*, pp. 49-50. Cf. 'Lines written a few miles above Tintern Abbey', ll. 42-50, in William Wordsworth, *Lyrical Ballads, and Other Poems, 1797-1900*, ed. James Butler and Karen Green (Ithaca, NY: Cornell University Press, 1992), p. 117.

Shelley, too, in the passage from the journal letter to Peacock, seems to describe a pause of the intellect filled by 'an extatic wonder, not unallied to madness' as the 'immensity of these aerial summits . . . suddenly burst upon the sight'. But Shelley's wonder is not quite the same as Gilpin's enthusiastic pleasure, precisely to the extent that it approximates madness, since for Shelley madness is not the suspension of mental operations but their (sometimes) temporary derangement. To be sure, in Shelley's poetry, many of his madmen and women are victims and sometimes unwitting agents of tyrannical power (Ahasuerus, Beatrice Cenci), but for others (Laon, Cythna, Prometheus) madness offers a new way of seeing, a positive impulse for social change, arising out of a dislocation of the relations between things and between the signs for things. In this latter sense, Shelley's confrontation of Mont Blanc becomes a moment fraught with danger and potential, for the subject confronting Mont Blanc like the mad person is responsible for reconstructing the disorientated object world, and can do so for good or ill.

I would insist upon the distinction between Gilpin's 'pause of intellect' and Shelley's 'extatic wonder' partly because madness does come to play such an important role in Shelley's work, particularly *The Revolt of Islam*, and also because the sudden prospect, when a scene bursts upon the sight, becomes a well-rehearsed moment in travel writing for the situation in which the disorientated subject refigures his or her metaphysical and cultural control (or lack thereof) over nature, the object world. Take for example, Helen Maria Williams's encounter with the falls of Schaffhausen in *A Tour in Switzerland* (1798):

> My heart swelled with expectation – our path, as if formed to give the scene its full effect, concealed for some time the river from our view; till we reached a wooden balcony, projecting on the edge of the water, and whence, just sheltered from the torrent, it burst in all its overwhelming wonders on the astonished sight . . . . Never, never, can I forget the sensations of that moment! when with a sort of annihilation of self, with every past impression erased from my memory, I felt as if my heart were bursting with emotions too strong to be sustained. – Oh, majestic torrent! which hast conveyed a new image of nature to my soul . . . .[53]

Or Hookham, from *A Walk through Switzerland* (1818):

> We had not long quitted the latter place, on our approach to Lausanne, when such a view of Alpine magnificence burst upon our sight . . . . Having no definite conception of what we were to behold, we gazed on the objects around us with doubt, and a disbelief of our senses. I have fancied that the unsubstantial visions of sleep were real – here I imagined that the substantial forms of things were visionary.[54]

---

[53] Williams, *A Tour*, 1: 59-60.
[54] Thomas Hookham, *A Walk through Switzerland, in September 1816* (London: Printed for T. Hookham, and Baldwin, Craddock and Joy, 1818), pp. 21-2.

In hindsight, both of these instances anticipate or recall moments of sudden vision in Shelley's poetry. Williams's self-annihilation followed by her vision of 'a new image of nature' reminds us of Rousseau's in 'The Triumph of Life', when his 'brain became as sand': 'so on my sight / Burst a new Vision never seen before' (*SPP*, ll. 405; 410-11). Hookham's 'unsubstantial visions', more immediate to our concerns here, recall Part III of 'Mont Blanc', when Shelley questions, 'or do I lie / In dream, and does the mightier world of sleep / Spread far around and inaccessibly / Its circles?' (*PS1*, B Text, ll. 54-7). Such parallels highlight the importance of disorientation as a prelude to higher visionary states. But they also emphasise the heightened sensibility of the beholder whose mind responds actively to whatever powers of sublimity nature can display, either by imitating in emotional receptivity the suddenness ('I felt as if my heart were *bursting*') or by abandoning the limited senses altogether for the imagination itself. Self-annihilation quickly gives way to self-congratulation. Williams goes on to reflect how sublime 'objects appear to belong to immortality; they call the musing mind ... to higher destinies and regions'.[55] Hookham, similarly, affirms his humanity in rather more social terms: 'The scenes of Switzerland make us feel our superior rank – our undivided empire over the animal creation – our intellectual alliance, although it may be remote, with the Great and Good of beings framed like ourselves'.[56]

An *Edinburgh Review* article on Richard Payne Knight's *An Analytic Inquiry into the Principles of Taste* (1805), cited by Peacock in *Headlong Hall* (1816) (*WTLP*, 1: 32 n.), touches the metaphysical and cultural implications of sublime encounter more directly, with a passage that would make a fit preface to Shelley's 'Mont Blanc':

> It is hard to say what others feel; but we have often experienced, that the sublime of natural objects, after the first effect of *unexpectedness* is over, leaves a kind of disappointment, a vacuity and want of satisfaction on the mind. It is not until our imaginations have infused life, and therefore power, into the still mass of nature, that we feel real emotions of sublimity. This we do, sometimes by impersonating the inanimate objects themselves; sometimes by associating real or fancied beings with the scenes which we behold. This is that, which distinguishes the delight of a rich and refined imagination, amidst the grandest scenery of Wales or Scotland, from the rude stare of a London cockney.[57]

For Shelley, the imagination is activated immediately; though the mind 'staggers' before sublime objects, what strikes it is like madness rather than disappointment. Otherwise, the reviewer has anticipated Shelley's strategies for 'infusing life' or 'power' into his poem by personifying the Ravine and Mountain, or by associating the latter with the Earthquake Daemon. The review also anticipates Shelley's

---

[55] Williams, *A Tour*, 1: 61.
[56] Hookham, *A Walk*, p. 24.
[57] Review of *An Analytic Inquiry into the Principles of Taste*, by Richard Payne Knight, *Edinburgh Review*, 7, no. 14 (Jan. 1806), p. 324.

conclusion: mental activity prevents 'vacuity' or, as Shelley puts it, 'vacancy'. The major difference is that Shelley's question at the end of 'Mont Blanc' remains a rhetorical affirmation of the imagination, for he never admits disappointment, want of satisfaction, or vacuity into the workings of his poetry or travel prose.

The *Edinburgh Review*'s easy transition from landscape description to matters of class and taste, the 'rich and refined imagination' opposed to 'the rude stare of the London Cockney', seems akin to Hookham's self-congratulatory reflections on rank, or even Williams's ability to recognise in unorganised nature a 'path formed to give the scene its full effect'. The review offers an important reminder that these writers are authorised by a sensibility that had formerly been the purview of the Grand Tourist, but was increasingly being appropriated by the professional classes.[58] Similarly, the proximity between strategies of description in travel writing and those in the more clearly class-bound theories of landscape improvement was not that great, for Knight's *Analysis*, as Shelley and Peacock surely understood, was as much a contribution to the one field as to the other.[59] Gilpin, Knight, and the reviewer lay claim as much as Williams, Hookham, or Shelley to a discourse of authorisation, a construction of an ideology of taste with implications to their respective formulations of identity. As John Barrell and Ann Bermingham have shown, such strategies of authorisation are founded on principles of exclusion or aesthetic idealisation, on structures of perception that encode political and class biases.[60] Nevertheless, Shelley reveals an authorial awareness of at least the problem of idealising through an aesthetic the place of real human beings – inhabitants, guides, and tourists – in the scenes he describes, even as he confirms in the aesthetic an ideal epistemological relation between mind and the object world.

'The Subject . . . Less Sublime': Aesthetic Vision and Social Reform

Thus far I have been discussing Shelley's aesthetic within parameters established by travel writers and landscape theorists, suggesting ways in which, even in 1816,

---

[58] See also Gillen D'Arcy Wood, *Shock of the Real: Romanticism and Visual Culture, 1760-1860* (New York: Palgrave, 2001), p. 13 and *passim*, for the threat and challenge posed by spectators of the London panorama to traditional notions of class sensibility. The panorama was popular across class lines, and spectators were admitted without distinction.

[59] Like the *Edinburgh Review* article, Peacock's *Headlong Hall* chides the analytical shortcomings of picturesque theory and theorists when measured against actual experience in a landscape: '"Pray, sir," said Mr. Milestone, "by what name do you distinguish this character ['unexpectedness'], when a person walks round the grounds a second time?"' (*WTLP*, 1: 31-2). In his 12 July 1816 letter from Geneva, Shelley inquired of Peacock 'the success of your Headlong Hall, of which I hear every day merited & indeed extravagant praise' (*SC* 571, 7: 27).

[60] See John Barrell, *The Idea of Landscape and the Sense of Place, 1730-1840: An Approach to the Poetry of John Clare* (Cambridge: Cambridge University Press, 1972) and Ann Bermingham, *Landscape and Ideology: The English Rustic Tradition, 1750-1860* (Berkeley: University of California Press, 1986).

this aesthetic was inseparable from Shelley's ideas of appropriation and identity, both personal, national, and international. Now I would like to turn to the revised work of 1817 – the *History of a Six Weeks Tour*, including the 'Letters from Geneva' and 'Mont Blanc' – in order to consider how this collection as a whole develops this aesthetic[61] while also trying to come to terms with the place in that aesthetic of human society. This is what Shelley refers to as 'the subject more mournful and less sublime; but such as neither the poet nor the philosopher should disdain to regard' (*HSWT*, p. 163). My contention is that Shelley resists this subject as poet and philosopher, tending instead to idealise and sublimate general human society into the epistemological confrontation of a solitary representative – 'my own, my human mind' – with nature. At the same time, the texts of the *History* implicitly provide a rationale for the movement to sublime regions and subjects by offering aesthetic vision as the cause and effect of social improvement. From the confrontation of the best and happiest minds with nature comes the best influence for reform.

This 'subject less sublime' immediately informs the 1814 journal as it appears in the *History*, though, to be sure, in something less than a philosophic manner. Despite some liberal comments on the parity between 'the lower orders in France' and 'the most well-bred English' (*HSWT*, p. 9) in terms of politeness, the journal records the travellers' disappointment that French manners 'are not English' (*HSWT*, p. 6), and then offers a similarly ambiguous assessment of the European peasantry. Beyond Paris, the dull, barren, comfortless, war-torn landscapes are discovered to be inhabited by unresponsive servile men, but the exceptions to this 'rule' prove difficult to explain. In Echemine, the travellers are surrounded by villagers, 'squalid with dirt, their countenances expressing every thing that is disgusting and brutal' (*HSWT*, pp. 23-4), while in the next village, Pavillon, they 'fancied [themselves] in another quarter of the globe', so improved these villagers were in 'cleanliness and hospitality' (*HSWT*, p. 25). In Switzerland, scenes which seem to be 'a fit cradle for a mind aspiring to high adventure and heroic deeds', instead nurture 'a people slow of comprehension and of action' (*HSWT*, p. 50), whose liberties are defended by force of habit rather than conscious demands.

As in other liberal tours of the period, there is some effort to mete out responsibility for the most brutal aspects of social life to the 'Gothic barbarism' (*HSWT*, p. 12) of the counter-revolutionary forces.[62] As for the contrast between Echemine and Pavillon, the journal poses a rhetorical question – 'What could occasion so great a difference?' (*HSWT*, p. 25) – but there is more than a hint of Arthur Young's similar query and conclusion: 'To what are we to attribute this difference in the manners of the lower people in the two kingdoms? To government'.[63] The sluggishness of both French and Swiss seems as much due to

---

[61] See also, Leighton, *Shelley and the Sublime*, p. 36.
[62] See *HSWT*, p. 87, and Morris Birkbeck, *Notes on a Journey through France*, 3rd edn (London, 1815), p. 84.
[63] Arthur Young, *Travels during the Years 1787, 1788, and 1789 . . . with a View of Ascertaining the Cultivation, Wealth, Resources, and National Prosperity of the Kingdom of France* (1792), reprinted in Pinkerton, ed., *General Collection*, 4: 192.

their segregation from a national and European economy as any essential propensities of their own, and government must take responsibility for the infrastructure of economic and cultural circulation, as Young had previously insisted. Moreover, the 1816 portion of the *History* makes plain that the greater 'equality of classes' remarked in France in 1814 and Geneva in 1816 are the 'consequence of republican institutions' (*HSWT*, p. 103) that survive their abolishment.[64] As a social landscape, Europe offers a progressivist tableau in which manners begin to register the effects of modernisation, despite their evident backwardness when compared to those of the travelling 'stranger'.

With the indictment of government in the *History* comes a more obvious and incisive traducement of French taste, associated with the monarchical privilege of pre- and post-revolutionary France. Following Wollstonecraft's cue in *Short Residence*, the journal casts Europe as seen through 'English eyes', and what these find pleasant are picturesque scenes. When the travellers visit the gardens of the Thuilleries, they find them 'formal, in the French fashion, the trees cut into shapes, and without grass' (*HSWT*, p. 11). At Vandeuvres, however, they 'walked in the grounds of a nobleman, laid out in the English taste, and terminated in a pretty wood' (*HSWT*, p. 28) – altogether a more appealing description, coupled with the barely concealed hint that French nobility is rendered more enlightened by its progressive penchant for the English picturesque in landscape gardening rather than for its own monarchical models of aesthetic control. While the *roturiers* may have benefited from pre-restoration political institutions, they are decidedly in the rearguard of taste. After a typically uninteresting journey through the unvaried lowlands between Bar-sur-Aube and Besançon, for example, the hilly country beyond the gates of the latter excites emotions in the travellers, pointedly contrasted with those of their guide:

> On quitting the walls, the road wound underneath a high precipice; on the other side the hills rose more gradually, and the green valley that intervened between them was watered by a pleasant river; before us rose an amphitheatre of hills covered with vines, but irregular and rocky . . . . This approach to mountain scenery filled us with delight; it was otherwise with our *voiturier*. (*HSWT*, pp. 31-2)

The *voiturier* features large in the account as an insensitive rustic, unable to appreciate the charms of his own country nor attend to the travellers' needs. His presence at the borders of the sublime reminds the reader of fetters with which political circumstances have bound the region and from which the travellers depart with relief.

The journal also presents travellers much more comfortable when a literary response can be savoured. High points include reading Tacitus by Lake Geneva, as

---

[64] Cf. *HSWT*, p. 116: 'The appearance of the inhabitants of Evian is more wretched, diseased and poor, than I ever recollect to have seen. The contrast indeed between the subjects of the King of Sardinia and the citizens of the independent republics of Switzerland, affords a powerful illustration of the blighting mischiefs of despotism, within the space of a few miles'.

106   *Shelley's Eye: Travel Writing and Aesthetic Vision*

Rousseau did before them, or Wollstonecraft's *Short Residence* along the Rhine in Germany.[65] Low points include many of their encounters with common men. The range of these responses comes together near the end of the Rhine voyage, in a passage that begins with a reflection reminiscent of Wollstonecraft's own encounter with those least 'alive to the sentiments inspired by tranquil country scenes'[66]:

> ... nothing could be more horribly disgusting than the lower order of smoking, drinking Germans who travelled with us; they swaggered and talked, and what was hideous to English eyes, kissed one another....

But then the travellers turn from the boat to the banks:

> The part of the Rhine down which we now glided, is that so beautifully described by Lord Byron in his third canto of *Childe Harold*. We read these verses with delight, as they conjured before us these lovely scenes with the truth and vividness of painting, and with the exquisite addition of glowing language and a warm imagination. We were carried down by a dangerously rapid current, and saw on either side of us hills covered with vines and trees, craggy cliffs crowned by desolate towers, and wooded islands, where picturesque ruins peeped from behind the foliage, and cast the shadows of their forms on the troubled waters, which distorted without deforming them. We heard the songs of the vintagers, and if surrounded by disgusting Germans, the sight was not so replete with enjoyment as I now fancy it to have been; yet memory, taking all the dark shades from the picture, presents this part of the Rhine to my remembrance as the loveliest paradise on earth. (*HSWT*, pp. 67-9)

The mirroring effect of the Rhine's troubled waters becomes a fit emblem for the manner in which the scene is distorted by the traveller's stubborn refusal to allow discomforts ('disgusting Germans') near at hand to overcome the pleasure of distant prospects and sounds (the song of the unseen 'vintagers' on the river banks). All is distorted by mediating lenses – memory, the picturesque, Byron's verse – and yet nothing deformed. Quite the contrary, since a scene of hellish disgust is transformed into the 'loveliest paradise', as the author reconfigures experience in words. Overall, the passage celebrates these powers of distortion for the beauty they leave intact, or create, and the workings of memory anticipates a fundamental principle in Shelley's theory of social reformation and the role of art therein: what lives on in the minds of men and women will be what changes them.[67] With the retrospective veneer thrown over the account of the experience

---

[65] For Rousseau's reading of Tacitus at Geneva, see *The Confessions*, trans. J. M. Cohen (London: Penguin, 1953), p. 368.

[66] Wollstonecraft expresses her horror at the 'smoking, drinking' Norwegian peasants: 'Nothing can be more disgusting than the rooms and men towards the evening: breath, teeth, clothes, and furniture, all are spoilt' (*LSND*, p. 135).

[67] See *Laon and Cythna*, Canto Second, where Cythna tells Laon: '... we meet again / Within the minds of men, whose lips shall bless / Our memory, and whose hopes its light

along the Rhine itself, the passage calls attention to the *History* as history, and history as art; temporal perspective becomes as positive an aesthetic value as painterly perspective, and both highlight the competing value of art over experience. Shelley, conspiring in Mary Shelley's elision of human degradation from the picture, thus refers to the scenes in his preface as 'beautiful in themselves, but which . . . a great Poet has clothed with the freshness of a diviner nature' (*HSWT*, p. v).[68]

By the end of 1817, Byron had usurped the role of 'great Poet' in Shelley's mind, and as Charles Robinson and Robert Brinkley have argued, Shelley's *History* encodes a dialogue with Byron over the extent of man's progressive powers of imagination and love – a 'high argument' conducted under the aegis of Wordsworth and taking into account the achievements of Rousseau and Gibbon. Robinson holds that under Shelley's Wordsworthian influence, Byron achieved in the summer of 1816 a temporary 'faith in man's imaginative fulfillment', and, inspired by the two poets' reading of Rousseau's *Julie* while touring Lake Geneva, an 'apprehen[sion of] the ideal of Love manifest within the beauty of Nature'.[69] Brinkley takes another tack, and regards the *History*, particularly Shelley's Geneva letter and 'Mont Blanc', as a context for and revision of 'poetry Byron had just published', particularly *Childe Harold* III and 'The Prisoner of Chillon'.[70] Sensitive to the relativity of Byron's conversion to Shelleyan or Wordsworthian or Coleridgean principles, Brinkley considers Shelley 'more insistent on the power of an individual creative mind' 'without reference to any third power, whether God, the universal mind, or the "something far more deeply interfused" of Tintern Abbey'.[71] Both regard Shelley's evaluation of Rousseau and Gibbon as a foundation for understanding Shelley's place among the canonical Romantics; his anxious relationship with Byron and 'the ongoing debate over the relative merits of their two major precursors, Coleridge and Wordsworth'.[72]

---

retain / When these dissevered bones are trodden in the plain' (*PS2*, II, ll. 1095-8). See also *The Defence of Poetry*: 'Poetry thus makes immortal all that is best and most beautiful in the world; it arrests the vanishing apparitions which haunt the interlunations of life, and veiling them or in language or in form sends them forth among mankind' (*SPP*, p. 532).

[68] The passage in question anticipates Letter IV where Shelley confronts Mont Blanc (the same moment discussed above), and Gilpin's observations on the 'pleasure in recollecting' again form an important context for Mary Shelley's discussion of memory. The 'delight' she recounts of remembering through the mediation of *Childe Harold* III also recalls Gilpin's comparison of 'the high delight . . . produced by the scenes of nature' with that excited by 'artificial objects': 'Here and there a capital picture will raise these emotions: but oftener the rough sketch of a capital master. This has sometimes an astonishing effect on the mind; giving the imagination an opening into all those glowing ideas, which inspired the artist; and which the imagination *only* can translate' (Gilpin, *Three Essays*, p. 50). See also, Mary Shelley's 28 May 1817 meditation on *Childe Harold* III: 'How a powerful mind can sanctify past scenes and recollections — ' (*MWSJ*, p. 172).

[69] Robinson, *Shelley and Byron*, p. 24.

[70] Robert Brinkley, 'Documenting Revision: Shelley's Lake Geneva Diary and the Dialogue with Byron in *History of a Six Weeks' Tour*', *Keats-Shelley Journal*, 39 (1990), p. 74.

[71] Brinkley, 'Documenting Revision', pp. 78-9.

[72] Brinkley, 'Documenting Revision', p. 78.

Shelley's language in the *History* is rife with Byronic and Wordsworthian echoes, resonances, and allusions, but the importance of Rousseau as the figure of the poet, perhaps even as a Byronic alter ego, must not be underestimated. When Shelley refers to 'Mellerie, and Clarens, and Chillon, and Vevai' as 'classic ground, peopled with tender and glorious imaginations of the present and the past' (*HSWT*, p. v) he surely has in mind both Byron and Rousseau – the former in his present capacity for altering the future, the latter as an example of one widely held responsible for ideas that 'set the world in flame' (*Byron PW*, 2: 106, *Childe Harold*, III, l. 764). To be sure, Shelley's originality as a travel writer was in his appropriation of a contemporary figure, Byron, for a discussion usually reserved for Rousseau, but we must not forget Shelley's faithfulness to the raptures of travellers over Rousseau's landmarks:

> This journey has been on every account delightful, but most especially, because then I first knew the divine beauty of Rousseau's imagination, as it exhibits itself in Julie. It is inconceivable what an enchantment the scene itself lends to those delineations, from which its own most touching charm arises. (*HSWT*, pp. 107-8)

For Shelley, unlike other sentimental tourists, Rousseau becomes a catalyst for his thinking on poetry and the creative imagination as, to borrow Wordsworth's phrase, 'a power like one of nature's',[73] disseminating its message to those equipped to better the lot of those who are out of keeping in the scenes that English eyes regard on their travels. Shelley's example of the Empress Marie Louise visiting Mellerie in tribute to Rousseau's St Preux is pertinent here, especially as it follows a political anecdote contrasting the 'wretched, diseased and poor . . . . subjects of the King of Sardinia and the citizens of the independent republics of Switzerland' to illustrate 'the blighting mischiefs of despotism, within the space of a few miles' (*HSWT*, p. 116). In such a context, Rousseau's influence as a republican theorist is aligned with his influence as a legislator of sentiment and opinion; poetry proves an equal to politics as a power for social change.

Shelley's continual attraction to 'one mind . . . so powerfully bright' (*HSWT*, p. 128) is a dominant theme in the *History*, one that Byron was not prepared to accept without demurring.[74] Shelley's attempt to meld epistemology with a theory of language, to naturalise art and aestheticise nature, could find only limited concordance with Byron's distrust of language and scepticism at the harmony of language and power. For Byron, Rousseau 'knew / How to make madness beautiful, and cast / O'er erring deeds and thoughts, a heavenly hue / Of words' (*Byron PW*, 2: 105, *Childe Harold*, III, ll. 729-32). For Shelley, however, Rousseau's was 'a mind so powerfully bright as to cast a shade of falsehood on the records that are called reality' (*HSWT*, p. 128). Byron's Rousseau makes an art of self-deception; Shelley's makes of art a new way of understanding the world.

---

[73] William Wordsworth, *The Prelude, 1799, 1805, 1850*, eds Jonathan Wordsworth, M. H. Abrams, and Stephen Gill (New York: Norton, 1979), 1805, XII, 312.

[74] See Brinkley, 'Documenting Revision', pp. 76-9.

Shelley's difference with his new friend on this subject, as Brinkley points out, may be seen through their dialogue on the relative powers of nature and art for impressing the mind with sublime associations, as well as their dialogue over the relative merits of Rousseau and Gibbon. Of the latter, Shelley's account of their visit to Gibbon's house and garden in Lausanne is most succinct:

> My companion gathered some acacia leaves to preserve in remembrance of [Gibbon]. I refrained from doing so, fearing to outrage the greater and more sacred name of Rousseau; the contemplation of whose imperishable creations had left no vacancy in my heart for mortal things. Gibbon had a cold and unimpassioned spirit. I never felt more inclination to rail at the prejudices which cling to such a thing, than now that Julie and Clarens, Lausanne and the Roman Empire, compelled me to a contrast between Rousseau and Gibbon. (*HSWT*, pp. 137-8)

Though Shelley was touched by the scene of 'the decayed summer-house where [Gibbon] finished his History, and the old acacias on the terrace, from which he saw Mont Blanc, after having written the last sentence' (*HSWT*, p. 137), *The Decline and Fall* itself invested no particular landscapes with human meaning. Gibbon, an avid reader of travels, did sketch out the shifting geographies of empire, and peopled them with portraits of the famous and notorious, but it remained for a 'poet' to give a heart to those places by tracing in landscapes, visionary or otherwise. The Roman Empire failed to come alive in the landscapes and human habitations (the 'mortal things') of Lausanne, as Julie did in Clarens, and through Shelley's sense of this we have a foreshadowing of how he will work to transform Gibbon (whom he never stopped reading) in the orientalist works to come: *The Revolt of Islam*, *Prometheus Unbound*, and *Hellas*. Gibbon provides Shelley fuel for his thinking about empire, Christianity, and Islam, but Rousseau offers him an example of how poetic language works to render these things permanent and make them work to the betterment of mankind.

The vacancy that Rousseau's work fills anticipates the vacancy imagination fills with unseen objects at the end of 'Mont Blanc', and as such illustrates Shelley's contention in the *Defence* that 'the great instrument of moral good is the imagination; and poetry administers to the effect by acting upon the cause' (*SPP*, p. 517). *History of a Six Weeks' Tour*, similarly, shows that poetry like Byron's or Rousseau's acts by superadding 'glowing language' to the objects it speaks of, just as Richard Payne Knight would have it that paintings, sculptures, and grottoes, allow us to see in nature the picturesque, the sculpturesque, and the grotesque.[75] Positioned at the end of the *History*, 'Mont Blanc' functions like an index to these concerns, occupied as it is with articulating nature and nature's own articulations – the many voices that become embodied in the texture of the landscape that Shelley confronts, creates, and moralises.

---

[75] Knight, *Analytic Inquiry*, pp. 190-91. Knight believes that Price's distinctions between the sublime, the picturesque, and the beautiful might be extended *ad infinitum* as long as one can come up with suitable adjectives – 'statuesque' and 'grotesque' he offers as existing additions. My point is that Shelley extends the principles of the picturesque to literature.

But Shelley's preface is potentially obfuscating in claiming that the poem was composed 'under the immediate impression of the deep and powerful feelings excited by the objects which it attempts to describe' (*HSWT*, p. vi). We need not turn to the textual history of the poem to realise that there is an important difference between the immediate impression of feelings and the immediate impression of objects themselves. Shelley's argument throughout the preface downplays the book as a record of particular scenes 'now so familiar to our countrymen' (*HSWT*, p. iii) and 'already rendered interesting' (*HSWT*, p. vi). Instead, he emphasises the secondary appropriations of those scenes by minds that move through them; his reader is called upon to follow and sympathise with the travellers' youth, enthusiasm, and feelings, and to review scenes 'clothed' by their perceptions. 'Mont Blanc' foregrounds less the presence of the tallest mountain in Europe sought out by countless English milords, than its metonymic presence as 'Lines Written in the Vale of Chamouni'. In the poem, Shelley continually defers agency to nature ('Nature was the poet') only to affirm the power of the human imagination to organise the unorganised, appropriate the unappropriable, and thus dictate the terms of reality.

The poem repeatedly points towards Rousseau's monumentalising power of imagination to 'cast a shade of falsehood on the records . . . called reality' (*HSWT*, p. 128). In fact, Shelley's preface to the *History* implicitly draws a parallel between Rousseau's *Julie* and Shelley's own poem. 'Mont Blanc', Shelley claims, was 'an undisciplined overflowing of the soul' (*HSWT*, p. vi), while *Julie* was 'an overflowing . . . of sublimest genius, and more than human sensibility' (*HSWT*, pp. 127-8). The 'overflowing' metaphor works in a similar manner as when Shelley discounts the 'vulgar error' that distinguishes poetry from prose in the later *Defence*. Representing Bacon's language as a *tertium aliquid*, Shelley writes that it 'distends, and then bursts the circumference of the hearer's mind, and pours itself forth together with it into the universal element with which it has perpetual sympathy' (*SPP*, p. 515). The overflowing here also resembles that which Shelley refuses to vulgarise in 'the raptures of travellers' (*HSWT*, p. 141), and the Bacon passage highlights the interchangeability of Shelley's discourse on the effects when Mont Blanc 'burst upon the sight' (*HSWT*, pp. 151-2) and his theories of poetic language. Sublime confrontation and true poetry, Shelley argues, destabilise the self by empowering self to range beyond epistemological limitations.[76] In this way, Shelley's intermingling meditations on the power of Rousseau, Mont Blanc, the mind, and nature, anticipate the progressivist arguments of the *Defence*.

---

[76] In 'Mont Blanc', Shelley expresses this idea in the lines, 'And *this*, the naked countenance of earth, / On which I gaze, even these primæval mountains / Teach the adverting mind' (*HSWT*, p. 180). The didactic power of the landscape is directly related to the 'adverting' power of the mind, and while 'advert' shares a root with 'avert', Shelley is being precise in allowing the gazer's mind to be looking towards the primeval sublimity it confronts. Still, Shelley exploits the 'avert' connotation for elsewhere in the *History* he emphasises how the imagination 'staggers' (*HSWT*, pp. 44; 149) when faced with the Alps. Even these instances, I would argue, retain a sense that the moment of staggering gives rise to an 'effort of the understanding' (*HSWT*, p. 44) or of the imagination.

The passage in the *History* where Shelley comments on the 'overflowing' of *Julie* has a history of its own that suggests another important way that the example of Rousseau lay behind Shelley's exploration of the mind's purchase on the object world in 'Mont Blanc'. In the 17 July 1816 manuscript letter to Peacock, Shelley discusses the significance of Rousseau's work in terms largely retained in the *History*, except for a crucial simile:

> I read Julie all day. I forgot its prejudices— it is an overflowing of sublimest genius & more than mortal sensibility.– It ought to be read amongst its own scenes which it has so wonderfully peopled. Mellerie, Chillon Clarens the mountains of La Valais & Savoy are monuments of the being of Rousseau. *like the path of a mighty river– whose waters are indeed exhausted but which has made a chasm among the mountains that will endure forever.* The feelings excited by this Romance have suited my creed, which strongly inclines to immaterialism
> —The beings who inhabit this romance, were created indeed by one mind—but a mind so powerfully bright as to cast a shade of falsehood on the records that are called reality.
> (*SC* 571, 7: 33; my italics)

The letter shows Shelley developing a topographical picture of Rousseau's genius, both in terms of the landscapes that intersect with Rousseau's creations and in terms of landscape tableaux that depict metaphorically the operations and strong effects of that genius. Rousseau becomes a river, exhausted because mortal, whose works are equal to the most powerful forces of nature, leaving their mark on those forces if only in the mind of the percipient. Though suppressed in the *History*, the simile does anticipate the kind of transference between Shelley's ideas of the powers of mind and those of nature that informs the analogy between the properties of mind and the Ravine of Arve in 'Mont Blanc'. The 'vast river' in the poem is much like the 'mighty river' of Rousseau's work; the 'Power in likeness of the Arve' that 'comes down / From the ice gulphs that gird his secret throne' (*HSWT*, p. 176) might well gloss Rousseau's mind 'so powerfully bright'. Rousseau's presence-in-absence in the poem must not be discounted.

At the point in Part II when Shelley turns to the 'Dizzy Ravine' to 'muse on my own separate phantasy' (*HSWT*, p. 177), the attentive reader of the *History* as a whole might well recall Shelley's earlier musings on the interchange between Rousseau's consciousness, his works, and the scenes around Lake Geneva. In the poem, Shelley's attempt at differentiation proves equally problematic, as he turns to

> My own, my human mind, which passively
> Now renders and receives fast influencings,
> Holding an unremitting interchange
> With the clear universe of things around[.] (*HSWT*, p. 177)

A letter to Hogg describing the Lake Geneva tour, however, provides the best evidence for Rousseau's interchange with Shelley's poem at this point:

I have seen Vevai, Clarens, Mellerie & have read La Nouvelle Heloise at these places a book which tho in some respects absurd & prejudiced, is yet the production of a mighty genius, & acquires an interest I had not concieved it to posess when *giving & receiving influences* from the scenes by which it was inspired. Rousseau is indeed in my mind the greatest man the world has produced since Milton — [.] (*SC* 335, 7: 719; my italics)

Shelley identifies himself with Rousseau, giving and receiving influences with immediate surroundings, which are in turn given duration through their respective works, 'Mont Blanc' and *Julie*. In this way, Shelley claims Mont Blanc for his vision, even as Rousseau has impressed Vevai, Clarens, Mellerie, and the surrounding mountains with his. But Shelley, unlike Rousseau, self-reflexively writes about the process by which these relations are formed even as he forms them. While Rousseau had become indistinguishable from his fictions, Shelley turns to the seemingly more direct interpenetration of 'my own, my human mind' with the 'clear universe of things around' (*HSWT*, p. 177), only to find that this primary relation becomes immediately immured in aesthetic response, 'the still cave of the witch Poesy' (*HSWT*, p. 177). The confusing syntax that follows the 'clear universe' lines has the corresponding effect of confusing the location of the Ravine, but the possibilities are the same for Shelley as for Rousseau: the ravine may exist in the mind, in the object world, in Poesy, in some combination of all of these, and lastly, in 'the deep and powerful feelings excited by the objects which [the Poem] attempts to describe' (*HSWT*, p. vi). Unable to quite disentangle those feelings from the objects nor from their corresponding associations, Shelley instead affirms the life of those feelings poised somewhere between their source in 'the breast' and their suspended animation in the pictures of memory: 'till the *breast / From* which they fled *recalls* them, thou are there!' (*HSWT*, p. 177; my italics). This is the life of the imagination which 'delights in personification' (*L*, 1: 101) so much as to give its creations a place outside the self – 'thou art there', 'the power is there' – while the dislocation and the deferral of that place in the unspecified 'there' prevents what Shelley calls in a note to *Queen Mab* the 'mistake of a metaphor for a real being' (*PSI*, p. 379, ll. 139-40).

'Mont Blanc' reconstitutes Shelley's presiding interest in the *History* with the Rousseauian subject position that interpenetrates the object world and becomes imaginatively part of it for the self and others. But this transference of Rousseauian properties to the poem is effective only insofar as Rousseau becomes the type of the Poet, manifestations of which include Wordsworth, Byron, and most importantly, Shelley himself. 'Mont Blanc' is a poem about poetic creation, and its effectiveness depends upon Shelley's assumption of Rousseau's powers. In other words, Shelley must become the 'one mind so powerfully bright' that he attributes to Rousseau. Indeed, so powerful is this 'one mind' that Wasserman and others have mistaken Shelley's imitation of its powers in 'Mont Blanc' as an affirmation of the transcendental One Mind, 'which constitutes total Existence and of which each individual mind is a portion'.[77] Instead, the poem begins within a

---

[77] Earl R. Wasserman, *Shelley: A Critical Reading* (Baltimore and London: Johns Hopkins University Press, 1971), p. 223.

personification; Shelley's 'human mind' has already effaced itself, and does not reassert its own presence until the lines in the middle of Part II where Shelley displaces Rousseau, and even then the hard-won subject position is lost in a creative harmony with landscape features. Part I, the vehicle to the Ravine tenor introduced at the beginning of Part II, substitutes a vital metaphoricity for any subject position, and 'the mind' through which the 'everlasting universe of things / Flows' (*HSWT*, p. [175]) is strictly neither Shelley's nor Rousseau's nor a pantheistic alternative, despite sharing qualities of all three. It is instead the mind already projected on the object world, on the site of Mont Blanc, as Shelley *enacts* the construction of the overarching analogy between the projection and the Ravine itself ('Thus thou, Ravine of Arve') (*HSWT*, p. 176). The fact that the completed analogy is largely a tautology – thus thou, Ravine of Arve are like the Arve raving through a ravine[78] – only emphasises the superadded 'interest' that natural phenomena receive from the tributes of thought animating them.

The elision of Rousseau, coupled with Shelley's own substitution of his own subject position for Rousseau's, forces the poem into an alliance with the materials of the *History* that precede it, but not only with those that deal with Rousseau or other poets like Byron, Wordsworth, Coleridge, or Wollstonecraft. In thematising the naturalisation of the imagination, Shelley also turns to the mountains, glaciers, and rivers as natural metaphors for the workings of genius, even as he sculpts the emblem of Rousseau's genius from the force of a river cutting a river valley. The 'ethereal waterfall' in Part II, 'whose veil / Robes some unsculptured image' (*HSWT*, p. 176) conversely epitomises the imaginative potential that the object world possesses for the mind prepared to perceive the relations between things mortal and material. In the *History*, the image is described as 'precisely resembling some colossal Egyptian statue of a female deity' (*HSWT*, p. 145), but the imprecision in the poem emphasises the transition between nature and culture, where nature's raw material is concealed and revealed by the imagination's first interpositions, as suggested by the metaphor of the veil. The poem at once takes Nature's inherent creativity more seriously, yet also relies in part on the context of the *History* as a whole to suggest the ironic alternative that Nature's creativity is always a metaphor for man's.

Similarly, 'Mont Blanc' is surcharged with 'voices' that make literal Shelley's claim in the preceding letter that 'Nature was the Poet'.[79] Turning the tables on

---

[78] See Ferguson, 'Shelley's *Mont Blanc*', p. 206.

[79] Shelley transforms human presences in the travel letters to natural ones in the poem. For example, the lines, 'the strange sleep / Which when the voices of the desart fail / Wraps all in its own deep eternity' (*HSWT*, pp. 176-7), are drawn from an experience mentioned in the *History* when Shelley reflects on his guides' voices in the profound stillness of the Alps: 'The natural silence of that uninhabited *desert* contrasted *strangely* with the *voices* of the men who conducted us, who, with animated tones and gestures, called to one another . . . creating disturbance, where but for them, there was none' (*HSWT*, p. 93; my italics). While human voices impress Shelley as being out of place in the landscape, the lines following his reference to the failing 'voices of the desart' in the poem emphasise the 'unresting sound' that otherwise animates nature. Shelley implies that the voices of the imagination are never out of place, for they are the life of the landscape, harmonising all disturbances.

poets like Rousseau who have infused nature with monuments to their own power, Shelley gives his wilderness

> ... a mysterious tongue
> Which teaches awful doubt, or faith so mild,
> So solemn, so serene, that man may be
> But for such faith with nature reconciled[.] (*HSWT*, p. 179)

Not stopping at this one-upmanship of Rousseau's Savoyard vicar, Shelley goes on to put Rousseau and his compeers, including Gibbon and the host of travel writers including Shelley himself, decidedly on the receiving end of such natural communication:

> Thou hast a voice, great Mountain, to repeal
> Large codes of fraud and woe; not understood
> By all, but which the wise, and great, and good
> Interpret, or make felt, or deeply feel. (*HSWT*, p. 179)

Like the other voices attributed to Nature in the poem, the wilderness and mountain speak non-verbally, and it remains for the interpreters to make felt that which they have felt, even as Shelley interprets his own experiences to Peacock and his readers. The poem ends on the same note. Although the animating 'power' of the universe is 'there' on high, Shelley pointedly envisions a region of silence and voicelessness surrounding 'the secret strength of things / Which governs thought' (*HSWT*, p. 182). In so doing, he emphasises the complicity of nature's non-verbal voice and human language, both subject to the same law, and structured out of the same space of silence and non-meaning. The final question, however, because of its sheer unanswerability affirms the role of the wise, great, and good for communicating what they imagine:

> And what were thou, and earth, and stars, and sea,
> If to the human mind's imaginings
> Silence and solitude were vacancy? (*HSWT*, p. 183)

Fittingly, the question enacts its own affirmation, for the documentary-like opener of Part V – 'Mont Blanc yet gleams on high:–the power is there' (*HSWT*, p. 182) – has become charged once again with the personifications that the imagination delights in; the third person subject returns to the evocative second person that characterises Shelley's address to the Ravine and Mountain elsewhere in the poem.

'Mont Blanc' and the *History* end, however, not with 'vacancy' but a misprint: Shelley includes a date for the poem which mistakenly places its composition on 'June 23, 1816', rather than July. While I would not want to claim that this date, which Mary overlooked in *Posthumous Poems*, is *not* an error, it does prove to be a very poignant one, since it directs the reader back to the Lake Geneva letter rather than the Chamounix letter. On the evening of the 23rd, Shelley relates his and

Byron's encounter with 'some children who were playing at a game like ninepins', most of whom 'appeared in an extraordinary way deformed and diseased' (*HSWT*, p. 110). One boy, however, is an exception. Shelley continues:

> His countenance was beautiful for the expression with which it *overflowed*. There was a mixture of pride and gentleness in his eyes and lips, the *indications of sensibility, which his education will probably pervert to misery or seduce to crime*; but there was more of gentleness than of pride, and it seemed that the pride was tamed from its original wildness by the habitual exercise of milder feelings. My companion gave him a piece of money, which he took without speaking, with a sweet smile of easy thankfulness, and then with an unembarrassed air turned to his play. *All this might scarcely be; but the imagination surely could not forbear to breathe into the most inanimate forms some likeness of its own visions*, on such a serene and glowing evening, in this remote and romantic village, beside the calm lake that bore us hither.
>
> (*HSWT*, pp. 110-12; my italics)

The boy is marked as a natural poet by the 'overflowing' metaphor so important to Shelley's conception of sublime and poetic experience, but Shelley then makes the point that such a sensibility is out of sync with the degradation of the people that inhabit sublime regions. Sensibility becomes the sign of civilisation, and if Shelley's subsequent doubt as to the reality of that which he sees is true, then those who possess it impose sensibility on nature and the natural. The imagination creates its own likeness in the inanimate – and not just in people but in landscapes. As a suppressed footnote to 'Mont Blanc', such a meditation becomes an apt reminder that sublime encounters sublimate the 'degraded', and such visions exert a power of their own over social realities. For Shelley, the aesthetic ontology of 'Mont Blanc' provides a way of thinking about social progress from a position of futurity even as his writing foregrounds itself as a history of the imagination's own self-composition.

Chapter 4

'Relics of Antiquity': Shelley's Classical Tour through Italy

> We often hear of persons disappointed by a first visit to Italy. This was not Shelley's case. The aspect of its nature, its sunny sky, its majestic storms, of the luxuriant vegetation of the country, and the noble marble-built cities, enchanted him. The sight of the works of art was full enjoyment and wonder. He had not studied pictures or statues before; he now did so with the eye of taste, that referred not to the rules of the schools, but to those of Nature and truth. The first entrance to Rome opened to him a scene of remains of antique grandeur that far surpassed his expectations; and the unspeakable beauty of Naples and its environs added to the impression he received of the transcendent and glorious beauty of Italy.
>
> (Mary Shelley, 'Note on Poems of 1818', *PW*, p. 570)

Within four months of the publication of *History of a Six Weeks' Tour* (1817), Shelley was on the road again, seeking in Italy relief from his worsening health.[1] On Thursday, 12 March 1818, the Shelley party sailed from Dover and, after a stormy crossing of barely three hours, arrived in Calais. They began a rapid journey south the next day, pausing at Lyon for four nights, where they made arrangements with a voiturier for the journey to Milan and again enjoyed their proximity to the Alps. Mont Blanc rose above the horizon and Mary Shelley recorded in her journal that 'the whole scene reminds us of Geneva' (*MWSJ*, p. 199). Two days later, they again set out 'towards the mountains whose white tops are seen at a distance' (*MWSJ*, p. 199), and on the third day, at Chambéry, Shelley took up the journal and wrote of their progress through 'the vallies of the Alps' and of their ascent into a ravine near Les Eschelles. This entry – his first since their return trip from Switzerland in September 1816 – also contained the seeds of *Prometheus Unbound*, the poem that occupied him until the close of 1819, and which was to embody and transform much of the imagery and experience of his

---

[1] As Nora Crook and Derek Guiton point out, 'southern Europe was the standard prescription for delicate constitutions and mysterious ailments'. In the months preceding Shelley's departure, he suffered from severe pains in his side, as well as a bout of ophthalmia. Shelley's doctor, William Lawrence, recommended a residence in Italy as the most effective remedy. See Crook and Guiton, *Shelley's Venomed Melody* (Cambridge: Cambridge University Press, 1986), pp. 107-13.

travels during that time.[2] 'The scene is like that described in the Prometheus of Aeschylus', Shelley wrote, 'Vast rifts & caverns in the granite precipices – wintry mountains with ice & snow above – the loud sounds of unseen waters within the caverns, & walls of topling [sic] rocks only to be scaled as he describes, by the winged chariot of the Ocean Nymphs' (*MWSJ*, p. 200).

This journal entry was to be the last of its kind; thenceforth he committed descriptive travel prose to his letters, mostly to Peacock, with whom Shelley had established a similar rapport during the Swiss tour. From Peacock, Shelley could expect a sympathetic ear, interested as much in his own doings as in what he saw, while Peacock's passion for the picturesque and his scholarly enthusiasm for the classics made him an ideal recipient of letters from Italy, the Mecca of nature and of art for travellers and connoisseurs. 'Behold us arrived at length at the end of our journey', Shelley reports on 6 April, stressing the immediate effects of climate on his well-being, 'Our journey was somewhat painful from the cold & in no manner interesting until we passed the Alps . . . but no sooner had we arrived in Italy than the loveliness of the earth & the serenity of the sky made the greatest difference in my sensations' (*L*, 2: 3). Already, Shelley responds to Italy aesthetically, sublimating temperature changes into 'loveliness', as if an atmosphere of beauty were correlative to the warmth that improves his physiological 'sensations'. He similarly heightens by association his first sightseeing impressions at Susa: 'the triumphal arch of Augustus . . . in the Greek taste', a female guide 'of light & graceful manners . . . in the style of Fuseli's Eve' (*L*, 2: 4). Subsequent letters to Peacock continue to explore the intensity and evanescence of aesthetic vision. The 20 April letter gives a highly picturesque account of the Shelleys' excursion from Milan to Lake Como in search of a house ('The union of culture & the untameable profusion & loveliness of nature is here so close that the line where they are divided can hardly be discovered') (*L*, 2: 7), and a sculpturesque description of Milan cathedral ('those groupes of dazzling spires . . . those sculptured shapes . . . beyond any thing I had imagined architecture capable of producing') (*L*, 2: 7-8). From Bologna in November, Shelley gives a virtuoso performance in art criticism, dwelling breathlessly on Raphael's *Cecilia* ('You forget that it is a picture as you look at it') (*L*, 2: 51), while his next letter describes a sublime vista at the Falls of Terni ('A thunder comes up from the abyss wonderful to hear') (*L*, 2: 56). From December to April 1819, Shelley wrote long journal letters to Peacock from Rome and Naples, recounting afresh the most famous tourist attractions in painting, sculpture, architecture, and landscape. In Rome, Shelley leaves indelible impressions of the Coliseum, the Roman Forum, the Baths of Caracalla, St Peter's, and the Pantheon; in Naples, he memorably describes excursions to Baiae Bay, Vesuvius, Paestum, and Pompeii.

The descriptive travel letters abruptly cease in June 1819 after the death of William, the Shelleys' eldest and last remaining child, in Rome. 'I do not as usual give you an account of my journey', he wrote Peacock from Leghorn (Livorno), 'for I had neither the health or spirits to take notes' (*L*, 2: 99). Nor did he resume a

---

[2] See *MWSL*, 1: 357, where Mary writes that 'la Montagne des Eschelles . . . gave S— [Shelley] the idea of his Prometheus'.

systematic travel correspondence thereafter. The fifteen surviving letters to Peacock between 6 April 1818 and 6 April 1819 thus comprise a unique collection within the Shelley canon that has received very little attention.[3] With the example of the *History of a Six Weeks' Tour* fresh in mind, Mary Shelley realised the letters' potential as materials for a travel book, and she instructed Peacock in a postscript from Bologna, 'take care of these . . . because I have no copies & I wish to transcribe them when I return to England' (*L*, 2: 54). Peacock himself responded enthusiastically to letters from Bologna and Rome, proclaiming, 'if you bring home a journal full of such descriptions of the remains of art and of the scenery in Italy they will attract a very great share of public attention' (*LTLP*, 1: 160). To this, Shelley responded modestly, 'I am more pleased to interest you than the many' (*L*, 2: 70), yet disingenuously, for he too would have been aware of the *History*'s precedent. When Mary Shelley finally did return to England, after Shelley's death, she made plans to reprint the letters as part of Shelley's *Posthumous Works*, a project that produced only *Posthumous Poems* (1824) before Timothy Shelley forestalled further publication.[4] At last, Shelley's 'Letters from Italy', including thirteen to Peacock, were published in Mary Shelley's edition, *Essays, Letters from Abroad, Translations and Fragments* in November 1839. Yet she herself recognised the special status of the 'long descriptive letters' that Shelley wrote 'during the first year of his residence in Italy, which, as compositions', she continues, 'are the most beautiful in the world, and show how truly he appreciated and studied the wonders of Nature and Art in that divine land' (*PW*, p. 270).[5]

Taken as a whole, the letter series gives an important insight into Shelley's *annus mirabilis*, for some of his best-known works from the period are imbued with a similar tourist ethos. *Lines Written among the Euganean Hills, October, 1818*, as I shall discuss below, meditates on the locality of Venice experienced by Shelley and frequently represented by travel writers; *Prometheus Unbound* draws heavily on Shelley's own letters to Peacock for its imagery, particularly those recounting his Neapolitan excursions; *Julian and Maddalo* and Shelley's fragmentary tale, 'The Coliseum', explore the political and aesthetic links between perspective and expression, travel observation and writing; *The Cenci* exploits Protestant perceptions of Italian Catholicism, a subject that had fascinated and

---

[3] Nicholas A. Joukovsky suggests that Shelley wrote eighteen letters to Peacock during this period. See his reconstruction of 'The Shelley-Peacock Correspondence, April 1818-April 1819' in *LTLP*, 1: lix.

[4] Joukovsky notes that Mary Shelley 'planned to include "Letters from Italy" in a volume of her husband's "Posthumous Works" projected in December 1823, and then in a separate volume of his prose works intended to follow the publication of his *Posthumous Poems* in June 1824'. Joukovsky's main source is Ingpen (*Shelley in England*, p. 577 n.) who quotes 'John Hunt's advertisements dated Dec. 1823 and Mar. 1824'. Joukovsky also cites Mary Shelley's Preface to *Posthumous Poems*, dated 1 June 1824, which states her intentions of bringing out a separate edition of prose. See 'Introduction', *LTLP*, 1: lvi-lvii; lvii n. 71.

[5] One of the few critics to comment on the letters, William M. Johnston remarks that they 'contain passages of incandescence that show the poet as a born travel writer'. See *In Search of Italy: Foreign Writers in Northern Italy Since 1800* (University Park and London: Pennsylvania State University Press, 1987), p. 186.

repulsed English tourists throughout the era of the Grand Tour.[6] The extent to which each of these works and Shelley's travel letters are involved in an intertextual exchange with contemporary travel writing on Italy is not always obvious, but there is little doubt that the Shelleys' absorption in travel culture produced such writing. Not only did they follow the beaten path to picturesque stations, museums, and galleries, but also they read guidebooks, reflected on the publications of other tourists, sketched, wrote journals and letters, and, most importantly, shared these works and ideas with each other. Claire Clairmont wrote travel compositions in a journal she kept of the Italian tour from their departure to the end of May 1818, when the party took up residence at Leghorn, and she resumed it in March 1819 at Rome.[7] While en route to Venice with Claire Clairmont in August 1818, Shelley crowded his intimate letter to Mary Shelley with descriptions of sights on the road to Florence, and first impressions of the city itself. Perhaps prompted by the example of Richard Belgrave Hoppner,[8] Mary Shelley resumed her studies in landscape drawing on the trip from Venice to Rome in 1818; in March 1819, at Rome, she began taking drawing lessons and practised in the Borghese Gardens and the Baths of Caracalla.[9] Around the same time, Shelley started to receive medical treatment from Dr John Bell, a renowned Scottish physician then resident in Italy. Bell frequently visited the Shelleys socially as well as professionally and may have shown or discussed his manuscript travel journal with Shelley, prompting Shelley that autumn to gather notes on sculptures in the Uffizi Gallery following Bell's methods.[10] Though Shelley ceased writing extended travel letters and gallery notes at the end of the year, Claire Clairmont planned and began drafting a travel book, 'Letters from Italy', from April to July 1820.[11] In May, the Shelleys convinced Maria and Thomas Gisborne

---

[6] Shelley wrote in his preface that the drama was based on a 'manuscript . . . communicated to me during my travels in Italy', and he explains the origins of his decision to write it in terms of his encounter with foreign attitudes, customs, and settings: 'this national and universal interest which the story produces and has produced for two centuries, and among all ranks of people in a great City, where the imagination is kept for ever active and awake, first suggested to me the conception of its fitness for a dramatic purpose' (*PS2*, pp. 727; 729).

[7] Several of Claire's entries in the earlier journal appear to be crafted in the manner of 'a retrospective travelogue, more like a letter or a travel article' (*SC* 448, 5: 460).

[8] Hoppner was the English Consul-General at Venice, son of a famous portrait painter, and an amateur painter himself. When Shelley first met him, Hoppner was just about to make a sketching tour of the Julian Alps. Hoppner also translated Urey Fedorovich Lisyansky's *A Voyage round the World, in the Years 1803, 1804, 1805, and 1806* (London, 1813).

[9] Mary Shelley began the lessons on 24 March 1818, probably under the tutelage of one Signor Delicati (*MWSJ*, p. 254, n. 4). Her interest in drawing, however, predates the Italian tour. She also took lessons in October 1816 while residing in Bath (*MWSJ*, p. 139, n. 1), and Michael Erkelenz suggests that some sketches of Lake Geneva from the previous summer in a shared notebook (Bodleian adds. e. 16) could possibly be by her. I am indebted to Nora Crook for bringing the strands of this history together.

[10] Bell's work was published posthumously as *Observations on Italy* (London, 1825).

[11] Only the table of contents survives. See *CCJ*, p. 98.

to write a journal of their travels to England, which the Shelleys expected to read when their friends returned.[12] As the Gisbornes reached Paris, Mary Shelley reminded them of their promise and urged them to send all their news: 'What think you of the Alps, and how did you cross Cenis? You who are travelling must write long letters, and we that stay at home must ask questions, having nothing better to do' (*MWSL*, 1: 145). Tourism and travel writing, so integral to the Shelleys' experience of Italy, becomes in this last instance a means of recreating England to the expatriate abroad.[13]

Nevertheless, most of Shelley's comments on travel and travel writing during this period serve to distance him from other tourists and travel writers. He decries against the English for being unpatriotic by travelling at a time when their efforts are needed 'in their own country' during the reform crisis ('Their conduct is wholly inexcusable') (*L*, 2: 9), and excuses himself on the grounds of poor health. He criticises the 'insupportable' manners of the 'rich English' at Rome, and condemns the 'spirit of the English abroad, as well as at home' (*L*, 2: 94) for their treatment of him as a social pariah, their inability to establish human contact outside the bounds of national prejudice.[14] With regard to travel writing, Shelley confesses shortcomings that limit his abilities to write in the genre. To Hogg, Shelley circumscribes his descriptive powers to landscape and art alone, rather than 'the human part of the experience of travelling; a thing of which I see little and understand less, and which if I saw and understood more I fear I should be little able to describe' (*L*, 2: 15).[15] To Peacock, Shelley stresses the obstacles preventing him from obtaining a fuller account of art and culture: 'the bodily fatigue of standing for hours in galleries' prevents him from seeing 'half that I ought', his isolation from society and inability to question the 'sullen & stupid' 'common Italians' prevents him from gathering 'information' (*L*, 2: 70). And then there is the problem of audience. Shelley would have it that he writes for the select few who can perceive beauty ('a perception of the beautiful charat[er]izes those who differ from ordinary men; & those who can perceive it would not buy enough to pay the printer') (*L*, 2: 70); he condemns popular travel writers for pandering to 'taste' at the expense of feeling, and manufacturing their diction accordingly. 'I am afraid of

---

[12] See *CCJ*, p. 8.

[13] English residents abroad were also supplied with images of 'home' in the form of news digests published in *Galignani's Messenger*, a popular Paris-based English language daily available in major cities throughout Europe. Galignani's Leghorn agent was the bookseller Glauco Masi, who later printed *The Cenci* for Shelley. The Shelleys began their subscription to the paper around March 1819, and Mary Shelley wrote to Maria Gisborne on 8 May 1820, 'you . . . perhaps will know more of the state of your Country from reading Galignani at Leghorn, than in England itself' (*MWSL*, 1: 145).

[14] For similar comments on the English community around Lake Geneva during the summer of 1816, see Shelley's letter to Teresa Guiccioli of ?9 August 1821 (*L*, 2: 325-9). Shelley refers to 'une colonie d'Anglais établis qui portent avec eux leurs préjugés mesquins et leur haine inquiète pour tous ceux qui les surpassent ou les évitent' (p. 326).

[15] Cf. Shelley's notions of travel during the summer of 1811, when he writes of a proposed journey to Wales: 'My excursion will be on foot for the purpose of better remarking the manners & dispositions of the peasantry' (To Elizabeth Hitchener, 25 June 1811; *L*, 1: 117).

stumbling upon their language when I enumerate what is so well known' (*L*, 2: 85), Shelley writes on the Palatine at Rome, and in the same letter again underlines his distinction from popular travel writers, 'Hobhouse, Eustace, & Forsyth', who retail 'all the shew-knowledge about it—"the common stuff of the earth"—' (*L*, 2: 89). For his part, Shelley explains, 'I have said what I feel without entering into any critical discussions of the ruins of Rome, & the mere outside of this inexhaustible mine of thought & feelings' (*L*, 2: 89). And again, in an earlier letter to Peacock, 'You know I always seek in what I see the manifestation of something beyond the present & tangible object' (*L*, 2: 47).

Taken together, these comments show that Shelley contrasted his own performance with a more public mode of travel writing, which he positions as an indefatigable archaeology, an excavation, classification, and analysis of the materials that make up a country, its people, and their art, much in the manner of Claire Clairmont's grand outline for her travel book: 'On the country of Italy', 'On the Manners & Customs including those of the Country & those of the town', 'On the Pictures & Statues', 'On the Music and the State of the Opera' (*CCJ*, p. 98). Yet in rejecting his ability to participate in such an encyclopaedic approach and instead carving out a separate space in which private impressions of art and landscape define his experience of Italy, Shelley joins a growing body of travel writers eager to prove the experience of Italy on their own pulses and distrustful of the monopolising pressures exerted by informational guidebooks over representation of the foreign. By 1820, John Scott suggested that 'such desultory communications' as Shelley's made up the 'great majority of recent tours and travels', and that the best of these derived their interest more from

> the novelty of the mental speculations, and in the freshness of the emotions suggested by strange objects, than in the mere action of that curiosity and surprise, which an accurate description of these is calculated to excite and gratify. He, therefore, "best shall paint them, who shall *feel* them most;" and it generally happens, that a more lively and faithful idea of foreign scenery is afforded by giving effusion to the workings of the mind of the observer under its view, than by a bare enumeration of its external points and features.[16]

Scott's terms here and elsewhere in his review of Henry Matthews's *The Diary of an Invalid* (1820) invoke what Nigel Leask has called the 'aesthetics of curiosity' developed in Lord Kames's *Elements of Criticism* (1762).[17] Kames argues that 'things rare and new' convert 'into a pleasure the fatigues and even perils of travelling' and that 'the emotion of wonder, raised by new and strange objects,

---

[16] [John Scott], Review of *The Diary of an Invalid: Being the Journal of a Tour in Pursuit of Health; in Portugal, Italy, Switzerland, and France*, by Henry Matthews, *London Magazine* (July 1820), pp. 60-61.

[17] Nigel Leask, *Curiosity and the Aesthetics of Travel Writing 1770-1840* (Cambridge: Cambridge University Press, 2002), p. 25.

inflames our curiosity to know more of them'.[18] By contrast, Scott uses the example of Matthews to illustrate Madame de Staël's assertion that travel 'is a "melancholy pleasure"', in which 'external excitements to wonder or curiosity' merely conceal the traveller's 'necessary alienation' or 'isolation in the midst of society', a situation made especially poignant in the case of an invalid traveller, consciousness of mortality, the leave-taking from all society.[19] This creates a gap between the motivations of travel ('curiosity') and the existential nature of travelling itself (physical and psychological detachment from known society); distance, speed of travel, ignorance of local languages and customs increase the traveller's sense of foreignness and exacerbate his or her sense of alienation. For Scott, travel writing that attempts to recreate only the excitements of curiosity through accurate representation ('bare enumeration of its external points') misrepresents the experience of the foreign. 'Accurate description' cannot give a 'faithful idea of foreign scenery' without a superadded representation of the subjective experience of distance, alienation, isolation, or death. Scott's attempt to desynonymise 'accuracy' and 'faithfulness' – terms closely linked in what Leask calls the eighteenth-century 'discourse of curiosity' – has the additional effect of underscoring the strong potential for disjunction between experience and representation of foreignness. If 'curiosity' is especially suited to represent 'the traveller's *desire* for the distant',[20] Scott relocates the interest of 'modern' travel writing to those emotional and speculative signs that distance always and ultimately eludes this desire. He also breaks down the fetish of accumulation, the idea that travel writing must account for everything worth seeing in order to satisfy its readers' insatiable curiosity. Instead, travel writing must expose the traveller's eye as well as its object if it is to be 'true' to the experience as well as to the objects of travelling. Shelley's eye, embedded in the landscape, again haunts the aesthetic problematic of post-Napoleonic travel (see fig. 1, p. 9).

Shelley's self-professed orientation to modern travel is ambivalent about the value of external objects, but like Scott he seeks an approach to travel that avoids guidebook inclusivity on the one hand and 'sentimental' or subjectivist exclusivity on the other.[21] To Godwin, Shelley remarked relatively early in his travels, 'We have as yet seen nothing of Italy, which marks it to us as the habitation of departed greatness . . . . Rome & Naples—even Florence are yet to see: and if we were to write you at present a history of our impressions it would give you no idea that we

---

[18] Henry Home (Lord Kames), *Elements of Criticism* [1762], 9th edn, 2 vols (Edinburgh, 1817), 1: 233; also quoted in Leask, *Curiosity*, p. 25.
[19] [Scott], Review of *The Diary of an Invalid*, pp. 59-60. See also Anna Louise Germaine de Staël-Holstein, *Corrine, or Italy*, trans. Sylvia Raphael (Oxford and New York: Oxford University Press, 1998), p. 8. For Scott's view of Oswald, Lord Nelvil as the type of the modern traveller, see below.
[20] Leask, *Curiosity*, p. 23.
[21] See Bruce Redford's account of William Beckford's *Dreams, Waking Thoughts, and Incidents* (1782) in *Venice and the Grand Tour* (New Haven and London, Yale University Press, 1996), pp. 105-15. Redford argues that Beckford draws on Philippe Jacques De Loutherbourg's Eidophusikon and develops a 'visionary way of gazing' that celebrates the Grand Tourist's sensibility over the objects of his gaze.

lived in Italy' (*L*, 2: 21). To 'see' Italy is to observe its ruins and works of art, yet 'impressions' rather than detailed descriptions will comprise a traveller's history. As much as Shelley criticises the 'shew-knowledge' of the guidebooks, he presumes to contest rather than reject the representation of the tour's standard objects. The 'history of our impressions' that Shelley gives between April 1818 and April 1819, therefore, responds creatively to the epistemological and aesthetic pressures felt by post-Napoleonic travellers and travel writers in Italy. He chooses the private letter as a mode of expression less inhibited by the genre and gender expectations imposed on published travel accounts – he crosses at will from 'masculine' discourses of classical and antiquarian inquiry to 'feminine' discourses of emotional response, for example, negotiating a space between John Chetwode Eustace's *A Classical Tour through Italy* (1813) and Marianne Baillie's *First Impressions on a Tour upon the Continent* (1819). Combining classical knowledge with aesthetic responsiveness, he emphasises the importance of feeling history through imaginative experience of the past, rather than through its recovery or reconstruction by antiquarian research. He undertakes an archaeology of the self and society as they are reflected in landscape and ruins, rather than a study of accumulated writings.

This chapter and the next consider these modes of travel writing as complex negotiations and choices made regarding observation and representation, seeing and writing, not merely within longstanding conventions of writing on the Italian tour, but within emerging discourses of travel responding to post-Napoleonic political and cultural conditions. Shelley is not unique among travel writers in seeing something 'beyond the present & tangible object', but what he sees and how he sees it become social and political acts defined against other, more public versions of the 'eye of taste' or the 'travellers' eye'. As Peacock demonstrated by sharing Shelley's travel letters with a circle of friends, even private communications depend upon wider contexts and conventions; in Mary Favret's words, 'by means of the angle of presentation, the letter becomes public property'.[22] As much as Shelley distinguishes himself from other travellers, his decisions on representation were not his alone to make, and the history of travel writing in the period will show that the forms of Shelley's travel writing are partly 'the endowment of the age' (*PS2*, p. 474) in which he lived. The first section of this chapter will look at the backdrop of popular travel writing on Italy, with particular emphasis on Eustace and Byron, the two most important modern travel writers for Shelley and his age. I then consider Shelley's specific response to these writers at the outset of his year's tour in a discussion of Shelley's *Lines Written among the Euganean Hills*. In the second half of the chapter, I focus on the letters to Peacock, isolating instances of aesthetic vision that help orientate Shelley's choices in representation against those of other travellers, similarly involved in endeavours to reconstruct a modern aesthetic responsiveness to landscape, architecture and art. I conclude with a consideration of 'The Coliseum', a work that acts as a fitting coda for the tour as far as Rome, for it is concerned with the limits

---

[22] Mary Favret, *Romantic Correspondence: Women, Politics & the Fiction of Letters* (Cambridge: Cambridge University Press, 1992), p. 2.

and limitlessness of travel representation when the traveller's eye is turned towards itself.

John Chetwode Eustace and the Italian Tour

In her review article, 'The English in Italy' (1826), Mary Shelley recounts how, when 'after many long years of war . . . our island prison was opened to us, and our watery exit from it was declared practicable, it was the paramount wish of every English heart . . . to hasten to the continent'. France was the first destination for the travelling hordes, but when it 'palled on our travelled appetites . . . Italy came into vogue'.[23] While it is difficult to ascertain how many tourists travelled to any given Continental destination in the post-war years,[24] British publishing trends reflect Mary Shelley's chronology. New travel books on France and Italy were scarce in the years preceding 1814, with an average of two a year from 1810. In 1814, at least twenty on France appeared, with another eighteen the following year. Though interest gradually abated, around six new titles appeared each year throughout the 1820s. Travel accounts on Italy peaked later. Around five appeared yearly between 1814-16, rising to nine between 1817-19,[25] then twenty-two in 1820. Though the trend was then downwards, nearly twice as many titles were published each year compared with those on France.[26] These patterns reflect those of Continental tourism and of vicarious demand at home by those who might not undertake tours themselves. Henry Aston Barker kept his finger on the pulse of this market with his

---

[23] Mary Shelley, 'The English in Italy', *Westminster Review* (Oct. 1826); quoted in *CCJ*, 'Appendix A', pp. 441-2.

[24] John Towner suggests that an average of 15,000-20,000 British tourists may have been abroad during the mid-eighteenth century (*An Historical Geography of Recreation and Tourism in the Western World, 1540-1940*, Chichester, John Wiley & Sons, 1996, p. 98). By contrast, Paul Gerbod reports that 15,512 British tourists and residents were present in Paris alone in 1815 ('Voyageurs et Résidents Britanniques en France au XIXe Siècle: Une Approche Statistique', *Acta Geographica*, 4.76 (1988), p. 22). J. R. Hale believes that numbers of continental tourists declined after the initial rush, but gives a figure of 2,000 British tourists present at Rome during winter 1818, with another 1,000 elsewhere in Italy ('Introduction', *The Italian Journal of Samuel Rogers*, ed. J. R. Hale, London, Faber and Faber, 1956, p. 60).

[25] Only four travel books on Italy appeared with British imprints in 1816: the second edition of Joseph Forsyth's *Remarks on Antiquities, Arts, and Letters, during an Excursion in Italy in the Years 1802 and 1803*; the second edition of J. Salmon's *A Description of the Works of Art of Ancient and Modern Rome*, first published in 1798; the third edition of Mariana Starke's *Travels in Italy*, first published in 1800; and a translation of Karl Theodor von Uklanski's *Travels in Upper Italy . . . in the Years 1807 and 1808*. None concern post-1814 tours.

[26] These figures are from my forthcoming *Bibliography of British Travel Writing, 1780-1840*, which includes a chronological listing of all titles pertaining to each country and region in Europe. It should be noted that here I refer to new titles only, including translations, but not new editions or reprints of previous works. Nevertheless, the trends remain the same when this additional body of writing is taken into consideration.

exhibitions at the Panoramas in Leicester Square and the Strand.[27] In 1815, he exhibited 360° views of Elba and Paris, capitalising on public interest in the fallen Napoleon and the imperial capital he had 'created'. In 1817, sensitive to the shifting vogue that Mary Shelley describes, Barker began exhibiting his view of Rome from the tower of the Capitol (the Shelleys visited it on 12 February 1818, a month before their departure for Italy) (*MWSJ*, p. 193). Views of Venice and Naples followed in 1819 and 1821 respectively, a concentration on Italian subjects that exactly follows and exploits travelling and publishing trends.[28]

In a letter to Thomas Moore from Venice, written in March of that pivotal year, 1817, Byron complained that Rome was 'pestilent with English . . . wishing to be at once cheap and magnificent': 'A man is a fool who travels now in France or Italy, till this tribe of wretches is swept home again. In two or three years the first rush will be over, and the Continent will be roomy and agreeable' (*Byron LJ*, 5: 187).[29] Byron himself did more than any living contemporary to heighten Italy's attraction by modelling the last canto of his semi-autobiographical bestseller, *Childe Harold* (1818), on his own tour from Venice to Rome in 1817. His travelling companion, John Cam Hobhouse, immediately published a volume of antiquarian research, *Historical Illustrations of the Fourth Canto of Childe Harold* (1818), supplementing the 135 pages of endnotes that accompanied the poem itself; tourists on the spot, including Shelley and Lady Morgan, soon began experiencing

---

[27] Henry Aston Barker inherited the Leicester Square panorama after his father, Robert Barker, died in 1806; Henry Aston Barker and John Burford took over the rival Strand panorama in 1817. See Richard Altick, *The Shows of London* (Cambridge, MA: Harvard University Press, 1978), p. 137.

[28] Visual and verbal reproductions of Roman antiquities predate these exhibitions. Between 1778 and 1785, Richard Dubourg exhibited cork models of classical sites at his aptly titled Classical Exhibition, Pall Mall, and a second, unrelated Dubourg began a similar exhibition in 1798 at Manchester Square, including a miniature Tivoli replete with 'copious foam and spray' – Wordsworth paid tribute to the minute accuracy of such models in *The Prelude*, VII, 265-80 (see Altick, *Shows*, pp. 115-16). Ramsay Richard Reinagle exhibited a panorama of Rome in 1802-1803 in the Strand, capitalising on interest generated by tourism during the Peace of Amiens. The Oxford and Cambridge prize poems, widely circulated during the early nineteenth century, also reflected French and British imperial interest in classical sculpture and architecture, and 'offered simulated or "virtual" excursions for the emerging middle classes who could not yet afford an actual trip to the continent' (Grant Scott, 'The Fragile Image: Felicia Hemans and Romantic Ekphrasis', in *Felicia Hemans: Reimagining Poetry in the Nineteenth Century*, eds Nanora Sweet and Julie Melnyk, London, Palgrave, 2001, p. 38). Those who could make the trip before 1816 found it more economical to visit Paris, where Napoleon had collected the plundered art of Italy for display to the nation (and exulting foreigners during the Peace of Amiens and again in 1814-15). The return of the works of art to Italy in 1816 was another motive for travellers to extend their tour to the south.

[29] In July 1818, Mary Shelley reported from Bagni di Lucca: 'we see none but English, we hear nothing but English spoken—The walks are filled with English Nurserymaids . . . & dashing staring English-women . . . on horseback' (*MWSL*, 1: 74).

Italian scenes in the light of Byron's self-involved descriptions.[30] Other 'first rush' tourists made their way into print after 1817, and there is little sense of belatedness in their accounts; if anything they suggest relief that accumulated writings of the pre-war generation might be discarded as outdated or quaint. Sir William Gell, who accompanied the Princess of Wales's entourage to Italy in 1814, became instrumental in continuing the French excavations at Pompeii, the account of which he published to great acclaim in *Pompeiana* (1817-19). Henry Matthews toured Italy in pursuit of health from 1817-19 and his *The Diary of an Invalid* (1820), praised by Byron, reached a fifth edition by 1825. The blind traveller, James Holman, began a three years tour of Europe in 1819 and published his debut travel book a few years later, *The Narrative of a Journey Undertaken in the Years 1819, 1820, & 1821, through France, Italy, Savoy, Switzerland, Parts of Germany Bordering on the Rhine, Holland, and the Netherlands* (1822; 5th edn, 1834). Between 1817 and 1822, numerous view books and sketching tours were published by artists and architects attracted by Italy's reputation for picturesque scenes and classical ruins, including Thomas Allason, Elisabeth Batty, James Hakewill, and Marianne Colston.[31] As the success of these attractive volumes indicates, Italy was above all seen as the homeland of classical and renaissance art, sculpture, and architecture, and no travel account on Italy was considered complete without its description of visits to museums, galleries, churches, and sites of classical antiquity.

Two accounts of tours conducted during the Peace of Amiens, but first published in 1813, became particularly influential: John Chetwode Eustace's *A Tour through Italy* and Joseph Forsyth's *Remarks on Antiquities, Arts, and Letters during an Excursion in Italy*. Reprinted in numerous editions, both inspired other 'classical tourists', including 'Henry Coxe', Sir Richard Colt Hoare, Stephen Weston, Charles Kelsall, and Peter Edmund Laurent.[32] While these men regarded travel writing as a masculine discourse and claimed to be updating values of the

---

[30] Capitalising on this tendency in the 1830s, the house of Murray repackaged a highly edited version of *Childe Harold* for its popular Murray Guides. For a discussion of this circulation of an 'atmospheric Byron', see James Buzard, *The Beaten Track: European Tourism, Literature, and the Ways to Culture, 1800-1918* (Oxford: Clarendon Press, 1993), pp. 125-30.

[31] See Thomas Allason, *Picturesque Views of the Antiquities of Pola, in Istria* (1819); Elisabeth Frances Batty, *Italian Scenery. From Drawings Made in 1817* (1820); James Hakewill, *A Picturesque Tour of Italy, from Drawings Made in 1816-1817* (1820); Marianne Colston, *Journal of a Tour in France, Switzerland, and Italy during the Years 1819, 20, and 21. Illustrated by Fifty Lithographic Prints, from Original Drawings* (2 vols, Paris, 1822).

[32] See Henry Coxe (possibly a pseudonym for John Millard), *Pictures of Italy; Being a Guide to the Antiquities and Curiosities of that Classical and Interesting Country* (1815); Sir Richard Colt Hoare, *A Classical Tour through Italy and Sicily* (1819); Stephen Weston, *Enchiridon Romæ: or, Manual of Detached Remarks on the Buildings, Pictures, Statues, Inscriptions, &c. of Ancient and Modern Rome* (1819); Charles Kelsall, *Classical Excursion from Rome to Arpino* (Geneva, 1820); Peter Edmund Laurent, *Recollections of a Classical Tour through Various parts of Greece, Turkey and Italy Made in the Years 1818 & 1819* (1821).

Grand Tour, a significant number of women travellers made their mark with accounts of Italy. Of the thirty-seven new travel books published by women between 1814 and 1822, ten concerned Italy, and of these five appeared in 1820 alone. In addition to Batty, Colston and Morgan, the following deserve particular mention: Maria Graham's *Three Months Passed in the Mountains East of Rome during the Year 1819* (1820; 2nd edn, 1821), Charlotte Eaton's *Rome in the Nineteenth Century* (3 vols, 1820; 4th edn, 1826), and Jane Waldie's *Sketches Descriptive of Italy in the Years 1816 and 1817* (1820). Finally, Mariana Starke's *Travels on the Continent Written for the Use and Particular Information of Travellers* (1820; 8th edn, 1832) under its more popular title, *Information and Directions for Travellers on the Continent*, became a standard guidebook throughout the 1820s.

By far the most influential of these travel accounts for post-Napoleonic British travellers was Eustace's *A Tour through Italy* (1813), or, as it became widely known after the second edition, *A Classical Tour through Italy*. 'The epithet *Classical*', writes Eustace, 'sufficiently points out its peculiar character, which is to trace the resemblance between Modern and Ancient Italy, and to take for guides and companions in the beginning of the nineteenth century, the writers that preceded or adorned the first' (*CT*, 1: vi). For James Buzard, this character seems hardly peculiar, for in his view 'the antiquarian interests of some eighteenth-century Grand Tourists survived most visibly' in Eustace.[33] Yet Eustace also offered contemporaries a new departure. He makes a point of rejecting the vade mecum of eighteenth-century Grand Tourist classicism, Addison's *Remarks on Several Parts of Italy* (1705), arguing that political and religious 'prejudice had narrowed' Addison's 'extensive views', rendering him 'not so much a Classic as a Whig traveller' (*CT*, 1: 28).[34] Eustace extends this charge of partisan and partial observation to almost the whole tradition of eighteenth-century travel writing on Italy, clearing the way for a classical revival in tourism to complement the Greek Revival in English architecture and culture. Classical tourism becomes an ideological contestation over the shape and meaning of history, over the transmission of aesthetic and political values from ancient to modern culture, and over the origins of these values in Greek, Roman, or Italian civilisation.

The example of France, especially revolutionary France, functions as Eustace's foil throughout the *Classical Tour*. He attacks not only travel writers who have perpetuated Addison's faults, but also those 'within the last ten years' who 'employed their journals as vehicles of revolutionary madness' (*CT*, 1: 30). Without much subtlety, Eustace presents everything French – French enlightenment philosophy and literature, French dynastic, republican and imperial politics – as founded on a false, superficial classicism, which the modern, post-Napoleonic classical tourist must purge by intellectually recolonising Europe,

---

[33] Buzard, *The Beaten Track*, p. 69.
[34] Katherine Turner has described Addison's *Remarks* as 'the most popular and influential eighteenth-century travel book' (*British Travel Writers in Europe, 1750-1800: Authorship, Gender and National Identity*, Aldershot, Ashgate, 2001, p. 26).

particularly Italy.[35] The critique extends backwards to include French neo-classicists of the seventeenth and eighteenth century, and Addison is also tarred with having constructed his aesthetics on the false refinements of Boileau. Eustace's more immediate target is French Revolutionary and Imperial appropriation of Roman iconography (and later Italian art works themselves) for national identity and aggrandisement.[36] His observations on classical sites often give way to reflections contrasting Roman magnificence with French insensitivity to classical culture, as in this account of the amateur theatrics of the French occupying army in Rome, 1797-98:

> ... they erected in the centre of the Coliseum a temporary theatre, where they acted various republican pieces .... *Voltaire*'s Brutus was a favourite tragedy, as may easily be imagined; and in order to give it more effect, it was resolved to transport the very statue of Pompey ... to the Coliseum, and to erect it on the stage. The colossal size ... and its extended arm, rendered it difficult to displace ... the arm was therefore sawed off for the conveyance, and put on again at the Coliseum .... So friendly to Pompey was the republican enthusiasm of the French! So favourable to the arts and antiquities of Rome is their Love of Liberty! (*CT*, 2: 32-3).[37]

Byron responds to the story by darkly contrasting Pompey's historical prowess with this ignoble afterlife – 'have ye been / Victors of countless kings, or puppets of a scene' (*Byron PW*, 2: 153, st. 87, l. 783) – and Hobhouse notes wryly that 'the republican tragedians had to plead that the arm was a restoration'.[38] For his part, Eustace offers no hint of exculpation; in his underlying typology, the French re-enact the Gothic invasion, ensuring the destruction rather than the glory of Rome. He frequently resorts to name-calling. The French are 'modern Vandals' (*CT*, 1: 64), 'the scourge of Italy' (*CT*, 2: 60) whose 'destroying spirit' (*CT*, 1: 209) and 'sacriligious rapine' (*CT*, 1: 303) are exemplified by numerous acts of wanton pillage befitting 'the Huns of Attila, or the Goths of Radagaisus' (*CT*, 1: 119). By contrast, the hermeneutic virtuosity of Eustace's self-sufficient classical tourist, disencumbered of accumulated travel writings and prepared by a liberal and classical education, models a post-Napoleonic imperial humanism, embodied in an ideal of British liberty, tolerance, and cosmopolitan responsibility. Unfashionably,

---

[35] See *CT*, 4: 338-9.

[36] See *CT*, 1: xvii. 'As long as religion and literature, civilization and independence are objects of estimation among men, so long must *revolutionary* France be remembered with horror and detestation'. For the appropriation of Roman iconography in architecture and fashion during the French Revolution, see Ronald Paulson, *Representations of Revolution (1789-1820)* (New Haven and London: Yale University Press, 1983), pp. 10-28, and Robert Rosenblum, *Transformations in Late Eighteenth Century Art* (Princeton: Princeton University Press, 1967), pp. 119-34.

[37] See also *CT*, 1: 114-15 for a description of the theatrical purposes to which the ancient amphitheatre at Verona was employed by the Emperor Joseph (bull-baiting), the Pope (benediction), and the French occupiers (pantomime and farce).

[38] Notes to *Childe Harold* IV, in *Byron PW*, 2: 249.

in an age when British visitors still 'came primarily to admire the past and to scorn the present',[39] the *Classical Tour* affirms the modern Italian's disposition and potential to share in this ideal. Defending Italian national character, religion, language, and art, the *Classical Tour* concludes by calling for a unified Italy to 'unite with Great Britain . . . in restoring and supporting that equilibrium of power so essential to the freedom and happiness of Europe' (*CT*, 4: 338).

Despite gestures towards a post-Napoleonic 'modernism', Eustace's patrician ideals would have been especially attractive to the university educated male elite, the same class that embodied the Grand Tour's ideals in the previous generation. Eustace himself dedicated his work 'solely to persons of a liberal education' who have acquired a 'bosom intimacy with the ancients' (*CT*, 1: 4, 5), and his frequent use of Latin quotations circumscribes his readership accordingly. When first published in 1813, the *Classical Tour*'s two weighty quarto volumes seemed destined for the fireside library rather than the traveller's carriage. Nevertheless, the *Classical Tour* was well positioned to bridge the gap between Grand Tourism and modern travel, once the Continent reopened to British travellers. Though not intended as a general guidebook, the *Classical Tour* surprisingly lent itself to that purpose, for Eustace had supplemented his classical observations with detailed itineraries, picturesque descriptions of the sites of classical renown, recommendations on viewpoints, and practical information, including routes, seasons for optimal travel, and modes of transportation. The third edition (4 vols, 1815) was published in a cheaper octavo format, 'for the more portable convenience of travellers',[40] and successive octavo editions were produced in 1817 (4th), 1819 (5th), and 1821 (6th). An American edition appeared in 1816, and from 1817 travellers could purchase a cheap Italian reprint at Leghorn replete with appendices containing an update on recent excavations in Pompeii, tables of posting routes between major cities and a list of respectable inns in each of the major towns.[41]

The Leghorn edition's practical format testifies to a widening readership, as the *Classical Tour* was developed and repackaged to appeal to all classes of tourists. Though Eustace's death at Naples in 1815 prevented him from completing an extension of his *Tour*, Sir Richard Colt Hoare published *A Classical Tour through Italy and Sicily; Tending to Illustrate Some Districts, Which Have Not Been Described by Mr. Eustace, in His Classical Tour* (1819). The publisher Joseph

---

[39] Frances Haskell, 'Preface' to *Grand Tour: The Lure of Italy in the Eighteenth Century*, eds Andrew Wilton and Ilaria Bignamini (London: Tate Gallery Publishing, 1996), p.10.

[40] Sir Richard Colt Hoare, *Hints to Travellers in Italy* (London: Printed by W. Bulmer and Co., 1815), p. 5 n. Buzard refers to 'Eustace's ponderous *Classical Tour* . . . in two to four weighty volumes' (*The Beaten Track*, p. 67), overestimating the bulk of the octavo editions, and generally underestimating the crucial impact of Eustace's classicism in the early nineteenth century.

[41] In his note to stanza 174 of *Childe Harold* IV, Hobhouse mentions a cheap Florentine reprint of Eustace abandoned before publication on the advice of returning travellers. Hobhouse uses the example to support his general disparagement of the *Classical Tour*, though the extant Leghorn edition attests to the demand from travellers on the spot for pirate editions of popular titles. See *Byron PW*, 2: 263.

Mawman brought out an expensive quarto edition combining the two tours in three volumes, and directed towards a genteel audience (Hoare's was also available on its own in two volumes quarto). The same year saw the appearance of two other books indebted to Eustace, but which aimed to broaden his appeal. The first, *Galignani's Traveller's Guide through Italy* (Paris, 1819), marketed itself as a digest of the most trusted authorities on Italy ('Carefully compiled from the Works of Coxe, Eustace, Forsythe, Reichard, etc.') and was intended as a portable guidebook. The second, James Hakewill's *A Picturesque Tour of Italy, from Drawings Made in 1816-1817* (1819) undertook to provide engravings of views mentioned by Eustace and ordered according to the itinerary of the *Classical Tour*, it 'being a popular work . . . in general circulation'.[42] Mawman appears to have hoped to extend that circulation with the 1821 edition of the *Classical Tour*, which for the first time included translations of the Greek and Latin quotations. This effort appears to have come too late, for no further edition of Eustace was called for until the Paris edition of 1837. Nevertheless, Eustace's *Classical Tour* had become itself a classic, a touchstone for future travel writers and artists.[43]

On the face of it, the *Classical Tour* seems an unlikely companion for Shelley, who had once notoriously described himself in the register of the Hotel d'Angleterre at Chamounix as 'δημοκρατικὸς, φιλάνθρωποτατος, και άθεος' (democrat, great lover of mankind, and atheist).[44] After all, Eustace was a Roman Catholic priest who had been the intimate of Edmund Burke. Yet Eustace was also considered a progressive, liberal-minded churchman. Born in Ireland around 1762, he was groomed for the Roman Catholic priesthood during a time of increasing agitation for Catholic emancipation.[45] Though he followed a strict course of religious education,[46] Eustace espoused latitudinarian beliefs that incited

---

[42] Hakewill, *Picturesque Tour*, [preface], n.p.

[43] View books on Italy continued to draw on Eustace into the 1830s. See Samuel Prout, *One Hundred and Four Views of Switzerland and Italy, Adapted to Illustrate Byron, Rogers, Eustace, and Other Works on Italy* (1833) and James Duffield Harding, *Seventy-Five Views of Italy and France, Adapted to Illustrate Byron, Rogers, Eustace, and All Works on Italy and France* (1834). An earlier, but curious example of Eustace's continued relevance to travel writing is *Voyages and Travels of Her Majesty, Caroline Queen of Great Britain* (1822), attributed to Louis Demont. This compilation somewhat belatedly hoped to exploit interest generated by Caroline's death in 1821. Purporting to be written by one in the Queen's service, the sections of the text on Italy include wholesale plagiarisms of Eustace's *Classical Tour*.

[44] See Gavin de Beer, 'An "Atheist" in the Alps', *Keats-Shelley Memorial Bulletin*, 9 (1958), p. 8.

[45] Eustace's only known religious tract is a popular polemic on Catholic emancipation, detailing the reasonableness of civil equality in England. See his *Answer to the Charge Delivered by the Lord Bishop of Lincoln to the Clergy of that Diocese, at the Triennial Visitation in the Year 1818* (1813).

[46] From 1767-74, he attended Sedgely Park School in Staffordshire, one of the first Catholic schools set up in England since the Reformation, and he finished his education at the English Benedictine convent of St Gregory at Douai. After returning to Ireland, he was ordained (c.1777).

controversy and influenced his decision to leave Ireland. In England, he became associated with the 'Blue book' faction of Catholic clerics, who favoured accommodations with the Anglican Church proposed by the Committee for Catholic Relief under the Pitt ministry. Dredging up this history in 1819, the ultramontane Vicar Apostolic, John Milner, accused the 'reverend tourist' of being among 'the betrayers of religion' for having formerly encouraged his English congregations to attend Anglican services, and, more recently, for filling his *Classical Tour* with an 'un-catholic and latitudinarian spirit . . . more dangerous, and therefore more censurable, in this age of irreligious indifferency, than if it broached half a dozen open heresies'.[47] Perhaps it was Eustace's tolerant attitude that allowed him to cross religious divides and become close to Burke in the 1790s.[48] Milner certainly accused Eustace of 'gadding with protestants through classical scenes', a reference to John Cust, Lord Brownlow, who accompanied Eustace and his pupil, Philip Roche, on their Grand Tour to Italy during the Peace of Amiens in 1802.[49] Though Shelley could hardly have known of this particular controversy surrounding the *Classical Tour*, his trip to Dublin in 1812 gave him first-hand experience in agitating for Catholic emancipation, and his rhetorical techniques in his *Address to the Irish People* involved clothing deist sentiments in Catholic language. In Italy, Shelley used Catholic rhetoric to critique the moral hypocrisy rooted in English Protestant society. As he writes in the preface to *The Cenci* (1819), 'religion in Italy is not, as in Protestant countries, a cloak to be worn on particular days; or a passport which those who do not wish to be railed at carry with them to exhibit . . . . It is interwoven with the whole fabric of life' (*PS2*, p. 732). '*We* Catholics', he later joked to Medwin, 'speak eternally and familiarly of the first person of the Trinity; and amongst *us* religion is more interwoven with . . . ordinary life' (*L*, 2: 219). In the *Classical Tour*, Eustace launches his defence of Italian Catholicism from the charges of Protestant travellers on exactly these grounds – that 'religious practices [are] *interwoven* in the life of an Italian, and incorporated with the whole business and very substance of his existence' (*CT*, 4: 247; my italics) – and he appeals to the common 'essence of Christianity' to link Protestants and Catholics: 'the three prime and all-enlivening virtues, of Faith, Hope, and of Charity' (*CT*, 4: 291).

---

[47] Letter, signed 'J. M. [John Milner]', *The Orthodox Journal*, VII, no. 73 (June 1819), p. 229; VII, no. 75 (August 1819), p. 303. The references to Eustace form part of a controversy between Milner and an anonymous correspondant, 'Candidus', in the pages of *The Orthodox Journal* between June 1819 and February 1820. Milner opened the series of exchanges with an attack on Eustace and other latitudinarians in a review of John Lingard's *A History of England* (1819). See also, Frederick Charles Husenbeth, *The Life of the Right Rev. John Milner* (Dublin, 1862), pp. 394-9.

[48] After Burke's death, Eustace published a heartfelt, if unambitious elegy on his friend. See *An Elegy to the Memory of the Right Honourable Edmund Burke* (London: Printed for F. and C. Rivington, 1798).

[49] *The Orthodox Review*, VII, no. 75 (August 1819), p. 303. Cust (afterwards Lord Brownlow, Lord Lieutenant of the County of Lincoln) and Robert Rushbrooke of Rushbroke Park, joined Eustace and Roche at Vienna.

Shelley may also have known of – or sensed – Eustace's Grecian sympathies. During the decade between Eustace's return from Italy until the publication of the *Classical Tour*, Eustace came under the influence of the Cambridge Hellenists, a group of Cambridge scholar-travellers who promoted the investigation of Greece. The Hellenists included such renowned travellers as the Reverend Edward Daniel Clarke (1769-1822), Thomas Hope (1769-1831), William Gell (1777-1836), Charles Kelsall (1782-1857), and William Wilkins (1788-1839).[50] Eustace resided at Jesus College from 1805, as tutor and chaplain to George Petre.[51] There he became particularly close to Clarke, the College's new senior tutor. By that time, Clarke had already completed his extensive travels through Europe and Asia Minor, an account of which he published between 1810 and 1823 (Mary Shelley read a good deal of Clarke's *Travels* after 1817, and Shelley expressed interest in the parts 'relating to Greece').[52] Brian Dolan has recently described Clarke as 'exemplary of the new, modern European traveller', one who attempted to reinvigorate British science and art through first-hand comparative studies of European cultures.[53] As a tutor at Cambridge, he promoted travel as the foundation for this progressive education by lecturing to acolytes and exhibiting his extensive collection of marbles, bought or pilfered during his travels. Byron (who matriculated at Trinity in 1805) and Hobhouse were possibly among those inspired by Clarke to visit Greece, and Eustace certainly was. Eustace and Petre set out around 1809, travelling 'to parts of *Dalmatia*, the Western Coasts of *Greece*, the *Ionian Islands*, to *Sicily*, *Malta*, &c' (*CT*, 1: xix-xx). Upon their return, Clarke encouraged Eustace to publish the manuscript journal of his earlier tour to Italy, and it was Clarke who negotiated terms with the publisher, Mawman. After Eustace's death of malaria in Naples, Clarke wrote, 'I feel the happier in reflecting that the monument he has left behind him, would, but for my exertions, have been buried with him'.[54]

Clarke's exertions may have included introducing Eustace to other Cambridge Hellenists, for Eustace's remarks on Greek culture emerge most clearly in the supporting matter – the introduction, conclusion, footnotes, and appendices – superadded to the journal that he probably drafted during the 1802-1803 tour itself, before his arrival at Cambridge. Taken together, however, the materials that make up the *Classical Tour* comprise a defence of Italy over Greece as the prime destination for the modern tourist who travels to ascertain the applicability of the past to the present. If Eustace allows the Greeks 'the first praise . . . as the inventors' of 'poetry, history, and grammar, architecture, painting, and sculpture'

---

[50] See David Watkin, *Thomas Hope 1769-1831 and the Neo-Classical Idea* (London: John Murray, 1968), pp. 64-75.
[51] Watkin, *Thomas Hope*, p. 68, and *DNB* on Eustace.
[52] For a summary of Mary Shelley's readings of Clarke, see *MWSJ*, p. 642; Shelley requested Clarke's *Travels* in a letter to Peacock from Livorno, 5 June 1818 (*L*, 2: 18).
[53] Brian Dolan, *Exploring European Frontiers: British Travellers in the Age of Enlightenment* (Basingstoke: Macmillan, 2000), p. 14.
[54] *The Life and Remains of the Rev. Edward Daniel Clarke, LL.D. Professor of Mineralogy in the University of Cambridge* (London, 1824), p. 625.

(*CT*, 4: 305), he celebrates Italy as 'the *parent* of all the sciences that enlighten, or all the arts that embellish human life' (*CT*, 4: 338-9, my italics). Eustace relocates Greek political values in republican Rome, and discovers the mechanism for their distribution in the succeeding imperial age. He traces the obscure channels by which Catholic Rome under Leo X preserved and perpetuated this inheritance, and argues that modern Italy was born with the Renaissance city states such as Venice or Genoa which, but for the French Revolution, would have inevitably reanimated the Roman spirit. Nevertheless, Eustace is also a Hellenist insofar as he values Rome in the light of Greek models of simplicity, beauty, and grandeur in art and modes of life. There is no contradiction in his recommendation of 'Stuart's Athens' (*CT*, 1: 15)[55] for its unsurpassed samples 'of Grecian art and of Attic taste' (*CT*, 1: 15) and his appreciation of cinquecento Church architecture, for his discourses on architecture always revert to Greek aesthetic values of simplicity and unity.

At times Eustace refashions Hellenist touchstones to emphasise their applicability to Italy. For example, he alludes in several places to Jean-Jacques Barthélemy's *Voyage du jeune Anacharsis en Grèce* (1788), a work Shelley consulted frequently between 22 June and 7 July 1818, while translating Plato's *Symposium* and before drafting *A Discourse on the Manners of the Ancient Greeks Relative to the Subject of Love*.[56] Anacharsis is an imaginary traveller from Scythia who tours Greece during the age of Pericles, discoursing with philosophers, poets, and legislators, while commenting on matters of geography, trade, political history, the arts, manners and customs of the inhabitants. As Jennifer Wallace points out, Barthélemy's travelogue 'sparked a debate across Europe about the nature of ancient Greek life, and provoked rival attempts to produce the authentic account', including works by Christoph Martin Wieland, A. W. Schlegel, and Shelley.[57] However, Eustace emphasises the French antiquarian's awe at the sublime picture of Italian civilisation as a complement to Grecian simplicity; in an appendix, the *Classical Tour* reproduces part of a memoir in which Barthélemy traces the origins of *Anacharsis* to his Italian tour of 1755. Contemplating the 'ancient splendour' of Italy, Barthélemy explains how he first conceived the plan of a travelogue set in the High Renaissance Italy of Leo X rather than Greece. Perhaps more revealing is Eustace's praise of William Wilkins's 'magnificent work', *The Antiquities of*

---

[55] James Stuart and Nicholas Revett, *The Antiquities of Athens*, 4 vols (London, 1762-1816). Eustace refers young readers to Charles Rollin's dissertation on classical architecture appended to *The Ancient History of the Egyptians, Carthaginians* (*CT*, 1:15). Shelley ordered this book on September 1815.

[56] In making the point that no modern writer has successfully represented the ancient Greeks 'precisely as they were', Shelley notes, 'Barthélemy cannot be denied the praise of industry and system; but he never forgets that he is a Christian and a Frenchman' (*A Discourse on the Manners of the Ancient Greeks Relative to the Subject of Love*, in *Prose*, p. 219). Shelley's sentiments echo those of A. W. Schlegel, who writes that *Anacharsis* relates 'not the travels of a young Scythian, but of an old Parisian' (*A Course of Lectures on Dramatic Art and Literature*, trans. John Black, 2 vols, London, 1815, 1: 47).

[57] Jennifer Wallace, *Shelley and Greece: Rethinking Romantic Hellenism* (Basingstoke: Macmillan Press, 1997), p. 9.

Magna Graecia (1807).[58] A Cambridge don, traveller, archaeologist, and architect, Wilkins became one of the leaders of the English Greek Revival. J. Mordaunt Crook observes that Wilkins 'took the architectural world by storm' with his Greek Doric design for Downing College, Cambridge, submitted after he returned from a three years' tour through Greece, Asia Minor, and Italy between 1801 and 1804. His influential *Antiquities* contained empirical descriptions and 'fine drawings . . . of the temples at Syracuse, Selinus, Agrigentum, Aegesta and Paestum',[59] and argued that the principles of Greek temple architecture – 'solidity, combined with simplicity and grace' – derived from 'one great model', namely, the Temple of Jerusalem mentioned in scriptures.[60] Wilkins's scientific data and his picturesque views combined to promote Italy as a palimpsest beneath which Grecian lineaments could be clearly discerned. Eustace refers to Wilkins in order to ally the *Classical Tour* with the Greek Revival's programme of reimagining the classical world in Grecian terms and applying these to contemporary tastes in literature, architecture, and fashion. Nevertheless, Eustace's emphasis on Italy attempts to wrest momentum from the more strict Greek revivalists. If, as Wallace has rightly observed, 'the official account of Greece did not yet exist',[61] Eustace shows how a re-evaluation of Italian as well as Greek classicism helped in shaping that account.

One of Eustace's more curious footnotes establishes a further link between Shelley and the *Classical Tour*. In his 'Preliminary Discourse', Eustace notes that

> . . . the best guide or rather companion which the traveller can take with him, is *Corinne ou l'Italie*, a work of singular beauty and eloquence. In it *Madame de Staël* does ample justice to the Italian character . . . she raises the reader above the common level of thought, and inspires him with that lofty temper of mind, without which we can neither discover nor relish the great and beautiful in art or in nature' (*CT*, 1: 30-31 n.).[62]

Madame de Staël's novel, *Corinne* (1807), which Shelley would read in Naples from 13-15 December 1818 (*MWSJ*, p. 243), 'achieved great authority as a guide not only to the sights but also to the new appropriate responses of the Italian tour'.[63] These responses involved what Chloe Chard calls the conversion of 'historical time into personal time', making 'the vestiges of antiquity more easily transportable into a private domain of emotional intimacy'.[64] Yet for Staël's heroine, the Anglo-Italian improvisatrice, emotion is always the reflex of her public role as interpreter of the past and poet of the present, expressing in

---

[58] Eustace and his companion on the Italian tour, John Cust of Trinity College, Cambridge, are among the list of subscribers to Wilkins's *Antiquities*.
[59] J. Mordaunt Crook, *The Greek Revival: Neo-Classical Attitudes in British Architecture 1760-1870* (London: John Murray, 1972), p. 47.
[60] William Wilkins, *The Antiquities of Magna Graecia* (Cambridge, 1807), pp. 59; vi.
[61] Wallace, *Shelley and Greece*, p. 9.
[62] Eustace added the footnote to the second edition of the *Classical Tour* (1814).
[63] Buzard, *The Beaten Track*, p. 111.
[64] Chloe Chard, *Pleasure and Guilt on the Grand Tour: Travel Writing and Imaginative Geography* (Manchester: Manchester University Press, 1999), pp. 133; 134.

spontaneous language what her auditors instinctively feel. Her dramatic function is cosmopolitan; she embodies in her occupation, her international parentage, and her longings for the English Lord Nelvil a link between North and South, ancient and modern, very much in keeping with Eustace's appeal for an European equilibrium formed by Great Britain and a newly-empowered Italian republic. For Eustace, Corinne's 'lofty temper' is also inseparable from the novel's politics, for Staël sets her plot before the French invasion, subtly repudiating (and foreshadowing) the destruction of cosmopolitan ideals under Napoleon, by whose orders Staël lived in exile during the years in which *Corinne* was written.

Such were the attractions that may have recommended Eustace to the Shelleys in August 1818. The *Classical Tour* held the pre-eminent reputation of contemporary travel accounts on Italy; it was underpinned by writings that were or would become important for Shelley; it intervened in the debate over the cultural and aesthetic applicability of the Greek Revival to contemporary Europe; and it attempted to empower the modern traveller and travellee as joint participants in developing Europe and its political future. Nevertheless, the Shelleys' overt responses to Eustace are almost entirely negative, often tinged with satire. Mary Shelley struck first in a letter to Maria Gisborne of 17 August, within a fortnight of Shelley's consultation:

> We have been reading Eustace's tour through Italy—I do not wonder the Italians reprinted it—among other select specimens of his way of thin[king] he says that the Romans did not derive their arts and learning from the Greeks—That the Italian ladies are chaste and the Lazzeeroni honest and industrious—And that as to assassination and highway robbery in Italy it is all a calumny—no such things were ever heard of—Italy was the garden of Eden and all the Italians Adams and Eves untill [sic] the Blasts of Hell (i.e. the French for by that polite name he designates them) came. (*MWSL*, 1: 78)

Mary Shelley's first 'select specimen', as I have suggested above, appears to be an almost wilful misreading of Eustace's subtler attitude towards the origins and propagation of the arts and sciences. Similarly, the other 'specimens' distort through one-sidedness the comparative methodology Eustace employs in his defence of modern Italians from the calumnies 'sung by poets, repeated by novelists, and copied . . . by ephemeral tourists' (*CT*, 4: 333). Italian women are no less chaste than women in other countries, he argues, particularly among 'the middling classes and the peasantry, the strength and the pride of a nation' (*CT*, 4: 321). The much maligned Lazzaroni of Naples, he asserts, lack the means not the disposition to work, while as a class they are known for their 'warm attachment to the cause of liberty' (*CT*, 3: 128). Acts of spontaneous violence Eustace attributes to the exigencies of climate and poor government, but argues that 'deliberate assassination is very uncommon' in Italy when compared with France or England (*CT*, 4: 331). Though Mary Shelley was on more solid ground when contrasting Eustace's warmth for the modern Italian and his fervent horror of the French, her

Miltonic conclusion overstates Eustace's position on Italy's cultural achievement and ripeness for nationhood before the 1797 French invasion.[65]

Shelley's first comment on Eustace was equally damning, though no less partial. At Bologna, his near total absorption in painting and Eustace's almost total neglect of it perhaps account for Shelley's snubbing reference in his journal letter to Peacock: 'Consult Eustace if you want to know nothing about Italy' (*L*, 2: 54).[66] While Shelley devoted his powers to describing the wonders of Guido and Raphael, Eustace peremptorily dismisses painting with a list of 'first masters', singling out Albano for colours and figures, but describing no individual paintings. Shelley pointedly lists Domenichino and Albano as those he 'cannot admire' – 'remember I dont pretend to taste' (*L*, 2: 52) – positioning Eustace oppositionally. Yet Shelley does agree with Eustace on general architectural features, and at times approximates Eustace's diction: both regard the Cathedral as worthy of notice only for 'a kind of shrine', which Eustace describes as an 'altar' (*L*, 2: 49; *CT*, 1: 259); both single out the Church of the Madonna for praise, particularly its view of the plains, mountains, and city (*L*, 2: 53; *CT*, 1: 261); and both disparage the two

---

[65] The phrase, '*blasts from hell*', appears in Eustace's account of Florence and the vale of Arno ('Happy will it be for the inhabitants, if its charms can resist the *blasts from hell*, which have passed the Alps and the Apennines, and now brood in tempests over the *Val d'Arno*') (*CT*, 3: 342). Mary Shelley's reference to Eden in this context parallels a review of the *Classical Tour* from *The British Review* in which the phrase is applied to French attacks on the Abbey of nearby Vallambrosa, 'the supposed original of Milton's description of Eden', subsequent to Eustace's visit (see no. 10, February 1814, p. 383). Lady Morgan recalls this article when facetiously observing that the Abbey had been restored 'to the delight of all picturesque and pious travellers, and to the consolation and triumph of that High Church publication – "*My Grandmother's Review – the British*"' (Sidney Owenson, Lady Morgan, *Italy*, 2 vols, London, Henry Colburn and Co., 1821, 2: 146). In a note to her quotation from Byron's notorious satire on the journal, Lady Morgan cites the review article and the phrase, attributing it to the reviewer rather than to Eustace. However, there is no evidence that Mary Shelley had read *The British Review* account of Eustace, and she may well have been responding to the obvious Miltonic resonance of the phrase in question.

[66] Frederic S. Colwell describes Eustace's account of Bologna as 'irritatingly sketchy, characteristically pietistic, and by Shelley's time . . . largely obsolete following the scattering and rearrangement of the Bolognese collections during and after the Napoleonic occupation' ('Shelley and Italian Painting', *Keats-Shelley Journal*, 29 (1980), pp. 49-50). In his notes to *Childe Harold* IV, Hobhouse considers Eustace 'entirely out of date' for another reason. He argues that Eustace's lament over the fall of papal government fails to account for the presence of a republican undercurrent in Bolognese society. While 'the tourist pours forth such strains of condolence and revenge, made louder by the borrowed trumpet of Mr. Burke . . . Bologna is at this moment . . . notorious amongst the states of Italy for its attachment to revolutionary principles . . . .' (*Byron PW*, 2: 263). Eustace begins his account of the city by quoting Burke's 'Third Letter on a Regicide Peace' (1797), which refers to Bologna as a 'free, fertile, and happy city' incorporated into a 'Jacobin ferocious Republick' (i.e. into the Cispadane Republic in October 1796). However, Eustace does address Bolognese republicanism, arguing that despite the city's submission to papal authority in the thirteenth century, it had always retained 'the essential forms of a republic' (*CT*, 1: 258) until the French replaced them with the mere name.

leaning towers, *Degli Asinelli* and *Dei Garisendi* – 'high ug{ly} things' to Shelley, 'deformed monuments of a barbarous age' to Eustace (*L*, 2: 53; *CT* 1: 262). And Shelley continued to consult Eustace at Rimini, on the banks of the Metaurus, at Spoleto, Terni, Rome, and Naples.[67] As late as 23 March 1819, during his second visit to Rome, Eustace looms up when Shelley expresses his fear of 'stumbling upon their [the tourists'] language' (*L*, 2: 85). Again, it is the language of Eustace that Shelley principally comes up against,[68] as when he describes Mount Palatine 'covered with shapeless masses of ruin' (*L*, 2: 85), echoing Eustace's 'mere heaps of ruins, so shapeless and scattered' (*CT*, 1: 378).

But for such echoes, Shelley offers what would seem his definitive rejection of Eustace and popular travel writing in the 23 March letter. Shelley's phrase, 'stumbling on their language', alludes to the stanzas in *Childe Harold* IV where Byron refers to Rome as 'the desert, where we steer / Stumbling o'er recollections' that deceive the antiquarian and tourist: 'now we clap / Our hands, and cry "Eureka!" it is clear – / When but some false mirage of ruin rises near' (*Byron PW*, 2: 151, st. 81, ll. 726-9). Later in the letter, Shelley makes explicit Byron's more subtle repudiation of the competitive efforts of travel writers to arrive at the historical and aesthetic 'truth' of Roman sights, without concurring with Byron's equally pessimistic pronouncement, 'we but *feel* our way to err' (st. 81, l. 723; my italics):

> I have said what I feel without entering into any critical discussions of the ruins of Rome, & the mere outside of this inexhaustible mine of thought & feeling.—Hobhouse, Eustace, & Forsyth will tell all the shew-knowledge about it—'the common stuff of the earth'—[.] (*L*, 2: 89)

Keith Crook suggests that 'Eustace was, for Shelley, fit only for pointing out what objects were to be seen ("shew-knowledge")'.[69] The reference, however, is more complex. First, Shelley again frames his remarks using a suppressed quotation from *Childe Harold* IV, where Byron depicts a moonlight view of the Coliseum: 'This long-explored but still *exhaustless mine / Of contemplation*' (st. 128, ll. 1150-51; my italics). In Byron's poem, 'lunar light' (st. 80, l. 719) transforms and idealises appearances, rendering the Coliseum a reflex of the contemplating

---

[67] It is likely that on the basis of Eustace's praise for the bridge at Rimini ('the best style of Roman architecture') (*CT*, 1: 279-80) that Shelley writes Peacock: 'Of course you have heard that there are a Roman Bridge & a Triumphal Arch at Rimini, & in what excellent taste they are built' (*L*, 2: 55). More decisively, Shelley's comments on Asdrubal's defeat on the banks of the Metaurus repeat what he had read in Eustace: 'it is said—you can refer to the book—that Livy has given a very exact & animated description of it. I forget all about it, but shall look as soon as our boxes are opened' (*L*, 2: 55). Cf. *CT*, 1: 287-8.

[68] 'The tourists tell you all about these things, & I am afraid of stumbling upon their language when I enumerate what is so well known' (*L*, 2: 85).

[69] 'Introduction', *Remarks on Antiquities, Arts, and Letters during an Excursion in Italy, in the Years 1802 and 1803 by Joseph Forsyth, Esq.*, ed. Keith Crook (Newark: University of Delaware Press, 2001), p. xvii.

subject: the ruined amphitheatre of cruel and murderous games, like corrupt and mortal man, is transformed by time and perspective into a symbol of unattainable perfection: 'There is given / Unto the things of earth, which time hath bent, / A spirit's feeling' (st. 129, ll. 1155-7). Shelley deploys this notion of temporal subjectivity and aesthetic vision to distinguish his and Byron's poetic tourism from the principal travel writers of the day, which, significantly, include Byron's own travelling companion and collaborator, John Cam Hobhouse. Yet Shelley's allusion to Byron also contains a rebuke; Shelley's refusal to enter 'critical discussions' departs from Byron's own sanctioning, insofar as Byron had allowed Hobhouse's commentaries to become inseparable from *Childe Harold* (Byron not only dedicated Canto IV to Hobhouse, but also subsumed his own few notes to those written by his companion).[70] Aligning Hobhouse with Eustace and Forsyth helps Shelley separate what he perceives as the impurities of popular tourism from Byron's (and his own) true achievement: popular tourism deals with surfaces, poetic tourism with the deep truth of things.

Second, Shelley's linking of Hobhouse, Eustace, and Forsyth gestures towards the politicisation of classical tourism that largely resulted from Hobhouse's attack on Eustace and praise of Forsyth in the concluding note to *Childe Harold* IV. As Crook has shown, Eustace's *Classical Tour* and Forsyth's *Remarks on Italy* were at first reviewed in a non-partisan spirit.[71] Despite its anti-Gallic bias, Eustace's book was highly esteemed by the Whig *Edinburgh Review*, but treated severely by the Tory *Quarterly Review*, which found Eustace's jingoism indiscriminate and inconsistent.[72] The High Church *British Critic*, meanwhile, was sympathetic to Eustace's advocacy of a unified Italy and to his latitudinarian religious tenets. It weighed in with a meticulous but overall favourable critique of the *Classical Tour*.[73] Both the *Edinburgh Review* and the *British Critic* reviewed Forsyth's *Remarks*. Both were more enthusiastic if less thorough in their evaluations.[74]

The publication of Byron's *Childe Harold* IV with its copious notes, and Hobhouse's *Historical Illustrations*, changed all this. In his references to Forsyth, Hobhouse offers unstinting praise, but reserves for Eustace an extended and blistering critique:

> The unction of the divine, and the exhortations of the moralist, may have made this work something more and better than a book of travels, but they have not made it a book of travels; and this observation applies more especially to that enticing method of

---

[70] See *Byron PW*, 2: 122: '. . . for the whole of the notes, excepting a few of the shortest, I am indebted to yourself'.

[71] Crook, 'Introduction', *Remarks on Antiquities*, pp. xxi-xxix. I am indebted to Crook's summary of the periodical reviews throughout this section, although I sometimes arrive at different conclusions from the evidence he presents.

[72] See *Edinburgh Review*, 21 (July 1813), pp. 378-424; *Quarterly Review*, 10 (Oct. 1813), pp. 222-50.

[73] See *British Critic*, 1 (Mar. 1814), pp. 246-63; continued (Apr. 1814), pp. 386-401.

[74] See *Edinburgh Review*, 22 (Jan. 1814), 376-85; *British Critic*, n.s., 7 (Jan. 1817), pp. 32-48.

instruction conveyed by the perpetual introduction of the same Gallic Helot to reel and bluster before the rising generation, and terrify it into decency by the display of all the excesses of the revolution. . . . [W]ho would choose to have the antipathies of any man, however just, for his travelling companions? A tourist, unless he aspires to the credit of prophecy, is not answerable for the changes which may take place in the country which he describes; but his reader may very fairly esteem all his political portraits and deductions as so much waste paper, the moment they cease to assist, and more particularly if they obstruct, his actual survey.

(Note to *Childe Harold* IV, *Byron PW*, 2: 262-3)

Hobhouse repeats the usual saws that travel writing should be accurate and instructive, assisting rather than obstructing the tourist's view of the foreign. The travel book's pedagogic function, he suggests, must not be occluded by ideological contestation. Yet his critique of superadded 'political portraits' is decidedly disingenuous, for Hobhouse interpolates his own republican ideological position into his notes.[75] What he calls Eustace's attempt to terrify 'the rising generation . . . into decency' becomes another example of what Byron identifies in the poem as a post-Napoleonic reactionary backlash; attempting to reassert pre-revolutionary values, the Congress of Vienna ultra-Royalists bequeath 'their hereditary rage / To the new race of inborn slaves' (st. 94, ll. 841-2). Elsewhere in the notes, Hobhouse draws a parallel with the resurgence of Papal government, what he calls the Jesuits 're-established in Italy . . . employed once more in moulding the minds of the rising generation, so as to receive the impressions of despotism' (*Byron PW*, 2: 238). In claiming that 'Mr. Eustace's Antigallican philippics [are] entirely out of date' (*Byron PW*, 2: 263), Hobhouse attempts to dislodge the *Classical Tour* from its pre-eminence by restoring it to a politicised context, less attractive to youthful liberals. Ironically, Hobhouse's call for non-political travel writing appears intended to remind reviewers of their polemical duties: 'If the conspiring voice of otherwise rival critics had not given considerable currency to the *Classical Tour*', Hobhouse notes, 'it would have been unnecessary to warn the reader' (*Byron PW*, 2: 263).

Hobhouse's ploy was only partly successful. His reputation as a reform politician – he ran for parliament as a Radical in February 1819 – ensured that his *Historical Illustrations* and notes to *Childe Harold* were roundly condemned in the Tory press, even when the safely exiled Byron received more generous treatment. In its May 1818 review of *Historical Illustrations*, *The British Critic* even reversed its favourable judgement of Forsyth and then ran a 'panegyric' on Eustace in September 1819, winnowing out the criticisms it had included in its first review of the *Classical Tour*.[76] On the radical side, Lady Morgan's travel book, *Italy* (1821), included a series of satirical comments on Eustace and voiced her support for

---

[75] See McGann's commentary, *Byron PW*, 2: 317-18.
[76] See *British Critic*, (May 1818); (Sep. 1819).

Hobhouse.[77] Other travellers of less determined politics transformed partisan sniping at Eustace into something of a vogue. Henry Matthews allows Eustace 'charm' but questions his 'accuracy': 'one is sometimes led to doubt, whether he really ever saw the places he describes'.[78] W. J. Monson cites an Italian archbishop for evidence that Eustace was 'an elegant enthusiast', over-colouring his prose.[79] Anna Jameson's persona in *Diary of an Ennuyée* (1826) throws down the *Classical Tour* 'with indignation, deeming all his verbiage the merest nonsense'.[80] Yet it is easy to overestimate the impact of Hobhouse's contrast between Eustace and Forsyth. Significant reviews carried defences of Eustace that refused to acknowledge a Eustace-Forsyth ideological split. The *Monthly Review* described Forsyth 'as a very agreeable and very fit accompaniment to the more extended tomes of Mr. Eustace'.[81] The *London Magazine* published a 'Vindication of Eustace' in May 1820, which refuted Hobhouse's charges in detail but which found no reason to mention Forsyth.[82] Even the extremely partisan 'Preface' to the sixth edition of the *Classical Tour* contains a detailed refutation of Hobhouse with only the barest references to Forsyth.[83]

Shelley's grouping of Hobhouse, Eustace, and Forsyth as equal purveyors of 'shew-knowledge' and 'common stuff' shows that Shelley refused to be drawn into similar polemics by Hobhouse's categories.[84] The three travel writers are reduced to one error: a shallow, one-dimensional aesthetic vision that abstracts the traveller

---

[77] Morgan adjudges 'HOBHOUSE'S ILLUSTRATIONS, one of the very few books on Italy distinguished by truth and originality' (*Italy*, 1: 249 n.). By contrast, the *Classical Tour* is a 'false, flimsy, and pompous work' demonstrating Eustace's 'utter ignorance of Italy' or 'his premeditated perversion of facts' (1: 57 n.). For an account of Morgan's running commentary on Eustace, see J. H. Whitfield, 'Mr. Eustace and Lady Morgan', in *Italian Studies Presented to E. R. Vincent on His Retirement from the Chair of Italian at Cambridge*, ed. C. P. Brand, K. Foster, and U. Limentani (Cambridge: W. Heffer and Sons, 1962), pp. 166-89.
[78] Henry Matthews, *The Diary of an Invalid Being the Journal of a Tour in Pursuit of Health in Portugal Italy Switzerland and France in the Years 1817 1818 and 1818*. 2nd edn (London: John Murray, 1820), p. 67.
[79] W. J. Monson, *Extracts from a Journal* (London: Rodwell and Martin, 1820), p. 87.
[80] Anna Jameson, *Diary of an Ennuyée*, new edn (London: Henry Colburn, 1826), p. 136.
[81] *The Monthly Review*, 89 (May 1819), p. 24; quoted in Crook, 'Introduction', *Remarks on Antiquities*, p. xxix.
[82] In several notes, the editor (John Scott) checks the anonymous correspondent's ardour in defence of Eustace: 'Mr. Hobhouse's remarks on Eustace seem to us frivolous, captious, and badly-motivated: but we are no sticklers for the accuracy of Eustace, or the utility of his work as a guide to Italy' (p. 533).
[83] Crook notes that the preface names 'Forsyth for errors and indirectly sneer[s] at him under the sobriquet of "another journalist"' ('Introduction', *Remarks on Antiquities*, p. xxi). While this is true, I would like to emphasise that the author does not take up Hobhouse's polemical use of Forsyth in any direct manner.
[84] 'Of Hobhouse I have a very slight opinion' (*L*, 2: 75), Shelley wrote to Peacock late in January 1819, referring primarily to Hobhouse's decision to contest the seat at Westminster vacated the previous year. Hobhouse ran as a Radical and was supported by Sir Francis Burdett.

from the scenes in which she or he travels. In addition, Shelley saw his own judgement as provisional until he had read more for himself, concluding with 'by the bye Forsyth is worth reading, as I judge {from a} chapter or two I have seen' (*L*, 2: 89).[85] Having dismissed on aesthetic grounds Hobhouse's attempt at fomenting controversy, Shelley returns to cultural criticism from a firmer vantage, less assailable by charges of political opportunism. Nevertheless, Eustace remained the most important travel writer of the triumvirate, even as Byron became the one with whom Shelley most closely identified as a counter to popular and populist 'shew-knowledge'. From August 1818 to March 1819, Shelley read Eustace oppositionally, reacting to his aesthetics and politics with frustration, but acknowledging in his exasperation and with his private debts that Eustace helped define the conversation on Italy with which modern travellers and cultural commentators were to be evaluated. Travelling, as it were, with his Byron in one hand and his Eustace in the other, Shelley observed and described Italian landscape, art, and culture, always conscious of his own interventions in the mapping of modern perceptions in an age of political and social transformation.

'The Lamp of learning': Aesthetic Vision and History in *Lines Written among the Euganean Hills*

Shelley's subtle evaluation of Byron, Hobhouse, and Eustace may be contrasted with Lady Morgan's remarks in *Italy*, where potential discrepancies between Byron and Hobhouse are glossed over in her critique of Eustace: '. . . the true character of [the *Classical Tour*] . . . is to be found in the 4th canto of Childe Harold, and Lord Byron's long residence in Italy, and his intimate knowledge of the country, leave his testimony, on this occasion, beyond appeal'.[86] For polemical reasons, Morgan allows Hobhouse to speak for and through Byron, a ventriloquism that Hobhouse later emphasised when claiming to have supplied guidance in the composition of the poem as well as notes to its contents.[87] Yet there is some evidence to suggest that Byron did not entirely share Hobhouse's opposition to Eustace. Bruce Redford argues that as a tourist Byron was much more willing to allow guidebooks their due without suborning them to political purposes; as Byron writes to Moore, 'Of Rome I say nothing; it is quite indescribable, and the Guidebook is as good as any other' (*Byron LJ*, 5: 227).[88] The 'Guidebook', as Redford asserts, was quite possibly Eustace's *Classical Tour*,[89] for which Byron

---

[85] I am indebted to Keith Crook for helping me rephrase this so as not to downplay the increasing regard in which Shelley and Mary Shelley held Forsyth's *Remarks*.
[86] Morgan, *Italy*, 1: 57 n.
[87] See Andrew Rutherford, 'The Influence of Hobhouse on *Childe Harold's Pilgrimage*, Canto IV', *Review of English Studies*, n.s., 12 (1961), p. 392. Rutherford argues that Hobhouse overestimated his contribution.
[88] See Redford, *Venice & the Grand Tour*, pp. 115-17.
[89] Redford suggests that Canto IV contains 'silent borrowings' from Eustace's *Classical Tour* (*Venice*, pp. 118 and 132, n. 26). However, Crook argues more convincingly that

took an interest in advance of its publication, perhaps reading a manuscript or proof copy in late May 1813.[90] Byron's Cambridge connections, including Eustace's patron Edward Daniel Clarke, would also have made the *Classical Tour* a likely travelling companion.[91]

There is no record of Shelley having discussed Eustace with Byron during the period of their renewed intimacy at Venice between 23 August and 31 October 1818. Yet readings of *Childe Harold* IV and the *Classical Tour* coincide at two principal junctures. The first is circumstantial. Mary Shelley remarked to Maria Gisborne that 'We have been reading Eustace's tour through Italy' on 17 August, the day Shelley left for Venice. The day he arrived, 23 August, Shelley notes that he and Byron discussed the 'fourth Canto which he says is very good, & indeed repeated some stanzas of great energy to me' (*L*, 2: 37). The second occurs after several worrisome weeks in which the Shelleys, installed at the villa in Este loaned to them by Byron, struggled with the grave illness and death of their youngest child, Clara. On the day Clara was buried on the Lido in Venice, 25 September, Shelley read Canto IV again with Byron. In the next few days, Mary Shelley read it too, and both Shelleys undertook a sightseeing tour of Venice, a desperate anodyne for their loss. Within a week of returning to Este on the 29th, Shelley began composing a retrospective poem on these experiences, *Lines Written among the Euganean Hills*. With its dense, allusive texture, the poem brings the *Classical Tour* and *Childe Harold* IV together for the first time in Shelley's writings. Yet unlike Mary Shelley's caustic paraphrase of 17 August, Shelley's poetic analysis of the *Classical Tour* engages seriously with Eustace's historiographical musings, often sympathetically, and weighs them against Byron's personalised account of Italy's past and present. Attracted and repulsed by Byron's historical-autobiographical meditation on the universality of human suffering and the waste of art, Shelley turns to Eustace for alternative models, synthesising through a Byron-Eustace dialectic his own cross-cultural understanding of the relation between the modern British sightseer and sights seen, the alienated subject and the outward signs of social, political, and intellectual mutability.

The 'great energy' of *Childe Harold* IV perhaps surprised Shelley, for Peacock's preliminary report had been disappointing. Canto IV was published in April 1818, while Shelley was preparing to leave Milan for the journey to Leghorn. On 30 May, Peacock wrote that the new canto was 'really too bad' and declared his

---

Byron actually refers to Forsyth's *Remarks* (p. xiv). To be fair, Byron never names the guidebook and his non-committal reference to it ('as good as any other') does not quite match the high estimation in which he held Forsyth's work. Byron's use of the word 'Guidebook' would suggest a more comprehensive travel account than that offered by Forsyth, as when Byron writes in a letter to Thomas Moore of 6 November 1816: 'I have seen the finest parts of Switzerland, the Rhine, the Rhone and the Swiss and Italian Lakes; for the beauties of which I refer you to the Guide-book' (*Byron LJ*, 5: 123-4).
[90] See *Byron LJ*, 3: 51.
[91] Byron and Hobhouse's tour of Greece in 1809-10 coincided with that of Eustace and Petre; all were associated with Cambridge and were likely to have known of each other, though there is no record of their paths ever crossing.

intention to target it in his satiric novel-in-progress, *Nightmare Abbey* (publ. Nov 1818): 'I cannot consent to be *auditor tantum* of this systematical "poisoning" of the "mind" of the "Reading Public"' (*LTLP*, 1: 123).[92] Knowingly, Peacock depicted a radical difference between Shelley and Byron. Making use of Shelley's 22 April travel letter from Milan, in which Shelley writes of the inexcusability of travel in times of domestic crisis and disparages Italians as 'stupid & shrivelled slaves' (*L*, 2: 9), Peacock has his interlocutors discuss the ethics of foreign travel. Scythrop, Shelley's alter ego, argues that Roman ruins are 'indexes to lost volumes of glory' that contrast pointedly with the national character of present inhabitants (*WTLP*, [3]: 102). The histories and accomplishments of the classical world do provide exempla for present political struggle, he concedes, but only in conditions where they are applicable: 'I should have no pleasure in visiting countries that are past all hope of regeneration'. Scythrop therefore urges the Byron figure, Mr Cypress, to devote his genius to his own country, where there is hope for political reform, but Cypress excuses himself with a typical but egotistical flourish: 'Sir, I have quarrelled with my wife; and a man who has quarrelled with his wife is absolved from all duty to his country' (*WTLP*, [3]: 102; 103). Scythrop's argument that the English national character (as opposed to that of the French) warrants hope for reform, provokes Cypress into the first of his dour paraphrases from Canto IV:

> I have no hope for myself or for others. Our life is a false nature; it is not in the harmony of things; it is an all-blasting upas, whose root is earth, and whose leaves are the skies which rain their poison-dews upon mankind. We wither from our youth; we grasp with unslaked thirst for unattainable good; lured from the first to the last by phantoms – love, fame, ambition, avarice – all idle, and all ill – one meteor of many names, that vanishes in the smoke of death. (*WTLP*, [3]: 104)[93]

To Mr Cypress's unmitigated pessimism on human nature and endeavour (expertly condensed by Peacock from stanzas 120-26 in *Childe Harold*), only the ameliorist, Mr Hilary, offers effective opposition. Hilary defends the ancients as inherently cheerful: 'To represent vice and misery as the necessary accompaniments of genius, is as mischievous as it is false, and the feeling is as unclassical as the language in which it is usually expressed'. He chides Cypress for chasing will-o'-the-wisps and railing at humanity when his efforts come to nothing: 'Ideal beauty is not the mind's creation: it is real beauty, refined and purified in the mind's alembic', or again, 'to make ideal beauty the shadow in the water, and, like the dog in the fable, to throw away the substance in catching at the shadow, is scarcely the characteristic of wisdom, whatever it be of genius'. But to such solid homespun truths, Cypress can only repeat his litany of gloom. Unphased by his critics, 'Mr. Cypress ... stepped ... into his ... travelling chariot ... to rake seas and rivers, lakes and canals, for the moon of ideal beauty' (*WTLP*, [3]: 105; 107; 109; 113).

---

[92] On 5 July Peacock included the canto in a parcel shipped to Shelley. Shelley did not receive this parcel until well after his meeting with Byron.

[93] Cypress paraphrases stanzas 124 and 126 of Canto IV.

Peacock's satire condemns Byron for absolving himself from political responsibility, for reading the past in terms of his own present suffering, history in terms of autobiography, and for abstracting idealism from its earthly sources. Even before Shelley read *Nightmare Abbey*, Peacock must have expressed the concerns of Chapter 11 to Shelley in a letter of 1 November, now lost, for Shelley's response seems particularly apt:

> I entirely agree with what you say about Childe Harold. The spirit in which it is written is, if insane, the most wicked & mischievous insanity that ever was given forth. It is a kind of obstinate & selfwilled folly in which he hardens himself. I remonstrated with him in vain on the tone of mind from which such a view of things alone arises. For . . . nothing can be less sublime than the true source of these expressions of contempt & desperation. . . . He is not yet an Italian & is heartily & deeply discontented with himself, & contemplating in the distorted mirror of his own thoughts, the nature & the destiny of man, what can he behold but objects of contempt & despair? (*L*, 2: 57-8)

Like Scythrop and so many other English tourists, Shelley indicates his contempt for the unregenerate modern Italian, and his horror that Byron has 'gone native'. Shelley priggishly charges Byron with adulterating his genius by consorting with common Italians. For Peacock and Shelley, Byron's aesthetic judgement – 'Of its own beauty is the mind diseased, / And fevers into false creation' (st. 122, l. 1090) – expresses this pathology, not the human condition. By contrast, Shelley's representations of nature and art on his Italian tour become part of his exploration of the ways in which cultural acts of seeing might be conduits of self-knowledge and self-improvement. His emotional state as he composed *Euganean Hills* may have made Byronic despair a tempting alternative, yet Shelley also had the classical tourist's example before him. As Eustace writes, thinking of Petrarch, 'Genius communicates its own dignity to every subject that it chooses to handle' (*CT*, 1: 196). Such sentiments apply to classical tourism more generally, for landscapes and the remains of sculpture or architecture rarely speak for themselves as ruins, but are always represented through classical literature and become imbued with its associations. Observation, in the *Classical Tour*, is the art of recovery hallowed by genius, rarely an elegy for irrevocable loss.

Euganean Hills explores the means by which tourists are attracted to objects, and the powers that tourist attractions exert over observers. This is not to say that Shelley's plangent opening conceit – 'Many a green isle needs must be / In the deep wide sea of misery' (*PS2*, ll. 1-2) – does not gesture towards the poem's more specific personal origins, but that the poem refuses to indulge itself with its opening visions of solitary extinction: the lone mariner's erasure by the 'unreposing wave' (l. 25) or the 'wretch' whose 'white skull and seven dry bones' inspires 'no lament' (ll. 45-65). Instead, Shelley turns from voyage to tour, from a landscape of privation to one rich in historical and literary associations, well known to tourists, and placed before the 'Reading Public' by Eustace's *Classical Tour* and Byron's *Childe Harold* IV. *Euganean Hills* transmutes the green isles that attract the mariner into various forms – the 'solitary hill' (l. 89) on which the speaker stands, Venice with its 'marble shrines' (l. 112), and 'many-domèd Padua' (l. 215) – and each becomes a monument where death and ruin give place meaning rather than a place of meaningless death. Meaning, however, is shown to be the poetic observer's hermeneutic privilege; the local inhabitant under Austrian occupation and the superficial tourist alike fail to see 'beyond the present & tangible object' (*L*, 2: 47), either oblivious to monuments of beauty, or failing to regard them as symbols of historical process, partaking of that which they represent. Shelley's ideal tourist is attracted to that which reflects his or her values and desires ('neither the eye nor the mind can see itself, unless reflected upon that which it resembles'; *SPP*, p. 520), so that observation is also always a form of self-identity. The poem's speaker models this way of seeing, an aesthetic vision that gives scope and organisation to the full range of associations available to the British traveller when regarding an attraction, including the palimpsest of writings that reproduce and disseminate the significance of place.

The 'Advertisement' to *Rosalind and Helen . . . with Other Poems*, the volume in which *Euganean Hills* first appeared, remarks that the poem 'was written after a day's excursion among those lovely mountains which surround what was once the retreat, and where is now the sepulchre, of Petrarch' (*PS2*, p. 427). The poem situates Shelley's eye on Monte Venda, the region's highest elevation, a panoramic viewpoint taking in the Alps, the 'olive-sandalled Apennines', Venice, and Padua. Besides Venice, not properly part of the Euganean hills, the region's chief tourist attraction was in fact 'Arqua where Petrarch's house & tomb are religiously preserved & visited' (*L*, 2: 43).[94] Consequently, a visit to Petrarch's villa and tomb dominates Eustace's section on the Euganean hills. Though hardly a classical writer, Petrarch 'engaged universal and unqualified admiration' for surpassing 'every public character' in 'pleasing manners', 'generous feelings', 'warm attachment', 'and in all the graceful, all the attractive accomplishments of life' (*CT*, 1: 193). Eustace locates Petrarch's greatest achievement in his Italian *canzoniere*, which sublimate his passion for his mistress, Laura, into universal ideals of love and beauty. Countering what he calls Gibbon's claim that Laura 'could have possessed few of the charms ascribed to her', Eustace argues that Petrarch delineated a species of beauty based less on the endowments of Laura's youth, than qualities of her 'expression', 'charms which emanate directly from the mind, and seem almost to enjoy some portion of its pure and imperishable nature' (*CT*, 1: 194). In every way, Eustace's Petrarch becomes an idealised inversion of Peacock's or Shelley's Byron – the republican poet, untainted by vulgar living, able to transform affairs of the heart into those of the mind, giving the place of his birth an aura of sacredness that attracts and humbles future literary travellers of all nations.[95] Shelley's strategy in the 'Advertisement' is both to flag up *Euganean*

---

[94] Shelley here echoes Eustace: 'This monument and his villa have been preserved by the people with a religious care, and continue even now to attract a number of literary visitants of all countries, who . . . fail not to pay their respects to the manes of Petrarca' (*CT*, 1: 187).
[95] My use of 'aura' here and below follows Dean MacCannell, who reverses Walter Benjamin's notion of aura as a residual uniqueness: 'The work becomes "authentic" only

Hills as a travel poem, drawing on associations of a well-known region, but also to foreground one of its poets who had literally 'grounded' the aesthetic ideals fostered by the poem itself. Seeing Petrarch's Arqua as a tourist attraction (like Rousseau's Geneva) testifies to the power of poetry to become what Dean Maccannell calls an institution of 'sight sacralization', returning significance to the objects from which it draws its imagery and inspiration.[96]

The 'Advertisement' belongs to a later stage of the poem's textual history, when it included the address to Venice and Byron that Shelley interpolated after December 1818, and which I will return to later. For now, I want to notice how these lines invoke a future Venice as an uninhabited sea-ruin, memorable only for having been the residence in exile of Byron, the 'tempest-cleaving Swan / Of the songs of Albion' (*PS2*, ll. 174-5). Shelley then addresses Byron specifically, flattering him by comparison to Homer, Shakespeare, and the bard of the Euganean Hills himself, Petrarch:

> As the love from Petrarch's urn
> Yet amid yon hills doth burn,
> A quenchless lamp by which the heart
> Sees things unearthly; – so thou art
> Mighty spirit – so shall be
> The City that did refuge thee. (ll. 200-205)

The Petrarch reference not only develops earlier allusions in the poem, but also relies on the touristic associations towards which the 'Advertisement' gestures.[97] Petrarch's achievement gives an aura to the Euganean hills that inspires 'literary visitants' (Eustace describes an act of homage he and his companions perform at Petrarch's tomb, applauded by locals), making the hills another form of Petrarchan text, the tourist another reader, and light a grammar. So shall Venice be to Byron, Shelley concludes, thinking of Byron posthumous reputation as the author of Venetian poems and as Europe's foremost poet. Venice becomes a new kind of text or tourist attraction. Its past faults are effaced by ruin and displaced by Byron's English 'lamp', by which the tourist 'sees'. Hence, poets influence the world by re-colonising places in their own image; the Venice-ruin speaks of a British national poetry's power to transcend and nullify foreign identities and boundaries. Great poets become intertwined with perception by imbuing objects with associations, so the 'heart sees' 'beyond the present & tangible object' by a light that appears to emanate from the object itself. Light is a crucial motif. The poem begins at sunrise, culminates with the dioramic effects of sunlight on the Venetian towers, and subsides as 'noon descends' (l. 320). As with 'the quenchless lamp' of poetry, the poem figures light as an external source that nevertheless represents inner qualities

---

after the first copy of it is produced. The reproductions *are* the aura' (*The Tourist: A New Theory of the Leisure Class*, Berkeley, University of California Press, 1999, p. 48).

[96] MacCannell, *The Tourist*, pp. 43-8.

[97] See Weinberg, *Shelley's Italian Experience*, pp. 28-9, for Shelley's 'adaptation of the Petrarchan conceit' of the '"mariner-ship-port" image cluster'.

of imagination.[98] Light represents equilibrium between the subject and object world that repudiates both Byronic solipsism and the empirical travel writer's quest for accuracy or objectivity.

Shelley's emphasis on how and what 'the heart / Sees' expresses his notions on the manner in which travel discourse frames or sublimates personal experience in social, political, or historical contexts. The poem begins with a tangle of personal allusions that resist decoding.[99] The 'green isle' motif may derive from the Rhine tour in summer 1814. On Mary Shelley's birthday that year, Shelley had noted in their shared journal how the river was 'full of little islands green & beautiful' contrasting with dangerous rapids (*MWSJ*, p. 21). The cryptic 'northern sea' (*PS2*, l. 45) of *Euganean Hills* recalls the 'northern shore' in 'Listen, listen, Mary mine – ', a fragment written during a passage through the Apennines of 4 May 1818, the anniversary of Shelley's first meeting with Mary Godwin. The 'northern sea' has also been associated with 'the Baltic or the Skagerrak, where Mary Wollstonecraft in her despair had often longed to die' (*PS2*, p. 428). On the Rhine tour, the day Shelley wrote of the 'green isles', Claire Clairmont recorded that Shelley began reading aloud Mary Wollstonecraft's *Letters Written during a Short Residence in Sweden, Norway, and Denmark*, a text Shelley refers to in several places in *Euganean Hills*. Clairmont also notes a curiosity, 'We saw a sea-mew & wonder[ed] much how came in a place so m[any] miles from the sea' (*CCJ*, p. 33) – one possible source for the sea-mews whose voices are heard 'o'er the billows of the gale' (*PS2*, l. 54). Taken together, these echoes recall shared experiences that had become the bases for travel writings, including *Alastor* and *History of a Six Weeks' Tour* as well as Wollstonecraft's *Short Residence*. Wollstonecraft's public traveller voice is of particular relevance here, for it not only underwrites much of the Shelleys' travel discourse, but it also reinscribes personal suffering beneath a narrative of cultural consolation. As I have already discussed in Chapter 2, Wollstonecraft's *Short Residence* studies the good that arises from the aesthetic transformation of harsh nature into accommodating dwelling places. *Euganean Hills*, then, is a pivotal poem. It looks back on the Rhine experience and its textual transformations and begins to draw them into relation with Italian tourism and travel writing. In each case, travel writing re-inscribes energies of imagination into narrative; personal history becomes a type of universal history; the self is mythologised as a microcosm of society in its most exalted mood.

Shelley's first meditation on the effacement of natural monuments, the unmarked places of death and loss, marks the thematic and allusive shift towards the poem's more public and political concerns:

> On the beach of a northern sea
> Which tempests shake eternally,
> As once the wretch there lay to sleep,

---

[98] See Donald H. Reiman. 'Structure, Symbol, and Theme in "Lines Written Among the Euganean Hills"', *PMLA*, 77 (1962), pp. 404-13.
[99] The 'Advertisement' suggests that the lines preserved 'at the request of a dear friend' (*PS2*, p. 427), i.e. Mary Shelley.

> Lies a solitary heap,
> One white skull and seven dry bones,
> On the margin of the stones . . . . (ll. 45-50)

As Kelvin Everest and Geoffrey Matthews observe, these mysterious lines have a 'personal as well as universal bearing', on the one hand gesturing towards the Wollstonecraft subtext, and on the other alluding to 'Sophocles's famous Chorus deploring human adversity in *Oedipus at Colonus* (1239-44)' (*PS2*, p. 428). Shelley's complex image clusters here also begin to draw in points of reference from Eustace's *Classical Tour*. The 'sea-mews' (*PS2*, l. 54) heard 'on the margin of the stones' (l. 50) are also found in Eustace, who uses the image to reflect the primitive state of Venice, poised on the knife-edge of history: 'That bold independence which filled a few lonely islands, the abode of sea-mews . . . is bowed into slavery; and the republic of Venice . . . is now an empty name' (*CT*, 1: 144). Shelley's allusion emphasises that the 'boundaries of the sea and land' (*PS2*, l. 52) are also boundaries between nature and history, and that the fate of 'the wretch' who 'lay to sleep' (l. 47) reflects a surrender of autonomy experienced by peoples as well as individuals. In this way, Shelley begins to layer the story of individuals (biography, autobiography) against that of nations (history).[100]

When the poem turns to the sunrise among the 'mountains Euganean' (l. 70)[101] with its rooks reflecting the changing light, the no less symbolic language further emphasises the trans-temporality of vision — what 'the heart sees' is repeated in patterns of history. Here, Shelley recalls Eustace's discussion of the Euganean hills as 'formerly . . . inhabited by a race of soothsayers' (*CT*, 1: 186). Eustace paraphrases Lucan's account of a seer who, 'seated on his native hill', relates a vision of the battle of Pharsalia on the very morning in which it occurred. Pharsalia, the battle in which Caesar's defeat of Pompey spelled the end of the Roman Republic, suggests a type of the civil 'fratricide' that subjugated 'the

---

[100] Reading through Eustace allows other political interpretations of lines that Shelley keeps deliberately unspecific. The 'empty name' of Venice resembles the empty skull on the northern shore. The cryptic 'one white skull and seven dry bones' (*PS2*, l. 49) might refer in part to Eustace's Venice and 'the Seven Ionian Islands . . . of the Venetian dominions, [that still] enjoy a nominal and precarious independence' (*CT*, 1: 178). From Eustace's perspective, Shelley's allegorical 'king' who 'in glory rides / Through the pomp of fratricides' (ll. 58-9) was '*Bonaparte*'. Referring to the French occupation of Venice in 1797, before the treaty of Campo-Formio apportioned the city to Austrian control, Eustace concludes that 'the causes . . . must be sought in the bosom of the republic itself'. He blames the 'nobles' who 'trembled for their Italian estates' for 'betray[ing] their country . . . to plunder, to slavery, and to indelible disgrace' (*CT*, 1: 181-2), despite the willingness of the people to fight. Such 'fratricide' led to the tragic pageant of the Venetians 'transport[ing] the armies of France from the mainland over the *Lagune* into the very heart of the city' (*CT*, 1: 181).

[101] Eustace also calls the hills 'mountains, for so they may justly be termed, if the enormous swell of the neighbouring Alps did not in appearance diminish their elevation' (*CT*, 1: 186).

second fated seat of independence and empire' (*CT*, 1: 164), Venice.[102] Shelley's speaker sees a more diurnal vision: the 'paean' of 'legioned rooks' that accompany the sunrise; the sun's reflection on their plumage; their flight down the hill as the morning vapours dissipate. Yet the language is suggestive. The 'legioned rooks' recall the Roman armies (Pompey 'once boasted that he could raise legions to his assistance by stamping on the ground with his foot'[103]); the rooks' 'plumes of purple grain' (*PS2*, l. 80) which 'gleam above the sunlight woods' (l. 82) before following 'down the dark steep' (l. 87) echo Lucan's description: 'When the doomed Pompeian soldiers descended from their position on the hills and faced the rising sun, the whole landscape shone with the glitter of their weapons'.[104] In Lucan's account, Pompey's legions bring under the Roman standard representatives of many peoples, 'the blood of all mankind', adding momentousness to the demise of the republic; Shelley transforms these into 'silent multitudes' (l. 83) of birds, silent because effaced from historical records. The visionary landscape transforms sunlight into a symbol, sight into what Eustace calls 'second sight', the local into the historical.

Visionary history in *Euganean Hills*, then, links Roman times to modern Venice and beyond to its possible futures. Venice comes into view 'under day's azure eyes' (l. 94), an image invoking Venice as a complex appearance, or object of aesthetic vision, contrasting with the clarity and serenity of the light that illumines it in the speaker's gaze. Shelley invokes Venice in a future anterior tense, described it as both 'Ocean's nursling' (l. 95) and 'Amphitrite's destined halls' (l. 97), originating from and fated to return to the sea. The synecdochical 'column, tower, and dome, and spire' (l. 106) represent the city in fragmented features that might also characterise a ruin, and its resemblance to 'obelisks of fire' further emphasise its quality as a monument-memorial. Fugue-like, the language recycles image patterns from the preceding Lucanic passage, as the vatic tourist envisions Venice, like the rooks, giving way to historical process. In the next section, Shelley reifies these ideas in an image of Venice as sea-ruin, almost effaced, 'save where many a palace gate / With green sea-flowers overgrown / . . . / Topples o'er the

---

[102] Book I of Lucan's *Pharsalia* opens with an echo of Shelley's lines, rendered thus in Robert Graves's translation: 'the whole struggle was indeed no better than one of licensed fratricide' (Lucan, *Pharsalia*, trans. Robert Graves, Harmondsworth, Penguin, 1956, p. 25); Caesar is thus another candidate for the King who rides in pomp and glory (ll. 58-9).

[103] *Lemprière's Classical Dictionary of Proper Names Mentioned in Ancient Authors Writ Large, with a Chronological Table*, 3rd edn (London: Routledge & Kegan Paul, 1984), p. 510, col. 2.

[104] Lucan, *Pharsalia*, VII. 207-38. Shelley read Lucan on 16 August (*MWSJ*, p. 223), the day before his departure for Venice. Weinberg observes that 'Lucan is remembered for his passionate defence of the Republican cause in the *Pharsalia*' (p. 296) and that Lucan VI, 496-9 and 744-8 are also sources for Demogorgon in *Prometheus Unbound*. See also Shelley's echoes of Lucan in his 'Ode to Naples', ll. 44-6, 'sunbright vapour, like the standard / Of some aetherial host'. For Shelley's earliest direct reference to Lucan's poem, see his letter to T. J. Hogg, August 1815 (*L*, 1: 429). E. B. Murray also notes a possible reference to *Pharsalia* in Shelley's fragmentary romance, *The Assassins* (1814-15) (*The Prose Works of Percy Bysshe Shelley*, Oxford, Clarendon Press, 1993, I, 388).

abandoned sea' (ll. 129-30). The ruin's appearance remains deceptive for some, as when the Italian 'fisher' looks upon it with superstitious dread. Yet Shelley is as much interested in the 'reading' of Venice by the modern tourist, the ways in which the poem's staged acts of observation resemble or differ from the superficial tourist's experience. 'Those who alone thy towers behold', Shelley writes in what I take as the poem's central passage,

> Quivering through aërial gold,
> As I now behold them here,
> Would imagine not they were
> Sepulchres . . . (ll. 142-6)

Historical vision, Shelley suggests, the eye gifted with seeing beyond the temporal 'present' as well as the 'tangible object', can regard the beauties of architecture as symbols rather than naive images.

Despite such claims for visionary exclusivity, Shelley closely follows Eustace's popular representations of Venice. Anticipating Shelley's layering of ancient and modern history, Eustace discusses Venice as embodying more than 'any city in Italy' 'the spirit of the ancient Romans' (*CT*, 1: 161). Founded as a Roman colony in 421, he argues, Venice assumed 'a striking resemblance to the great parent Republic' ennobled by 'the same spirit of liberty' (*CT*, 1: 162). In the well-worn tradition of the Grand Tourists, Eustace goes on to indicate the path by which liberty degenerates into licentiousness.[105] Threatened by the Doge's bid for absolute sovereignty, the 'aristocratic party' at first usurps power from the people. Over time, the nobility becomes complacent through commercial and military success, considering 'pleasure . . . the only object of pursuit', while republican pageantry satisfies 'the Venetian commonalty': 'This once proud and potent republic, like some of the degenerate Emperors of Rome, seemed to prefer the glories of the theatre to those of the field, and willingly rested its modern claim to consideration, on the pre-eminent exhibitions of its well-known carnival' (*CT*, 1: 180). For eighteenth-century tourists, the highlight and sum of this composite myth of Venetian glory and decadence was the ceremony in which the city was wed to the sea, the 'Sposalizio al Mar', which began the Feast of the Ascension.[106] For Eustace, and Byron for that matter, the French destruction of the Bucentaur, the ornate galley of state at the centre of these ceremonies, becomes a symbol of Venice's terminal decline under the occupation of successive northern powers, first France and then Austria.[107]

Shelley focuses more specifically on the semiotics of Venice in decline and he refuses to particularise tourist attractions; rather than reviewing sights like St Mark's or the Doge's Palace, he instead treats Venice as a first impression, a 'sungirt City' (*PS2*, l. 115), on which the effects of light play and suggest shadowy

---

[105] See Redford, *Venice*, p. 57.
[106] Redford, *Venice*, p. 58.
[107] Byron's *Childe Harold* IV begins with a vision of Venice in the past tense: 'She looks a sea Cybele, fresh from ocean, / . . . / And such she was' (*Byron PW*, 2: 125, st. 2, ll. 10-14).

'Relics of Antiquity': Shelley's Classical Tour through Italy 151

counter-meanings. He again takes his cue from Eustace, who subordinates his treatment of Venetian landmarks to historical and political sketches of the past and present:

> But, why enlarge on the beauty, on the magnificence, on the glories of Venice? or, why describe its palaces, its churches, its monuments? That Liberty which raised these pompous edifices in a swampy marsh, and opened such scenes of grandeur in the middle of a pool, is now no more! That bold independence which filled a few lonely islands, the abode of sea-mews and cormorants, with population and with commerce, is bowed to slavery; and the republic of Venice, with all its bright series of triumphs, is now an empty name. The City, with its walls and towers, and streets, still remains; but the spirit that animated the mass is fled. *Jacet ingens littore truncus.* (*CT*, 1: 177-8)

I have already suggested the importance of this passage for Shelley's layering of personal and political imagery in the earlier part of *Euganean Hills*. After line 115, the echoes are even more prominent. Shelley's 'power that raised thee here' (*PS2*, l. 119), Eustace names as 'Liberty'. The 'drear ruin . . . now' (l. 121) draws on Eustace's 'now an empty name'; 'conquest-branded brow' (l. 122) inverts 'bold independence'. Shelley's Venice is 'stooping to the slave of slaves' (l. 123), Eustace's 'is bowed to slavery'; the 'sea-mew' (l. 125) reappears in an appropriate place. Even Shelley's image of 'thine isles depopulate' (l. 127) with its ruined 'palace gate' (l. 129) and its superstitious 'fisher' (l. 134) glosses Eustace's conclusion: 'the population of Venice . . . will diminish, till . . . this city shall become a superb solitude, whose lonely grandeur will remind the traveller, that Venice was once great, and independent' (*CT*, 1: 182-3).

Shelley's 'fisher on his watery way' (l. 134), introduced in lieu of Eustace's 'traveller', indicates a disagreement in emphasis. Shelley's future Venetian is unregenerate, superstitious, unable to read the moral of ruins or be changed by them (for ruined palaces, like Ozymandias's bust in the desert, can subvert the powers that put them there). Shelley presents modern Venetians in the poem with even less sympathy. They first appear as monstrous offspring when he describes Venice as 'a peopled labyrinth of walls' (l. 95), an allusion to the famous labyrinth built to house the Minotaur.[108] In the lines following the 'fisher', the people are merely 'human forms, / Like pollution-nourished worms' that 'to the corpse of greatness cling (ll. 146-8). Writing to Peacock on 8 October, Shelley follows Eustace in tracing the origins of this corruption from the time when 'oligarchy usurped the rights of the people' and, most recently to 'the French, and especially the Austrian yoke' (*L*, 2: 43). But unlike Eustace, Shelley pours scorn on the moral state of the modern inhabitants under these conditions: 'I had no conception of the excess to which avarice, cowardice, superstition, ignorance, passionless lust, & all the inexpressible brutalities which degrade human nature could be carried, until I had lived a few days among the Venetians' (*L*, 2: 43). His judgement that Venice is

---

[108] In Greek myth, Minos builds the labyrinth to hide the Minotaur, the offspring produced from the unnatural union of Queen Pasiphae and a bull.

no longer 'worth our regret as a nation' is reinforced by his stern command to Venice and her 'sister band' in the poem: 'If [Freedom should] not [awake], perish thou and they, – Clouds which stain truth's rising day' (ll. 160-61).

Eustace resists generalising on the state of the Italian people, let alone the Venetians. His harshest judgements – e.g. 'luxury corrupted every mind, and unbraced every sinew' (*CT*, 1: 179) – apply to the Venetian nobility, whom he holds responsible for corrupting civic responsibility and practicing the politics of appeasement. Yet he devotes a sizeable 'Dissertation' in the last volume of the *Classical Tour* for the purpose of defending the modern Italian from the aspersions of English travellers and ascertaining the likely future of Italy as a modern European state. Rather than interring the 'corpse of greatness' (*PS2*, l. 148) *pace* Shelley, Eustace discovers 'all the materials of greatness' (*CT*, 4: 148) ready for use should Italy reassume her place in the family of nations. Though Eustace does entertain the notion that the Italians might be 'doomed still to bear the foreign yoke' (*CT*, 4: 337), he reconciles himself to it by asserting that Italy will always assume 'the milder but more useful sovereignty of the intellectual world' as 'parent of all the sciences that enlighten, or all the arts that embellish human life' (*CT*, 4: 338-9).[109] If, on the other hand, Italy succeeds in asserting its independence, Eustace believes that 'Europe might confidently expect to see the spirit and the glory of Rome again revive' (*CT*, 4: 337-8). Shelley was thinking of Eustace's dissertation when posing the condition that, 'if Freedom should awake', Venice and the city republics 'might adorn this sunny land, / Twining memories of old time / With new virtues' (*PS2*, ll. 150-59), and when considering the idea of a federated Italy.[110] But Shelley expresses little of Eustace's confidence in the Italian people, their prospects, or their legacy. His command, 'If not, perish . . . Earth can spare ye' (ll. 160-63), shifts emphasis from what the Italians might offer the world towards a more cosmopolitan formulation. Venice is expendable; 'Liberty' may even '*Hallow* . . . [its] watery bier' (l. 120; my italics). In a philosophical view of reform, Venice might even be more significant as a ruin than as the abode of a regenerated people.[111]

At the moment of envisioning Venice's extinction, Shelley first turns to *Childe Harold*. In stanzas 96-8, Byron addresses the post-Waterloo reformer's question of how freedom can be reasserted when restored 'tyranny' seems most unassailable: 'Can tyrants but by tyrants conquered be[?]' (*Byron PW*, 2: 156). He cites the

---

[109] 'But, if some happy combination of events should deliver her from foreign influence and unite her many states once more under one head, or at least one common cause, the cause of independence and of liberty, then Europe might confidently expect to see the spirit and the glory of Rome again revive' (*CT*, 4: 337-8).

[110] Cf. Shelley's image of 'thy sister band' (l. 156) with Eustace's reflections on the possibility of 'a sort of federal union' (*CT*, 4: 155) of city states.

[111] Cf. Shelley's judgement on Rome on 6 April 1819: '& were all that *is* extinguished, that which *has been*, the ruins & the sculptures would remain' (*L*, 2: 93). While Shelley's lines in *Euganean Hills* are directed against the Venetians in particular – whom he considered to have brought out the worst in Byron's character – later experiences of Italian society did little to improve the temper of his feelings about Italian manners.

failures of revolutionary France – the Terror, the rise of Napoleon and his assumption of imperial 'pageant' – as excuses for European governments to justify 'the eternal thrall / Which nips life's tree', but he forcefully asserts a counter-hope that liberation struggle provides a deeper structure than that suggested by recent historical appearances: 'Yet, Freedom! yet thy banner, torn, but flying, / Streams like the thunder-storm *against* the wind' (*Byron PW*, 2: 157). Shelley later used these lines as an epigraph for 'Ode to Liberty' (1820), but in *Euganean Hills* he alludes to the organic metaphor that follows. Byron affirms that though Freedom's 'tree hath lost its blossom', 'the seed we find / Sown deep, even in the bosom of the North; / So shall a better spring less bitter fruit bring forth' (*Byron PW*, 2: 157). Shelley redeploys this flower-blossom motif, affirming with Byron that 'from your [Venice's] dust new nations spring / With more kindly blossoming' (*PS2*, 165-6). With Byron's backing, Shelley checks Eustace's enthusiasm for Italy (which, it must be said, Byron partly shared[112]), transferring hope to 'the North', or Britain. Under this neo-colonial idea of nation building, the north will reinvigorate the south if the south cannot do it itself. The lines Shelley added in December locate the motivating force of nation-building in a kind of aesthetic resuscitation. The northern poet, identified as Byron, 'clothes' (*PS2*, l. 170) the south, covering 'the tattered pall of time' (l. 172). He usurps the place that Eustace had pointedly given to Aldus Manutius, the translator of Pindar, Aeschylus, Sophocles, Euripides, Herodotus, Thucydides, Demosthenes, Plato, and Aristotle.[113] This is surprising, given Shelley's own Grecian proclivities, but Shelley wishes to reinforce his aesthetic historiography. That is, Britain embodies and exports through its exiled poet the Grecian values that the illustrious foreigner, Manutius, first brought to Venice (but which the Venetians proved unable to emulate). Poetry expressed by the 'sunlike soul[s]' (l. 193), who appear at various junctures in history, is 'a quenchless lamp' (l. 202) that alters perception. However, this becomes the expression of the free, and Shelley discountenances the possibility of a modern Venetian poet through a circular logic of social-historical conditioning ('rather say / . . . thy sins and slaveries foul / Overcloud a sunlike soul?; ll. 191-3).

The Padua tableau (ll. 206-84) repeats the structures and many of the conclusions of the Venice sections. It continues to rely on the Eustace-Byron dialectic for its points of reference, though this time Eustace rather than Byron informs the poem's central affirmations. The section begins with another image of 'thought-winged liberty' abandoning Venice ('the beams of morn lie dead / On the towers of Venice'; ll. 211-12). Padua too suffers under 'the brutal Celt' (l. 223), and Shelley introduces its domains with a vignette of Austrian economic oppression. The region looks fertile, but lacks prosperity; it is a 'peopled

---

[112] Like Eustace, Byron affirms that one 'is struck with the extraordinary capacity of this people, or . . . their *capabilities*, . . . their "longing after immortality", – the immortality of independence' (*Byron PW*, 2: 123).

[113] 'But it would be difficult to say whether the exertions of any individual . . . ever shed so much lustre on the place of their residence as that which Venice derives from the reputation of a stranger, who voluntarily selected it for his abode' (*CT*, 1: 164-5).

solitude'.[114] The peasant 'heaps his grain / In the garners of his foe' (ll. 218-19); the vintage feeds a northern intemperance; nothing returns to the local economy (Lady Morgan describes a similar scene near Narni, 'where gloom and poverty tell their tale . . . while Nature laughs in the vallies beneath, and plenty loads the carrier's team with corn and wine for distant lands').[115] Eustace notes that Padua's environs give 'the traveller an idea of plenty and of population' (*CT*, 1: 187), but elsewhere indicates that Italian cities without independence are soon depopulated. In the 'Dissertation', he considers this at length, declaring that 'population and cultivation may be considered as the most prominent indications of prosperity' (*CT*, 4: 341). Shelley, who was reading Malthus alongside Eustace, would have found in Eustace nothing to counter Malthus's 'inference' that 'misery is the check that represses the superior power of population and keeps its effects equal to the means of subsistence'.[116] But Eustace does articulate an idea that population represents the equilibrium between morality and reproduction, sustained by productivity.[117] He locates the roots of depopulation in ancient Rome under the emperors, citing the misery caused by civil wars, 'a general spirit of libertinism', 'accumulation of landed property', and 'operation of the military system' (*CT*, 4: 343; 348; 351). Like Morgan, Shelley lays depopulation firmly at the door of the absentee Austrian landlord; like Eustace, he indicts the enabling institutions of Austrian occupation.

Paralleling the conclusion to the lines on Venice and freedom (*PS2*, ll. 142-66), the first Padua section ends with a suggestion that there is a time limit to occupation, if not to moral regeneration: the Austrian usurpation of agricultural productivity creates conditions for rebellion ('destruction's harvest home'; l. 230). Yet this time, Shelley turns to Byron's bleaker stanzas in *Childe Harold* on the

---

[114] Shelley may be recalling a phrase Eustace applies to Venice: ' . . . if the present order of things should unfortunately continue, [the population of Venice] will diminish, till, deserted like Sienna and Pisa, this city shall become *a superb solitude*, whose lonely grandeur will remind the traveller that Venice was once great, and independent' (*CT*, 1: 182-3; my italics).
[115] Morgan, *Italy*, 2: 165-6.
[116] Thomas Malthus, *An Essay on the Principle of Population*, ed. Antony Flew (London: Penguin, 1970), p. 82. On the front pastedown of a notebook used in 1818-19 (Bodleian MS. Shelley e. 4), Shelley has written 'French Malthus' above 'English Eustace', partly a reference to the languages in which Shelley read their works. On 8 October 1818, Shelley reported to Peacock, 'I have just read Malthus in a french translation. Malthus is a very clever man, & the world would be a great gainer if it would seriously take his lessons into consideration . . . but what on earth does he mean by some of his inferences!' (*L*, 2: 43). In particular, Shelley objected that Malthus's proposals penalised the poor without addressing the usurpation of scarce resources by the rich. See *Philosophical View of Reform* in *Prose*, pp. 247-8, especially the echoes of *Euganean Hills*, ll. 218-19 ('whose plenty is garnered up in the strongholds of their tyrants').
[117] Eustace's analysis of population may have been a direct reply to Malthus, whom Eustace is likely to have known at Cambridge. Malthus accompanied Eustace's patron, Edward Daniel Clarke, on the outset of his European tour in 1801 (the same tour that provided Malthus with statistical material for subsequent editions of the *Principle of Population*). Malthus also held a fellowship at Jesus College, Cambridge, until 1804, the year Eustace took up residence there.

cyclical nature of violence in history. Again reflecting on the parallels between Roman history and revolutionary France, Byron represents Napoleon as a 'bastard Caesar', epitomising a destructive human urge to imitate 'the things they fear'd' (*Byron PW*, 2: 154, st. 90, ll. 802-3; st. 89, l. 796). The great examples, to Byron, prove the rule: 'for this the tears / And blood of earth flow on as they have flowed, / An universal deluge' (st. 92, ll. 824-6). Echoing this, and Byron's rhetorical question, 'What from this barren being do we reap? / Our senses narrow, and our reason frail' (st. 93, ll. 829-30), Shelley answers catechistically, 'Men must reap the things they sow, / Force from force must ever flow' (*PS2*, ll. 231-2). But the formulaic, aphoristic response itself indicates Shelley's lack of conviction. Instead, he resists Byron's remediless vision of 'opinion [as] an omnipotence' (*Byron PW*, st. 93, l. 833) that prevents revolutionary change, and Byron's overall degenerative psycho-historiography:

> And thus they plod in sluggish misery,
> Rotting from sire to son, and age to age,
> Proud of their trampled nature, and so die,
> Bequeathing their hereditary rage
> To the new race of inborn slaves, who wage
> War for their chains . . . . (*Byron PW*, 2: 155, st. 94, ll. 838-43)

Shelley counters by lamenting that ''tis a bitter woe / That love or reason cannot change / The despot's rage, the slave's revenge' (*PS2*, ll. 233-5) – and by exploring in the poem as a whole the conditions in which love and reason *can* change history. The solution he posits against Byron remains the same as that posited with Byron's help in the Venice section, namely, that international tourism, the ability to see beyond the limits of self and society, allows one to practise the perceptual politics that redeem custom. In *Euganean Hills*, Shelley reads *Childe Harold* as a profoundly self-divided poem, both worthy of the satire to which Peacock subjects it, yet containing moments in which hopes for political renewal are paramount.

Eustace's depiction of Padua helps Shelley to make the point that its oppression (like Venice's) is intricately involved with its decline as a world centre for the arts and the circulation of ideas. The 'quenchless lamp' of poetry is contrasted to Padua's extinguished 'lamp of learning' – 'In thine halls the lamp of learning, / Padua, now no more is burning' (ll. 256-7) – the primary reference being to Padua's 'internationally famous eleventh-century University' (*PS2*, p. 439 n). For Eustace, Padua and its university represent the transmission and continuity of knowledge from Roman to modern times:

During the various revolutions that followed the fall and dismemberment of the Roman empire, Padua, in the intervals of reposes that followed each successive shock, endeavoured to repair the shattered temple of the Muses, and to revive the *sacred fire* of knowledge. (*CT*, 1: 153; my italics)

The university attracted 'prodigious numbers of students from all, even the most remote countries' (cf. Shelley's 'Once *remotest* nations came / To adore the *sacred flame*'; ll. 260-61, my italics), among whom were Italians, Dalmatians, Greek and Latin Christians, Turks, Persians, and Arabians (*CT*, 1: 154). Through the work of illustrious students such as Petrarch, Columbus, and Galileo, the university acts as a conduit to modernity, a propagator of arts and sciences that were to revolutionise the perception of the world through poetry, geography, and astronomy. Eustace attributes the university's decline paradoxically to its success. 'The establishment of similar institutions in other countries, and . . . the general multiplication of the means of knowledge' (*CT*, 1: 155) shifts the cultural centre northwards, particularly to the universities of Edinburgh and Göttingen.

Shelley's phrasing, 'new fires from *antique* light' (*PS2*, l. 265; my italics) also gestures towards Eustace's analogy between the university and the 'extension of [the Roman] empire (*CT*, 1: 344).[118] Reflecting on the meaning of Rome to the modern tourist, Eustace asserts the inextricability of Roman thought and culture from northern psychology: 'The name of Rome echoes in our ears from our infancy . . . and our first and most delightful years are passed among her orators, poets, and historians' (*CT*, 1: 343). The power of Roman culture over the individual reflects its power over European society, which Eustace attributes to the means by which empire shapes consciousness in its own image. Rome becomes 'the instrument of communicating to Europe, and to a considerable portion of the globe, the three greatest blessings of which human nature is susceptible – Civilization, Science, and Religion' (*CT*, 1: 343-4). 'Eastern monarchies' keep people in 'abject slavery', 'Greek republics confined their blessings of liberty within their own precincts', but Rome considers 'conquered countries as so many nurseries of citizens' (*CT*, 1: 344). 'With her laws and franchises she communicated to them her arts and sciences; wherever Roman eagles penetrated schools were opened' (*CT*, 1: 344); architecture, sculpture, and painting 'decorate the capitals of the most distant provinces' (*CT*, 1: 344-5). This process of 'civilizing and polishing mankind' prepares the way for Christianity (*CT*, 1: 346) and Rome becomes the 'metropolis of the world' 'the "Holy City," the "Light of Nations," the "Parent of Mankind"' (*CT*, 1: 346). Even during decline of empire, apostles and teachers took over from armies, spreading civilisation:

> . . . the Latin muses, which had followed the Roman eagles in their victorious flight, now accompanied her humble missionaries . . . and with them penetrated into the swamps of Batavia, the forests of Germany, and the mountains of Caledonia. Schools, that vied in learning and celebrity with the seminaries of the south, rose in these

---

[118] Leask, *Curiosity*, pp. 2-3, argues that Shelley's use of 'antique' in 'Ozymandias' allows him both 'to "temporalize" peoples and topographies with reference to Europe's classical past' and pun on the term 'antick', meaning 'grotesque, in composition or shape; grouped or figured with fantastic incongruity; bizarre' (*OED*). While Leask is concerned with 'extra-European antique lands' (p. 3), his analysis applies to *Euganean Hills* if we consider 'antique light' to refer not only to the Greek and Roman sources of civilisation, but also to the 'remotest nations' that come to the University at Padua.

benighted regions, and diffused the beams of science . . . even to the polar circles. Thus the predictions of the Roman poets were fulfilled . . . and their immortal compositions were rehearsed in the remote islands of the Hebrides, and in the once impenetrable forests of Scandinavia. (*CT*, 1: 343)

As *A Philosophical View of Reform* and other writings show, Shelley rejected Eustace's faith in Christianity as an uncomplicated force for propagating virtue. Nevertheless, *Euganean Hills* refigures Eustace's Scandinavian forest clearance with a Norwegian forest fire. The ignorant woodman-tyrant 'trample[s] out' the fire of culture-liberty, but the sparks have already caught in the wider forest-world; its 'myriad tongues victorious' (*PS2*, l. 278) present a Maenedic inversion of Eustace's 'consenting nations . . . of the civilized world' (*CT*, 1: 350). The woodman-tyrant now 'sees' his imminent extinction by a new light, though hardly the unquenchable lamp of poesy. Shelley's more particular source for the simile is the *Short Residence*, in which Wollstonecraft describes how Norwegian farmers start forest fires by burning stubble: 'the soil, as well as the trees, is swept away by the destructive torrent; and the country, despoiled of beauty and riches, is left to mourn for ages' (*LSND*, p. 173). Wollstonecraft's Norwegian peasants are characterised by their privative understanding, 'bastilled by nature' (*LSND*, p. 133). Lacking connection with the ideas of equality fermenting in the Parisian centre, the peasant expresses the force of tyranny in unconscious ways, all involving the spoliation of 'beauty and riches', aesthetic and economic signs of international cultural circulation. Shelley's flames implicitly extend Wollstonecraft's analysis of French Revolutionary Europe to wider contexts. The upheaval that starts from below ('mighty trunks are torn / By the fire thus lowly born'; *PS2*, ll. 273-4) compresses in its imagery the Jacobin terror and Napoleon's might (Napoleon's own *roturier* origins were often emphasised in the period). 'Howling through the darkened sky' (l. 277), the flames imitate a mob, the correlative to Byron's 'hereditary rage'; it is not at all obvious that tyranny will be replaced by anything better. Thus, though Shelley may take his cue from Eustace, Wollstonecraft and Byron are present too, helping to complicate Eustace's chart of republican progress by applying the example of France as a positive as well as a negative agent of social change. But all three writers lead to an impasse; Shelley's layering of history cannot prove that the forces at work against tyranny promise an escape from the cycles of tyranny.

What escape there is, Shelley locates in individual experience and perception. As the poem advances towards its conclusion, the light no longer illumines Venice and Padua, but falls on and around the observing subject – 'Noon descends *around me now*' (l. 285; my italics) – reintegrated with the world through a heightened perception of it, an aesthetic vision. For the first time, allusions to the strife of history are absent. The 'overflowing sky' (l. 293) contains none of the fires or intense sun-scapes of previous lines, and all is muted, vaporous, dissolved, a 'light and fragrance' (l. 290) that unifies a landscape in which Venice and Padua have been curiously effaced. Even the few reminders of present and past human activity – the trellised vines and 'hoary tower' (l. 303) – are considered as deictic structures, 'pointing' light into dark patches. Various effects of light lead the eye over and through the panoramic distances: the 'vaporous amethyst' (l. 288) tint stretching from horizon to zenith; the plain with its 'gleaming' (l. 298) frost; the 'hoary tower' and 'glimmering' (l. 305) flower at the point of view; the more distant Apennines 'dimly islanded' (l. 307), the snowy Alps. Shifting from light as optical presence to light as trope, the eye then turns inward towards 'living things each one; / And my spirit which so long / Darkened this swift stream of song' (ll. 310-12). Grammatically and thematically, object world and subject are 'interpenetrated . . . / By the glory of the sky' (ll. 313-14), though Shelley refuses to equate 'glory' with light, lest vision be reduced to the visual. 'Love', 'light', 'harmony', 'odour', 'the soul of all', or 'the mind' are instead offered as possible explanations for the unity effect. Positioned most prominently, the last in this list is qualified as 'the mind *which feeds* this verse / *Peopling* the lone universe' (ll. 318-19; my italics). The suggestion is that observing and writing ('perception and expression' in *A Defence*) express the highest operations of the mind in its social mode, for Shelley's image finally gestures back to the poem's previous reflections on the propagation of knowledge and art. Mind 'feeds' verse, and populates the universe in an anti-Malthusian gesture. It is opposed to misery, the Malthusian check, and can arise out of misery. It is the main force of cultural empire, the motivating spirit of progress.

The 'windless bower' (*PS2*, l. 344), with which the poem concludes, refigures and idealises the scene of vision from the previous section, where the poet stands in the 'windless air' beneath a 'hoary tower' (ll. 303-4). Yet if the first setting represents an ideal present of unified tourist perception, the second is an ideal past, where the 'earth [may] grow young again' (l. 373), rejuvenated and able to rejuvenate all discord and suffering. The 'memories of old time' (l. 158), the ruins and monuments, that complicated the tourist's perception of Venice's present and future are erased, or replaced by 'wild sea-murmurs' and the 'old forests echoing round', images resonant of beginnings. The 'pollution-nourished worms' (l. 147) of Venice are reintroduced to the scene in the guise of 'the polluting multitudes' (l. 356), and the bower softens them until their 'rage' is 'subdued' (l. 357) by the perfect economy of art. The 'musical' object world interacts and complements the 'melodies' of the 'inspired soul' (ll. 363-5), and love is the natural expression of this harmony. Without history and its reminders, 'they [the polluting multitudes], not it [the bower] would change' (l. 370). The cycle of oppression is broken, and the 'pomp of fratricides' (l. 59) that opened the poem is replaced by a 'mild brotherhood' (l. 369). In the poem's entire context, Shelley's 'bower' becomes a self-regenerating architecture without ruins, a beautiful ideal of human community beyond violence. Though gesturing beyond Byron's 'hereditary rage', the utopian vision more particularly rejuvenates its own imagery – forests, sea, and multitudes – without the texture of allusion to Byron, Eustace, or Wollstonecraft that characterised earlier sections. For the first and last time, the verse strains towards a pure form, beyond intertextuality, where public place can be defined and delimited by the ideals of private communion. For once, all depends on the model of 'me, and those I love' (l. 343), no longer upon tourists trying to make sense of a strange yet familiar land.

How much of this was written in October cannot be ascertained with certainty, but Shelley's negotiations with Byron's and Eustace's travel discourse continued as the Shelley party embarked on the tour to Rome and then Naples. At first, the Shelleys proceeded in Byron's footsteps, leaving Este on 5 November and arriving at Ferrara on the 6th. On the 7th they visited the Public Library which held a manuscript collection of works by Ariosto and Tasso, and which housed Ariosto's tomb. From there, they went on to visit the Tasso's prison cell at the Hospital of Santa Anna, where Shelley cut away a fragment of the door as a souvenir for Peacock.[119] Eustace had bypassed Ferrara as containing little of interest to the classical tourist. Byron, however, had visited the same sites in April 1817, and had devoted stanzas 35-41 of *Childe Harold* to Ferrara and its poets. As John Scott suspected, Hobhouse's notes align Tasso as a type of Byron, the exiled poet and republican martyr to tyranny.[120] The analogy was sufficiently evident to Shelley, too, for in his letter to Peacock he notes that 'Tasso's situation was widely different from that of any persecuted being of the present day, for from the depth of dungeons public opinion might now . . . startle the oppressor' (*L*, 2: 47). Though Shelley might well have associated the 'persecuted being' with himself rather than Byron, only Byron commanded a popular audience.[121] Like Scott, Shelley suggests that the Tasso-Byron analogy underestimates the impact of poetry on politics and falsely absolves Byron from exerting a more powerful influence on the age; though exiled in Venice, Byron still might write poetry worthy of his genius and his status – another parallel with Peacock's position in *Nightmare Abbey*.

From Ferrara, Shelley travelled to Bologna, arriving on the 8th. Again Shelley read Byron's fourth canto aloud (*MWSJ*, p. 235), before a full day of sightseeing on the 9th. *Childe Harold*, however, is silent on Bologna and its art treasures; explaining his neglect of statuary and painting in Florence, Byron's speaker somewhat disingenuously claims, 'I have been accustomed to entwine / My thoughts with Nature rather in the fields, / Than art in galleries' (*Byron PW*, 2: 144). Eustace too neglected the galleries, though the chief attractions for many contemporary tourists were the superb collections of the Accadèmia di Belle Arti, the Mariscalchi Palace, and the Ercolani Palace.[122] There is then nothing unusual

---

[119] See John Cam Hobhouse, *Historical Illustrations of the Fourth Canto of Child Harold* (London: John Murray, 1818), p. 6: 'The bedstead, so they tell, has been carried off piecemeal, and the door half cut away by the devotion of those whom "the verse and prose" of the prisoner have brought to Ferrara'.

[120] John Scott, *Sketches of Manners, Scenery, & c. in the French Provinces, Switzerland, and Italy*, 2nd edn (London, 1821), pp. 314-15. Scott was particularly critical of Hobhouse's insinuation that Byron's treatment by his wife, Annabella, amounted to 'domestic treason' (p. 314). See also *Byron PW*, 2: 317-18.

[121] Shelley's exuberant response to Tasso's 'free & flowing' handwriting in a manuscript of *Jerusalem Delivered*, however, would suggest self-identification, given Shelley's reputation for obscurity and his limited readership: 'It is the symbol of an intense & earnest mind exceeding at times its own depth, and admonished to return by the chillness of the waters of oblivion striking upon its adventurous feet' (*L*, 2: 47).

[122] For a reconstruction of Shelley's gallery itinerary and the significance to him of individual paintings, see Colwell, 'Shelley and Italian Painting', pp. 43-66.

about Shelley's decision to focus his journal letter to Peacock on that of which Eustace and Byron are strangely silent, but Shelley continues to address his literary interlocutors through allusive engagement.[123]

The Bologna letter is also where Shelley first registered in a postscript his impatience with Eustace: 'Consult Eustace if you want to know nothing about Italy' (*L*, 2: 54). Shelley wrote this after Mary Shelley had transcribed his descriptions of paintings from the previous day. Cross-writing over this transcription, Shelley reported on his activities of the 10th: the second visit to 'those divine pictures of Raphael & Guido', the day trip to the Chapel of the Madonna, Monte del Guardia, and 'a moonlight walk through Bologna'. The itinerary suggests that he again had recourse to the *Classical Tour*, as does a 'melancholy' reflection on the restoration of pictures that 'had been pierced by the French bayonets' – a charge similar to one Eustace makes in several places.[124] Unlike Eustace, however, Shelley does not dwell with outrage on modern attempts to demolish what 'time, war, and barbarism had spared' (*CT*, 1: 293-4).[125] Instead, he moralises on the perishable nature of art. Art is only as permanent as the materials from which it is made, except books which can be 'produced & reproduced forever'. As for lost painters (and writers) from the ancient world:

> The material part indeed of these works must perish, but they survive in the mind of man, & the remembrances connected with them are transmitted from generation to generation. The poet embodies them in his creation, the systems of philosophers are modelled to gentleness by their contemplation, opinion the legislator is infected with their influence; men become better & wiser, and the unseen seeds are perhaps thus sown which shall produce a plant more excellent even that [than] that from which they fell.
>
> (*L*, 2: 53)

The notion that classical values in art improve life is fundamental to the argument of the *Classical Tour*, and Shelley was attracted to Eustace's ideas on the transmission of culture 'from generation to generation', as we have seen. Yet Shelley's historical vision here becomes more fully integrated with a psychology of perception in which vision is more than the sum of what is seen. Seeing plants 'unseen seeds' in the poet, philosopher, and legislator. Thinking thus, Shelley delineates his own touristic gaze as an aesthetic vision, always sensitive to the reflexive power of the perceived to 'influence' or 'infect' the perceiver. Eustace's refusal to contemplate the wonders of Bolognese painting, and his attention instead to discursive and expository matter, must have struck Shelley as a failure of imagination. To know *something* of Italy, Shelley concludes, one must focus on natural spectacle, significant ruins, and objects of art, as an inter-art exploration of the authenticity of creativity.

---

[123] See my discussion of Shelley's description of Raphael's 'St Cecilia' in Chapter 5, pp. 192-4, below.
[124] See *CT*, 1: 119. See Morgan, *Italy*, 1: 80-81.
[125] Here, Eustace refers specifically to Lord Elgin's removal of the marbles from the Parthenon.

Public Consumption and Private Vision: The Cascata delle Marmore

By the end of 1818, when Shelley had almost reached the southernmost point of his Italian travels – only Paestum remained – he had begun to give a shape to his classical tour. Writing to Hogg, a somewhat neglected correspondent, Shelley directed him to Peacock for details, but summed up:

> The more I see of this astonishing country the more do the wonders of nature, the voluptuous softness of its climate, the wrecks of all that was most magnificent and lovely in antient art strike me with admiration. . . . I have seen Rome, the bay of Baia, Vesuvius, the cataract of Terni. (*L*, 2: 68)

The Cataract of Terni, locally known as the Cascata delle Marmore, is the only site north of Rome to make Shelley's list of 'essential Italy', but he was not alone in singling it out. In Augustus von Kotzebue's *Travels through Italy* (1806), the Cascata is 'one of the three objects which will indelibly impress on my mind the recollection of Italy' (the others being 'flaming Vesuvius' and 'subterraneous Pompeii').[126] For Eustace, the falls were 'one of the noblest objects . . . in the world' (*CT*, 1: 327); Byron called the Cascata 'a matchless cataract' in *Childe Harold* (1818), 'worth all the cascades and torrents of Switzerland put together' (*Byron PW*, 2: 148, l. 639; 2: 248, l. 639 n). For most of Shelley's contemporaries on the tour, the Cascata epitomised picturesque viewing; the united beauty and sublimity in Italian landscape that attracted the English to Italy in the twilight of the Grand Tour.

Like many tourists, Kotzebue and Shelley enthused over the spectacle's power, but were more vague about its artifice. The falls were the product of a grandiose public works project undertaken by the Roman consul, Curius Dentatus, to improve drainage in the Velino river lands, a fact behind Addison's comparison in *Remarks on Italy* (1705), 'I think there is something more astonishing in this *Cascade*, than in all the water-works of Versailles'.[127] Addison's pleasure in the victory of ancient over modern hydraulics complements his wider attention to the Cascata's classical literary associations, particularly Virgil's lines on the Fury Alecto's descent into Hell in *Æneid*, Book VII. By mid-century, however, the taste for the sublime began to eclipse classical references, and Tobias Smollett complains that though 'an object of tremendous sublimity: yet great part of its effect is lost, for want of a proper point of view'.[128] In 1781, Pope Pius VI rectified this by building viewing huts to shelter tourists; and he improved the Roman flood

---

[126] August Friedrich Ferdinand von Kotzebue, *Travels through Italy in the Years 1804 and 1805*, 4 vols (London: Printed for Richard Phillips, 1806), 4: 165.

[127] Joseph Addison, *Remarks on Several Parts of Italy in the Years 1701, 1702, 1703*, in *The Miscellaneous Works of Joseph Addison*, vol. 2, ed. A. C. Guthkelch (London: G. Bell and Sons Ltd, 1914), p. 83.

[128] Tobias Smollett, *Travels through France and Italy [1765]*, ed. Frank Felsenstein (Oxford: Oxford University Press, 1979), p. 295.

defences by widening the Velino's artificial channel.[129] Although Italian tourism slowed to a trickle during the French Revolution and Napoleonic wars, the infrastructure was in place to accommodate the tourist hordes after 1815. Those who came to sketch or paint followed the lower path along the Nera to a picturesque viewpoint directly opposite the falls; those who came to gaze and feel, chose the bird's-eye view above, following the steep road from Terni or approaching along the channel from Lake Pie de Lugo.[130] By Shelley's time, the Papal Government exercised a monopoly on tourist guides and vehicular hire, leasing the rights to an innkeeper. Lady Morgan reports in *Italy* (1821) that she was unable to enjoy 'the splendid *spectacle*' because 'the mules and carriages [were] hired out'; her own driver could not venture without risking a prison sentence, for, he explained, 'none could go there but the POPE's hacks'[131] (the Shelleys circumvented this by visiting on foot). Lady Morgan's experience testifies to that new aspect of tourism – traffic. Candid travel writers mentioned the presence of fellow sightseers, as when Eustace describes sharing a platform with two Roman artists. Shelley, however, ignores fellow tourists and locals, concentrating instead on the views, where the observing eye is transfixed, astonished or activated by the sublime object of its gaze.

Shelley's description of the Cascata differs from those of other travel writers by delaying his account of the approach to the falls until *after* he has sketched his impressions of them. Even Kotzebue guides his reader along the upper road and then recounts the discomforts of 'a quarter . . . hour's walk', the noise of the torrent intensifying, before the stage is set for sudden vision. 'But who could here think of any inconvenience for the first ten minutes? and who could, even at the end of twenty-four hours, conceive the idea of describing this spectacle?', he questions, before doing so.[132] Shelley waited forty-eight hours. In the journal letter comprising his journey from Bologna to Rome, he gives this account:

> From Spoleto we went to Terni, and saw the Cataract of the Velino. The glaciers of Montanvert & the source of the Arveiron is the grandest spectacle I ever saw. This is the second. Imagine a river sixty feet in breadth, with a vast volume of waters, the outlet of a great lake among the higher mountains, falling 300 feet into a sightless gulph of snow white vapour which bursts up forever & forever from a circle of black crags, & thence leaping downwards make 5 or 6 other cataracts each 50 or 100 feet high which exhibit on a smaller scale & with beautiful & sublime variety the same appearances. But words, and far less could painting, will not express it. Stand upon the brink of the platform of cliff which is directly opposite. You see the evermoving water stream down. It comes in thick & tawny folds flaking off like solid snow gliding down a mountain. It does not seem hollow within, but without it is unequal like the folding of linen thrown carelessly

---

[129] See *CT*, 1: 331 n.
[130] See John Smith, *Select Views in Italy, with Topographical and Historical Descriptions in English and French* (London: W. Bulmer and Co., 1796), plate 15.
[131] Morgan, *Italy*, 2: 164.
[132] Kotzebue, *Travels through Italy*, 4: 163.

down. Your eye follows it & it is lost below, not in the black rocks which gird it around but in its own foam & spray, in the cloudlike vapours boiling up from below, which is not like rain nor mist nor spray nor foam, but water in a shape wholly unlike any thing I ever saw before. It is as white as snow, but thick & impenetrable to the eye. The very imagination is bewildered in it. A thunder comes up from the abyss wonderful to hear; for though it ever sounds it is never the same, but modulated by the changing motion rises & falls intermittingly. We past half an hour in one spot looking at it, & thought but a few minutes had gone by.— (*L*, 2: 55-6)

Only at this point does Shelley start describing the walk to the viewing platform, rejecting travel writers' more usual reliance on narrative strategies for building suspense. The only context provided is the opening comparison with 'the glaciers of Montanvert', and then the descriptive tumult begins.

Shelley's sudden focus on the falls – their dimensions, features, and effects on the imagination – exemplifies his 'aesthetic vision', his apparent subordination of social, political, and commonplace commentary, to the appreciation of the attraction itself. His tableau engages contemporary travel most obviously in its challenge to artists, whom Shelley considers less able to represent the 'changing motion' of external phenomena than poets. Again he had been reading and following Eustace's tour, and he may have been responding to Eustace's failure to privilege his own word-painting over the works of artists who share (and had shared) the lower viewpoint (not to mention Byron and Hobhouse's actual preference for this vantage).[133] But Shelley also gestures towards a wider debate about the verbal and visual techniques of travel writers and landscape artists. Kotzebue represents one extreme when he appends a list of those 'who are *not* to read this work', including 'all artists; or judges of the arts' who are 'fond of *viewing* performances of merit, but not reading *descriptions*'.[134] At the other extreme is Francis Nicholson's *The Practice of Drawing and Painting Landscape from Nature* (1820), which decries the 'mere literary man' who dares break the familial bonds of the sister arts. 'Verbal description of scenery . . . without graphic illustration, is at best very imperfect, and is frequently made more so by . . . vague terms and indiscriminate admiration', when the tourist displays his 'powers of description' at the expense of 'those who follow in his track'.[135] For Nicholson, the artist aims for 'correctness of form and truth of character' by eschewing 'servile attention to detail', instead capturing the 'permanent features of the subject' 'impressed upon and retained by the memory'.[136] Written from memory, Shelley's

---

[133] See *CT*, 1: 327: 'This point enables you to see, with much advantage, the second fall, when the river bursting from the basin into which it was first precipitated, tumbles over a ridge of broken rocks in various sheets half veiled in spray or foam. Hence are taken most of the views hitherto published, and when we visited it, we found two Roman artists employed on the spot'.

[134] Kotzebue, *Travels through Italy*, 1: iii-iv.

[135] Francis Nicholson, *The Practice of Drawing and Painting Landscape from Nature, in Water Colours* (London: Printed for the Author by J. Booth, 1820), pp. ii; ii-iii.

[136] Nicholson, *Practice of Drawing*, pp. 16; 33; 38.

tableau mediates the interart rivalry by disputing such animadversions against detail (Shelley's careful recording of dimensions and his search for precise language distinguishes his from most contemporary descriptions of the Cascata), while self-consciously *rejecting* the picturesque viewpoint. Though he did visit the lower platform from which 'most of the views hitherto published' (*CT*, 1: 327) had been taken, Shelley constructs his impressions largely from the vantage of the 'Belvedere superiore' constructed by the Pope in 1781.[137]

Shelley's aesthetic vision might be theorised as part of the idealising narrative of Romantic travel, the turn from empirical to subjective, emotive response; the rise of 'literary' as opposed to scientific or ethnological rhetoric in travel writing; or the construction of what Elizabeth Bohls has called the masculinist 'aesthetic disinterestedness' operating within picturesque discourse.[138] However, Nigel Leask has very recently reminded us that 'the standard account of "romantic travel writing" is in need of serious revision'[139] not least because hegemonic conceptualisations of Romantic culture, anachronistically constructed after the Romantic period, have delimited our understanding of generic and stylistic cross-currents, fanned by commercial pressures, at historical junctures. In another recent study, *The Visual and Verbal Sketch in British Romanticism* (1998), Richard Sha has suggested a way beyond 'the received view . . . that Romantic aesthetics displaces . . . historical particularities'.[140] Sha describes the culture wars between Royal Academician proponents of 'finished' art, and those who promoted the 'sketch' as inherently valuable (Sir Joshua Reynolds and William Gilpin representing the two sides). For Gilpin, the sketch becomes potential aesthetic property for the middle classes (anyone can do it with leisure to travel), and arguments for its equal or greater value than finished painting hinge on its immediacy; executed 'on the spot', the sketch becomes a 'portable inscription that bears the imprint and authority of nature'.[141] By the early nineteenth century, the sketch's commodification in picturesque tours, popular prints, and topographical poetry, ensured that the 'display of privacy'[142] had a very public function, despite continued resistance from the Royal Academy.

Shelley's aesthetic vision – his emphasis on perspective and detail, for example – not only engages with contemporary debates on accuracy and 'truthfulness' in verbal and visual arts, but might also be considered as a specific response to conditions in which the commodification of tourism, travel writing, and visual

---

[137] See Mary Shelley's scale of appreciation on the spot: 'Visit the celebrated waterfall first from below where we see it as a fine painting & afterwards from above where it is more beautiful than any painting' (*MWSJ*, p. 237). Shelley's preliminary description is a composite one, drawing on his reading (he did not visit the 'great lake among the higher mountains') and his vantages at both the lower and upper viewing stations.

[138] Elizabeth A. Bohls, *Women Travel Writers and the Language of Aesthetics, 1716-1818* (Cambridge: Cambridge University Press, 1995), p. 67.

[139] Leask, *Curiosity*, p. 6.

[140] Richard Sha, *The Visual and Verbal Sketch in British Romanticism* (Philadelphia: University of Pennsylvania Press, 1998), p. 17.

[141] Sha, *Visual and Verbal Sketch*, p. 57.

[142] Sha, *Visual and Verbal Sketch*, p. 27.

representation apply new pressures on the aesthetic and political values associated with the Italian tour in post-Napoleonic Europe. Elsewhere in his Italian letters, Shelley deploys a disclaimer ('remember, I dont pretend to taste') (*L*, 2: 52) signifying his resistance to popular modes of tourism, yet resistance bespeaks awareness of and positioning against them. Shelley's tourist sensibility encounters the same problems as his politics; how to define a popular equality in representation and expression subject neither to demagoguery nor market forces. His assertion of a private aesthetic vision cannot be so easily divorced from the contexts of public consumption for which it was partly intended.

The Italian Canto of Byron's *Childe Harold*, published in April 1818, was again at the centre of public consciousness. With a print run of 10,000, the canto made an instant impression on the Italian tour, providing 'sketches' that became modern touchstones for arguments about 'accuracy' and 'faithfulness'. In 1821, Lady Morgan refers her readers to Byron's stanzas on the Cascata when she is unable to visit; the same year, William Lisle Bowles used *Childe Harold* IV to dispute with Byron whether travellers (and readers) found sublime and beautiful representations of art more poetical than those of nature (he concludes that artificial sublimities in Byron's poem could not compare with Niagara).[143] In 1823, an American traveller, the Reverend Matthias Bruen, quotes Byron's version of the Cascata in another extended comparison between it and Niagara, the Virgil and the Homer of waterfalls, attempting to restore both to a moral frame, which Bruen felt mass tourism had begun to neglect.[144] Anna Jameson and William Hazlitt cite Byron's stanzas to highlight the incommensurability of representation and experience; 'the poetry is fine, but not like', remarked Hazlitt, while Jameson, frustrated with Byron and Eustace's efforts, lamented:

> . . . it *is* nonsense to attempt to image in words an individual scene like this. When we have made out our description as accurately as possible, it would do as well for any other cataract in the world . . .[145]

With each reference, Byron's Terni stanzas increase their cultural capital. Associated with the modern experience of the falls, Byron begins to stand in for Virgil (a ground that Eustace helps prepare by rejecting the relevance of Virgil's Alecto lines to the setting).[146] This is most clearly seen when comparing two openings from view books that, in their earliest editions, are separated by little over twenty years. The first, entitled 'Cascade of Terni', comes from John Smith's *Select Views in Italy, with Topographical and Historical Descriptions in English*

---

[143] William Lisle Bowles, *Two Letters to Lord Byron*, in *The Pamphleteer*, vol. 18, no. 36 (1821), pp. 331-91.
[144] Matthias Bruen, *Essays, Descriptive and Moral; on Scenes in Italy, Switzerland, and France. By an American* (Edinburgh: Archibald Constable and Co., 1823).
[145] William Hazlitt, *Notes on a Journey through France and Italy*, in *The Complete Works of William Hazlitt*, ed. P. P. Howe, vol. 17 (London: Dent, 1933), p. 258; Jameson, *Diary of an Ennuyée*, p. 137.
[146] See *CT*, 1: 331-3.

and French (1816) (see fig. 2), a reprint of a drawing engraved for the 1792 edition of the collection.[147] The text first provides establishing details, emphasising picturesque and sublime features: the 'thick forest' of undecaying 'verdure', the three hundred foot precipice down which the Nera 'rushes'; the mists below 'like the clouds of smoke ascending from some vast furnace', and the sub-falls 'boiling and foaming . . . down the valley'. Then Smith turns to literary touchstones, referring to Addison's assertion that Virgil had this cascade in mind when describing Alecto's descent into hell. Dryden's translation is duly cited and the text ends with further allusion to Virgil. The accompanying plate details numerous picturesque effects, including gazing figures both at the upper station, and again silhouetted in the foreground from the artist's point of view – but there is correspondingly no sign of the Pope's rural architecture. These are tourists who, like the artist, have entered into the sublime space of danger, precariously poised above a maelstrom of mists and surging violence of waters that underwrite the relevance of Addison's classical vision in an age of picturesque travel.

The second opening comes from James Hakewill's *A Picturesque Tour through Italy, from Drawings Made in 1816-17* (1820), published by John Murray (see fig. 3).[148] In the plate, 'picturesqueness' is under new pressure (Does the picturesque represent nature artfully, or art naturally? How accurate should 'picturesque perspective' be?). The mist that dominates Smith's sublime rendering gives way to Hakewill's textured falls and centred iris, while objects, even in the distance, are more distinct. Overall, power is transferred from formlessness to a combination of form and vertical perspective. In addition, the painter's eye melds with the viewer's (there are no surrogate figures in this foreground); the only figures visible are displaced to the middle distance, ascending a path, perhaps towards the Pope's belvedere, now clearly distinguished. The accompanying text devotes less space to establishing details, and moves straight to 'a great modern poet' who need not be named (and there is no mention of Virgil). Hakewill's updated classicism embraces modern science in the next paragraph, giving three versions of the iris (painting, poetry, optics), all of which problematise notions of perspective and accuracy. In the concluding paragraph, Hakewill emphasises the deception of appearances; what seems like natural sublimity is owing to 'human art'. A final touch refers readers to passages in popular travel books, Eustace and Joseph Forsyth's *Remarks on Italy*: Eustace describes the Cascata painstakingly, attempting to capture the scene in words; Forsyth merely remarks, 'all must have been so often described, that I leave

---

[147] John 'Warwick' Smith, 1749-1831, was born in Cumberland and trained as a topographical artist. The engravings for *Select Views* were based on drawings made during a tour of Italy in 1776-81. *Select Views* itself was initially published in two volumes, the first appearing in 1792 and the second in 1796.

[148] Hakewill's engravings were first published in parts by subscription from 1 May 1818. Murray advertised them as 'Hakewill's Views of Italy, Illustrative of Addison, Eustace, and Forsyth' in the endpapers of Byron's *Childe Harold's Pilgrimage. Canto the Fourth* (1818). The similarity between the layout of Hakewill's *Picturesque Tour* and Smith's *Select Views* (1816) suggests that Murray was following Smith's proven formula.

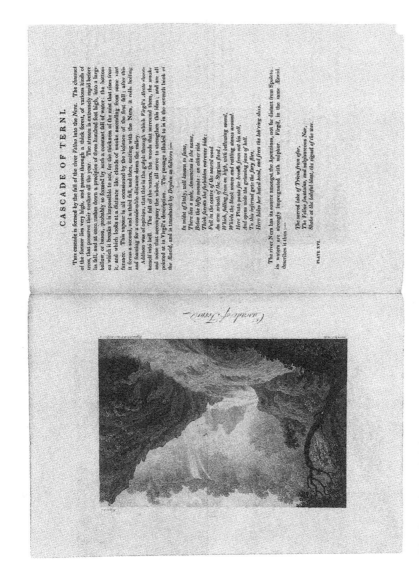

Fig. 2. 'Cascade of Terni': plate 16 and facing page from *Select Views in Italy ... by John Smith, 1816.* Bodleian reference (shelfmark) 20503 d. 55.

CASCADE OF TERNI.

This Cascade of Terni is called, in the truly descriptive language of Italy, the *Cascata del Marmore*; a torrent, precipitating itself over a cliff of two hundred feet in height, into an abyss that the eye almost dreads to look upon. The beauty and horror of such a scene cannot be better represented than in the words of a great modern poet:

> Lo! where it comes like an eternity,
> As if to sweep down all things in its track,
> Charming the eye with dread—a matchless cataract,
> Horribly beautiful! but on the verge,
> From side to side, beneath the glittering morn
> An Iris sits amidst the infernal surge.—
> *Childe Harold, Canto iv. lxix-lx.*

The Iris, as is well known, is but an image of the sun, in which the rays are divided into their several component colours by the refractive power of the watery particles of the spray that is produced; a common accompaniment of water-falls at certain periods of the day, though no where more strikingly exhibited than here, and it has accordingly attracted general observation, from the age of Pliny to our own time. *Vellus—in trea nullo non die apparere arcus.* —Plin. Hist. Nat. ii. 62.

The rough face of the cliff, and the groves that fringe its edge, and, in short, the whole country around, wears an appearance that may be termed, even in Italy, singularly wild and beautiful; yet we find that we owe to human art that which constitutes the chief feature of the scene. We are informed, in a letter of Cicero to Atticus, that the channel conducting the stream to the precipice, was made under the direction of M. Curius, in order to drain the marshes of the country above. Cicero was requested by the people of *Reate*, to plead their cause against the inhabitants of *Interamnæ*, considering themselves injured by the loss of the water, whatever benefits might have accrued to others. The river above is the *Velino* (*Velinus*), and that below, which receives the cascade, is the *Nera* (*Nar*). Reatini ne sua Tempo diceret,

Fig. 3. 'Cascade of Terni': plate 7 and facing page from *A Picturesque Tour of Italy, from Drawings by J. Hakewill*, 1820. Bodleian reference (shelfmark) 20503 d. 44.

them in silent admiration'.[149]

Hakewill announces that 'the public eye' (his phrase) can never be satiated with Italian scenes, because of the many possible combinations of picturesque detail. His views, he writes, are 'correct portraits' distinguished by 'accuracy and fidelity', 'arranged according to the line of . . . Eustace's tour, as being a popular work . . . in general circulation'.[150] The commercial tension between popular appeal and fidelity, art and accuracy, is palpable, and Hakewill's acknowledgement of J. M. W. Turner for the engravings conceals a further irony. Turner's watercolours (and the engravings taken from them) were based on Hakewill's *camera lucida* sketches made during his 1816-17 tour. The *camera lucida* was invented by William Hyde Wollaston (1766-1828) in 1806 for 'drawing in true perspective, and for copying, reducing, or enlarging other drawings'. The device consisted of 'a small prism lens, hung on a stand, [that] projected the image of the object at which it had been "aimed" downward onto a sheet of paper'.[151]

Hitherto, those who wished to obtain this kind of mimetic accuracy were forced, like the Abyssinian traveller James Bruce, to rely on the *camera obscura*, a bulky device consisting of a dark box within which an inverted image was projected through an aperture. As Nigel Leask describes it, Bruce's camera 'was a 6-foot diameter hexagon with a conical top'[152] which Bruce himself compared to 'a summer house' in which 'the draughtsman sat unseen'.[153] By contrast, the *camera lucida* was portable and could be set up almost anywhere in the field (see fig. 4), eroding the division between the views and viewpoints of scientific and aesthetic observers. If Jonathan Crary is correct in arguing that the *camera obscura* represents a paradigm of eighteenth-century notions on the relation between the autonomous subjectivity of the observer and the object, then the *camera lucida* might represent the paradigm shift better than his example of the later stereoscope. With the *camera lucida*, the observer becomes reinscribed into the landscape, affected by natural light, wind and weather, and newly self-aware of corporeality of vision.[154] This 'modern' observer is both in and outside of the scene in a new way that allows, potentially, the radical admixture of science and spontaneity.

Hakewill's decision to employ the 'line' of Eustace as an organising principle reveals another way in which science and spontaneity are subject to commercial

---

[149] Joseph Forsyth, *Remarks on Antiquities*, p. 175.

[150] Hakewill, *Picturesque Tour*, [preface], n.p.

[151] Horst de la Croix, Richard G. Tansey, and Diane Kirkpatrick, *Gardner's Art through the Ages*, 9th edn (Fort Worth, TX: Harcourt Brace Jovanovich, 1991), II, 891. Sir William Gell also used 'the prism of Dr Wollaston', as he referred to the *camera lucida*, for his drawings of Pompeii in 1814-19, published with acclaim in his *Pompeiana* (1817-19). See, 'Introduction', *Sir William Gell in Italy: Letters to the Society of Dilettanti, 1831-1835*, ed. Edith Clay in collaboration with Martin Frederiksen (London: Hamish Hamilton, 1976), pp. 23; 29-30.

[152] Leask, *Curiosity*, p. 71.

[153] James Bruce, *Travels to Discover the Source of the Nile*, 5 vols (Edinburgh, 1790), vol. 1, p. ix; quoted in Leask, *Curiosity and the Aesthetics of Travel Writing*, p. 71.

[154] See Jonathan Crary, *Techniques of the Observer: On Vision and Modernity in the Nineteenth Century* (Cambridge, MA: MIT Press, 1990), pp. 7-8; 38-9.

Fig. 4. Frontispiece from *Description of the Camera Lucida . . . by G. Dolland, 1830*. Bodleian reference (shelfmark) G. Pamph. 2312 (5).

and generic pressures. Despite the endless permutations of the picturesque and the public appetite for them, Hakewill relies on Eustace to authenticate and 'arrange' his viewpoints even as he supplements and re-motivates Eustace's classical tourism in terms of the picturesque, a belletrist aesthetic in keeping with literary trends in travel writing of the 1820s, but outside of Eustace's own purview. For similar ends, Hakewill obscures his *camera lucida*, nowhere acknowledging his use of the technology, instead paying tribute to Turner, as mentioned above. When Turner was commissioned in 1818 to make up his watercolours from Hakewill's *camera lucida* sketches 'as an aid to the illustration'[155] of the *Picturesque Tour*, he himself had not yet visited Italy (he did so only in the *following* year, 1819). In the absence of personal experience, Turner depended on Hakewill's originals and on his own reading, which may have included Byron's *Childe Harold* IV (Murray was Hakewill's publisher too). The published plates, then, represent a layering of truth and imagination and an argument for truth in imagination; the attendant texts provide contexts in optics and *belle lettres* that do little to disentangle the claims of either.

Basil Hall, another traveller who used the *camera lucida*, later remarked: 'It ought to be a rule strictly adhered to by all sketchers with the Camera, never to touch those drawings done with it . . . There is a truth, and what is called a *feeling*

---

[155] Graham Reynolds, *Turner* (London: Thames and Hudson, 1969), p. 109.

of accuracy about the work performed in this way, which, any after touches ... are sure to injure'.[156] Writing a decade later, Hall celebrated the liberation of amateur and professional artists alike by the camera, which would raise the standards of each, and render obsolete 'those frigid caricatures of nature, which now disgust us almost every time we open an Album'.[157] To the professional, Hall recommends a fluid technique for tracing the camera image, an avoidance of 'minute particulars' and attention to 'conspicuous shades': 'In this way the sketch will convey, upon the whole, a more correct idea to the mind of another person, than if twice the pains had been taken to render all its parts rigidly correct'.[158] Hall thus shares with Hakewill a desire to liberate the public eye without overly compromising modern values of artistic originality. Like John Scott, whose rejection of 'bare enumeration' of 'external points and features' I have cited in the opening section of this chapter, Hall argues for a phenomenological aesthetic of truth that challenges the pre-eminence of scientific objectivity for reproducing reality, yet an aesthetic that arises out of scientific perspective.

Shelley values a reproducibility that intensifies aesthetic vision and in *A Defence of Poetry* (1821) this becomes the function of poetic mimesis. In a passage on the drama, Shelley figures the interactions between poetic apperception and the truth of representation using an optical metaphor that recalls in some ways the operations of Wollaston's *camera lucida*:

> The drama, so long as it continues to express poetry, is as a prismatic and many-sided mirror, which collects the brightest rays of human nature and divides and reproduces them from the simplicity of these elementary forms, and touches them with majesty and beauty, and multiplies all that it reflects, and endows it with the power of propagating its like wherever it may fall. (*SPP*, p. 520)

The prismatic device of drama, however, has other properties; it adds to truth the aesthetic accuracy that remains the prerogative of Hall's professional artist. For Mary Shelley, Shelley's travel descriptions recall less the prism of the *camera lucida* than the darkened mirror of the *camera obscura*. 'The eminent German writer, Jean Paul Richter,' she writes in the preface to *Essays, Letters from Abroad* (1839),

---

[156] *Description of the Camera Lucida, and Instrument for Drawing in True Perspective, and for Copying, Reducing, or Enlarging Other Drawings. To Which Is Added, by Permission, A Letter on the Use of the Camera, by Capt. Basil Hall, R.N., F.R.S.* (London: G. Dollond, ?1830), p. 9; my italics.

[157] *Description of the Camera Lucida*, p. 10. See also Hall's *Forty Etchings, from Sketches Made with the Camera Lucida, in North America, in 1827 and 1828* (Edinburgh and London, 1829), p. ii: 'In short, if Dr. Wollaston, by this invention, have not actually discovered a Royal Road to Drawing, he has at least succeeded in Macadamising the way already known!'.

[158] *Description of the Camera Lucida*, p. 11.

says, that "to describe any scene well, the poet must make the bosom of a man his *camera obscura*, and look at it through *this*." Shelley pursues this method in all his descriptions; he always, as he says himself, looks beyond the actual object, for an internal meaning, typified, illustrated, or caused, by the external appearance.[159]

In his travel description of the Cascata, Shelley also experiments with versions of accuracy and reproducibility, though he is less confident about the propagating powers of this art, commenting as he does to Peacock on his circumscribed audience – 'those who differ from ordinary men' by having 'a perception of the beautiful'. Yet in Peacock, the classicist and man of letters, Shelley embodies an ideal auditor with whom he might engage in the task of remodifying the elements of modern Italian tourism. For Shelley, the sublimity of the Cascata delle Marmore resists all attempts to contain them (from papal privatisation to the mass tourist experience), and fails to compromise the revolutionary potential of an aesthetic sensibility that can be communicated to like-minded others. The private travel letter establishes this sympathy in a way that modes of public consumption cannot. Shelley's dismissal of popular travel writers as purveyors of 'shew-knowledge' (*L*, 2: 89), then, is also about a tourism that establishes its promise, like the lower falls of Terni, 'on a smaller scale'.

'Ruins of Human Power': Rome and the Coliseum

Shelley's first vision of Rome was from the tower of the Capitol, a bird's-eye vantage that disclosed the wonders of the ancient and modern city: The Triumphal Arch of Septimus Severus, The Temple of Peace, The Colosseum, The Forum, The Palatine Hill, Caracalla's Baths, The Tomb of Cecilia Metella, St Peter's, The Vatican Palace, The Castle of St Angelo, The Pantheon, The Porta del Populo, The Capitolan Hill, The Trajan Column, and much more. Before ascending the tower, he might have purchased a six-penny guidebook in which each of these objects was described; for a shilling he might have had a more historically detailed version with reflections on the depredations caused by the French occupying army during the Napoleonic wars.[160] However, Shelley may equally have spurned the pamphlet, relying only on his eye and the conversation of his companions.

The date was 12 February 1818, one month before his departure for Italy. Shelley, Peacock, Mary Shelley, and Claire Clairmont spent part of the day visiting Henry Aston Barker and Robert Burford's Panorama in the Strand, which had been showing the 'View of Rome, Taken from the Tower of the Capitol' since August

---

[159] Percy Bysshe Shelley, *Essays, Letters from Abroad, Translations and Fragments*, ed. Mary Shelley, 2 vols (London: Edward Moxon, 1840 [i.e. 1839]), 1: xxi.
[160] *An Explanation of the View of Rome, Taken from the Tower of the Capitol. Now Exhibiting at H. A. Barker and J. Burford's Panorama, Near the New Church, in the Strand*. [n.p.], 1817; R. R. Reinagle, *An Explanation of the View of Rome, Taken from the Tower of the Capitol* (Smithfield: Printed by J. Adlard, Duke-Street).

1817.[161] Patented by Robert Barker in 1787, the popular panorama worked by an optical trick. From the street, spectators walked down a dim passage, emerging onto a better lit viewing platform, where the differential caused their surroundings to appear as if in daylight. A canopy prevented them from seeing skylights; instead they gazed towards the colossal 360° painting whose proportions and true perspectives startled them with its verisimilitude. The entire production aimed at this effect. Artists 'on the spot' prepared preliminary sketches using the latest optical tools, including the *camera obscura* and the *camera lucida*. A team of copyists and foremen then supervised the transference of the sketches, as perspective lines were altered to fit a convex cylindrical canvas. Over several months, artists filled in outlines with oils, working on rolling platforms. The finished work was then hung in the panorama rotunda and a false foreground prepared.[162] The printed guidebooks gave no information about the process of composition, but focused on the objects themselves, providing historical and cultural information. This was virtual tourism, as *Blackwood's Magazine* wryly suggested in a review of Barker and Burford's Panorama of Pompeii in 1824:

> Panoramas are among the happiest contrivances for saving time and expense in this age of contrivances. What cost a couple of hundred pounds and half a year half a century ago, now costs a shilling and a quarter of an hour. Throwing out of the old account the innumerable miseries of travel, the insolence of public functionaries, the roguery of innkeepers, the visitations of banditti, charged to the muzzle with sabre, pistol, and scapulary, and the rascality of the custom-house officers, who plunder, passport in the hand, the indescribable *desagremens* of Italian cookery, and the insufferable annoyances of that epitome of abomination, an Italian bed.
>
> Now the affair is settled in a summary manner. The mountain or the sea, the classic vale or the ancient city, is transported to us on the wings of the wind . . . . There is no exaggeration in talking of those things as really existing. *Berkeley* was a metaphysician; and therefore his word goes for nothing but waste of brains, time, and printing-ink; but if we have not the waters of the Lake of Geneva, and the bricks and mortar of the little Greek town, tangible by our hands, we have them tangible by the eye . . . .[163]

Whether Shelley ever reflected on the applicability of his belief that 'nothing exists but as it is perceived' (*Prose*, p. 173) to this manifestation of Berkeleyan metaphysics cannot be known, for Shelley did not record his response to the panorama of Rome.[164] However, the panorama does illustrate another possible

---

[161] See Ralph Hyde, *Panoramania!: The Art and Entertainment of the 'All-Embracing' View* (London: Trefoil Publications, 1988), p. 74.

[162] For a full account of production techniques, see Stephan Oettermann, *The Panorama: History of a Mass Medium*, trans. Deborah Lucas Schneider (New York: Zone Books, 1997), pp. 51-9.

[163] 'Pompeii', *Blackwood's Edinburgh Magazine*, 15 (Apr. 1824), pp. 472-3; See also Altick, *Shows*, p. 181.

[164] His letter to Hogg of 21 December 1818 indicates that Shelley's keen interest in optical contrivances stopped short of their popular applications: 'Your kalleidoscope spread like the

version of what Shelley meant by 'shew-knowledge' when rejecting the literary efforts of popular travel writers. The 'shew' Rome reduces experience to static vision, an anthology of geographical features and edifices, a template for recognition and rehearsal; the virtual tourist, like the Grand Tourist, gains cultural accreditation for having seen the 'eternal city' by an authorised view. Stephan Oetterman has argued that 'the choice [of standpoint] was highly symbolic'.[165] Panoramas placed spectators in positions of eminence that emphasised their commanding presence and national stature. In the 'View of Rome', the Capitol represents a compendium of Rome's mythical and historical past (see fig. 5). As Eustace recounts, it had been 'the seat of the tutelar deities of the empire' (*CT*, 1: 361), including Jupiter Capitolinus ('wielding the sceptre of the universe'; *CT* 1: 363), while the Palazzo Senatorio with its tower was 'the palace of the Roman people, the seat of their power, and the residence of their magistrates' (*CT*, 1: 367). For the British citizen to access this viewpoint, without having to leave England, served to remind them of their privileged position in the new seat of empire and liberty. However, this democratisation of space provoked the panorama's critics. The usurpation of the Grand Tourist's position by anyone with a spare shilling meant an unwelcome mixing of classes, which the guidebooks did nothing to alleviate. The difference between the six-penny and the shilling guide is one of quantity. The shilling pamphlet merely expands on the shorter version, often adding information about what is not seen; the more affluent visitor might read of what was inside a church as well as of its history, but learns nothing qualitatively different.

The panorama of Rome effected travel writing. Eustace, for example, performs due oblations before St Peter's upon his arrival at Rome, as might be expected from a Catholic priest. His account proper then begins with an elaborate panoramic view: 'from St. Peter's we hastened to the capital, and ascending the tower, seated ourselves under the shade of its pinnacle, and fixed our eyes on the view beneath and round us' (*CT*, 1: 354-5). For panorama-goers like Shelley, Eustace's establishing shot would have been completely familiar, down to the canopy overhead, though in this instance Eustace may have influenced Barker and Burford's Panorama as much as it him.[166] Another travel writer who uses panorama was Charlotte Eaton, whose *Rome in the Nineteenth Century* (1820) recounts a tour

---

pestilence at Livorno. A few weeks after I sent your description to a young English mechanist of that town, I heard that the whole population were given up to Kalleidoscopism. It was like the fever which seized the Abderites who wandered about the streets repeating some verses of Euripides' (*L*, 2: 69). Abder was a town in Thrace whose inhabitants were proverbial for stupidity caused by pestilential air. The kaleidoscope ('to see beautiful forms') was invented by David Brewster (1781-1868) in 1816 and often imitated.
[165] Oettermann, *The Panorama*, p. 21.
[166] Eustace's panorama evinces an awareness of the structure and viewpoint of the London panoramas, and he may well have seen a panorama of Rome painted by Richard Reinagle around 1802, though whether Reinagle used the 'Tower of the Capitol' as his viewpoint cannot be established with certainty. The Bodleian Library does holds a pamphlet, *An Explanation of the View of Rome, Taken from the Tower of the Capitol. By R. R. Reinagle*, tentatively dated 1803, though this may be another guide to the 1817-18 exhibition.

'Relics of Antiquity': Shelley's Classical Tour through Italy

Fig. 5. Fold-out map from *An Explanation of the View of Rome . . . by R. R. Reinagle, 1817*. Bodleian reference (shelfmark) 17006 d. 235 (4).

in 1817 and 1818 nearly overlapping Shelley's own. After describing the approach to Rome, Eaton begins her account of the city with two 'first impressions' chapters on the centres of her enthusiasm: 'St Peter's', 'the Modern Capitol', 'The Forum' and 'the Coliseum'. Then comes a chapter entitled like its famous namesake, 'View of Rome from the Tower of the Capitol'. As a whole, Eaton's *Rome* is similarly structured to Eustace's *Classical Tour*. After the all-embracing view, Eustace pursues a thematic path through the ancient and modern city, beginning with each of the seven hills and then grouping observations of 'churches, monuments, tombs, hills, and fields' (*CT*, 1: 360 n.). Eaton follows her panorama with a fairly methodical account of principal groupings of classical structures, with volume two devoted to temples, baths, and tombs.

Eaton's book differs from Eustace's in the degree to which she allows enthusiasm to colour her reflections. In the panorama chapter, for example, Eaton dizzyingly spirals outwards, beginning with immediate objects of interest at each compass point, then turning round the middle distance until she reaches 'the classic mountains that bounded the blue horizon'.[167] Through rapid accumulation of detail, she disorders the sense of control that the panorama's circularity might otherwise impose, though Eaton may also wish to capture something of the 'see-sickness' experienced by some visitors to the Strand.[168] Even as John Ruskin later remarked that actual travel made the panorama's 'deep wonder become fathomless',[169] Eaton attempts to represent to her show-going public the excesses of authenticity on the spot. Shelley makes similar comments on another show. Visiting the statue of Castor and Pollux at the Quirinal fountain, he recalls Canova's reproductions in London:

> These figures combine the irresistible energy with the sublime & perfect loveliness supposed to have belonged to the divine nature. . . . The countenances at so great a height are scarcely visible & I have a better idea of that of which we saw the cast together in London than of the other. But the sublime and living majesty of their limbs & mien . . . seen in the blue sky of Italy, & overlooking the City of Rome, surrounded by the light & the music of that chrystalline fountain, no cast can com[m]unicate. (*L*, 2: 88-9).[170]

If cast and panorama represent 'shews', and the Panorama 'explanation' (along with travel writings of Eustace, Hobhouse, and Forsyth) 'shew knowledge',

---

[167] Charlotte Eaton, *Rome in the Nineteenth Century*, 3 vols (Edinburgh, 1820), 1: 146.
[168] Oettermann describes how many visitors to the panorama experienced feelings of nausea that he describes as 'see-sickness' (*The Panorama*, pp. 12-13).
[169] John Ruskin, *Praeterita* (Oxford: Oxford University Press, 1989), p. 106.
[170] Shelley and Peacock saw Canova's casts of Phidias's Castor, probably at the British Museum (see *MWSJ*, p. 193, n. 6; *CCJ*, p. 84). The casts were evidently part of a touring exhibition, hence the catalogue, *Royal Mews Gallery Exhibition of the Celebrated Heroic Equestrian Group of Monte Cavallo at Rome, with Other Statues . . . also a . . . Collection of Cabinet Pictures* (London, 1816).

Shelley may be seen to be arguing for the value of authentic travel and expression. The experience of travel brings ideas to life; travel writing must do the same.

Like Eaton's, then, Shelley's account of Rome takes place against a backdrop of 'virtual' travel. Shelley writes to one with whom he had already 'seen' Rome at the Panorama, at the British Museum, at other exhibits, and through a common course of classical reading. However, Shelley staunchly refuses to acknowledge any benefits to panoramic vision, and avoids the establishing tableau (as he did when setting up his sublime encounter at the Cascata). Instead, he reproduces Rome through selective sightseeing. Though his Roman letters at times suggest a linear logic in his ordering of objects, as in his account of the Roman Forum, he prefers a more open plan; as he writes of the Baths of Caracalla: 'I speak of these things not in the order in which I visited them, but in that of the impressions which they made on me, or perhaps as chance directs' (*L*, 2: 85). In his first Roman letter, written from Naples on 17 or 18 December, Coliseum displaces Tower as the centre of interest. Eaton, who uses the Coliseum as a structural motif in her book, leads her reader 'round the vast circle',[171] as does Eustace, before entering. Shelley, however, quickly establishes a viewpoint *within* the structure, emphasising the spectator's disorientation, his or her lack of control over the sublime object:

> The Coliseum is unlike any work of human hands I ever saw before. It is of enormous height & circuit & the arches built of massy stones are piled on one another, & jut into the blue air shattered into the forms of overhanging rocks. It has been changed by time into the image of an amphitheatre of rocky hills overgrown by the wild-olive the myrtle & the fig tree, & threaded by little paths which wind among its ruined stairs & immeasurable galleries; the copse-wood overshadows you as you wander through its labyrinths & the wild weeds of this climate of flowers bloom under your feet. The arena is covered with grass, & pierces like the skirts of a natural plain the chasms of the broken arches around. But a small part of the exterior circumference remains, it is exquisitely light & beautiful, & the effect of the perfection of its architecture adorned with ranges of Corinthian pilasters supporting a bold cornice, is such as to diminish the effect of its greatness. The interior is all ruin. I can scarcely believe that when encrusted with Dorian marble & ornamented by columns of Egyptian granite its effect could have been so sublime & so impressive as in its present state. It is open to the sky, & it was the clear & sunny weather of the end of November in this climate when we visited it day after day. (*L*, 2: 58-9)

This remarkable description emphasises how great architectural ruins become subject to natural processes until they become almost indistinguishable from sublime and beautiful objects in nature.[172] Shelley strips the Coliseum of features

---

[171] Eaton, *Rome*, 1: 134.

[172] Cf. Shelley's description of the intact Roman aqueduct at Spoleto: 'I never saw a more impressive picture; in which the shapes of nature are of the grandest order, but over which the creations of man sublime from their antiquity & greatness seem to predominate' (*L*, 2: 55).

that impressed other travellers. Equally enthusiastic about the 'mighty Coliseum', Eaton nevertheless points out the fourteen Stations of the Cross ranged around the ellipse, 'the huge black cross' in the centre, and another on the 'external elevation preserved entire', all 'grievously offending the protestant eye of taste'.[173] Shelley's eye elides the Christian iconography altogether, and his notice of the elevation pointedly stops at the 'Corinthian pilasters' and 'bold cornice'. Eaton condemns 'a little public garden' laid out in the French taste at the 'base of the Coliseum': 'I . . . longed to grub them all up by the roots, to carry off every vestige of the trim paling, and bring destruction upon all the smooth gravel walks'.[174] Shelley's eye obliges, laying down winding paths, wild weeds, and flowers that 'bloom under your feet'. Eaton leads her reader up a 'temporary wooden staircase' that gives access to the 'highest practicable point of the edifice'.[175] Shelley mentions only 'ruined stairs' and 'immeasurable galleries'. As for the upper tour, we are already there; his detail about the 'Corinthian pilasters' refers to the order of the fourth and highest level of the structure (Shelley does not mention the other three).[176]

Nor does Shelley supplement the pictorial with the historical. Reinagle's *Explanation of the View of Rome* merges architectural detail with the history of the Coliseum's construction and preservation, and, describing the arena's dimensions, relates the gladiatorial blood sports that took place there.[177] Eaton devotes a separate chapter to the structure's history, emphasising how 'the beauty and refinement of the arts which adorn it, form a striking contrast to the barbarism of the purposes for which it was erected', a fact, she claims, the eye cannot ignore: 'all beautiful as it is, we must ever regard it with mingled admiration and horror'.[178] By contrast, Shelley's focus on material presence – the way the ruin engages the eye and leads it beyond signs of construction, function, and appropriation – emphasise how the Coliseum escapes history: it is 'unlike any work of human hands'. His vision resembles Byron's in *Manfred*, where the Coliseum is 'a noble wreck, in ruinous perfection'.[179] In Byron's poem, the moon acts the part of Shelley's eye:

---

[173] Eaton, *Rome*, 1: 134-5.
[174] Eaton, *Rome*, 1: 136.
[175] Eaton, *Rome*, 1: 136.
[176] Eaton also condemns the architectural taste of the elevation, but argues that 'the fault lies in the Doric' (*Rome*, 2: 58).
[177] R. R. Reinagle, *An Explanation of the View of Rome, Taken from the Tower of the Capitol. Now Exhibiting at the Panorama, near the New Church, in the Strand* (Smithfield: Printed by J. Adlard, [n.d.]), pp. 8-9.
[178] Eaton, *Rome*, 2: 57-58; 2: 71. Eaton's sentiments are anticipated by, among others, Aubrey George Spencer in his poem, *The Coliseum; of A Letter from Rome* (Norwich, 1818), and Byron in *Childe Harold* IV (1818).
[179] More immediately, Shelley invokes the Coliseum lines in *Childe Harold* IV as indicated by his suppressed allusion to them in the letter to Peacock: 'We staid there [Rome] only a week intending to return at the end of February & devote two or three months to its *mines of inexhaustible contemplation*' (*L*, 2: 58; my italics). Cf. *Childe Harold* IV, ll. 1150-51 (*Byron PW*, 2: 167).

> And thou didst shine, thou rolling moon, upon
> All this, and cast a wide and tender light,
> Which soften'd down the hoar austerity
> Of rugged desolation, and fill'd up,
> As 'twere, anew, the gaps of centuries;
> Leaving that beautiful which still was so,
> And making that which was not....
>
> (*Byron PW*, 4: 98, III, iv. 31-7)[180]

However, Byron undercuts Manfred's vision with a sense that the aesthetic has been turned into another form of tyranny; the Coliseum exacts 'silent worship' (III, iv. 38) of the past, while 'the dead ... rule / Our spirits from their urns' (III, iv. 40-41). Eaton, too, believes that 'at Rome, it is not the present or the future that occupies us, but the past'.[181] Against these forms of representation, Shelley's aesthetic vision of a present in which cosmic replaces human history serves his more progressive ideals.

On 25 November, the day before he departed for Naples, Shelley began writing a romance, 'The Coliseum'.[182] The fragment develops his aesthetic idealism and is also an important meditation on authentic perception and expression, a counter to the 'shew-knowledge' of superficial tourism. The principal characters are a blind man and his daughter, Helen, who find themselves among the Coliseum ruins during Holy Week. Much of the fragment consists of the father 'contemplating this monument ... in the mirror of [his] daughter's mind' (*Prose*, p. 228), or, in her words, for Helen describes what he cannot see. As such, daughter and father refract the relationship between tourist, travel writer, and reader: the father plays Peacock to Helen's Shelley. However, it is not quite this simple. In overwriting his daughter's visual descriptions, transforming immediate impressions into prose poetry, the father becomes Shelley's ideal reader; one who reads creatively. But he also reflects a more complex form of associative impressionism that reflects

---

[180] Shelley echoes these *Manfred* lines more directly when describing the Baths of Caracalla: 'Around rise other crags & other peaks all arrayed & the deformity of their vast *desolation softened down* by the undecaying investiture of nature. Come to Rome. It is a scene by which expression is overpowered' (*L*, 2: 85; my italics). Another who agreed that Byron had overpowered expression was Henry Matthews: 'what can I say of the Coliseum? It must be *seen*; to describe it I should have thought impossible, – if I had not read Manfred .... His description is the very thing itself' (*Diary of an Invalid*, p. 155).

[181] Eaton, *Rome*, 1: xii.

[182] I have retained Shelley's spelling for the amphitheatre ('Coliseum') even though the Latin form ('Colosseum') has been used in *Prose*. Until Timothy Clark's article, 'Shelley's "The Coliseum" and the Sublime', *Durham University Journal*, 85 (July 1993), pp. 225-35, critical analysis of the fragment was at best sketchy. Clark's analysis has similarities with mine, though I differ in my relation of the fragment to Shelley's letter to Peacock on the same subject. More recently, Kevin Binfield has usefully argued that the fragment 'proposes a rhetorical solution to the problem of history', an argument that also complements my approach. See '"May they be divided never": Ethics, History, and the Rhetorical Imagination in Shelley's "The Coliseum"', *Keats-Shelley Journal*, 46 (1997), pp. 125-47.

Shelley's technique in describing the same scenes to Peacock. The fragment effectively theorises Shelley's practice as a travel writer.

The narrative begins by distinguishing between popular and authentic tourism. The father and Helen have just arrived at Rome, but they do not seek out the Vatican festivities 'with all the foreigners who flock from all parts of the earth' (*Prose*, p. 224); instead they follow Sir Richard Colt Hoare's advice and head straight for the Coliseum.[183] Without guidebooks, they stumble on their destination before realising what in fact it is, choosing the ruined 'southern part' over the intact northern elevation. Selecting, like Eaton at the Temple of Concord, a seat on 'a fallen column',[184] they sit 'as in silent contemplation'. Yet the father is at peace within his own mind, while Helen's eyes are fixed on his lips, which 'filled the silent air with smiles, not reflected from external forms' (*Prose*, p. 224). The father resembles a statue, 'a Praxitelean image of the greatest of poets' (*Prose*, p. 224), and with his daughter makes a group. Shelley thus establishes a scene of writing that initially privileges art over scenery, subject over object.

The pair are then accosted by 'a figure only visible at Rome in night or solitude . . . amid the desolated temples of the Forum' (*Prose*, p. 224). Eaton describes a similar encounter when a convent bell tolls midnight and 'a figure glided from the shade of the Temple of Concord . . . and disappeared among the trees'. Her phantom appears while she is moralising on oblivion and memory, what is lost and what survives the ruins of power, and the figure seems a visitant from that past or something generated from 'the rules of romance'.[185] Shelley's youthful figure similarly represents the genius of the place; he wears 'an ancient chlamys' and 'ivory sandals, delicately sculptured' (*Prose*, p. 224). He also resembles a disaffected Grand Tourist, remade in the image of the Greek Revival. He is pointedly dissociated from modern Italians 'whose language he seemed scarcely to understand', and aligned with the classical world ('he spoke Latin, and especially Greek') and European refinement ('[he] was occasionally seen to converse with some accomplished foreigner') (*Prose*, p. 224). Though ultimately an undeveloped character, the stranger embodies features of the father (both are described in terms of sculpture) and Helen (both have deep reflective eyes) and unites them: 'a timid expression of womanish tenderness . . . which contrasted, yet intermingled strangely, with the abstracted and fearless character' (*Prose*, p. 224). Despite these requisites, he misreads father and daughter as modern tourists unaffected by the Coliseum. Like Prometheus and other Shelleyan misperceivers, the enlightened youth must learn yet one lesson more in how to see with a worthy eye.

If lesson there was to be, it remains outside the scope of the fragment. Instead, Shelley creates a dialectical demonstration of tourist perception and expression,

---

[183] Hoare, *Hints to Travellers in Italy*, p. 27. Like his characters, Shelley visited the Coliseum on Good Friday in 1819, but otherwise spent Holy Week mingling with other tourists at St Peter's and the Vatican. See *MWSJ*, pp. 256-7.

[184] Cf. Eaton, *Rome*, 1: 126-7: 'I seated myself on the fragment of a broken column at the base of the Temple of Concord, and as I gazed on the ruins around me, the remembrance of the scenes . . . forced on my mind . . . the eternal truth . . . '.

[185] Eaton, *Rome*, 3: 423.

observation and writing, performed by the blind father and Helen. Shelley begins by analysing how touristic encounter resists and enables accurate discourse. To her father's question, 'Why have you been silent now?', Helen gives a multi-part answer: 'first the wonder and pleasure of the sight, then the words of the stranger, and then thinking on what he had said, and how he had looked — and now . . . your own words' (*Prose*, p. 225). The first impediment is the incommensurability of language to experience, what leads Eaton to exclaim, 'no monument of human power . . . ever spoke so forcibly to the heart, or awakened feelings so powerful and unutterable'.[186] Next, Helen comes up against the stranger's information, 'these are the ruins of the Coliseum' (*Prose*, p. 225), a knowledge that overwrites onto affective experience overdetermined cultural representations, accumulated in histories and travel accounts. Finally, Helen's father reminds her of the travel writer's duty, to 'describe . . . objects that give you delight' and 'to array them in the soft radiance of your words' (*Prose*, p. 225). Freed from the burden of accounting for everything, Helen proceeds exactly in the mode of Shelley's addresses to Peacock, as when Shelley wrote from Geneva in 1816: 'I will simply detail to you, all that . . . if related . . . could enable you to conceive of what we have done or seen . . . ' (*L*, 1: 495).

Compared with Shelley's description of the Coliseum in his letter to Peacock, Helen's seems more literal, though not unenthusiastic. Shelley's letter quickly achieves a metaphorical register: 'arches built of massy stones are piled on one another, & jut into the blue air shattered into the forms of overhanging rocks . . . the image of an amphitheatre of rocky hills'. Helen deploys the same imagery denotatively and causally: 'a great circle of arches built upon arches, and shattered stones lie around, that once made a part of the solid wall' (*Prose*, p. 225). By contrast, her father represents an imaginative aesthetic that is dependent on visual accuracy for its 'truth'. He transforms Helen's 'bright-green mossy ground' into 'lawny dells . . . in the Alps of Savoy'; her 'arches built of massy stone' into 'great wrecked arches, the shattered masses of precipitous ruin . . . like chasms' (*Prose*, p. 226). His well-stocked mind accumulates imagery from past travels (presumably supplied by Helen on former occasions) as well as from other, more arcane sources (natural science, myth). From the foundations Helen provides, he creates new ideas and more imaginative combinations, as when he refigures chasms into 'caverns such as the untamed elephant might choose, amid the Indian wilderness, wherein to hide her cubs' (*Prose*, p. 226).[187] Helen responds, 'your words image forth what I would have expressed, but . . . could not' (*Prose*, p. 226). Kevin Binfield argues that this is because Helen is a materialist 'subject to the distortions that tradition works upon perception' while her father represents Shelley's disavowal of Holbach's materialism for a 'notion of sensory self-reliance' derived from Locke.[188] However, Binfield ignores the father's acknowledgement of 'the soft

---

[186] Eaton, *Rome*, 1: 132.
[187] Cf. *HSWT*, p. 179: 'Is this the scene / Where old Earthquake-dæmon taught her young / Ruin?'.
[188] Binfield, 'Ethics, History, and the Rhetorical Imagination in Shelley's "The Coliseum"', pp. 130-32.

radiance of [Helen's] words' and the 'dear dependence' (*Prose*, p. 225) they enforce. Rather, Shelley brings out the relationship between close observation and imaginative associative writing. Prompted by her father, Helen is perfectly capable of achieving a middle register, a synthesis of the observant and imaginative summed up in her exclamations, 'I see — I feel its clear and piercing beams fill the universe' (*Prose*, p. 226). 'Seeing-Feeling' represents the style of discourse that Shelley aims at in his own travel descriptions, and this is what John Scott had referred to when discussing the travel writer's faithfulness to the foreign: 'He, therefore, "best shall paint them, who shall *feel* them most"'.[189]

'The Coliseum' also offers an explanation of the political and social importance of aesthetic vision; its view of history, as Binfield rightly observes, is 'perceptual *and* ethical'.[190] In his romance and his travel letters, Shelley hardly acknowledges the Coliseum's gladiatorial past, in contrast to Eaton, Eustace, Barker, and even Byron. The exception is an important footnote to the father's associative reading in the fragment:

> Nor does a recollection of the use to which it may have been destined interfere with these emotions. Time has thrown its purple shadow athwart this scene, and no more is visible than the broad and everlasting character of human strength and genius, that pledge of all that is to be admirable and lovely in ages yet to come. . . . (*Prose*, p. 226)

Timothy Clark reads this as unsatisfactory compensation: 'in his excitement about the gorgeous ruins', Shelley had been 'too hasty to forget aspects of Roman History'.[191] However, Shelley consistently elides historical events in his travel letters, attending to the ways in which the visible and the imagined in tandem encompass history's lessons. In 'The Coliseum', historical memory merely supplements imagery – 'We do not forget these things' insists Shelley at the end of his note – and Shelley focuses on time's transformation of event into effect. The 'energy & error' (*L*, 2: 86) represented by historical oppressions become refined by ruins into tributes:

> It is because we enter into the meditations, designs, and destinies of something beyond ourselves that the contemplation of the ruins of human power excites an elevating sense of awfulness and beauty. It is therefore that the ocean, the glacier, the cataract, the tempest, the volcano have each a spirit which animates the extremities of our frame with tingling joy. . . . And this is Love. (*Prose*, p. 227)

---

[189] [Scott], Review of *The Diary of an Invalid*, p. 60.

[190] Binfield, 'Ethics, History, and the Rhetorical Imagination in Shelley's "The Coliseum"', p. 138 (my italics). Cf. Clark, 'Shelley's "The Coliseum" and the Sublime', p. 228: 'The major innovation [in 'The Coliseum'] . . . is the degree to which the ruins serve as the basis not for a reconstruction of the past, but paradoxically . . . for a powerful configuration of the future'.

[191] Clark, 'Shelley's "The Coliseum" and the Sublime', p. 233.

In *A Defence of Poetry*, composed in February-March 1821, the 'something' is changed to someone: 'The great secret of morals is Love; or a going out of our own nature, and an identification of ourselves with the beautiful which exists in thought, action, or person, not our own' (*SPP*, p. 517). Shelley's theory of the imagination begins as a theory of tourist perception that sublimates historical motive into natural phenomena. 'Going out of our own nature' can also mean going into nature and history through faithful observation and art.

In their intergenerational and interpersonal love, the father-daughter relationship models aesthetic ideals of visual and visionary communion.[192] It is not too much to see in their collaborative relationship an emblem also of Shelley and Mary Shelley, when one considers their joint publication, *History of a Six Weeks Tour*. The *History* is one of the very few travel books to be published jointly by male and female authors, as internal evidence indicated to readers despite the Shelleys' decision to omit their names from the title page.[193] With its complex textual history including Mary Shelley's many revisions of Shelley's journals and letters, the *History* collaboration potentially melds and harmonises gendered discourses, much as Helen achieves a middle ground between the visual and imaginative with her 'see-feel' discourse. Eaton's similar attempt to bridge gender divides is relevant here. In her preface, Eaton represents herself as a scholar whose very leisure (as a woman) allows her to study on the spot, rather than merely applying a preformed classical education to the objects of her gaze. Studying while observing and feeling Rome, she promotes herself as the corrector of Eustace, while implicitly transforming her dispute about 'accuracy' into a dispute about the style of travel and travel writing. Participating in observation, Eaton thus has no caveats about railing against antiquarians while arguing with them for the 'true' historical meanings of sights; nor does she find it a double standard to combine enthusiasm with analysis. Symptomatic of her approach, the Coliseum appears in her book in different guises: first as a platform for sentimental moralising on history; then as a subject for historical analysis, and in the final volume as the place of leave-taking, haunted by her phantom figure of romance. Helen's 'see-feel' ideal in Shelley's fragment captures Eaton's sense of participating and feeling, producing accuracy that at once outstrips Eustace and the popular Panorama, with which she too competes.

---

[192] As Clark points out, the 'dialogue between father and daughter on commemoration and death' echoes and follows the pattern of 'Tintern Abbey' ('Shelley's "The Coliseum" and the Sublime', p. 233). However, Helen is not a passive receptacle of another's visions or memories (as is the 'Dorothy' figure in Wordsworth's poem) but an active participant in the creation of the scene.

[193] Only two other travel books before the *History* can be said to represent such a collaboration: John Parker and Mary Ann Parker's *A Voyage round the World, in the Gorgon Man of War. Performed and Written by Captain John Parker, His Widow, for the Advantage of a Numerous Family* (1795) and John Henry Manners and Elizabeth Manners's *Journal of a Trip to Paris by the Duke and Duchess of Rutland, July 1814* (London, [1814]). *Journal of a Trip*, however, appears to be largely the work of John Henry Manners, with Elizabeth Manners supplying drawings for coloured plates accompanying the text.

Mary Shelley's contribution to 'The Coliseum' collaboration was a counter-narrative romance fragment, 'Valerius: The Reanimated Roman' (1819).[194] 'Valerius' develops Shelley's motif of the displaced historical 'figure', in this case a Republic-era Roman reanimated in the nineteenth century. Valerius's perspective on the ruins of Rome resembles Eaton's from the Temple of Concord, when around her she sees 'the contrast of past greatness with present degradation'.[195] Yet Valerius cannot reconcile his view of Roman greatness with any of its post-Republican incarnations: Imperial, Christian, or modern. He thus regards the Coliseum, a structure that antedates his 'death', as the 'Type of Rome': 'degraded by a hateful superstition' yet 'still awakening in the imaginations of men all that can purify and ennoble the mind'.[196] Imagination is not enough, and Valerius's mood, like Eaton's, is always elegiac. To oppose such jaundice, Mary Shelley introduces Isabell Harley, a foreign resident who undertakes to show Valerius Rome in the Coliseum's spirit: 'When I visit the Coliseum, I do not think of Vespasian who built it or of the blood of gladiators and beasts which contaminated it, but I worship the spirit of antient Rome and of those noble heroes . . . who have enlightened the whole world'.[197] She takes him to another Shelleyan haunt, the Baths of Caracalla, where they ascend to the uppermost galleries and view a panoramic Rome. The experiment is a failure. Prepared differently, they see differently. Valerius contemplates a 'void'; Isabell a spirit of the past mingling with, though ultimately separated from, the modern city. Holding in tension Shelley's optimism through Isabell and Eaton's pessimism through Valerius, Mary Shelley's story is a fragment without resolution, but unlike Shelley's, one in which aesthetic vision provides no easy solutions for the Italian present. Both Valerius and Isabella see the present as a foreign land, and neither can escape their necessary alienation from it.

---

[194] Following arguments by Elizabeth Nitchie and Jean de Palacio, Charles E. Robinson accepts that 'Valerius' was written in 1819 and is based on Mary Shelley's visits to the various Roman sites in the Spring of that year. See Mary Shelley, *Collected Tales and Stories*, ed. Charles E. Robinson (Baltimore and London: Johns Hopkins University Press, 1976), p. 397.
[195] Eaton, *Rome*, 1: 126.
[196] Mary Shelley, 'Valerius', in *Collected Tales*, p. 335.
[197] Mary Shelley, 'Valerius', in *Collected Tales*, p. 340.

Chapter 5

'The Emblem of Italy':
Two-Fold Vision in *Prometheus Unbound*

There are two Italies; one composed of the green earth & transparent sea and the mighty ruins of ancient times, and aerial mountains, & the warm & radiant atmosphere which is interfused through all things. The other consists of the Italians of the present day, their works and ways. The one is the most sublime & lovely contemplation that can be conceived by the imagination of man; the other the most degraded disgusting & odious.
(Shelley, 'To Thomas Jefferson Hogg', 21 December 1818; *L*, 2: 67)

Reading Madam de Staël's *Corinne, or Italy* (1807) in Naples while anticipating a more intimate acquaintance with Rome, Shelley seems to have been impressed by the descriptions of 'the majestic and eloquent desolation of what Corinna calls the "City of the Dead"' (*L*, 2: 68). For Staël, Rome forms the fitting scene for the first confrontation of her heroine, the Italian improvisatrice, Corinne, and the Scottish gentleman, Oswald Lord Nelvil, not least because touring the ruins of Rome allows the two to achieve a 'lofty temper of mind' (*CT*, 1: 30-31 n) against which the demands of their respective national characters can be judged. Corinne undertakes to show Oswald Rome, to view 'our artistic masterpieces or the ancient ruins that teach us history through the imagination and feelings'. The lesson has its application to the present, for one 'may study the human spirit . . . in the different qualities of the arts, the buildings, and the ruins': '[Rome] is not simply a collection of dwellings; it is the history of the world, represented by different symbols and portrayed in different forms'.[1] Yet the world that Corinne and Oswald manage to create for themselves proves to be less than the zenith of the mind's progress, for Oswald is drawn inexorably back to England out of a sense of duty to his deceased father, who would have opposed Oswald's desired union with Corinne. Oswald ends up marrying Corinne's younger, fully English half-sister. Corinne's nerve fails at the crucial juncture when she imagines too vividly that Oswald's affections have been diverted from her. As Kenneth Churchill sums up, the novel raises 'the important theme of the mutual destructiveness of northern ideals of duty and domesticity and spontaneous southern vivacity'.[2]

---

[1] Anna Louise Germaine de Staël-Holstein, *Corrine, or Italy*, trans. and ed. Sylvia Raphael (Oxford: Oxford University Press, 1998), pp. 51; 82.
[2] Kenneth Churchill, *Italy and English Literature, 1764-1930* (London: Macmillan, 1980), p. 25.

The historicity of Italy in the imagination, as well as the individual mind's failure to actualise the ends it imagines, interests Shelley during his Italian tour, as is indicated by the proximity of *Corinne* to *Julian and Maddalo*.[3] Both works present the confrontation of a Briton with an Italian on Italian soil, rich with heritage, and both detail the failed ideals of unity, friendship, and international understanding that the confrontation seems briefly to nurture. In *Corinne*, Oswald is the more 'Byronic' character, racked by guilt and moroseness. By contrast, Corinne is ready to seize on reminders in ruins or art that 'there is in man an eternal power, a divine spark . . . and that you must never weary of kindling it in yourself and of reviving it in others'.[4] She thus attempts to draw Oswald from regarding the world in the distorted mirror of himself:

> 'My dear Oswald', said Corinne, 'you do not like the arts in themselves, but only because of their relationship to the heart or the mind. You are only moved by what recalls your heart's suffering. . . . the arts which appeal to the eye, although they may represent the ideal, please and interest us only when our hearts are at peace and our imaginations completely free'.[5]

Her argument closely resembles Shelley's criticism of Byron's 'tone of mind' in *Childe Harold* IV, and it is not difficult to see the similarity of her position to that of Julian in *Julian and Maddalo*. Through the figure of Corinne, Staël also achieves an intimation of the internationalist synthesis that Shelley argues for in his deployment of national encounter in the English Julian's confrontation with the Italian Maddalo. Corinne herself turns out to be the product of the union between a Scottish nobleman and an Italian, though raised predominately in Italy. Crucial to the complication in the plot, Corinne's hybridity at once gestures towards the fruitful unity of culture and towards the fatal limitations of her English stock; the desire of the North to reclaim its southern roots, and northern frigidity when faced with the South's warm response. For Shelley, the revivification of English culture's receptiveness would prove an important task, and one that he sought to actualise in his encounters with landscape, painting, and the plastic arts during his Italian tour.[6]

Nevertheless, Shelley's travel letters to Peacock between 6 April 1818 and 6 April 1819 do not dramatise a North-South divide as do *Julian and Maddalo* and

---

[3] In detailing the evidence for the date of composition of *Julian and Maddalo*, Alan M. Weinberg follows Matthews and Reiman in rejecting Shelley's claim that the poem was written at Este. If Matthews is correct in his belief that it was composed 'in or after December 1818 that is, either at Naples or Rome' (Weinberg, *Shelley's Italian Experience*, London, Macmillan, 1991, p. 45), then *Corinne* may have been a more crucial influence than has been hitherto credited.
[4] Staël-Holstein, *Corrine*, p. 65.
[5] Staël-Holstein, *Corrine*, p. 146.
[6] Cf. James Buzard, *The Beaten Track: European Tourism, Literature, and the Ways to Culture, 1800-1918* (Oxford: Clarendon Press, 1993), p. 113, on the 'revivificationists', including Staël, Goethe, and Rousseau.

Staël's *Corinne*. Instead, the letters record the confrontation and development of Shelley's aesthetic sensibility with the variety of sights approached by chance, or, more commonly, sought out in response to previous travellers, artists, and critics. Like Byron's, Staël's, and Eustace's Italy, Shelley's is a topography privileged with superlative instances of nature, art, and culture, that bear comparison with whatever the rest of Europe can offer in likeness, with the exception in Shelley's case of nature's energies expressed in the glaciers of Chamounix. But also like Byron, Staël, and Eustace, Shelley focuses his attention on Italy as foremost a place of art and artists, drawing on the landscapes for inspiration, giving in return to Italy the unity that modern political divisions deny it, and anticipating the apotheosis of world culture for which it forms the stem, if not the root. As such, Shelley's travel letters contain descriptions of landscapes that provide backdrops and commentaries on his other tableaux of painting, sculpture, architecture, and culture.

Eustace, who gives comparatively less space to landscape description than Shelley, reminds us in a short disquisition on 'scenery' that for most travellers Italy was the homeland of picturesque painting and therefore a natural place to look for scenes arranged like art. In his view, Italian landscape is especially amenable to 'an eye accustomed to contemplat[ing] prospects' because pure atmospheric conditions render visible even distant or obscure objects. Italy is 'a region, in which nature seems to have collected all her means of ornament, all her arts of pleasing' and the eye is suitably attracted by ever 'varied prospects'. He describes Italy as 'the school for painters, whether natives or foreigners' and he divides the topography south of Rome under the headings of the eighteenth century's most famous representatives of picturesque painting. Poussin (the Sabine Hills), Claude Lorraine (the Apennine range between Rome and Naples), and Salvatore Rosa (Calabria) mark with their imitative genius the gradations of territory from the picturesque to the sublime (*CT*, 4: 143-4).

Shelley's letters appropriately become more attuned to landscape as he moves south. With Eustace, he gives Italy as a whole its due for natural beauty in theory, but in practice saves his enthusiasm for the regions with the greatest reputation for picturesque beauty in nature: 'I reserve wonder for Naples' (*L*, 2: 43), Shelley writes from Este. Appropriately, Shelley's first Neapolitan letter (17 or 18 December 1818) contains the one landscape description of all the letters that rivals that of the Cascata delle Marmore: his picture of Vesuvius. The letter as a whole falls into two parts: an account of Shelley's sightseeing in Rome and an account of his Neapolitan excursions. It begins with Shelley's impressions on the hurried trip from Rome; he 'could just observe that the wild beauty of the scenery & the barbarian ferocity of the inhabitants progressively increased' (*L*, 2: 60), thus affirming Eustace's topography of the picturesque. But nothing better expresses the function of picturesque beauty than Shelley's own gloss on the relation between the landscape and its inhabitants. After describing an assassination he witnesses upon entering Naples, Shelley remarks: 'But external nature in these delightful regions contrasts with & compensates for the deformity & degradation of humanity' (*L*, 2: 60). The compensation is for the traveller alone, of course, who pursues the picturesque beyond or beneath the modern cities. The contrast, however, gestures towards the system of relations that forms the moral and political side of the traveller's or spectator's aesthetic appreciations.

As in the Cascata letter, Shelley's Vesuvius occupies the climactic position in a longer narrative of an excursion, in this case, the day trips around Naples, much of which follow Eustace in exploring the classical associations of various sites: *La Scuolo di Virgilio*, the Elysian Fields, and Lake Avernus.[7] Though Shelley's classical tourism is here much more sketchy than Eustace's detailed undertaking, it complements his landscape aesthetic, for Shelley continually seeks effects that heighten his perceptions, be they painterly or intertextual. The tone of disappointment that hangs over some of these excursions is testimony to this. Both the Elysian Fields and Solfatara strike Shelley as incommensurate with their poetic renderings. Of the latter, Shelley writes: 'the verses of the poet [Petronius] are infinitely finer than what he describes' (*L*, 2: 62).[8] Similarly, on Baiae Bay, Shelley remarks the contrast between the disappointing views on shore and those from their boat, where 'the colours of the water & the air breathe over all things here the radiance of their own beauty' (*L*, 2: 61). The account of these day trips ends with a moonlight return that also emphasises those effects of light and atmosphere that Eustace, too, in his dissertation on scenery, had noted as being characteristics of picturesque beauty: 'we returned by moonlight to Naples in our boat; what colours then were in the sky, what radiance in the evening star, & how the moon was encompassed by a light unknown to our regions!—' (*L*, 2: 62).

Against this backdrop, Vesuvius usurps even the place of the Cascata delle Marmore:

> Vesuvius is, after the glaciers the most impressive expression of the energies of nature I ever saw. It has not the immeasurable greatness the overpowering magnificence, nor above all the radiant beauty of the glaciers, but it has all their character of tremendous & irresistible strength. (*L*, 2: 62)

The absence of 'radiance' – a term that Shelley associates with picturesque beauty throughout the travel letters – signals a landscape that resists all appropriation or containment; we are in the presence of uncompromising sublimity, 'the most horrible chaos that can be imagined, riven into ghastly chasms' (*L*, 2: 62). Shelley's diction echoes 'Mont Blanc' where similar forces are summed up in the Earthquake-daemon lines, 'how hideously / Its shapes are heaped around! rude, bare, and high, / Ghastly, and scarred, and riven!' (*PS1*, B Text, ll. 69-71). The point is the same; Shelley wishes to demarcate 'the limits of the dead and living world' (l. 113). Also like 'Mont Blanc', and in keeping with its frame in the travel narrative, the Vesuvius description returns to the transforming presence of atmosphere with all its usual associations of picturesque effect. As nightfall

---

[7] Cf. *CT*, 2: 385; 2: 414-16; 2: 400ff.

[8] Shelley's disappointments are in part anticipated by Eustace, who writes of the Elysian Fields: 'The truth is, Virgil improves and embellishes whatever he touches; kindled by the contemplation of nature, his genius rises above her, and gives to her features, charms and beauties of his own creation' (*CT*, 2: 415-16).

approaches, Shelley's diction returns to the moonlight mode: 'the effect of the fire became more beautiful. We were as it were surrounded by streams & cataracts of a red & *radiant* fire' (*L*, 2: 63; my italics). In this light, Shelley concludes his sketch with a vignette that demonstrates how the scenes of nature contrast and compensate for human 'degradation':

> Our Guides on this occasion were complete Savages. You have no idea of the horrible cries which they suddenly utter, no one knows why, the clamour the vociferation & the tumult. . . . Nothing however can be more picturesque than the gestures & physiognomies of these savage people. And when in the darkness of night they unexpectedly begin to sing in chorus some fragment of their wild & but [sic] sweet national music, the effect is exceedingly fine— [.] (*L*, 2: 63)

Shelley is at his farthest from sympathy with actual people when deploying the accustomed picturesque response, and yet in so doing he creates a nationalist myth. Treating the Guides' otherness in the same vein as the natural otherness of Vesuvius, Shelley distances himself and his readers from their sudden utterances (like volcanic eruptions) with his incomprehension: 'no one knows why'. But in his record of the 'effects' of this by night, he transforms the horrible cries into 'sweet national music', the clamour into a chorus. Like the ruins of nature and empire that surround them, the music remains fragmented, awaiting the revolution of sensibility that will bring them to the observer's level of cultural refinement.[9] If the 'chaos' of Vesuvius militates against history, aesthetic mediation restores historicity to experience with the promise of a future shadowed forth in the present.

Shelley's picturesque representation of the guides, their 'gestures and physiognomies', is one of the only instances in the letters when people are included in landscapes. This is not the case with painting, for Shelley's gallery gazing takes in studies of grouped figures from history, religion, and myth, especially in the work of Raphael, Michelangelo, Correggio, Guido Reni, and others, the standard fare of travellers in Italy. Though Shelley's descriptions of such paintings may seem at several removes from his landscape descriptions, they share important similarities. For one, his critical notes on painting are as sensitive to form, arrangement, and opposition, as are his landscape descriptions of the natural and man-made objects that make up a scene. More crucially, Shelley's critical vocabulary favours the effects of light, colour, and atmosphere when referring to beauty. According to Frederick Colwell, Shelley's art criticism evinces a 'fascination with aerial forms' that is 'the stock in trade of Shelley's poetic

---

[9] In the 'Ode to Naples' (1820), Shelley also uses the picturesque to delineate revolutionary change associated with adjacent scenes. His introductory note to the poem states: 'The Author has connected many recollections of his visit to Pompeii and Baiae with the enthusiasm excited by the intelligence of the proclamation of a Constitutional Government at Naples. This has given a tinge of picturesque and descriptive imagery to the introductory Epodes which depicture these scenes, and some of the majestic feelings permanently connected with the scene of this animating event' (*PW*, p. 616).

vocabulary'.[10] Shelley's landscape and art criticism, in fact, suggest that he is forging one aesthetic for all human *techne* rather than merely deploying poetic sensibilities upon the sister arts. The terms of this aesthetic are evident in the resemblance between Shelley's landscape descriptions and his criticisms of painting. In both, Shelley is especially concerned with aesthetic effects which capture the effacement of subjectivity; that is, with establishing the percipient's mediation with the scene in question, often objectified in painting in terms of the painted figures' own mediation with their surroundings.

Shelley's descriptive meditations on painting and landscape implicitly, and at times explicitly, critique Byron's unorthodox analysis of 'ideal beauty' – what Peacock addresses in *Nightmare Abbey* when Mr. Glowry mutters his paraphrase of *Childe Harold*: 'The mind is diseased of its own beauty, and fevers into false creation' (i.e. 'Of its own beauty is the mind diseased, / And fevers into false creation'). Articulated in the Egeria fountain lines that Shelley thought so exceptional,[11] Byron's reflections on idealism challenged current thinking on ancient art brought to the fore by the Parliamentary debate in 1816 over the aesthetic value of the Elgin marbles, a prelude to their purchase for the nation. Proponents like Benjamin Robert Hayden argued that the marbles were 'more classically Greek than the Hellenistic Laocoon and the Belvedere Apollo',[12] but what 'classically Greek' actually meant was debated in terms drawn from the theories of Winckelmann and his followers, particularly A. W. Schlegel. In John Black's translation of *Lectures*, which Shelley used, Schlegel wrote: 'The Greeks . . . succeeded in combining in the most perfect manner in their art ideality with reality, or, dropping school terms, an elevation more than human with all the truth of life, and all the energy of bodily qualities'.[13] This mixing of real and ideal became fundamental to the anti-academic arguments of Haydon, Hazlitt, and Coleridge, who all found that the Elgin marbles revivified the Royal Academy's sterile notions on classical beauty.[14] Schlegel's theory was also developmental; if classical art and poetry was 'complete in itself', the modern or 'Romantic' expressed the ruptures introduced by Christian dualism, the striving to rejoin the spiritual and sensual. In *Childe Harold*, Byron develops Schlegel's notion of the modern experience of 'internal discord'[15] into a pathology of desire not limited to the moderns alone: art across the ages reflects nothing more than a 'desiring

---

[10] Frederick S. Colwell, 'Shelley and Italian Painting', *Keats-Shelley Journal*, 29 (1980), p. 60. See also, Weinberg, *Shelley's Italian Experience*, pp. 114-16.

[11] See *L*, 2: 44, where Shelley refers to 'those beautiful stanzas in the 4th Canto about the Nymph Egeria'.

[12] Nancy Moore Goslee, *Uriel's Eye: Miltonic Stationing and Statuary in Blake, Keats, and Shelley* (University of Alabama Press, 1985), p. 75.

[13] A. W. Schlegel, *A Course of Lectures on Dramatic Art and Literature*, trans. John Black, 2 vols (London, 1815), 1: 73; also cited by Goslee, *Uriel's Eye*, p. 75.

[14] See Jennifer Wallace, *Shelley and Greece: Rethinking Romantic Hellenism* (Basingstoke: Macmillan Press, 1997), pp. 154-5. See also, Gillen D'Arcy Wood, *The Shock of the Real: Romanticism and Visual Culture, 1760-1860* (New York: Palgrave, 2001), p. 245, n. 34 on the 'historical shift from literary classicism in England to its modern, material-visual phase'.

[15] Schlegel, *Lectures*, 1: 16; quoted in Goslee, *Uriel's Eye*, p. 72.

phantasy' (*Byron PW*, 2: 164) with no relation to the real or human. The artist and spectator value 'ideal' art insofar as it idealises and makes presentable in sensuous form something that they both lack. The Elgin marbles were more redolent to Byron as fragments, reflecting the unattainable object of desire, than they would have been in their pristine state. The modern condition and the human condition, Byron asserts, is to be 'a ruin amidst ruins' (*Byron PW*, 2: 132).

Shelley visited the Elgin marbles at the British Museum on 13 February 1818, before leaving for Italy, and Schlegel's *Lectures* formed part of his reading matter while en route. Though he did not begin reading Winckelmann until December, Shelley would have been familiar with Winckelmann's ideas through many possible intermediaries.[16] While Shelley recorded nothing of his response to the marbles, his pronouncements on statuary and painting in 1818-19 suggest his engagement with current aesthetic debates. In his *Discourse on the Manners of the Ancient Greeks*, for example, he notes how 'the ruins of a fine statue' 'obscurely suggest to us the grandeur of the whole' (*Prose*, p. 217). Later, in Florence, he pronounces that 'one of my chief {aims} in Italy' is 'the observing in statuary & painting the degree in which, & the rules according to which, that ideal beauty of which we have so intense yet so obscure an apprehension is *realized* in external forms' (*L*, 2: 126; my italics). In both instances, the work of art, whether ruined or 'whole', gestures 'obscurely' to a higher level of completion and unity.[17] Yet Shelley emphasises the intensity with which external forms 'realise' this gesture rather than its futility. Like Schlegel, he seeks to theorise art's combination of a reality effect with 'more than human' ideals, but he departs from both Schlegel and Byron by refusing to sever 'modern' creativity and the experience of art from classical models of excellence.[18] Rather than 'internal discord' or 'desire'

---

[16] There is no evidence that Shelley consulted Winckelmann before 24 December 1818 when he began reading Winckelmann's *Geschichte der Kunst des Altherthums* (1764) almost daily until 3 January 1819. Before then, Shelley may have imbibed Winckelmann's ideas through intermediaries such as Byron, Schlegel, and Coleridge. In particular, Byron's passage on the Laocoön in *Childe Harold* IV suggests a propinquity with Winckelmann that Shelley would later reject in his own note on the statue, composed after his reading of Winckelmann: 'Byron thinks that Laocoön's anguish is absorbed in that of his children, that a mortal's agony is blending with an immortal's patience. Not so. Intense physical suffering ... seems the predominant and overwhelming emotion' (*Prose*, p. 344).

[17] Shelley's thinking here parallels Winckelmann, who argues that the Grecian artist composes his works out of a Platonic intuition of 'something more than nature': 'Sensuous beauty was the model for the beauty of nature; ideal beauty for its sublimer features – the former for the human, the latter for the divine' (Johann Joachim Winckelmann, *Thoughts on the Imitation of the Painting and Sculpture of the Greeks*, trans. H. B. Nisbet, in *German Aesthetic and Literary Criticism*, ed. H. B. Nisbet, Cambridge, Cambridge University Press, 1985, pp. 35; 37).

[18] In his discussion of Raphael's 'St Cecilia', discussed below, Shelley reveals a close sympathy (or at least symmetry) with Winckelmann. Cecilia's 'countenance ... calmed by the depth of its passion & rapture' gestures towards and inverts the surface-depth terms of Winckelmann's famous reference to 'noble simplicity and tranquil grandeur' in Greek sculpture and painting: 'Just as the depths of the sea remain forever calm, however much the surface may rage, so does the expression of the Greek figures, however strong their

representing the spirit of art, Shelley turns to the self-replicating notion of 'rapture', a state that resembles the traveller's experience of the 'interpenetration' of subject and object with which *Euganean Hills* concludes.

In Bologna, Shelley regards painting in these terms. Correggio's 'The Saviour' depicts a Christ 'dilated with expression', 'heavy . . . with the weight of the rapture of the spirit' (*L*, 2: 49), while the colouring is 'absorbed' and 'penetrated' by 'every thing' (*L*, 2: 50). Guido's 'Christ Crucified' harmonises its subject matter with 'colours of a diviner nature, yet most like natures self' (*L*, 2: 50). Most of all, Shelley was impressed by Raphael's 'St Cecilia', one of the most important cultural objects for travellers to Bologna:

> You forget that it is a picture as you look at it, and yet it is most unlike any of those things which we call reality. It is of the inspired and ideal kind, and seems to have been conceived & executed in a similar state of feeling to that which produced among the antients those perfect specimens of poetry & sculpture which are the baffling models of suc[c]eeding generations. There is an unity & perfection in it of an incommunicable kind. The central figure St. Cæcilia *seems rapt in such inspiration as produced her image in the painters mind*, her deep dark eloquent eyes lifted up, her chesnut hair flung back from her forehead, one hand upon her bosom, her countenance as it were *calmed by the depth of its passion & rapture, & penetrated throughout with the warm & radiant light of life.* . . . Of the colouring I do not speak, it eclipses nature, yet it has all its truth & softness. (*L*, 2: 51-2; my italics)

Shelley's aesthetic appreciation of the painting's 'unity & perfection' coupled with his awareness of it as 'of an incommunicable kind' recalls his own exclamation when confronted with the sublimity of Mont Blanc: 'remember this was all *one* scene' (*HSWT*, p. 152; my italics). The painting successfully resists language and imitation ('the baffling models'), yet features associated with the beautiful contain its expression: calmness, softness, unity, and perfection. Shelley's analogy between the spectator's, the artist's, and the subject's rapture recalls the disorientated but positive receptiveness that characterises the raptures of travellers. St Cecilia's rapture points towards its sublime object as do her lifted eyes, and yet the rapture calms and inspires; similarly, Raphael 'rapt in such inspiration' receives and successfully translates its image; Shelley, the spectator, forgets 'that it is a picture' in the presence of an artist who like Rousseau 'cast[s] a shade of falsehood on the records that are called reality' (*HSWT*, p. 128). Implicitly, Shelley contrasts the 'state of feeling' with the 'tone of mind' that produced *Childe Harold*, for Shelley's image of the saint 'rapt in such inspiration as produced her image in the painter's mind' effectively counters Byron's image of the artist's 'mind diseased', fevering into 'false creation' by seizing on forms that exist 'in him alone'.

---

passions, reveal a great and dignified soul' (Winckelmann, *Thoughts*, pp. 33; 42). For a discussion of Winckelmann's creation of an aesthetic history of modernity out of Greek models, see David Ferris, *Silent Urns: Romanticism, Hellenism, Modernity* (Stanford: Stanford University Press, 2000), pp. 16-51.

Shelley's attraction to the Winckelmann camp put him in opposition to Reynolds's *Discourses on Art*, which Eustace takes for granted as one of the traveller's prerequisites for art appreciation (*CT*, 1: 18-19). Reynolds's commentary on the 'grand style' in Italian art did much for putting specific artists and works on travellers' itineraries. In particular, Reynolds's weighing of the respective merits of Raphael and Michelangelo, the two clear leaders in his hierarchy of taste, provided a conceptual backdrop for discussions on how and to what degree 'the greatest art . . . successfully unites the universal and the particular'.[19] If, as Colwell suggests, Raphael became increasingly associated with 'classical ideals' and Michelangelo with 'the stormy province of turbulent feeling',[20] Shelley's own break with 'taste' could not be more striking or revealing. While Shelley exalted Raphael, he found the more 'romantic' Michelangelo unpalatable because too particular, as his first reaction upon seeing a cartoon for 'The Judgement' in Naples attests:

> I cannot but think the genius of this artist highly overrated. He has not only no temperance no modesty no feeling for the just boundaries of art, (and in these respects an admirable genius may err) but he has no sense of beauty, and to want this is to want the essence of the creative power of mind. What is terror without a contrast with & connection with loveliness? How well Dante understood this secret, Dante with whom this artist has been so presumptuously compared! (*L*, 2: 80)

This damning criticism of Michelangelo gets to the heart of Shelley's unified aesthetic, especially since Shelley makes connections across the arts in his reference to Dante and in his general dictum that to want a sense of beauty is 'to want the essence of the creative power of mind'. For Shelley, Michelangelo's Christ, 'in an attitude of haranguing the assembly', ought to have been 'terrible yet lovely'; his Elect, like 'very ordinary people', ought to have been 'radiant with . . . everlasting light' (*L*, 2: 80; 81). While 'the region of the artist's exclusive power', Shelley feels, is 'Hell & Death', the moral sense that he derives from the whole as an 'infernal tragedy' results from this crucial absence of ideal beauty. Of course, in distinguishing the beautiful from the particular, Shelley develops a concept of beauty that has a social and cultural dimension, insofar as it is analogous to his disdain for the ordinary Italians mentioned so often in the letters. But for Shelley, this would only further emphasise the value of beauty in art for modelling a humanistic alternative to the present. The effect of beauteous art on the spectator is crucial, since, for Shelley, art has the power to make the spectator realise in

---

[19] Walter Jackson Bate, 'Introduction [to Sir Joshua Reynolds]', in *Criticism: The Major Texts* (San Diego: Harcourt Brace Jovanovich, 1970), p. 254. As Bate points out, this concern is characteristic especially of the later discourses which anticipate Romantic concerns with emotional immediacy and imaginative insight.
[20] Colwell, 'Shelley and Italian Painting', pp. 45-6.

himself the ideals that it depicts.[21] Correspondingly, the representability of those ideals becomes the best indication to the spectator that they *are* realisable, if only in the unspecified future.

Both Shelley's painting and landscape studies emphasise the 'contrast and connection' between the beautiful and the sublime, and the primary role of beauty in mediating aesthetic experience with the spectator. Given this parallel, it is not at all surprising that Shelley regards art and nature as 'contrasts and compensations' for human degradation and deformity, nor that the two operating in tandem with each other or with other kinds of aesthetic experience might shadow forth the great societies of the past on the screen of the future. Such are Shelley's reflections on the public and private spaces at Pompeii, where natural surroundings are integrated with painting and, what is more, architectural space. In his 23-24 January 1819 letter, Shelley conducts Peacock on an imaginary walk through the miraculously preserved streets and apartments of Pompeii, and describes the 'admirable plan' of the private dwellings, situated around courtyards with fountains, mosaics and paintings:

> There is an ideal life in the forms of these paintings of an incomparable loveliness, though most are evidently the work of very inferior artists. It seems as if from the atmosphere of mental beauty which surrounds them, every human being caught a splendour not his own. (*L*, 2: 72)

In 'Mont Blanc', which Shelley here echoes, the Ravine of Arve had been responsible for 'lending splendour' while human thought brought 'its tribute . . . / . . . with a sound but half its own' (*PS1*, B Text, ll. 4-6). In the new context, 'the everlasting universe of things / [that] flows through the mind' (ll. 1-2) becomes the 'atmosphere of mental beauty' expressed in painting and architecture. As Shelley develops his narrative of the tour to Pompeii, it becomes evident that these arts

---

[21] 'On the Medusa of Leonardo da Vinci in the Florentine Gallery', though of a slightly later date than the tour in question, captures the sense of the contiguity of the sublime with the beautiful in art, as well as the way the yoking of the two acts on the spectator:

> Yet it is less the horror than the grace
> Which turns the gazer's spirit into stone,
> Whereon the lineaments of that dead face
> Are graven, till the characters be grown
> Into itself, and thought no more can trace;
> 'Tis the melodious hue of beauty thrown
> Athwart the darkness and the glare of pain,
> Which humanize and harmonize the strain. (*PW*, p. 582)

In depicting the way in which the gazer is transformed into the likeness of the object of his gaze, even as engraving becomes organic growth, Shelley relates the death of Medusa's victims to the life of the painting in the spectator's mind. Terror is transformed by 'the melodious hue of beauty'.

supplement rather than replace the role of Nature in 'Mont Blanc', and they do so especially because they externalise and refine the epistemological flux described in the poem. If in the mind the 'universe of things' reflects gloom as well as lends splendour, in the atmosphere outside mental beauty it can only do the latter.

But if, as in Shelley's view of Spoleto, the works of man seem at times to predominate over Nature, this is only to the extent that these works harmonise with Nature, and become elemental expressions of human desire to be commensurate to the infinitude that lay beyond the bounds of impressions, and which the very excess of sensation indicates. When Shelley turns his attentions to ruins, the moral of his strain often turns on the harmony of original architectural forms with surrounding nature, where ruins attest to the holistic relation between man and nature in an earlier state of society (made accessible to the classical tourist). Thus, at Pompeii, Shelley's descriptions of such sights as the Temple of Jupiter envision the columned ruins as frames and 'portals' for the same natural views that impressed the ancients: 'They lived in harmony with nature, & the interstices of their incomparable columns, were portals as it were to admit the spirit of beauty which animates this glorious universe to visit those whom it inspired' (*L*, 2: 73). This leads Shelley to describe the interpenetration in architecture of art and nature:

> I now understand why the Greeks were such great Poets, & above all I can account, it seems to me, for the harmony the unity the perfection the uniform excellence of all their works of art. They lived in a perpetual commerce with external nature and nourished themselves upon the spirit of its forms. Their theatres were all open to the mountains & the sky. Their columns that ideal type of a sacred forest with its roof of interwoven tracery admitted the light & wind, the odour & the freshness of the country penetrated the cities. Their temples were mostly upaithric; & the flying clouds the stars or the deep sky were seen above. (*L*, 2: 74-5)

The 'sacred forest' of columns metaphor recalls the forest-like bower that the Narrator in *Alastor* weaves for the Poet, for that too contained elemental architectural forms, as we have seen: pyramid, arch, and dome (*PS1*, ll. 433-5). And that too is figured with a 'roof of interwoven tracery' that admits 'speck[s] / Of azure sky, darting between their chasms' (ll. 460-61). Even in the earlier poem, Shelley conceived of a prefigurative interpenetration of culture with nature, though the *Alastor* Poet, unlike the Greeks, had slipped beyond 'commerce' with society and the external world, and became wasted rather than nourished by 'the spirit of [their] forms'. By contrast, Shelley's Greeks express their most social being – in the theatre, the temple, and the city – under the auspices of a fundamental connection or economy with the external world. 'All their works of art' contain and idealise this unity of social, intellectual, and spiritual existence.

The Grecian orientation of Shelley's historiographical imaginings is unmistakeable in such fine strokes as the poet figure's special adeptness with the Greek language in 'The Coliseum' or in Shelley's bolder utterances on Pompeii's

Greek connections – 'If such is Pompeii, what was Athens' (*L*, 2: 73).[22] A similar enthusiasm colours his account in the 25 February letter of an all too brief journey to Paestum, where Shelley was enthralled with the temples of this outpost of Magna Graecia (see *L*, 2: 78-80). Even when Shelley turns fully to Rome in the last two letters of the series, his admiration for the ruins, sculptures, fountains, and monuments of the Latin and modern world is subtly measured against the more ancient standards of *upaithric* harmony. Shelley's long, fanciful description of the Baths of Caracalla that opens his account of Rome in the 23 March letter thus echoes his rendering of the Coliseum, emphasising 'their vast desolation softened down by the undecaying investiture of nature' (*L*, 2: 85): ruins that have escaped temporality and in doing so reconstitute the aesthetic origins of Grecian culture. At other points, Shelley does admire the monuments of imperial Rome, but in locating them in history, he is continually aware of the degree in which they express 'that mixture of energy & error' (*L*, 2: 86) when art is yoked to temporal politics, as in the triumphal arch of Constantine. Moreover, Shelley proves more of a classical tourist than even Eustace, who is keen to give churches place over and above temples, Christian art over Pagan, as landmarks of achievement. By contrast, Shelley is ever conscious of what he sees as an aesthetic fall brought on by the advent of Christianity. Christianity is 'a religion the destroyer of those arts which would have rendered so base a spoliation unnecessary' (*L*, 2: 86); as an institution it militates against the historiography implicit in the natural harmonies of art.

This aesthetic and historiographical argument is embodied in Shelley's comparison of St Peter's with the Pantheon. Of the first, Eustace's praise is unstinting: 'the whole of this most majestic fabric opened itself at once to the sight, and filled the eye and the imagination with magnitude, proportion, riches, and grandeur' (*CT*, 1: 354). In his well-known stanzas on 'piecemeal' perception in *Childe Harold* IV, Byron writes that 'of temples old, or altars new', St Peter's 'standest alone – with nothing like to thee' (*Byron PW*, 2: 176, st. 154, ll. 1378-9). He goes on to entertain the ultimately thwarted possibility that it gives the human mind some intimation of immortality:

> ... this
> Outshining and o'erwhelming edifice
> Fools our fond gaze, and greatest of the great
> Defies at first our Nature's littleness,
> Till, growing with its growth, we thus dilate
> Our spirits to the size of that they contemplate.
> (*Byron PW*, 2: 177, st. 158, ll. 1417-22)

Shelley for once finds himself checking Byron's hopeful enthusiasm. In the letter, he responds that the interior of St Paul's 'exhibits littleness on a large scale'

---

[22] By contrast, Eustace is affected by the sense in which Pompeii captures the experience of a Roman city, and he suggests a connection between the townscapes of that example and modern Italian cities. See *CT*, 3:56.

'The Emblem of Italy': Two-Fold Vision in Prometheus Unbound 197

(*L*, 2: 87). Aesthetically, Shelley's point is that this 'fane of living religion' 'is in every respect opposed to antique taste', but behind this criticism is his belief that taste reflects the authenticity of consciousness achieved in a historical epoch. The littleness that Shelley identifies is not that of 'our Nature', but that of our historicity, which can only be defied at the origins of aesthetic harmony or in its future. 'The effect of the Pantheon', Shelley thus holds,

> is totally the reverse of that of St. Peter's. Though not a fourth part of the size, it is as it were the visible image of the universe; in the perfection of its proportions, as when you regard the unmeasured dome of Heaven, the idea of magnitude is swallowed up & lost. It is open to the sky, & its wide dome is lighted by the ever changing illumination of the air. The clouds of noon fly over it and at night the keen stars are seen thro the azure darkness hanging immoveably, or driving after the driving moon among the clouds.
>
> (*L*, 2: 87-8)

Building on his observations of the Grecian ruins of Paestum, Shelley explores the 'delusion of perspective' that 'overpowers the idea of relative greatness, by establishing within itself a system of relations, destructive of your idea of its relation with other objects, on which our ideas of size depend' (*L*, 2: 80). The artist's ability to contain the illimitable and create such a delusion proves to be a virtuoso performance by Shelley's terms, if we remember his aesthetic idealisation of moments of containment, as when the lower cataracts of Terni image the more sublime upper fall 'on a smaller scale'. It is another case of ancient art, or the principles of ancient art, modelling the self-representing aspects of nature in the artist's own representations.

In the final letter of the series, Shelley turns his attention to the modern city of Rome. He had again changed his mind about the women; they have become 'gentle savages' or 'uncorrupted children' (*L*, 2: 92; 93), decidedly not up to refined European standards, but reminiscent of a Roman past. Shelley's descriptions of their 'sculptural' features show a marked similarity with his art criticism. However, the modern city is as expendable as Venice. 'Rome is eternal', Shelley writes, but his meaning is limited: '& were all that *is* extinguished, that which *has been*, the ruins & the sculptures would remain, & Raphael & Guido be alone regretted of all that Xtianity had suffered to spring forth from its dark & pernicious Chaos' (*L*, 2: 93). Shelley then describes a scene outside St Peter's of 'about 300 fettered criminals at work':

> The iron discord of those innumerable chains clanks up into the sonorous air, and produces, contrasted with the musical dashing of the fountains, & the deep azure beauty of the sky & the magnif[ic]ence of the architecture around a conflict of sensations allied to madness. It is the emblem of Italy: moral degradation contrasted with the glory of nature & the arts. (*L*, 2: 93-4)

As a summary of Shelley's classical tour through Italy, nothing could be more poignant. Shelley not only identifies the arts that captured most of his attention as the true embodiment of moral improvement, but locates the social-political divisions that militate against improvement before the foremost edifice of Christian faith in Rome, St Peter's. The 'madness' of the scene recalls an earlier moment 'not unallied to madness', the moment when Shelley faces Mont Blanc in the earlier *History of a Six Weeks' Tour*. As in the earlier case, this appears to be a creative madness; that confirmation of the 'mixture of energy & error' (*L*, 2: 86) that must be overcome by the combination of 'irresistible energy with sublime & perfect loveliness' in art.

Shelley's 'emblem of Italy' recalls his picture of universal apotheosis in *Prometheus Unbound*, Acts I-III, the poem for which Shelley announces the completion in the same letter. The madness might well be Prometheus's own when confronted by the Furies who, crowding behind Mercury, Ione wonders at:

> And who are those hydra tresses
> And *iron wings that climb the wind*,
> Whom the frowning God represses
> Like vapours steaming up behind,
> *Clanging loud, an endless crowd* – (*PS2*, Act I, ll. 326-30; my italics)

Though it is as likely that these lines lay behind Shelley's description of the 'iron discord' of the prisoner's 'innumerable chains' which 'clanks up into the sonorous air' (*L*, 2: 93) as the other way around, the parallel still suggests the consanguinity between Shelley's Italian experience and his meta-cultural thinking in the poem which occupied him from at least September 1818. The Furies that rise up before the giver of science and the arts, Prometheus, do indeed cause the conflict of sensations that Shelley allies with madness in the letter. As Prometheus puts it (ironically inverting Byron's lines on the dilation of spirit before the edifice of St Peter's):

> Whilst I behold such execrable shapes
> Methinks I grow like what I contemplate,
> And laugh and stare in loathsome sympathy. (*PS2*, I, 449-51)

But madness cannot ultimately affect one 'within whose mind sits peace serene / As light in the sun, throned' (I, 430-31); though tortured, Prometheus remains firm and embodies within himself the 'glory of the arts' against every form of 'moral degradation' the Furies can present him with.[23] If Shelley contrasts the prisoners with 'the musical dashing of fountains, & the deep azure beauty of the sky'

---

[23] Prometheus's response to the 'emblem' (*PS2*, I, 594) of the crucifixion resembles Shelley's in the 9 November letter from Bologna: 'One gets tired . . . of seeing that monotonous & agonized form forever exhibited in one prescriptive attitude of torture' (*L*, 2: 50). While in no position to deliver such calm criticism, Prometheus engages in a little revisionism of his own by demanding that the Furies' tableau be recomposed in a more ideal attitude: 'Fix, fix those tortured orbs in peace and death, / So thy sick throes shake not that crucifix, / So those pale fingers play not with thy gore' (I, 600-602).

(*L*, 2: 93), it is perfectly fitting that, beyond the power of the Furies, the prisoner Prometheus should receive the ministrations of 'a troop of spirits . . . / . . . in spring's delightful weather, / Thronging in the blue air!', and of those others who approach 'like fountain-vapours' (I, 664-6; 667).

According to Shelley, *Prometheus Unbound* owes a great deal to Italy, its blue sky, its seasons of rebirth, and the presence of its classical reminders of the past. As he writes in the preface:

> This Poem was chiefly written upon the mountainous ruins of the Baths of Caracalla, among the flowery glades, and thickets of odoriferous blossoming trees, which are extended in ever winding labyrinths upon its immense platforms and dizzy arches suspended in the air. The bright blue sky of Rome, and the effects of the vigorous awakening of spring in that divinest climate, and the new life with which it drenches the spirits even to intoxication, were the inspiration of this drama. (*PS2*, p. 473, ll. 37-43)

In her note to the poem, Mary Shelley takes Shelley's claims for inspiration quite literally, and so distinguishes between poets who 'clothe the ideal with familiar and sensible imagery' and Shelley who 'loved to idealize the real' (*PW*, p. 272):

> The charm of the Roman climate helped to clothe his thoughts in greater beauty than they had ever worn before. And, as he wandered among the ruins made one with Nature in their decay, or gazed on the Praxitelean shapes that throng the Vatican, the Capitol, and the palaces of Rome, his soul imbibed forms of loveliness which became a portion of itself. There are many passages in the *Prometheus* which show the intense delight he received from such studies, and give back the impression with a beauty of poetical description peculiarly his own. (*PW*, p. 274)

Geoffrey Matthews and Alan Weinberg have noted parallels and echoes between the geographical setting of Act II, Scenes ii-v and Shelley's descriptions of his excursions around Naples to Vesuvius and to the other areas of volcanic and subterranean activity 'which had been identified, since the days of antiquity, with uprisings, revolution, prophecy, inspiration, and rebirth'.[24] Similarly, Donald Reiman has described the composite sources for two architectural tableaux in Act III, Scene iv. The first, Shelley's rendering of the Spirit of the Hour's temple in the sun (*PS2*, III, iv, 111-21), combines his impressions of *La Salle della Biga* in the Vatican Museum with those of the Pantheon as expressed in the 23 March 1819 letter from Rome. The second (III, iv, 164-79), towards the conclusion of the Spirit's speech and thus the end of the Act, also synthesises impressions from the 23 March letter in describing the 'thrones, altars, judgement-seats, and prisons'

---

[24] Weinberg, *Shelley's Italian Experience*, p. 108, and pp. 108-111, *passim*. See also Geoffrey Matthews, 'A Volcano's Voice in Shelley', *Journal of English Literary History*, 24.3 (Sep. 1957), pp. 191-228.

which 'Stand, not o'erthrown, but unregarded now' (ll. 164; 179).[25] In addition to these sources and those I've suggested above, one might turn to Shelley's rendering of Pompeii (*L*, 2: 73) for Asia's description of the first cities after Prometheus's teachings ('Cities then / Were built, and through their snow-like columns flowed / The warm winds, and the azure ether shone, / And the blue sea and shadowy hills were seen'; II, iv, 94-7); or to his impressions of the 'winged figures of Victory' and the statues of Castor and Pollux (*L*, 2: 86; 89) for models of the 'wild-eyed charioteer[s]' (II, iv, 129-40; 156-62), one of whom conducts Asia and Panthea from the cave of Demogorgon.[26]

In 'idealizing the real', however, Shelley draws on his Italian impressions as 'the history of the world, represented by different symbols and portrayed in different forms'.[27] As a classical tourist, he explores the historicity of that which he observes, and this consciousness underlies the transformative nature of *Prometheus Unbound*, expressed in the poem's continuous re-imaginings of the past in the present and future. In a related discussion, Karl Kroeber identifies 'the poet's vision as an interfusing of visible and visionary, perceptible *is*, reconstructed *was*, envisioned *might be*'.[28] Reading a poem so concerned with the 'might be' as *Prometheus Unbound* in terms of Shelley's Italian travel experiences of the 'is' and 'was', one is continually aware of this temporal layering of imagery, form, and meaning. For instance, the utopia of the reunited Prometheus and Asia in Act III, as Reiman shows, is constructed out of the imagery of Shelley's Roman and Neapolitan excursions, while these same materials become used in the travel writing as emblems of Grecian influence or interconnection. Formally, Shelley's 'Lyrical Drama' also establishes its debt to Greece as a recasting of Aeschylus's lost drama in terms relevant to the post-French-Revolutionary present, not to mention Shelley's discussion of his 'imagery ... drawn from the operations of the human mind' (*PS2*, p. 472, ll. 44-5) with its precedent first in the imagery of the 'Greek poets', and later in that of Dante and Shakespeare. Here again an Italian mediation is noticeable, especially in the figure of Dante, whose *Commedia*

---

[25] Reiman, 'Roman Scenes in *Prometheus Unbound* III. iv', *Philological Quarterly*, 46 (1 Jan. 1967), pp. 69-78. See also Weinberg, *Shelley's Italian Experience*, pp. 111-13.

[26] Besides those of painting and the plastic arts, Shelley's impressions of landscape are likely to have their parallels in the poem, especially in the vegetative profusion that characterises the 'destined cave' where Prometheus and Asia retire in Act III. In a general sense, one is reminded of Shelley's long imaginative recreation of the Baths of Caracalla with its 'towers & labyrinthine recesses hidden & woven over by the wild growth of weeds & ivy' (*L*, 2: 84). At least one specific image, the 'odour-faded blooms / Which star the winds with points of coloured light / ... and bright, golden globes / Of fruit, suspended in their own green heaven' (III, iii, 137-40), can be found in the letters (*L*, 2: 78: 'golden globes ... & dark green leaves'; and *L*, 2: 83: 'On one side precipitous mountains whose bases slope into an inclined plane of olive & orange copses, the latter forming as it were an *emerald sky of leaves starred* with the innumerable globes of their ripening fruit whose rich splendour contrasted with the deep green foliage'; my italics).

[27] Staël-Holstein, *Corinne*, p. 82.

[28] Karl Kroeber, 'Experience as History: Shelley's Venice, Turner's Carthage', *English Literary History*, 41 (1974), p. 324.

Weinberg convincingly establishes as a vital structural forerunner of *Prometheus Unbound*.[29] More strikingly, Shelley's epigraph to the drama captures his archaeological vision. The lines he quotes are from Aeschylus's lost drama, *Epigoni*, as reproduced in Cicero's *Tusculan Disputations*, and may be rendered, 'Do you hear this, Amphiaraus, in your home beneath the earth?' (*PS2*, p. 471 n). On both the level of meaning and of form the quotation suggests the historical transference that underlies so much of Shelley's classical tourism; Cicero at once preserves and distorts the lost Greek text in the Latin, while Shelley contextualises and transforms its chthonic statement into an emblem of cultural transmission, figured partly in his own character 'Earth' from which all things proceed or take place (including Prometheus and Asia's temple and cave, and Demogorgon's abyss).

While concerned with history, historicity, and the end of history, *Prometheus Unbound* also concentrates on the problem of representation that preoccupied Shelley in his discussion of landscape, art, and architecture on the Italian tour. This dual concern in the poem reflects that of the prose, wherein Shelley explores the combinations of sublimity with beauty, and art with nature, in an effort to come to terms with an aesthetic sensibility at the root of history, motivating the present, and anticipating the future; in short, that 'ideal beauty' which 'compensates' those already privileged with a sufficiently refined sensibility (the 'citizens of the world') for the degradation of the European present. As in his sketch of the blind man and daughter in 'The Coliseum', Shelley attempts to recreate in *Prometheus* a world which 'excites an elevating sense of awfulness and beauty' (*Prose*, p. 227), but he again affirms that this is a world of representation as much as unmediated perception. To 'elevate' man, the essential opposition between nature and art must be done away with; an impossibility outside representation, and even then, Shelley leaves open in *his* art space for a metaphysical, noumenal reality.

In the most important sense, Prometheus and Asia mediate between the human and the divine, the temporal and the eternal, the real and the ideal. Prometheus, as Asia puts it to Demogorgon, 'gave man speech, and speech created thought / Which is the measure of the universe' (*PS2*, II, iv, 72-3) – not to mention his supplementary gifts of science, poetry, music, painting, sculpture, medicine, astronomy, navigation and architecture (II, iv, 74-97). The primacy of speech before thought, naming before ideating, measuring before comprehending, identifies man as a representational thinker. Likewise, each of the arts and sciences 'given' by Prometheus act on and elevate an initially passive, mimetic creature; for example, music 'lifted up the listening spirit / Until it walked' (II, iv, 77-8), while 'human hands first mimicked and then mocked, / With moulded limbs more lovely than its own, / The human form' (II, iv, 80-82).[30] Thus identified with the arts and sciences, Prometheus embodies this representational consciousness. Act I turns on his need to recall his own speech, objectified in the phantasm of Jupiter, and his renunciation of the curse follows from his recognising in this anti-image his own

---

[29] Weinberg, *Shelley's Italian Experience*, pp. 118-34.

[30] See the preface: 'As to imitation, poetry is a mimetic art. It creates, but it creates by combination and representation' (*PS2*, p. 474, ll. 88-9).

language's complicity with Jupiter's tyranny. Similar acts of reading occur as Prometheus confronts the visions fostered by the Furies and 'see[s] more clear / [The Tyrant's] works within my woe-illumèd mind' (I, 636-7). Even after his release, Prometheus envisions his retirement as a place of 'combination and representation' (*PS2*, p. 474, l. 88-9). Not only will he, Asia, and her 'sister nymphs' 'entangle buds and flowers . . . / . . . and make / Strange combinations out of common things' (III, iii, 30-32), but they will also receive 'the echoes of the human world' (III, iii, 44):

> And lovely apparitions – dim at first
> Then radiant, as the mind, arising bright
> From the embrace of beauty whence the forms
> Of which these are the phantoms, casts on them
> The gathered rays which are reality –
> Shall visit us, the progeny immortal
> Of Painting, Sculpture, and rapt Poesy,
> And arts, though unimagined, yet to be. (III, iii, 49-56)

As Shelley's precise but difficult syntax suggests, these 'echoes' are representations of representations, the 'phantoms' of the 'forms' of human art.[31] This is only fitting for the metaphysical realm which Shelley images. More crucially, Shelley emphasises the divinity of human art by depicting its reflex in the figure of Prometheus the maker. Prometheus is not beyond art'; he is its embodiment. On earth, Shelley's earth, art is the mind's 'embrace of beauty' clothed with the 'rays which are reality', though Shelley's confusing antecedents characteristically emphasise the interchange between his ideal of beauty and the object world, itself brought before the eye by the reflection of light.

If Shelley envisions Prometheus as the representative of Culture (art and science), Asia may be seen as Nature. But such an overly emblematic reading would miss Asia's aesthetic character, especially in its tension with the unrepresentability of absolute sublimity figured in Demogorgon, whom Asia counter-balances in Act II. In III, iii, Prometheus calls Asia 'thou light of life, / Shadow of beauty unbeheld' (*PS2*, ll. 6-7), associating her with the 'elevating spirit' of human art discussed above, or with 'the awful shadow of some unseen Power' (*PS1*, B Text, l. 1) in the 'Hymn to Intellectual Beauty'. Asia reinforces Shelley's idea of the essential contiguity or connection between the sublime and the beautiful, referred to in the travel letters during the excursion to the Falls of Terni. In 'her transforming presence' (*PS2*, I, 832) the sublime 'scene of her sad exile – rugged once / And desolate and frozen like this ravine [i.e. the scene of Act I]', is 'now invested with fair flowers and herbs, / And haunted by sweet airs and sounds' (I, 827-30). By contrast, Demogorgon's cave is a place beyond

---

[31] This is Shelley at his most un-Platonic. Far from lamenting poetry as a representation of a representation, Shelley sees a progressive function in this distortion, and moreover locates his 'forms' not in some metaphysical universal, but in 'reality'.

representation where 'the deep truth is imageless' (II, iv, 116), but which, following Matthews, is best associated with Vesuvius, the most extreme form of sublimity in the travel letters. Nevertheless, Asia mediates Demogorgon's 'deep truth' even as the lower Falls of Terni mediate the great cataract above. To Demogorgon, 'a voice / Is wanting' (II, iv, 115-16) except insofar as Asia can supply it: 'So much I asked before, and my heart gave / The response thou hast given; and of such truths / Each to itself must be the oracle' (II, iv, 121-3).

With the union of Asia and Prometheus in Act III, where Shelley had ended his poem before a fourth act was envisaged, Shelley brings his classical tour through Italy to its culmination. In his own 'rapt poesy', Shelley weaves a harmony of nature and art that rescues classical culture from Eustace's appropriation of it for Roman and Christian values; that challenges Byron's reading of ruins and landscapes; that refigures Staël's celebration of modern Italy's claims for a rejuvenated political and cultural life. The Cavern and Temple which forms Prometheus's and Asia's dowry from The Earth represent the co-eternal value of the profusion of nature and the perfection of art, much like Shelley's picture of Spoleto, but for the question of predominance that occupied him then. Also like the Baths of Caracalla or the Coliseum, which so delighted Shelley, the Cave and Temple have earned their perfection by outlasting the human error that created them as spaces or expressions of its own pathology. The Earth thus tells Prometheus and Asia:

> ... There is a Cavern where my spirit
> Was panted forth in anguish whilst thy pain
> Made my heart mad, and those who did inhale it
> Became mad too, and built a temple there,
> And spoke, and were oracular, and lured
> The erring nations round to mutual war,
> And faithless faith.... (*PS2*, III, iii, 124-30)

Though clearly a reference to the Grotto of the Sibyl outside Naples, Shelley locates the oracular spot 'beyond Indus, and its tribute rivers' (III, iii, 155), where the Cave has returned to nature, its 'ivy tangling wild' (III, iii, 136). The Temple likewise can be seen imaged 'on unerasing waves' (III, iii, 160) in a pool:

> Distinct with column, arch, and architrave,
> And palm-like capital, and over-wrought,
> And populous most with living imagery –
> Praxitelean shapes, whose marble smiles
> Fill the hushed air with everlasting love. (III, iii, 162-6)

Unlike his depiction of the Baths of Caracalla or the Coliseum, Shelley's transformed scene reconstructs ruins, and art becomes co-eternal with nature. The Corinthian architecture remains distinct, the Praxitelean sculpture lives, and the pool continues to represent the representation undisturbed by the time measured out by its own waves. At the Baths, Shelley describes a scene in which 'the deformity of their vast desolation [is] softened down by the undecaying investiture of nature':

> ... by the path through the blooming copse wood you come to a little mossy lawn, surrounded by the wild shrubs; it is overgrown with anemones, wall flowers & violets whose stalks pierce the starry moss, & with radiant blue flowers whose names I know not, & which scatter thro the air the divinest odour which as you recline under the shade of the ruin produces a sensation of voluptuous faintness like the combinations of sweet music. (*L*, 2: 85)

In *Prometheus Unbound*, ruins made whole take on nature's 'undecaying investiture' and shirk all deformity, rivalling the flower's 'divinest odours' with 'everlasting love'. Cavern and Temple continue to affirm the interdependence and interpenetration of the natural and human out of which Shelley, the sceptical idealist, constructs an ultimately social vision of utopia on the foundations of Western culture.

Chapter 6

'Empire o'er the Unborn World': Shelley's Hellas

We are all Greeks—our laws, our literature, our religion, our arts have their root in Greece. But for Greece, Rome, the instructor, the conqueror, or the metropolis of our ancestors would have spread no illumination with her arms, and we might still have been savages, and idolaters . . . . (Preface to *Hellas*, 1821; *SPP*, p. 431)

Birkbeck's Notes on America have fixed the public attention on that country in an unprecedented degree. He has emigrated with his whole family from a farm which he occupied in Surrey to the north-western territory where he has purchased a *prairie* of 4000 acres at the usual government price of two dollars an acre. Multitudes are following his example even from this neighbourhood. . . . the picture he presents of the march of population and cultivation beyond the Ohio is one of the most wonderful spectacles ever yet presented to the mind's eye of philosophy.

(Peacock, 'To P. B. Shelley', 15 September 1818, *LTLP*, 1: 152)

When Shelley received Morris Birkbeck's *Notes on a Journey in America* (1818) in a shipment of books and miscellany from Peacock in June 1819, he replied that the volume 'interested me exceedingly' (*L*, 2: 99); otherwise there is no further mention of Birkbeck in the letters or in Mary Shelley's journals, nor are there any direct references to the work in Shelley's subsequent poetry and prose writings.[1] Yet it is instructive to imagine Shelley turning from his study of painting, sculpture, and the ruins of classical civilisation in Italy to the contemplation of a transatlantic colonial venture that had such an impact among his contemporaries in Britain.[2] While Shelley refigured the ends of Western culture in *Prometheus*

---

[1] In the same passage relating to *Notes*, Shelley does mention Birkbeck's follow-up volume, *Letters from Illinois* (1818), as 'stupid' but 'useful' (*L*, 2: 99). Mary Shelley also lists Birkbeck's volumes among those books they especially desired Maria Gisborne to forward to Florence (5 October 1819, *MWSL*, 1: 110).

[2] According to Carol Kyros Walker, Birkbeck's *Notes* reached eleven editions between 1817 (the date of the first American edition) and 1819, while the *Letters from Illinois* sold out seven editions in 1818 alone. These accounts inspired numerous emigrants, including George and Georgiana Keats, to try their fortunes in America's Illinois territory. See *Walking North with Keats* (New Haven and London: Yale University Press, 1992), p. 10. For a more detailed account of Birkbeck's undertaking and its impact on British radical

Unbound as a Grecian apotheosis, where 'man remains, / Sceptreless, free, uncircumscribed: – but man: / Equal, unclassed, tribeless and nationless' (*PS2*, III, iv, 193-5), Birkbeck's planned community in the Illinois territory of America seemed to promise for many such a paradise on earth, though circumscribed by the national boundaries of a fledgling republic. Birkbeck's vision, like Shelley's, was an answer to the French Revolution's failure to transform European economic and political systems on republican and egalitarian principles; his America was a space in which the Revolution's promise could be re-enacted without a history of oppression to impede the transition between old ways and the new.[3] Like Shelley, Birkbeck imagined an undiscovered land, tenantless and fertile, in which the productions and populations of civilisation could take root and flower without constraint, or the need for Malthusian restraint.[4]

Birkbeck's community would have appealed to Shelley because it appeared to be grounded on fundamental human relations before they had been occluded by what Shelley refers to in *A Philosophical View of Reform* (1819) as an oligarchic 'double aristocracy', employing the structures of credit, finance, and government to perpetuate the imbalance of wealth and property (*Prose*, pp. 244-6). In Shelley's view, new moneyed interests had joined hereditary landowners to defraud labourers of the value they produce. Birkbeck's American wilderness opens up a space where labour could create and control surplus value for the benefit of the

---

discourse, see James Chandler, *England in 1819: The Politics of Literary Culture and the Case of Romantic Historicism* (Chicago and London: University of Chicago Press, 1998), pp. 454-9.

[3] Two important qualifications to this statement must be noted. First, Birkbeck elsewhere proves less convinced that the French Revolution had been an entire failure. Impressed by agricultural developments during his tour of France, he concludes: 'When capital, in the hands of well educated men, begins to be directed to rural affairs, a foundation is laid for a better state of society. A broad foundation of this sort is, I have been informed, already laid in France. Thanks to the Revolution!' (*Notes on a Journey through France*, 3rd edn, London, 1815, pp. 27-8). Second, Birkbeck's sense of America being free from a history of oppression applies largely to the territories. In *Notes on a Journey in America*, his choice of Illinois as a destination reflects his impassioned stance against slavery: 'All America is now suffering in morals through the baneful influence of negro slavery, partially tolerated, corrupting justice at the very source' (Birkbeck, *Notes on a Journey in America, from the Coast of Virginia to the Territory of Illinois*, London, 1818, p. 24). In the free territories, Birkbeck hoped to found a community outside this influence. On the oppression of Native Americans, he says little; that the 'wilderness' he colonises may have had inhabitants before him is beyond the concerns of the 'civilized' colonialist.

[4] In depicting 'the march of population and cultivation', as Peacock puts it, Birkbeck's *Notes* becomes a reply to Malthus's *Essay on the Principle of Population* (1798), which Shelley, Godwin, and other liberals saw as one of the greatest theoretical challenges to the philosophy of progressivist reform. For Birkbeck, procreation ensures rather than merely accompanies cultivation of the wilderness, and is described as a positive virtue in the *Notes*; Birkbeck criticises religious groups like the Shakers and Harmonites for practising 'unnatural restraint' in their outposts, a clear attack on the Malthusian principle of 'moral restraint' that Shelley also discusses in *A Philosophical View of Reform* (1820). See Morris Birkbeck, *America*, p. 140, and *Prose*, pp. 247-8.

community and every member in it. He appeals to agriculturalists to join his flight from English society and the 'approaching crisis – either of anarchy or despotism' – that he, like Shelley, anticipated as a result of England's severe national debt after the French wars:[5]

> The social compact here [in the Illinois Territory] is not the confederacy of a few to reduce the many into subjection, but is indeed, and in truth, among these simple republicans, a combination of talents, moral and physical, by which the good of all is promoted in perfect accordance with individual interest. It is, in fact, a better, because a more simple state than was ever pourtrayed by an Utopian theorist.[6]

Like Shelley, Birkbeck insists that 'man remains, / . . . but man' (*PS2*, III, iv, 193-4) with 'irregular and rude passions, and gross propensities and follies'. Though his portrait of 'the real world' be 'no poetical Arcadia',[7] it captures the same tension between the ideal and real that we find in Shelley's *Prometheus Unbound* and *A Philosophical View*. Shelley too considered the social state of England to be precarious, at 'a crisis in its destiny' (*Prose*, p. 239), and in these two works respectively, he sought to imagine a non-profit based economy 'where all things flow to all' (*PS2*, *Prometheus Unbound*, IV, 402) and to analyse the unreformed world from which inequality would have to be uprooted. Birkbeck's experiment might well have seemed a bridge between these two versions of the world, based as it was on Birkbeck's own liberal consciousness of 'simple' republicanism, operating naturally where 'the good of all' is 'individual interest'. When Birkbeck writes that 'The world we have left at so remote a distance . . . seems to my imagination, like a past scene, and its transactions, as matter rather of history, than of present interest', Shelley may well have sympathised with the delusion, so well does Birkbeck's 'history' accord with Shelley's own vision of the future.[8] In Birkbeck's account, Shelley may have seen those 'gigantic shadows which futurity casts upon the present' (*SPP*, p. 535) and which are reflected in his own poetry and prose.

Birkbeck's pioneering 'spirit of emigration'[9] captures the temporal and spatial progress that Shelley explores in such works as *Alastor* and *Prometheus Unbound*. Like the *Alastor* Poet, Birkbeck's emigrant travels to the wilderness, the 'undiscovered lands', and recapitulates the earliest stages of society even as he carries to the new places a sense of space that derives from refinement that, he argues, only civilised life can promote. The poet-traveller at once experiences and

---

[5] Birkbeck, *America*, p. 8. From the summer of 1819, Shelley's letters show his increasing sense of the urgent economic and political situation in England in terms that very much resemble Birkbeck's. Cf. *L*, 2: 115: 'England seems to be in a very disturbed state, if we may judg{e b}y some Paris Papers. . . . But the change should commence among the higher orders, or anarchy will only be the last flash before despotism. I wonder & tremble'.
[6] Birkbeck, *America*, pp. 114-15.
[7] Birkbeck, *America*, p. 115.
[8] Birkbeck, *America*, pp. 158-9.
[9] Birkbeck, *America*, p. 84.

reconstructs the unknown, at once sheds the burdens and plants the seeds of civilisation beyond its pales. Of the outward journey, Birkbeck writes memorably:

> We have now fairly turned our backs on the old world, and find ourselves in the very stream of emigration. Old America seems to be breaking up, and moving westward. We are seldom out of sight, as we travel on this grand track, toward the Ohio, of family groups, behind and before us, some with a view to a particular spot, close to a brother perhaps, or a friend, who has gone before, and reported well of the country. Many like ourselves, when they arrive in the wilderness, will find no lodge prepared for them.[10]

Having attained the last outposts before the wilderness, he finds 'a country beautiful, and fertile, and affording to a plain industrious and thriving population, all that nature has decreed for the comfort of man'.[11] The land is 'fully appropriated and thickly settled' unlike those tracts of 'unappropriated earth' (*Excursion*, III, 137 [939]) sought out by Wordsworth's Solitary in *The Excursion*. But for Birkbeck, this is the very promise of the wilderness; the wilderness presents the ideal conditions for the exercise and exaltation of cultural values. If Wordsworth's Solitary and Shelley's *Alastor* Poet mistakenly shed the vantage of civilisation in pursuit of reforms to it, if they mistake nature for the 'state of nature', Birkbeck labours under no such illusion. His is a colonial imagination, undistracted by the quest for 'that pure Archetype of human greatness' (*Excursion*, III, 138 [951]) in primitive man. Instead, Birkbeck recognises or creates the conditions in nature for an end to nature's otherness, and a place for the colonial agriculturalist to recreate the civilisation he has left behind, forging a new archetype of greatness.

Birkbeck argues that a picturesque sensibility distinguishes the English immigrant from the American settlers that preceded him in schemes of cultivation. Like Shelley's *Alastor* Narrator, or Shelley himself in 'Mont Blanc', Birkbeck gives 'the wilderness . . . a mysterious tongue' (*PS1*, B Text, l. 76) that can only be interpreted by those like himself who bring with them a sufficient level of aesthetic refinement.[12] The colonial agriculturalist has the dual responsibility of fostering that refinement through the cultivation of nature, while anticipating it by his aesthetic appropriation of waste ground under categories that celebrate both nature's resistance to appropriation and the powers of mind that aesthetically reproduce that resistance in landscape improvement, painting, or architecture:

---

[10] Birkbeck, *America*, pp. 31-2.

[11] Birkbeck, *America*, p. 52.

[12] Cf. T. J. Hogg, 'To Thomas Love Peacock', *New Shelley Letters*, ed. W. S. Scott, 1948; quoted in Timothy Webb, *The Violet in the Crucible: Shelley and Translation* (Oxford: Clarendon Press, 1976), pp. 61-2: 'The vulgarity of America as depicted in Ashe's travels and shewn by all other communications from that country, and which in a great measure arises from ignorance of Classical Literature, is so disgusting that we shrink from it with horror and take refuge in the ruins of ancient taste and elegance'.

> In their irregular outline of woodland and their undulating surface, these tracts . . . exhibit every beauty, fresh from the hand of nature, which art often labours in vain to produce; but there are no organs of perception, no faculties as yet prepared in this country, for the enjoyment of these exquisite combinations.
>
> The grand in scenery, I have been shocked to hear, by American lips, called disgusting, because the surface would be too rude for the plough; and the epithet of *elegant* is used on every occasion of commendation but that to which it is appropriate in the English language.
>
> *An elegant improvement* is a cabin of rude logs, and a few acres with the trees cut down to the height of three feet, and surrounded by a worm-fence, or zig-zag railing . . . . The word implies eligibility or usefulness in America, but has nothing to do with taste . . . – the idea has not yet reached them. Nature has not yet displayed to them those charms of distant and various prospect, which will delight the future inhabitants of this noble country.[13]

Birkbeck pinpoints the American inability to look on nature with what Gilpin calls the 'picturesque eye'. As Gilpin argues, 'it is not it's [sic] business to consider matters of utility. It has nothing to do with the affairs of the plough, and the spade; but merely examines the face of nature as a beautiful object'.[14] But in celebrating pleasure or 'delight', Birkbeck is careful to emphasise the natural abundance of a social organisation based on a solid foundation of agricultural utility. If Birkbeck's picturesque has 'nothing to do with . . . the plough', it is because the plough cannot function in the grand scenes, where the terrain itself resists cultivation; if distant prospects are valued, it is because they can be viewed from the vantage of a cultivated field. Indeed, behind Birkbeck's jibe at the 'cabin of rude logs' lay a vision of English models of landscape improvement, with elegant country houses graded into working farms by picturesque lawns and woods. Like Arthur Young before him, Birkbeck's economic vision of the just society combines pleasure and utility and is ratified by this combination. The mark of the just society is the leisure and refinement produced by surplus labour value; a state which, as Shelley puts it in *A Philosophical View*, 'might have made every peasant's cottage, surrounded with its garden, a little paradise of comfort, with every convenience desirable in civilised life; neat tables and chairs, and good beds, and a nice collection of useful books' (*Prose*, p. 249).

Birkbeck's economic ideal proves very congenial to both Shelley's *A Philosophical View* as well as his more utopian vision in *Prometheus Unbound*, so much so that one suspects the Sussex gentleman landowner's son of being something of an agriculturalist in his own right.[15] As Donald Reiman argues,

---

[13] Birkbeck, *America*, pp. 133-4.

[14] William Gilpin, *Remarks on Forest Scenery, and Other Woodland Views, Relative Chiefly to Picturesque Beauty*, 2 vols (London, 1791), 1: 298.

[15] Shelley did show a keen interest in agriculture not long after his reading of Birkbeck. Early in 1820, Shelley began an intimacy with George William Tighe, who 'encouraged Shelley to read Davy's lectures on agriculture, and to consider the problems set by

Shelley's thinking emphasises 'forms characteristic of and beneficial to the agricultural estate system of the eighteenth century and earlier', also espoused by 'reactionary' figures like Wordsworth, Coleridge, and William Cobbett, not to mention Birkbeck or Arthur Young.[16] In *A Philosophical View*, Shelley is therefore particularly harsh towards capitalist commercial interests, those whom he refers to as 'a set of pelting wretches in whose employment there is nothing to exercise, even to their distortion, the more majestic faculties of the soul' (*Prose*, p. 245). Such interests are twice damned: first, for exploiting labour value, and again for lacking the aesthetic sensibility that Birkbeck suggests as the hallmark of the civilised agrarian. By contrast, Shelley does allow his *landed* aristocrat at least some of that ennobling sensibility, even though he argues throughout for a classless society based on labour and the equal distribution of wealth; Shelley regards the end of reforms as some sort of 'levelling of inordinate wealth, and an agrarian distribution' (*Prose*, p. 252) of estates and waste lands, with 'equality of possessions . . . the last result of the utmost refinements of civilization' (*Prose*, p. 253). Like Birkbeck, Shelley envisions an unalienated labour force, working the land or providing useful manufactures or services, free from a system that allows or encourages poverty, and ennobled by literature and sensibility.[17] However, in the absence of that ideal infrastructure, literature and sensibility yet provide sustenance to those powers of the human spirit that might make the future state possible.

In Shelley's vision of that alternative, utopian economy in *Prometheus Unbound* I-III (1818-19), he describes a universal harmony that would eliminate all alienation, be it of the labourer from labour, the Greek from the Asian, or man from his 'Gods'. This 'new world order' does not mean an end to agrarian production or exchange of signs, produce, or even manufactured goods, but it does mean an end to the deceit involved in the one-way flow of wealth from the worker

---

Malthusian social theory in terms of population figures and food production' (Richard Holmes, *Shelley: The Pursuit*, London, Quartet Books, 1976, p. 576). On 13 April 1820, Shelley writes: 'I have been thinking & talking & reading Agriculture this last week' (*L*, 2: 182).

[16] Donald Reiman, 'Shelley as Agrarian Reactionary', *Keats-Shelley Memorial Bulletin*, 30 (1979), pp. 5-6.

[17] In *A Philosophical View*, Shelley rigidly distinguishes between the property of productive labour and that of accumulating capitalists. Especially in his catalogue of the former occupations do we see the proximity of Shelley's ideal society to that which Birkbeck describes in the agrarian townships at the colonial edges of America: 'When I speak of persons of property I mean not every man who possesses any right of property; I mean the rich. Every man whose scope in society has a plebian and intelligible utility, whose personal exertions are more valuable to him than his capital; every tradesman who is not a monopolist, all surgeons and physicians and those mechanics and editors and literary men and artists, and farmers, all those persons whose profits spring from honorably and honestly exerting their own skill and wisdom or strength in greater abundance than from the employment of money to take advantage of the necessity of the starvation of their fellow citizens for their profit, or those who pay, as well as those more obviously understood by the laboring classes, the interest of the national debt' (*Prose*, p. 250).

to the ruling oligarchy under the pretence of mutual benefit. The result is a non-profit economy, where 'all things flow to all' (IV, 402), and where the sign of transaction itself has undergone a transformation. If precious metals or paper bills stamped by the government were once the 'signs of labour and the titles to an unequal distribution of property' (*Prose*, p. 243), now they are abandoned for another currency that mediates between the producer and the consumer without an appropriating intercessor. In Act III, works of art symbolically take on this role between man and the Prometheans, becoming:

> .... the mediators
> Of that best worship, love, by him and us
> Given and returned . . . (III, iii, 58-60)

The temple-cave to which Prometheus and Asia retire represents a place of leisure and non-intervention in human affairs. Because of a universal exchange of love, work and intervention give place to a creative anarchy, where art connects man to his gods without subordinating him.

This aesthetic economy is, to borrow Jean Baudrillard's phrase, 'the mirror of production'.[18] For Shelley, leisure is the state of aesthetic production and exchange, which, in ministering to man's moral and intellectual needs, is at once a source and a result of civilisation. Its equally important counterpart, labour, allows material production, ministers to man's physical needs, and creates leisure time. As Shelley writes in the Notes to *Queen Mab*, 'a state which should combine the advantages of both [labour and leisure] would be subjected to the evils of neither'.[19] In *Prometheus Unbound*, Shelley focuses on leisure and art not because labour is unimportant, but because he would like to privilege aesthetic production as the best measure of mankind's moral and political evolution, while the poem anticipates this outcome by presenting, in Shelley's words, 'beautiful idealisms of moral excellence' (*PS2*, p. 475, l. 126). Labour exists at the margins of the text and is shadowed in the economic diction with which Shelley describes the production and exchange of art. Though this is 'another paradigm that fixes the hegemony of a temporal order which is always merely that of production',[20] Shelley is not as disappointed in the fact as Baudrillard would be, or as would the revolutionary-minded who insist that Shelley models for them the Apocalyptic promises of Socialism.[21] Shelley's symbolic economies are not meant to move us beyond political economy, but to refigure it in its idealised primitivist origin. As early as

---

[18] Jean Baudrillard, *The Mirror of Production*, trans. Mark Poster (St Louis: Telos Press, 1975).

[19] Shelley writes that 'labour is required for physical, and leisure for moral improvement' and that 'a state which should combine the advantages of both, would be subjected to the evils of neither' (*PS1*, p. 366, ll. 52-7). This has been achieved in *Prometheus Unbound* where all share both labour and leisure.

[20] Baudrillard, *Mirror*, p. 40.

[21] Cf. Edward Aveling and Eleanor Marx Aveling, *Shelley's Socialism*, repr. 1888 edn (London: The Journeyman Press, 1975).

Queen Mab (1813), Shelley is concerned with the nexus between 'the state of nature' and collectivised man as the *topos* for the analysis of inequality and alternative economies. In *Prometheus Unbound*, Shelley looks forward by looking backward, and defines utopia in a rediscovered relationship between nature and mind, with labour as the mediator between material and aesthetic being. Though this state of being seems to take place in an undefined future, the implication remains that such revolutionary choices were possible at the dawn of civilisation,[22] or, as Birkbeck's colonialist vision suggests, at the outposts of culture, where agriculture provided the first step in recreating a system of labour relations free from the conditions which drove emigrants like Birkbeck himself from Europe.

Notes on a Journey in America, then, is more than a guidebook; like *Prometheus Unbound* and *A Philosophical View of Reform*, it is a critique of history and political economy as well as a utopian prognosis. Like Shelley's, Birkbeck's humanism is imperial; the future is a meta-cultural, unified exertion of control over nature and the self by collective forces. For the *Edinburgh Review*, Birkbeck's account inspired a sense that that future lay in the infant grasp of America, an imperial power that the Old World had not sufficiently reckoned with:

> It is impossible to close this interesting volume, without casting our eyes upon the marvellous empire of which Mr. Birkbeck paints the growth in colours far more striking than any heretofore used in portraying it. Where is this prodigious increase of numbers, this vast extension of dominion, to end? What bounds has Nature set to the progress of this mighty nation? .... We perceive a nation rapidly *progressing* (as they themselves term it in language borrowed from our own great poet) towards universal dominion over the New World.[23]

Birkbeck's actual orientation is European. Not only does he plan to restock the American prairies with free Englishman, prepared like himself with the practical know-how as well as the aesthetic vision with which to appropriate the wilderness, but he envisions his ultimate success in a re-establishment of the European cultural circulation he ostensibly leaves behind. In a reflection that recalls Shelley's 1816 dream of 'following great rivers' (*SC* 571, 7: 27) on a tour of the great centres of civilisation, Birkbeck writes:

> We are also less reluctant at extending our views westward, on considering that the time is fast approaching, when the grand intercourse with Europe, will not be, as at present, through eastern America, but through the great rivers which communicate by the

---

[22] Shelley's story thus highlights Prometheus's civilising gifts of language, science, and arts, and the spirit in which these were given. The 'action' consists of Prometheus's reconsideration of the 'giving' of the gift, and of how easily this simple act can be transformed into a complex, destructive form of exchange.

[23] Review of *Notes on a Journey in America, from the Coast of Virginia to the Territory of Illinois*, by Morris Birkbeck, *Edinburgh Review*, 29 (June 1818), pp. 137-8.

Mississippi with the ocean, at New Orleans. In this view, we approximate to Europe, as we proceed to the west.[24]

Birkbeck may sign himself at the end of his book as 'an American', but he cannot shake free from the colonial imagination of a new society nurtured and succoured by the old. If westward expansion was to end in 'universal domination over the New World' the terms of this universalism would be forged on the ideals and models of the Old World, itself unable or unwilling to move beyond the political and economic inequalities that had ruined its own promise. For Birkbeck, Gibbon's prophecy had come true: the Old World had been overrun by a kind of self-generated barbarism, and 'Europe would revive and flourish' in America.[25]

For Shelley, 'America holds forth the victorious example of an immensely populous and . . . a highly civilized community administered according to republican forms' (*Prose*, p. 234), and has the place of pride before France in Shelley's world survey of the progress of reform in *A Philosophical View*. Shelley too makes the connection between America's success and, as he puts it, the 'state of public opinion in Europe of which it was the first result' (*Prose*, p. 235). As Shelley extends his gaze eastwards, it becomes clear that he believes that emancipation and freedom are coterminous with a very Euro-centric ideal of civilisation. His comments on India are particularly revealing. The 'slavery' of the Indians, he hopes, will be mitigated over time by the very impositions of their European colonisers. While typically recognising the hypocrisy behind European practice of institutionalised religion, Shelley nevertheless argues that the colonial importation of Christianity would have a beneficial effect on the Indian consciousness, allowing the 'backward' native to tap into the progressive Western philosophies embodied in the teachings of Christ:

> . . . even if the doctrines of Jesus do not penetrate through the darkness of that which those who profess to be his followers call Christianity, there will yet be a number of social forms modelled upon those European feelings from which it has taken its color substituted to those according to which they [the Indian people] are at present cramped, and from which, when the time for complete emancipation shall arrive, their disengagement may be less difficult, and under which their progress to it may be the less imperceptibly slow. (*Prose*, p. 238)

While Shelley does not strictly advocate the colonialism of a conquering and occupying force, he can yet see it in a larger progressivist context in which the force of European culture mitigates and transcends European violence or coercion. Having culturally anticipated the future of all free peoples, Europe cannot escape the destiny of freedom itself, nor can it forbear the legislation of the world, no

---

[24] Birkbeck, *America*, p. 84.
[25] Edward Gibbon, *The Decline and Fall of the Roman Empire*, 3 vols (New York: The Modern Library, [n.d]), 2: 441.

matter what form the world circulation of its culture and ideas takes: trade, emigration, conquest, or colonialism.

In the more idealised terms of *Prometheus Unbound*, Prometheus's union with Asia represents the superimposition of Grecian cultural origins throughout continental Asia. Already, the drama occupies and recapitulates the space of a former conquest, that of Dionysius.[26] In Euripides' *The Bacchae*, Dionysius brings his intoxicating message of godhood to Thebes after conquering Asia, and it is in Thebes that he meets resistance in the person of Pentheus. For his disbelief, Pentheus suffers dismemberment at the hands of his mother, Agave. Shelley's Maenad imagery invokes this violence as a madness that shook the world of tyranny with 'the voice which is contagion to the world' (*PS2*, II, iii, 10), but as the Earth's parallel description of the maddening oracular vapours of the Cave suggests, this contagion is still complicit with 'mutual war, / And faithless faith' (III, iii, 129-30). Prometheus and Asia, however, temper the maenad-like wildness of the East by overcoming Jupiter and tyranny amidst the Caucuses before returning triumphant back to Greece. Leaving 'Bacchic Nysa, Maenad-haunted mountain' behind them, they travel to 'the destined cave' where they will live in love and harmony (III, iii, 152-7). As mediating presences, Prometheus and Asia celebrate their marriage between East and West by returning to the origins of the aesthetic and cultural being with which they have occupied and transformed their eastern empire.

Though there is very little geographical movement in the drama, the implied journeys of Prometheus and Asia are very important as journeys, for travel and travellers, colonial expeditions and colonisers, become the bearers of the cultural circulation that *Prometheus Unbound* celebrates and anticipates. In *A Philosophical View*, it is the 'native Indians . . . competent knowledge in the arts and philosophy of Europe' (*Prose*, p. 238) that gives colonialism a Promethean quality, and despite Shelley's call for 'a system of arts and literature of their own' (*Prose*, p. 238), he is hardly troubled by the kind of melting pot vision that seems so much opposed to the nationalism he would write so movingly about in *Hellas* (1821):

> . . . the Turkish Empire is in its last stage of ruin, and it cannot be doubted but that the time is approaching when the deserts of Asia Minor and of Greece will be colonized by the overflowing populations of countries less enslaved and debased, and that the climate and the scenery will not remain forever the spoil of wild beasts and unlettered Tartars.
>
> (*Prose*, p. 239)

Substitute backwoodsman and American Indians for 'unlettered Tartars', and the sentiments could be those of Birkbeck regarding the overflow of Europe and a European sensibility into the wilderness of beauty, where but for these emigrants

---

[26] For a discussion of the parallels between the Dionysus of Orphic cults and Shelley's Prometheus, see Stuart Curran, *Shelley's Annus Mirabilis* (San Marino, CA: Huntington Library, 1975), pp. 91-4.

there would be none. Whether colonists or colonial ideas bring about such progress, Shelley's Euro-centric criteria remain constant, as in this final example:

> Egypt having but a nominal dependence upon Constantinople is under the government of Ottoman Bey, a person of enlightened views who is introducing European literature and arts, and is thus beginning that change which Time, the great innovator, will accomplish in that degraded country; [and] by the same means its sublime enduring monuments may excite lofty emotions in the hearts of the posterity of those who now contemplate them without admiration. (*Prose*, p. 239)

Again one might recall Birkbeck's predictions on how the sensibility introduced into the wilderness by his followers 'will delight the future inhabitants of this noble country'.[27] As in his prognosis for India, Shelley believes that 'European literature and arts' anticipate and promote the moral and cultural evolution of any nation state, precisely because all nation states occupy one scale of civilisation. This ethnographic historiography allows Shelley, like Birkbeck, to elide the ends of nationalism and history into the nationlessness of *Prometheus Unbound*. Significantly, Shelley's support for nationalist movements in Spain, Naples, Genoa, and Greece is conditional to his belief in those movements as subject to 'progress', and not to any inherent belief in the necessity of self-government for an ethnic, religious, or culture group. By the same token, neither Shelley's dismay at Napoleon's imperial pretensions, nor his optimism at the decline of Ottoman imperial influence, suggest that Shelley's politics are anti-imperialist; instead he favours an 'enlightened' imperialism in which neo-Grecian cultural and political values are exported to the world.

While Birkbeck 'approximate[s] to Europe, as [he] proceed[s] to the west', Shelley more often looks to the East for signs of European progress, partly because he wants to explore the means by which European sources rejuvenate the regions from which mankind was thought to have taken its origins, and partly because one of those sources had such leverage on Shelley's imaginative and intellectual life: Greece. Birkbeck was fascinated by the prospect of making a new start, of wiping the slate clean, but in order to reconstitute the past in a more egalitarian present. For Shelley, the sense of history and historical continuity was more pressing and, as we have seen, the closer he physically travelled to the places of classical fame, the more his thoughts turned to Greece, first as the parent of the highest aesthetic, political, and social sensibilities of mankind, and later, with *Hellas*, as the place where these classical values could again be imagined in a modern nation state. Mark Kipperman argues that 'bourgeois nationalism at this time must have seemed the most radical position capable, at a revolutionary moment, of articulating social ideals based on the most enduring yet progressive principles of European civilization'.[28] But, as *A Philosophical View* may indicate, Shelley would regard

---

[27] Birkbeck, *America*, p. 134.
[28] Mark Kipperman, 'Macropolitics of Utopia: Shelley's *Hellas* in Context', *Macropolitics of Nineteenth-Century Literature: Nationalism, Exoticism, Imperialism*, eds Jonathan Arac and Harriet Ritvo (Philadelphia: University of Pennsylvania Press, 1991), p. 92.

nations as transient as empires, so long as they are based on coercive economic, religious, or military power structures rather than on the free circulation of physical necessities and moral refinement. For Shelley, the Greek Revolution becomes the most radical revolutionary moment after the French Revolution precisely because of Greece's imperial heritage, not in terms of arms, but of 'thought's empire over thought' (*The Triumph of Life*, *SPP*, l. 211). As a place for utopia, Greece's function as a nation is largely metonymic of a larger progressive movement in the affairs of humankind.

Shelley's Grecian orientation emerges most strikingly out of his classical tour through Italy, which itself owes something to Shelley's early foundations as a classical scholar and, more importantly, to his researches as an adult in the company of Peacock and Leigh Hunt. As Timothy Webb points out, Shelley made no distinction between Greek and Latin literature in a letter to Godwin of July 1812, in which he also states that 'the evils of acquiring Greek & Latin considerably overbalance the benefits' (*L*, 1: 316). Under the influence of Peacock from 1813, however, Shelley's sea change began; Peacock appears to have imparted his enthusiasm for Greek literature to Shelley, who began to rank the Greek over the Latin authors, and to regulate his reading on Peacock's suggestions.[29] But as Webb also acknowledges, Shelley's Grecian commitment was further nurtured by his association with Hogg and Hunt. Hunt in particular may have helped Shelley regard the Greeks as 'a well adjusted race who had lived in harmony with nature'.[30] By the time he left for Italy in 1818, Shelley was a committed Grecian, well primed to seek out the traces of Greek civilisation in the ruins of Rome and Naples.

Shelley did not wait for his first sight of Pompeii, Paestum, or the Pantheon in Rome to form his opinions about the aesthetic harmony of Grecian forms with nature; the Italian tour was instead prefaced by Shelley's study of Grecian manners in his translation of Plato's *Symposium* in July 1818, and his composition of a kind of introduction to that piece completed the following month, namely, *A Discourse on the Manners of the Ancient Greeks Relative to the Subject of Love*.[31] With this essay 'upon the cause of some differences of sentiment between the antients & moderns' (*L*, 2: 22), Shelley prepared himself for the enthusiasm which he would bring to the ruins of Magna Graecia by extolling the ancient Greeks as 'on the whole the most perfect specimens of humanity of whom we have authentic record' (*Prose*, p. 219) and claiming for their art 'a sympathetic connection' with this overflowing of 'cultivation and refinement' (*Prose*, pp. 217; 221). To such records, the present proves indebted:

> The modern nations of the civilized world owe the progress which they have made . . . to what is called the revival of learning; that is, the study of writers of the age which

---

[29] Webb, *Violet*, pp. 53-6.
[30] Webb, *Violet*, p. 59.
[31] See *L*, 2: 26 [To Thomas Love Peacock, 25 July 1818]: 'I employed my mornings . . . in translating the *Symposium*, which I accomplished in ten days. Mary is now transcribing it, and I am writing a prefatory essay. I have been reading scarcely anything but Greek . . .'.

preceded and immediately followed the government of Pericles, or of subsequent writers, who were, so to speak, the rivers flowing from those immortal fountains.

(*Prose*, pp. 218-19)

Where he finds the ancients wanting is in their support of the institution of slavery and in their degradation of women to nearly the status of slaves. Shelley correspondingly theorises that Greek homosexuality, the presence of which in the *Symposium* he endeavoured to account for, represented a reflex expression of love in such conditions; if 'civilized' love is 'the universal thirst for a communion not merely of the senses but of our whole nature, intellectual, imaginative, and sensitive' (*Prose*, p. 220), then Greek society had disqualified the female sex from fulfilling the criteria. In this respect, the modern European has begun to outstrip the ancient Greek:

> They both had arrived at that epoch of refinement, when sentimental love becomes an imperious want of the heart and of the mind . . . . In modern Europe the sexual and intellectual claims of love, by the more equal cultivation of the two sexes, so far converge towards one point as to produce, in the attempt to unite them, no gross violation in the established nature of man. (*Prose*, p. 221)

The concept of love, so central to Shelley's work, is here perhaps most fully developed; it unites all the social functions of human 'nature' by perpetuating the species even as it satisfies the sensibilities of refinement. The ideally heterosexual *Alastor* Poet by these terms resembles more the ancients than the moderns; in leaving the vantage of modern civilisation he yet relentlessly pursues its intellectual without satisfying its physical requisitions.

In *A Discourse*, Greece also offers the intensity of intellectual harmony without the complete social and political transformation that Shelley looks to the European and American future to provide. Similarly, the sites of Magna Graecia that Shelley traverses in his travels provide him with evidence of this intellectual harmony in the aesthetic situation of the remains of Grecian art. But as a modern *topos*, Greece itself eluded Shelley. *A Discourse* concerns itself primarily with a European rather than a strictly Grecian modernity, and, if Shelley's reference to Greece as a 'desert' in *A Philosophical View* is anything to go by, it is unlikely that Shelley would yet have included the modern Greek in the scale of refinement that defined the modernity he has in mind; indeed, the Greeks would be in good company, with the other French, Swiss, and Italian *roturiers* who appear so frequently in Shelley's travel writings as examples of human degradation. Even the Greek canto of Byron's *Childe Harold*, for all its pro-Hellenic sentiment, would have confirmed this exclusion for Shelley, the armchair traveller. Byron, who like Shelley would cast off his earlier pessimism once faced by the phenomenon of philhellenism in response to the Greek Revolution, was then less sanguine about the analogy between the ancients and moderns that would later be promoted with such force:

> Fair Greece! sad relic of departed worth!
> Immortal, though no more! though fallen, great!
> Who now shall lead thy scatter'd children forth,
> And long accustom'd bondage uncreate?
>
> <div style="text-align: right">(<i>Byron PW</i>, 2: 68, st. 73, ll. 693-6)</div>

Byron's long note to the stanza provides an answer to the rhetorical question; the new Moses will not be Greek:

> The English have at last compassionated their Negroes, and under a less bigoted government may probably one day release their Catholic brethren: but the interposition of foreigners alone can emancipate the Greeks, who, otherwise, appear to have as small a chance of redemption from the Turks, as the Jews have from mankind in general.
>
> <div style="text-align: right">(<i>Byron PW</i>, 2: 202)</div>

In terms that anticipate Shelley's colonialist argument in *A Philosophical View*, Byron also writes:

> The Greeks will never be independent; they will never be sovereigns as heretofore, and God forbid they ever should! but they may be subjects without being slaves. Our colonies are not independent, but they are free and industrious, and such may Greece be hereafter. (*Byron PW*, 2: 201)

To be fair, in promoting the Greeks' ability to become a 'useful dependency' (*Byron PW*, 2: 202), Byron felt he was countering the wholesale condemnation of the modern Greeks on the one hand, and the too idealistic celebration of their classical pedigree on the other, that characterised late eighteenth-century and early nineteenth-century travel literature on Greece.[32] Claiming the authority of a traveller who had *lived* among those he observes, Byron opposes those he felt had merely passed through the region or who had a particular axe to grind, and offers, on the whole, a balanced view of a people over a thousand years distant from their classical ancestors and subject to hundreds of years under a foreign yoke.

Besides *Childe Harold*, Shelley probably consulted Edward Daniel Clarke on Greece. Mary records her own diligent reading of Clarke's voluminous *Travels in*

---

[32] Byron singles out William Eton (*A Survey of the Turkish Empire*, 1798) and C. S. Sonnini (*Travels in Greece*, 1801) as travellers who 'have led us astray by their panegyrics and projects'; De Pauw (unidentified) and Thomas Thornton (*The Present State of Turkey*, 1807), by contrast, 'have debased the Greeks beyond their demerits' (*Byron PW*, 2: 201). Robert Eisner points out that the Russian-provoked failed uprising of 1770 fuelled both camps. The idealists responded to 'classical place names in the columns of newspapers and periodicals [that] raised the expectation that modern Greeks *should* behave like ancients and recover their freedom'. The other camp, which included Voltaire and much of the European press, scorned the Greeks as 'degenerate' for giving up too easily and slaughtering innocents when the advantage was temporarily in their favour. See Robert Eisner, *Travelers to an Antique Land* (Ann Arbor: University of Michigan Press, 1993), pp. 79-80.

Various Countries of Europe, Asia, and Africa (1810-23) between 7 January and 5 February 1818 (she reads *Childe Harold* II on 29 January) (*MWSJ*, pp. 189-92).[33] Writing from Livorno on 5 June 1818, Shelley specifically requests Peacock to 'enclose the 2 last parts of Clarkes travels relating to Greece' (*L*, 2: 18).[34] The parts in question record Clarke's travels first from Constantinople to Palestine and Egypt via the Eastern Aegean islands, then to Athens and the Pelopponesus, and finally from Athens in a meandering route through Marathon, Thebes, Delphi, Thessalonica, back to Constantinople. Referring to then unpublished journals by travellers like Robert Walpole and J. B. S. Morritt, not to mention Byron's *Childe Harold*, Clarke's narrative forms one of the most compendious accounts of a region comparatively less known to readers than the rest of Europe. The *Edinburgh Review*, for one, followed the progress of the collection closely and enthusiastically deemed Clarke 'one of the most enlightened travellers of the present times'.[35]

But the picture of Greece that this 'enlightened traveller' offered would have done little to raise Shelley's expectations for the modern Greeks. Clarke treats their customs with bemused paternalism or even derision, with the model of the ancients as a standard against which they are always found wanting; describing a dance performed by some Athenian 'matrons', for example, Clarke writes: 'In all this there was nothing that could remind us, even by the most distant similitude, of the graceful appearance presented by the female Bacchanals, as they are represented upon Grecian vases'.[36] Indeed, Clarke proves far more interested in antiquarian and topographical inquiries than in studying the manners of the moderns throughout the *Travels*. He enters the fray over the topographical accuracy of Homer's account of Troy with relish, explores the sites of ancient ruins with indefatigable energy, and litters his pages with inscriptions copied from ancient tablets. He is perhaps best known for his carrying off the sacred 'statue of Ceres' from Eleusis, a feat of which he boasts to a horrified native at the beginning of Section the Third, and he appears constantly on the lookout for similar deals in 'marbles' for export to England.

Clarke's achievement lay in the thoroughness with which he surveys regions, while his descriptions colour landscapes of classical renown with a picturesque

---

[33] We cannot be certain whether Shelley read Clarke at this time. Mary Shelley does not mark Clarke's *Travels* as a book also read by Shelley in her reading list for 1818 (*MWSJ*, p. 265). Moreover, Shelley was suffering from bouts of ophthalmia during some of this period. However, it is likely that Shelley would have become acquainted with the contents of the volumes at very least through conversation. Mary Shelley may also have read parts of Clarke aloud to Shelley during his illnesses.

[34] It is not clear whether Shelley wanted all of 'Part the Second' of *Travels*, which consists of three folio volumes on 'Greece, Egypt, and the Holy Land', or whether he was requesting only the last two sections of the part. Each volume of 'Part the Second' makes up a 'Section' in Clarke's scheme of subdivision, but each of these contains material relating to Greece. Section the first was published in 1812, the second in 1814, and the third in 1816.

[35] Review of *Travels in Various Countries of Europe, Asia, and Africa*, by Edward Daniel Clarke, *Edinburgh Review*, 21 (Feb. 1813), p. 131.

[36] Edward Daniel Clarke, *Travels in Various Countries*, Part the Second, Section the Third (London: T. Cadell and W. Davies, 1816), p. 6.

sensibility. Yet this luxuriance can be quite detached from the actual inhabitants, whose presence, while acknowledged, appears less essential to the effect for which Clarke strives:

> In the channel between Chios and the opposite peninsula of Erythrae, the scenery is perhaps unequalled by any thing in the Archipelago; not only from the grandeur, height and magnitude, or the gigantic masses presented on the coast, but from the extreme richness and fertility of the island filled with flowery, luxuriant, and odoriferous plants, and presenting a magnificent slope, covered with gardens from the water's edge. Trees bending with fruit; the citron, the orange, the mulberry, and the *Lentiscus*, or Mastic tree, are seen forming extensive groves and in the midst of these appears the town of Scio.[37]

Quite carried away by this vision of golden age plenitude, Clarke extols Chios as 'the Paradise of Modern Greece', and he relates a story of 'an Englishman of the name of Baimbridge, who had searched all Europe for a healthy place to end his days', came at last to Chios at the age of seventy-four and lived another two decades, nurtured by the chosen climate. Even the classical age ratifies the 'favoured island': 'According to Plutarch, there was no instance of adultery in Chios, during the space of seven hundred years'.[38]

Chios inspires Clarke's most idealising powers of description, more so than other *topoi* among the Aegean islands or the Anatolian and Grecian mainlands. It is a space that transcends Greek manners, which themselves come in for a great deal of criticism elsewhere in *Travels*, and it is a space where all the requisites of civilisation are satisfied despite being located beyond its pale – a sort of Shangri-La accessible only to the adventurous traveller in distant parts. As such, Clarke's account of Chios helps contextualise Shelley's most powerful idealisation of Greece before modern Greece came to the fore of his consciousness with the events leading up to the composition of *Hellas*. In *Epipsychidion*, Greece is the destination proposed by the speaker for his ultimate union with the captive Emily, precisely because it represents a space within, yet on the periphery of history where the conditions for social being might be re-imagined, or re-enacted. The isle the Poet describes recalls Clarke's Chios, that 'Paradise of Modern Greece':

> It is an isle under Ionian skies,
> Beautiful as a wreck of Paradise,
> And, for the harbours are not safe and good,
> This land would have remained a solitude
> But for some pastoral people native there,
> Who from the Elysian, clear, and golden air
> Draw the last spirit of the age of gold,
> Simple and spirited; innocent and bold. (*SPP*, ll. 422-9)

---

[37] Clarke, *Travels*, Pt. 2, Sect. 1 (1812), pp. 184-7.
[38] Clarke, *Travels*, Pt. 2, Sect. 1 (1812), pp. 189; 192.

Clarke's Chios may be more populated that Shelley's Ionian isle,[39] and may boast harbours 'safe and good', but both are depicted as veritable Paradises, connecting the promise of perfection with its achievement in an Elysian past; both allow the traveller-coloniser to revivify the 'spirit of the age of gold'. Clark's Chios is a 'favoured island'; Shelley's isle is 'a favoured place' (l. 461).[40] Clarke's is 'filled with flowery, luxuriant, and odoriferous plants' and the traveller inhales 'spicy odours, wafted from cliffs and groves'. Shelley's 'is heavy with the scent of lemon-flowers' which, with 'moss violets and jonquils', 'dart their arrowy odour through the brain / 'Till you might faint with that delicious pain' (ll. 447; 450; 451-2). Chios, as Baimbridge found, was 'a healthy place' that prolonged his life.[41] On Shelley's isle, 'Famine or Blight, / Pestilence, War and Earthquake, never light' (ll. 461-2).

Shelley's isle need not be indebted to Clarke's Chios, but Shelley's aesthetic idealisation of Greece does suggest points of similarity with the classical traveller's account of the modern region. In point of fact, Shelley locates his island south of Chios. As the 'Advertisement' describes it:

> The Writer of the following Lines died at Florence, as he was preparing for a voyage to one of the wildest of the Sporades, which he had bought, and where he had fitted up the ruins of an old building, and where it was his hope to have realised a scheme of life, suited perhaps to that happier and better world of which he is now an inhabitant, but hardly practicable in this. (*SPP*, p. 392)

According to Clarke, the Sporades derived their appellation 'from the irregularity wherein they are here scattered' and some 'are not laid down in any chart' – the perfect place for the Poet's utopian retirement. More perfect, indeed, because of the contiguity of the modern to the ancient space, for though uncharted, there is 'no part of the coast, where a gulph, bay, river, or promontory, can be pointed at, on which some vestige of former ages may but be discerned'.[42] Thus the writer's ruins share with the island itself the uncertainty of place, having been built beyond the memory of the 'rustic island-people' 'in the world's young prime' (*SPP*, ll. 485; 489), but so integrated with the luxuriance of nature as to represent the pure union of human and natural creativity:

> It scarce seems now a wreck of human art,
> But, as it were Titanic; in the heart
> Of Earth having assumed its form, then grown
> Out of the mountains, from the living stone,
> Lifting itself in caverns light and high:

---

[39] As Reiman and Fraistat note, the term 'Ionian' here refers to 'the western coast of Asia Minor, together with the adjacent islands in the Aegean Sea, which had been colonized by Greeks who spoke the Ionian dialect' (*SPP*, p. 403, n. 5).
[40] Clarke, *Travels*, Pt. 2, Sect. 1 (1812), p. 189.
[41] Clarke, *Travels*, Pt. 2, Sect. 1 (1812), pp. 186; 188; 189.
[42] Clarke, *Travels*, Pt. 2, Sect. 1 (1812), pp. 213 n. 2; 220.

> For all the antique and learned imagery
> Has been erased, and in the place of it
> The ivy and the wild-vine interknit
> The volumes of their many twining stems . . . . (ll. 493-501)

Like the Coliseum or the Baths of Caracalla in Rome, the ruin assumes the form of nature, naturalising art and the ideals of art. But unlike those expressions of 'energy & error' (*L*, 2: 86), this is 'a wreck of human art' which originally expressed an age 'ere crime / Had been invented' (ll. 488-9), and, as such, its significance has not changed in spite of the erasure of its language: even in the space of erasure the ivy and wild-vine 'write' their volumes. The island is a palimpsest on which ancient art and nature record successive narratives, each as ideal as the other and each forming an interpenetration of meaning.

The language of nature and naturalised art proves insufficient for the full actualisation of the utopian scene, once colonised by the Poet and Emily. The Poet also brings to the self-contained island the best of modern culture, or the means of making it:

> . . . I have fitted up some chambers there
> Looking towards the golden Eastern air,
> And level with the living winds, which flow
> Like waves above the living waves below. —
> I have sent books and music there, and all
> Those instruments with which high spirits call
> The future from its cradle, and the past
> Out of its grave, and make the present last
> In thoughts and joys which sleep, but cannot die,
> Folded within their own eternity. (ll. 515-24)

Books, music, and instruments (of music, painting, and writing) here fulfil a similar role as 'European literature and arts' in *A Philosophical View of Reform*; in both instances, imported culture helps incorporate space into a teleological view of history, and affirms that the users of such culture are the 'high spirits' who best actualise these ends. As colonists who rule over their island solitude, the Poet and Emily, like Prometheus and Asia, must become fully incorporated in and representative of time past, present, and future. While the ivy naturalises art by erasing it, the new human agents must ensure that that erasure is never complete, so that nature can contain or supplement human endeavour, but never obliterate it. For all Shelley's tendency to imagine a Grecian space 'looking towards the golden Eastern air' as the place of utopia, there is more at stake than the mere associations the region maintains with the ancients. The presence of modern culture alone can authorise space as 'place'.

The Poet's 'fitting' of chambers with culture closely recalls the gesture which Maddalo makes to the Maniac in *Julian and Maddalo*. After the Maniac 'grew wild' (*PS2*, l. 249) upon being left by his mysterious French consort, Maddalo takes pity on him:

> . . . so I fitted up for him
> These rooms besides the sea, to please his whim,
> And sent him busts and books and urns for flowers
> Which had adorned his life in happier hours,
> And instruments of music . . . . (ll. 252-6)

The parallel reminds us of the way that both poems develop Shelley's idea of civilised love that I have discussed above with reference to *A Discourse on the Manners of the Ancient Greeks*. If love is 'the universal thirst for a communion not merely of the senses but of our whole nature, intellectual, imaginative, and sensitive' (*Prose*, p. 220), then the two situations – rooms open to sea winds, and full of the objects of cultural expression – represent the full range of those requisitions. For the Maniac, Maddalo's gift must compensate him for his lost communion in love, while for the Poet of *Epipsychidion*, the chambers by the sea will fulfil the domestic wants of his absolute union of love with Emily. In *Julian and Maddalo*, the Maniac's madness comes upon him as he moves beyond social being into a state of wildness which is also a state of being in an at least metaphoric wilderness, beyond the foundations of civilised economy and value: after the woman leaves him, he wanders 'about yon lonely isles of desart sand / 'Till he grew wild – he had no cash or land' (ll. 248-9). With Maddalo's help, he rebuilds society within a chamber of the madhouse open to the elements, but amidst those who are positioned even further than himself beyond civilisation and reason. Situated so, the music he creates, like the monologues he utters, is fragmented, yet powerful enough to beguile the inmates 'into strange silence' (ll. 227). In *Epipsychidion*, the Poet and Emily would fully colonise their lonely island, which far from being a wilderness, contains all the conditions for social being with none of its problems.

The orientation of *Epipsychidion* towards a border region at the edges of social life may appear in the broadest sense to reconfigure the border regions that Shelley deploys in *Julian and Maddalo*, *Alastor*, and 'Mont Blanc', but Shelley's choice of the Sporades in *Epipsychidion* seems to be influenced by his ever-developing sense of Greece as a cultural centre of the ancient world, exercising leverage on the present and the future. Shelley's attention was also drawn to Greece as a possible destination for his own travels; the voyage mentioned in the 'Advertisement' to *Epipsychidion* has its type in one that Shelley was preparing with his cousin Thomas Medwin that would have taken in an itinerary remarkably similar to that of Clarke in the part of his book 'relating to Greece'.[43] To Claire Clairmont, Shelley wrote on 29 October 1820: 'We [Shelley and Medwin] have also been talking of a

---

[43] *Epipsychidion* was composed between late November 1820, when Shelley first met Teresa Viviani, and 16 February 1821, when Shelley sent the fair copy to Ollier (*SPP*, p. 391). The Grecian scheme was thus well under way by the time Shelley turned his attention to the poem.

plan to be accomplished with a friend of his, a man of large fortune, who will be at Leghorn next Spring, and who designs to visit Greece, Syria, and Egypt in his own Ship' (*L*, 2: 242). However, the plan seems to have been hatched even earlier, as Shelley inquired of Byron some six weeks before, 'If I were to go to Levant & Greece, could you be of any service to me?' (17 September 1820; *L*, 2: 237). Though by 20 January 1821 Shelley and Medwin seem to have run into troubles ('The Greek expedition appears to be broken up') (*L*, 2: 257), Shelley had not entirely given up hope with the scheme until 4 April, when world affairs put an end to the dreams of tourists. To Medwin himself, Shelley writes: 'Greece has risen in this moment to vindicate its freedom. . . . Massacres of the Turks have begun in various parts.—This is a sufficient objection to our Grecian project even if other circumstances would permit my being one of the party.—There is nothing I so earnestly desired as to visit Greece; but the fates do not seem propitious to my desires' (*L*, 2: 280).

The massacres that Shelley speaks of were more than the troublesome intrusion of politics on a classical tourist's dream of exploring the remnants of the golden age. As tempting as such a vision of Greece would have been for Shelley – and *Epipsychidion* shows just how tempting it was – the new political situation brought Greece back to the present for Shelley; for the first time he had to reckon with the inhabitants of Greece not as those he had once likened to 'unlettered Tartars', but as Europeans with a claim to nationhood. This new orientation would have been abetted by new acquaintances. In December 1820, the Shelleys were first introduced to a circle of Greek expatriates, including Prince Alexander Mavrocordatos, the future president of the first constitutional government of Greece. Until Mavrocordatos left Italy to join the Revolution on 26 June 1821, he was a frequent visitor; Mary Shelley in particular became close to him and began learning Greek in exchange for English lessons.[44] While Shelley's feelings for Mavrocordatos are at time lukewarm, perhaps tainted with jealousy,[45] Shelley would have found in Mavrocordatos the antithesis to the Greeks that travel literature so often portrayed as cringing savages.[46] Besides being Shelley's social equal, Mavrocordatos was well-educated, literary, and had developed a disposition

---

[44] See Herbert Huscher, 'Alexander Mavrocordato, Friend of the Shelleys', *Keats-Shelley Memorial Bulletin*, 16 (1965), pp. 29-38. Huscher points out that Mary 'records his visits in her Journal on no less than 67 days, sometimes two or three on one day, and also walks with him' (p. 31).

[45] See *L*, 2: 292: 'The Greek Prince comes sometimes, & I reproach my own savage disposition that so agreable accomplished and aimiable [a] person is not more agreable to me'.

[46] Clarke includes in his *Travels* an extract from Robert Walpole's then unpublished travel journal in which Walpole evaluates the modern Greek character thus: 'No people living under the same climate, and in the same country, can be so opposite as the Greeks and Turks. There is in the former a cringing manner, and yet a forwardness, disgusting to the gravity and seriousness of the latter . . . ' (Clarke, *Travels*, Pt. 2, Sect. 1, 1812, pp. 186-7 n.).

towards European manners, having studied in Pisa and having perhaps adopted something of a European dress.[47]

With *Hellas*, which was dedicated to Mavrocordatos, Shelley brings the modern Greek fully into the fold of Europe. Not only does he point out the origins of European manners in the culture of the ancient Greeks ('We are all Greeks . . .'), but he also gives modern Greeks the pedigree so often denied them, not least of all by Byron and Clarke:

> The modern Greek is the descendant of those glorious beings whom the imagination almost refuses to figure to itself as belonging to our Kind, and he inherits much of their sensibility, their rapidity of conception, their enthusiasm and their courage. If in many instances he is degraded, by moral and political slavery to the practise of the basest vices it engenders, and that below the level of ordinary degradation; let us reflect that the corruption of the best produces the worst, and that habits which subsist only in relation to a peculiar state of social institution may be expected to cease so soon as that relation is dissolved. In fact, the Greeks, since the admirable novel of *Anastasius* could have been a faithful picture of their manners, have undergone most important changes; the flower of their Youth, returning to their Country from the universities of Italy, Germany and France have communicated to their fellow citizens the latest results of that social perfection of which their ancestors were the original source. The university of Chios contained before the breaking out of the Revolution eight hundred students, and among them several Germans and Americans. (*SPP*, pp. 431-2)

The Chios reference was topical. In April 1820, the *London Magazine* reported that the 'the Greek printing office' at Chios began 'its labours' with 'an excellent discourse by Professor Bambas, at the opening of the great college of Chios'. The new press, the article continues, 'bids fair to become the means of distributing throughout Greece a succession of important works, destined to contribute to the revival of the literature of that classic country'.[48] That the modern Greeks are 'the descendants of that nation to which [Europeans] owe their civilization' (*SPP*, p. 431), Shelley's preface reiterates at various points, but this passage makes clear that Greece's humanist commerce with Europe makes the difference between Greeks who can claim their heritage and Greeks who must be merely symbols of that heritage to others. Like Mavrocordatos, whom Shelley surely has in mind, 'the flower of their Youth' become Greek by first 'approximating Europe' and recolonising their own country under social models tried in the wider revolutionary European theatre (Mavrocordatos himself studied law, medicine, and military strategy at the University of Pisa).[49] Hellas does not provide the inspiration for its

---

[47] Huscher, 'Alexander Mavrocordato', pp. 29-32. Huscher notes that 'Mavrocordato was often scoffed at by his rival leaders of peasant stock like Colocotronis because he used to wear European clothes'.
[48] *London Magazine*, 1.4 (Apr. 1820), p. 468.
[49] Huscher, 'Alexander Mavrocordato', p. 29.

own birth in and of itself until the Greeks have been taught to perceive it, hence Shelley's emphasis on university education.

With the example of Mavrocordatos as the most tangible representative of this new modern Greek before him, Shelley's marker of the 'old' Greek, Thomas Hope's *Anastasius* (1819), must have struck him as a poignant contrast, especially since Shelley's knowledge of Greece at the time was largely based on second-hand 'newspaper erudition' (*SPP*, p. 431). The full title of the novel shows how well suited it was for such a contrast: *Anastasius: or, Memoirs of a Greek; Written at the Close of the Eighteenth Century*. The action properly begins in the aftermath of the Greek uprising in the Morea, or Pelopponesus, of 1770 and traces the travels of Anastasius, who narrates his own story, over much of the territory that interested Clarke; in the first volume alone, Anastasius describes his travels from his home on Chios to the Morea, from thence to Constantinople, and finally from Constantinople via the eastern Aegean to Alexandria and Cairo.[50] Anastasius's Hogarthian progress proves to be one of steady moral and political decline. The son of a Drogueman (interpreter) to the French Consul at Chios, Anastasius early on feels the effects of his father's ambiguous identity as a privileged Greek with an official position in the Ottoman administration. His boyish fantasies of leading the future revolution provoke a muted response:

> In my fits of heroism, I swore to treat the Turks as he [Achilles] had done the Trojans, and for a time dreamt of nothing but putting to the sword the whole Seraglio – dwarfs, eunuchs, and all. These dreams my parents highly admired, but advised me not to divulge. 'Just rancour', they said, 'should be bottled up, to give it more strength'. – Upon this principle they cringed to the ground to every Moslemin they met.[51]

After consummating a youthful passion with the daughter of the French Consul whom he has no intention of marrying, Anastasius flees Chios by shipping aboard a merchantman. In exercising this tyranny over an innocent girl, however unconscious, Anastasius symbolically turns the tables on himself and he soon becomes 'the slave of every common sailor'.[52] After a series of mishaps in which the ship is taken by pirates and in turn captured by a Turkish frigate, Anastasius's lament quickly gets to the heart of the novel's theme: 'thus was I, hapless Greek, compelled, in the space of four days, to bear the yoke of four different nations –

---

[50] The itinerary and details were drawn from Hope's own travels in these regions between 1787 and 1795. In a letter published in *Blackwood's Edinburgh Magazine*, 10 (Oct. 1821), p. 312, Hope explained, 'I resided nearly a twelve month in Constantinople; visited the arsenal and bagnio frequently; witnessed the festival of St. George; saw Rhodes, was in Egypt, in Syria, and in every other place which I have attempted to describe minutely in *Anastasius*' (quoted in David Watkin, *Thomas Hope 1769-1831 and the Neo-Classical Idea*, London, John Murray, 1968, p. 5).

[51] Thomas Hope, *Anastasius: or Memoirs of a Greek; Written at the Close of the Eighteenth Century*, 3 vols (London: John Murray, 1819), 1: 10.

[52] Hope, *Anastasius*, 1: 23.

French, Venetians, Maynotes, and Turks'.[53] The novel as a whole traces the many forms of slavery the 'hapless Greek' suffers under, particularly those forms of which he has the greatest share in producing or perpetuating. *Anastasius* becomes a pathology of servility in which masters and slaves, as Shelley puts it, 'for ever play / A losing game into each other's hands' (*PS1*, III, 172-3).

While Shelley was first reading *Anastasias* in mid-August 1821, he remarked to Mary Shelley: 'One would think that Albè [Byron] had taken his idea of the 3 last cantos of Don Juan from this book. . . . It is a very powerful & very entertaining novel—& a faithful picture they say of modern Greek manners' (*L*, 2: 332). The parallels between the novel and Byron's *Don Juan*, Cantos III-V (1821) are indeed striking, for Byron's hero seems like Anastasius delivered by circumstances into the hands of pirates, slave drivers, and lovers, and both heroes are drawn inexorably to Constantinople. Byron's sketch of the Greeks themselves also matches Hope's, particularly as represented in Haidee's 'piratical papa', Lambros:

> He was a man of strange temperament,
>   Of mild demeanour though of savage mood,
> . . . .
> Quick to perceive, and strong to bear, and meant
>   For something better, if not wholly good;
> His country's wrongs and his despair to save her
> Had stung him from a slave to an enslaver.
>   (*Byron PW*, 5: 177, st. 53, ll. 417-18; 421-4)

Something of the same temperament can be discerned in Anastasius, whose patriotic boyhood fantasies are soon replaced by his thirst for greatness close to the centres of Ottoman power. Not only does he become the understudy of a powerful Drogueman, Mavroyeni, but in this capacity takes up arms against the Arnaoot enemies of the Porte and nearly (accidentally) converts to Islam. However, Mavroyeni himself best represents the slave-turned-enslaver role that Anastasius covets. A Phanariot grandee, Mavroyeni enjoys wealth and power as intermediary between a great Pasha, Hassan-bey, and the Greeks over which he rules; Mavroyeni's is a kind of double life, both Greek and *de facto* Turk, both oppressed and oppressor.

Like Hope's Mavroyeni, Mavrocordatos would have known the pressures of this double life; Mavrocordatos himself was a Phanariot and 'his forbears and relations of his family had been in the service of the Sublime Porte as chief interpreters and later as Hospodars or Grand Bans of Valachia and Moldavia'.[54] But one might speculate that, for Shelley, the differential between Mavroyeni's 'losing game' and Mavrocordatos's liberating spirit may have been an important factor in his changing regard for *Anastasius*, from a 'faithful picture' of modern

---

[53] Hope, *Anastasius*, 1: 25.
[54] Huscher, 'Alexander Mavrocordato', p. 29.

Greek manners to a history of those manners before 'most important changes' had rendered them obsolete. Shelley may well have come to believe that Mavrocordatos's position in the Ottoman empire would be the means of ending its imperial power; by allowing educated Greeks to mediate relations with Europe, the Turks would allow the mediators to become crucially influenced by that which they mediate. On the other hand, Shelley's appeal to *Anastasius* as history may have served a subversive purpose of his own. If, as Carl Woodring argues, *Hellas* 'bore the clear intent to celebrate the rising of the Greeks in such a way as to arouse English interest, English funds, and patriotic shame', then the more one like Mavrocordatos could be made to appear the rule rather than the exception to Greek manners, the better.[55] In emphasising the European intellectual contribution to the renovation of the modern Greeks, Shelley may have been soliciting material contributions from Europeans.

Even if Shelley regarded *Anastasius* as a more 'faithful picture' of modern Greek manners on the whole, he would have been hardly comfortable with Mavroyeni's set speech on the subject, no matter how central to the novel. Chiding Anastasius's mortification at the servile bearing of the Greeks at Constantinople, Mavroyeni responds with an impassioned argument for the unity of the Greek character from ancient to modern times, from Cairo to Constantinople:

> ... the core is the same as in the days of Pericles. Credulity, versatility, and thirst for distinction from the earliest periods formed, still form, and ever will form the basis of the Greek character; and the dissimilarity in the external appearances of the nation arises, not from any radical change in its temper and disposition, but only from the incidental variation in the means through which the same propensities are gratified .... The [ancient Greeks] were staunch patriots at home, and subtle courtiers in Persia; the [modern Greeks] defy the Turks in Mayno, and fawn upon them at the Fanar .... When patriotism, public spirit, and pre-eminence in arts, science, literature, and warfare were the roads to distinction, the Greeks shone the first of patriots, of heroes, of painters, or poets, and of philosophers. Now that craft and subtlety, adulation and intrigue are the only paths to greatness, these same Greeks are – what you see them![56]

This essential compatibility of the Greek peoples might have formed the basis for an argument for a Greek nation, but not the one Shelley envisions in *Hellas*, for by his terms of reference, Mavroyeni has misread the past in terms of the present, the ancient Greeks in terms of the moderns. While Shelley recognises shortcomings of social conditions in *A Discourse on the Manners of the Ancient Greeks*, he also argues for the necessary interconnection between the achievements of a people and their level of refinement in social being, or civilisation: what he calls in the preface to *Prometheus Unbound* 'the equilibrium between institutions and opinions' (*PS2*, p. 474, l. 86). What would link the modern Greeks to each other and to their

---

[55] Carl Woodring, *Politics in English Romantic Poetry* (Cambridge, MA: Harvard University Press, 1970), p. 315.
[56] Hope, *Anastasius*, 1: 83-5.

ancestors in the age of Pericles would be their more universal participation in the restoration of that equilibrium in revolutionary Europe. Similarly, the mere 'thirst for distinction' that Mavroyeni postulates as the common denominator of the Greek people's past and present gives way, in Shelley's view, to an 'inextinguishable thirst for immortality' (*SPP*, p. 462, 'NOTE 2') that characterises all men and women. The argument of *Hellas* continually reaffirms Shelley's thinking on the essential social being of man (cf. *Prose*, p. 220) and the compatibility of the modern Greek with the highest levels of European society.

If the preface to *Hellas* suggests how the Ionian isle of *Epipsychidion* might be peopled in lieu of rough shepherds or western colonists, the poem itself contains little more to embellish the prospect. The only Greeks that appear are the 'Chorus of Greek Captive Women' and, in the reports of Hassan and the messengers, various nameless embodiments of the Greek Revolutionary spirit. Shelley is also little concerned with developing an idealised picturesque topography of Greece. The 'action' takes place in the vague terraces and chambers of the Seraglio in Constantinople, where news of naval and military engagements come in from various parts of the Grecian theatre of war, not to mention reports of rebellion at other edges of the Ottoman empire. Shelley, who relied on 'newspaper erudition' and his own Greek contacts for information, was in fact hardly in a position to suggest more than the ripeness of the Greek people from Crete to Wallachia for the assumption of the privileges of being one people in one nation, and the corresponding overripeness of the Ottoman empire, already under strains that would tear it apart.[57] Greece exists in the drama as 'Hellas', a concept emerging in the dreams and imaginations of the Ottoman leader, Mahmud, as he foretells the end of his empire even in the face of temporary victory against the Grecian foe.

Rather than providing details about Hellas or the specific means by which it will be brought about, Shelley sought to explore the psychology and historiography that would explain the decline and fall of empires. To the first of these themes, Hope's *Anastasius* and the remarks of travellers like Clarke would have contributed powerful ethnographical evidence for the interchange between the roles of master and slave, king and subject, that had interested Shelley since *Queen Mab*, and which radicals like Wollstonecraft regarded as the explanation for the failure of a historical upheaval like the French Revolution to achieve its full promise of emancipation; subjects who are conditioned by tyranny can never

---

[57] Responding to a similar statement by Jerome McGann, Kipperman usefully reminds us how 'such an outcome could [not] have been clear (or historically inevitable) *from the perspective of 1821*' (Kipperman, 'Macropolitics', p. 87). But Kipperman's criticism of McGann for stressing the contiguity of Shelley's poem with European imperialism rather than its local radicalism as a nationalist poem is over-subtle. Shelley is addressing a cause rejected by the imperial powers in 1821, but on the basis of arguments and structures of thought underpinning imperial power itself. Kipperman's argument comes back to this position, but only after he has validated Shelley's Romantic ideology as *essentially* radical because expressed in art rather than a more 'objective' discourse: 'In 1821 Shelley's idealism was *both* atemporal *and* rooted in historical progressivism in a way that only art and not politics can be' (p. 91).

become citizens. In superadding a historiographical narrative, Shelley sketches an ideal revolution that anticipates and explains the breaking free from this conditioning. The point is made quite subtly in the opening chorus, in which a solitary Indian and a group of Greek captive women attend the sleeping Mahmud. With this tableau, Shelley suggests at least three states of the consciousness of oppression:

> CHORUS OF GREEK CAPTIVE WOMEN.
> We strew these opiate flowers
>   On thy restless pillow, —
> They were stript from Orient bowers,
>   By the Indian billow.
>   Be thy sleep
>   Calm and deep,
> Like theirs who fell, not ours who weep!
>
> INDIAN.
> Away, unlovely dreams!
>   Away, false shapes of sleep!
> Be his, as Heaven seems
>   Clear and bright and deep!
> Soft as love, and calm as death,
> Sweet as a summer night without a breath. (*SPP*, ll. 1-13)

Though captive, the Greek women have achieved the highest consciousness of liberty and its subtle antithesis, tyranny. Their language objectifies the lessons of conscience drawn from the violence of imperial conquest; the 'opiate flowers' may induce oblivion, but an oblivion that only conceals the flowers' meaning as trophies of Oriental conquest ('*stript* from Orient bowers') from the conqueror himself. The captive women do not urge violence in turn on Mahmud, but promote his sleep that they may sing 'songs consecrate to truth and liberty' ('To Wordsworth'; *PS1*, l. 12). They know that conscience will take care of the tyrant – and it does, for Mahmud's dream turns out to be the prophetic image of his own downfall and that of all tyrannical empires. It is otherwise for the Indian, the subject of the imperial violence that the captive women recount. The Indian represents a people more thoroughly oppressed because unaware of their own oppression. The 'false shapes' she would chase away from Mahmud's sleep turn out to represent the truth; the heaven that 'seems / Clear and bright and deep' ultimately proves 'blood-red' (*SPP*, l. 341). A slave as much to appearances as to tyranny, the Indian would spurn the very revolution that would free her.

While the Greek Captive Women sing of freedom's progress from the state of chaos to the European present, Mahmud dreams; his awakened conscience confirms in sleep the historiographical narrative chanted over him. Of course, Mahmud does not quite remember his dream upon waking, but he begins to perceive in appearances the reality that eludes the Indian. 'The times do cast strange shadows / On those who watch and who must rule their course' (ll. 124-5), he explains to Hassan, who has remarked Mahmud's waking emotions. When Hassan extols the Ottoman power with which the Greeks must reckon, Mahmud proves already infected by a premonition of the transience of empire and imperial power:

> Look, Hassan, on yon crescent moon emblazoned
> Upon that shattered flag of fiery cloud
> Which leads the rear of the departing day,
> Wan emblem of an empire fading now. (ll. 337-40)

The emblematic nature of Mahmud's recognition is crucial: the change that takes place is taking place in representation, as the conscience-stricken Mahmud loses his imperial control over the objects of perception as well as his subjects.[58] Similar 'signs' appear continually: the sunset 'emblem' follows hard on the dream images that haunt Mahmud throughout the text – metaphors of the self-same loss – and Mahmud later recognises his phantom double, Mahomet, as the 'Imperial shadow of the thing I am' (*SPP*, l. 900). The Second Messenger, likewise, describes Ali Pasha as 'a crownless metaphor of empire' (l. 567), unwittingly reinforcing Mahmud's own recognitions past and to come. The Messenger continues:

> His *name*, that *shadow* of his withered might,
> Holds our besieging army *like a spell*
> In prey to Famine, Pest, and Mutiny;
> He, bastioned in his citadel, looks forth
> Joyless upon the sapphire lake that *mirrors*
> The ruins of the city where he reigned
> Childless and sceptreless. (ll. 568-73; my italics)

---

[58] Cf. *Laon and Cythna*, where Shelley describes the principle of Evil in Canto 1 in terms that anticipate Mahmud's situation:

> 'His spirit is their power, and they his slaves
> In air, and light, and thought, and language dwell;
> And keep their state from palaces to graves,
> In all resorts of men – invisible,
> But when, in ebon mirror, Nightmare fell
> To tyrant or imposter bids them rise,
> Black-wingèd demon forms . . . . (*PS2*, I, ll. 388-94)

The previous stanza describes the invisible power as 'those subtle nets which snare the living and the dead' (I, l. 387). In *Hellas*, Shelley allows both Mahmud and the Greek captive women to perceive the power, not only in dreams, but in all figurative perceptions: emblems, metaphors, and songs. Shelley's drama involves the renewal of language, freed from the kind of oblivion represented by the Indian.

Ali Pasha is a metaphor of empire, Shelley suggests, because he embodies both the power over representation that characterises the tyrant and, at the same time, the self-destructive principle that the exercise of such power entails. The Turkish army is stopped in its tracks, in awe of a name, a metaphor; but even so, the soldiers contribute to their own and Mahmud's destruction. Meanwhile, Ali himself – joyless, childless, and sceptreless – embodies absolute power that cannot be self-renovating or regenerating. Like Mahmud's vision of the sky-emblem, Ali sees the image of his own impotence in the 'sapphire lake', as nature wrests control over representation from the tyrants.

As the Greek captive women sing of the progress of liberty throughout history, and Mahmud increasingly recognises the instability of empire in the present, a progressivist historiography emerges as the 'argument' of *Hellas*. On the one hand, the transience of empire invokes the power of time to reduce all works of pride to dust. Ahasuerus thus instructs Mahmud in the art of dream reading: 'Thou mayest behold / How cities, on which empire sleeps enthroned, / Bow their tower'd crests to Mutability' (ll. 844-6). On the other hand, Shelley's message is not merely that 'Nought may endure but Mutability' ('Mutability', *PS1*, l. 16); he instead configures Mutability as the complement of thought. As Ahasuerus also instructs Mahmud:

> Mistake me not! All is contained in each.
> Dodona's forest to an acorn's cup
> Is that which has been, or will be, to that
> Which is — the absent to the present. Thought
> Alone, and its quick elements, Will, Passion,
> Reason, Imagination, cannot die;
> They are, what that which they regard, appears.
> The stuff whence mutability can weave
> All that it hath dominion o'er, worlds, worms,
> Empires and superstitions . . . . (*SPP*, ll. 792-801)

That this 'lesson' contains examples of Shelley's ambiguous use of syntax and antecedents is not surprising, given the scrupulous scepticism with which he deals with ultimate power elsewhere, as in 'Mont Blanc', but these features reward unpacking. The first difficulty is in the line 'They are, what that which they regard, appears, / The stuff . . . '. 'They' and 'stuff' must refer to the 'elements', which in turn constitute 'thought'. Hence, 'mutability' 'weaves' its objects not out of the external universe of things that thought regards, but out of thought itself (or, to be precise, the elements that constitute thought). By implication, what connects the present to the past, living men and women to their ancestors, is not a materialist relation to the world, but traces of intellectual being. The second difficulty with the passage potentially reinforces this reading. The antecedent of 'it' in the penultimate line calls into doubt what has dominion over the appearances of history: 'mutability' or 'the stuff'. Shelley, I think, has it both ways. The dominion of 'mutability' defuses the claim for idealism, while the dominion of 'thought' allows Shelley to locate the source of progressivism in the 'great' and pervasive thought of the ancient Greeks.

The Dodona's cup lines are as close as Shelley comes in *Hellas* to offering a metaphysics of history. As in *Prometheus Unbound*, Shelley wishes instead to present 'beautiful idealisms of moral excellence' (*PS2*, p. 475, l. 126), and he is not too particular whether the principle of dominion be figured as thought, mutability, liberty, or, as in his earlier 'Ode to Liberty', the 'spirit' of liberty. With this last figure, however, Shelley looks to the future in *Hellas* in terms that confirm that it is an imperial spirit that will replace empire. After Mahmud sees the 'emblem of empire' in the fiery sunset, he tells Hassan:

> The spirit that lifts the slave before his lord
> talks through the capitals of armed kings
> And spreads his ensign in the wilderness . . . . (*SPP*, ll. 351-3)

The spirit of liberty not only renovates metropolitan inequalities between tyrant and slave, but also 'spreads his *ensign* in the wilderness'; 'the *flag* of fiery cloud' that spells the doom of the Ottoman empire is unfurled elsewhere as the spirit reappropriates the powers over representation that Mahmud had usurped. Following Mahmud's trope of the flag 'which leads the rear of the departing day' (l. 339), the 'place' of the wilderness, and the new day, will be in the West, perhaps, indeed, Birkbeck's Illinois Territory or similar spaces where civilisation is born anew.

This recollection of Birkbeck is apt, since America features in *Hellas* as a space of hope, should Europe fail to nurture revolutionary promise on its own shores. In the great historiographical vision of the opening chorus, America is 'far Atlantis', the 'second sun' that rekindles the contemporary revolutionary spirit that the drama celebrates:

> Then Night fell — and as from night
> Re-assuming fiery flight
> From the West swift Freedom came
> Against the course of Heaven and doom,
> A second sun arrayed in flame
> To burn, to kindle, to illume.
> From far Atlantis its young beams
> Chased the shadows and the dreams . . . . (*SPP*, ll. 64-71)

Equally as prominent is America's role at the end of *Hellas* as 'the Evening-land' (l. 1030), where Freedom might flee if the revolutionary spirit were quenched in Europe. As much as the drama focuses on Greece as the latest site of that spirit, America exists on its margins as the space out of which civilisation can best be recreated, as from the wilderness that meets the Westward expansion of the republic. Indeed, it is the wilderness that gives America its special status, for only there can the experiment of social being be tried again without the history of oppression that troubled Shelley in *A Philosophical View of Reform*.

By the same token, 'young Atlantis' is not merely an idealised imperial space like Birkbeck's Illinois, but it is also the young empire that the *Edinburgh Review* recognised, with potential as much for ill as for good. Shelley compares it to Rome:

> Through exile, persecution and despair,
> Rome was, and young Atlantis shall become
> The wonder, or the terror or the tomb
> Of all whose step wakes Power lulled in her savage lair. (ll. 992-5)

The image recalls Eustace's *Classical Tour*, which speculates on the transience of all power, but particularly that of Britain: 'Empire has hitherto rolled westward . . . it is still on the wing; and whether it be destined to retrace its steps to the East, or to continue its flight to Transatlantic regions, the days of England's glory have their number . . .' (*CT*, 1: 23). *Hellas* offers another substitution. As the preface makes clear, behind Rome lay Greece: 'But for Greece, Rome, the instructor, the conqueror, or the metropolis of our ancestors would have spread no illumination with her arms, and we might still have been savages, and idolaters . . .' (*SPP*, p. 431). By analogy, 'young Atlantis' will transform savages to citizens by waking the power of social institution in the wilderness.[59] But the analogy holds good in two further points. First, those 'whose step wakes Power' move at the edges of empire, and are thus positioned as both antecedent to power and as awaiting its outcomes: they are also the embodiments of Greece, as the full context of the passage makes clear. Second, like Rome, America has the potential to become the 'terror or the tomb' of the free, as well as 'the wonder'. While advocating imperial cultural values, Shelley must in the end be sceptical of empire itself.

So the 'Brighter Hellas' that Shelley invokes is not necessarily America; instead, it is whatever empire will truly reconstitute Hellas of the Age of Pericles:

> But Greece and her foundations are
> Built below the tide of war,
> Based on the chrystalline sea
> Of thought and its eternity;
> Her citizens, imperial spirits,
>   Rule the present from the past,
> On all this world of men inherits
>   Their seal is set — (*SPP*, ll. 696-703)

> If Greece must be
> A wreck, yet shall its fragments reassemble

---

[59] Power over 'savagery' (an ideologically loaded term) can, as we have seen, take many forms, including the fostering of a picturesque aesthetic and aesthetic sensibility or 'taste'.

>   And build themselves again impregnably
>   In a diviner clime .... (ll. 1002-5)

Combining imperial and republican rhetoric, Shelley represents the embodiments of eternal thought as 'citizens, imperial spirits', under a republic that exports its values through all time. Their 'seal' ensures their triumph over representation, a triumph confirmed by the emblems, metaphors, and shadows that all signify the transience of evil throughout the drama. There is something inexorable about this imperial spirit, whose fragments 'reassemble / And build themselves' without the need for other agency.

In this way, Shelley universalises the cultural imperative of the Periclean age, creating in so doing a totalising history of the progress of civilisation. In promoting the modern Greek cause, Shelley develops a world historical vision that gives pride of place to the Hellas of the past and the 'Brighter Hellas' of the future, purged of the last anomalies of inequality that he had described in *A Discourse on the Manners of the Ancient Greeks*. The cause of modern Greece become indistinguishable from that of America or Europe, and the same renovating spirit will gradually transform the 'enslaved countries' of Asia. The message of the 'Sacred Legion' of the Battle of Dragashan at the heart of *Hellas* delocalises the Greek Revolution and the demise of the Ottoman empire in the broadest terms:

>   Nature from all her boundaries is moved
>   Against ye; — Time has found ye light as foam;
>   The Earth rebels; and Good and Evil stake
>   Their empire o'er the unborn world of men
>   On this one cast; — but ere the die be thrown
>   The renovated Genius of our race,
>   Proud umpire of the impious game, descends,
>   A seraph-winged Victory, bestriding
>   The tempest of the Omnipotence of God
>   Which sweeps all things to their appointed doom
>   And you to oblivion! (ll. 441-51)

Nature, Good, Evil – the stakes are universals, but the 'renovated Genius' is Greek. Hassan, who dramatically conveys the speech, validates the Revolution by the very enthusiasm with which he utters it, and Mahmud fittingly chides him: 'Your heart is Greek, Hassan' (*SPP*, l. 455). And, of course, as Shelley has it, 'We are all Greeks'; the victory of culture will be in the re-establishing of its dominion, whether this be in 'the birth of this old world' (l. 746) or in 'the unborn world' to come.

Ironically, *Hellas* becomes more openly ideological even as it argues for a transcendence of ideology. Ideology foregrounds itself first insofar as the work can be recognised as liberal propaganda on behalf of the Greek Revolution, with Shelley recognising the need for stirring up English grassroots support in order to provide material aid for the Greeks themselves, and, more importantly, to apply pressure on the English government to end its non-interventionist policy ('What little interest this Poem may ever excite, depends upon it's [sic] *immediate publication*') (*L*, 2: 365). But even as Shelley makes his case on this level, he also foregrounds an imperial ideology with its roots in the cultural achievements of Grecian society, interpreted and improved since 'the revival of learning', and which must 'wake' the wilderness of America, the 'decayed' civilisations of the far East, and, of course, Europe itself from monarchical oppression and economic exploitation. In the end, Shelley suggests, Europe itself owes its origins to Greece and has created the conditions for the perfection of Greece – and *Hellas* is hyperconscious of this vision.

Shelley's travel writings also develop the terms of this imperial imagination, as I have argued throughout this study. Drawing on discourses found in much of the period's travel literature (e.g. manners and national character, Rousseauian primitivism, the sublime, the beautiful, and the picturesque), Shelley constructs in his own literature of travel an aesthetic vision that privileges the appropriation of wilderness, landscape, and, ultimately, the nation state itself, as a reflex of an originary appropriation idealised in republican Greece. *Hellas* is both the culmination of this vision of a free space of world legislation, and the marker of the point to which all his travels were conducted, past which he could not go. With the dissolution of Shelley and Medwin's plans to visit Greece, Shelley's wider travels also drew to an effective close. Pisa became Shelley's home and his travel letters became fewer and less descriptive. Yet to the end of his life, Shelley never ceased refining and reflecting on his aesthetic vision, using the problematic of tourist perception and travel writing as a discursive foil. Even 'The Triumph of Life', Shelley's last great poem, begins with a setting of mass tourism where hordes of travellers are seen following a beaten path, unaware that their responses to nature and culture are circumscribed by custom, leading them to death. The narrator, like Shelley, finds himself 'beside a public way', potentially implicated in the acts of observation that lead the tourists on, yet searching for a vision that will prevent him from suffering a similar fate. Both a spectator of and a reluctant participant in travel culture, Shelley holds the mirror of his eye up to the scene of observation and expression, hoping to see the deep structure of his age, and to reform its future.

Bibliography

Primary Sources

A Tour through Part of France, Containing a Description of Paris, Cherbourg, and Ermenonville, with A Rhapsody, Composed at the Tomb of Rousseau. London: Printed for T. Cadell, 1789.

Addison, Joseph. *Remarks on Several Parts of Italy in the Years 1701, 1702, 1703* (1705). In *The Miscellaneous Works of Joseph Addison*. Ed. A. C. Guthkelch. Vol. 2. London: G. Bell and Sons Ltd, 1914.

Alison, Archibald. *Travels in France, during the Years 1814-15. Comprising a Residence at Paris, during the Stay of the Allied Armies, and at Aix, at the Period of the Landing of Bonaparte*. 2 vols. London: Printed for Longman, Hurst, Rees, Orme, and Brown, 1815.

An Explanation of the View of Rome, Taken from the Tower of the Capitol. Now Exhibiting at H. A. Barker and J. Burford's Panorama, Near the New Church, in the Strand. [n.p.], 1817.

Allason, Thomas. *Picturesque Views of the Antiquities of Pola, in Istria*. London: John Murray, 1819

Baillie, Mariane. *First Impressions on a Tour upon the Continent*. London: John Murray, 1819.

Barthélemy, Jean-Jacques. *Travels of Anacharsis the Younger in Greece, during the Middle of the Fourth Century before the Christian Aera*. Trans. from French. 5th edn. 6 vols. London: J. Mawman, 1817.

Batty, Elisabeth Frances. *Italian Scenery. From Drawings Made in 1817*. London: Rodwell & Martin, 1820.

Bell, John. *Observations on Italy*. Edinburgh: William Blackwood; London: T. Cadell, 1825.

Birkbeck, Morris. *Extracts from a Supplementary Letter from the Illinois; An Address to British Emigrants; and A Reply to the Remarks of William Cobbett, Esq*. 2nd edn. London: Printed for James Ridgway, 1819.

—. *Notes on a Journey in America, from the Coast of Virginia to the Territory of the Illinois*. London, 1818.

—. *Letters from Illinois*. London: Printed for Taylor and Hessey, 1818.

—. *Notes on a Journey through France, from Dieppe through Paris and Lyons, to the Pyrenees, and back through Toulouse in July, August, and September, 1814*. 3rd edn. London: Printed by W. Phillips, 1815.

Blagdon, Francis William. *Paris as It Was and as It Is; or, A Sketch of the French Capital, Illustrative of the Effects of the Revolution, with Respect to Sciences, Literature, Arts, Religion, Education, Manners, and Amusements . . . In a Series of Letters, Written by an English Traveller, during the Years 1801-2, to a Friend in London*. 2 vols. London: C. and R. Baldwin, 1803.

Bowles, William Lisle. *Two Letters to Lord Byron*, in *The Pamphleteer*, vol. 18, no. 36 (1821), pp. 331-91.

Burke, Edmund. *The Writings and Speeches of Edmund Burke*. Gen. ed. Paul Langford. 9 vols. Oxford: Clarendon Press, 1981-2000.

—. *Reflections on the Revolution in France.* Ed. J. G. A. Pocock. Indianapolis: Hackett Publishing Company, 1987.
—. *The Correspondence of Edmund Burke.* Eds Alfred Cobban and Robert A. Smith. Vol. 6. London: Cambridge University Press, 1967.
Brydone, Patrick. *A Tour through Sicily and Malta, in a Series of Letters to William Beckford.* 3rd edn. 2 vols. London: Printed for W. Strahan; and T. Cadell, 1774.
Byron, George Gordon, Lord. *Lord Byron: The Complete Poetical Works.* Ed. Jerome J. McGann. 7 vols. Oxford: Oxford University Press, 1980-93.
—. *Byron's Letters and Journals.* Ed. Leslie Marchand. 12 vols. Cambridge, MA: Harvard University Press, 1973-82.
—. *Childe Harold's Pilgrimage. Canto the Fourth.* London: John Murray, 1818.
Bruen, Matthias. *Essays, Descriptive and Moral; on Scenes in Italy, Switzerland, and France. By an American.* Edinburgh: Archibald Constable and Co., 1823.
Carr, John, Sir. *The Stranger in France.* 2nd edn. London: J. Johnson, 1807.
Clairmont, Claire. *The Journals of Claire Clairmont.* Ed. Marion Kingston Stocking, with the assistance of David Mackenzie Stocking. Cambridge, MA: Harvard University Press, 1968.
Clubbe, William. *The Omnium: Containing the Journal of a Late Three Days Tour to France.* Ipswich, 1798.
Coleridge, Samuel Taylor. *Biographia Literaria.* 2 vols in 1. Eds James Engel and W. Jackson Bate. Princeton: Princeton University Press, 1983.
—. *Coleridge: Poetical Works.* Ed. Ernest Hartley Coleridge. Oxford: Oxford University Press, 1969.
Colston, Marianne. *Journal of a Tour in France, Switzerland, and Italy during the Years 1819, 20, and 21. Illustrated by Fifty Lithographic Prints, from Original Drawings Taken in Italy, the Alps, and the Pyrenees.* 2 vols. Paris: A. and W. Galignani, 1822.
Coxe, Henry [pseud. for John Millard?]. *Pictures of Italy; Being a Guide to the Antiquities and Curiosities of that Classical and Interesting Country.* London, 1815.
Cunningham, J. W. *Cautions to Continental Travellers.* London, 1818.
Demont, Louise. *Voyages and Travels of Her Majesty, Caroline Queen of Great Britain.* London: Jones & Co., 1822.
Description of the Camera Lucida, and Instrument for Drawing in True Perspective, and for Copying, Reducing, or Enlarging Other Drawings. To Which Is Added, by Permission, A Letter on the Use of the Camera, by Capt. Basil Hall, R.N., F.R.S. London: G. Dollond, [1830?].
Devonshire, Georgina, Duchess of. *The Passage of the Mountain of Saint Gothard, a Poem.* London: For Prosper and Co., 1802.
Duppa, Richard. *A Journal of the Most Remarkable Occurences that Took Place in Rome: upon the Subversion of the Ecclesiastical Government, in 1798.* London: Printed for G. G. and J. Robinson, 1799.
Eaton, Charlotte Anne. *Rome in the Nineteenth Century; Containing a Complete Account of the Ruins of the Ancient City, the Remains of the Middle Ages, and the Monuments of Modern Times. With Remarks on the Fine Arts, on the State of Society, and on the Religious Ceremonies, Manners, and Customs, of the Modern Romans. In a Series of Letters Written during a Residence at Rome, in the Years 1817 and 1818.* 3 vols. Edinburgh: Archibald Constable and Co; London: Hurst, Robinson, and Co., 1820.
Escape from France: A Narrative of the Hardships and Sufferings of Several British Subjects Who Effected Their Escape from Verdun. With an Appendix, Containing Observations on the Policy and Conduct of Buonaparte towards British Subjects. London: Vernor, Hood, and Sharpe, 1811.

Eustace, John Chetwode. *A Classical Tour through Italy*. 3rd edn, rev. and enl. 4 vols. London: Printed for J. Mawman, 1815.

—. *A Classical Tour through Italy. An MDCCCII*. 4th edn, rev., corr. and amended. 4 vols. Leghorn: Glauca Masi, 1818.

—. *Answer to the Charge Delivered by the Lord Bishop of Lincoln to the Clergy of that Diocese, at the Triennial Visitation in the Year 1818*. London: J. Mawman, 1813.

—. *An Elegy to the Memory of the Right Honourable Edmund Burke*. London: Printed for F. and C. Rivington, 1798.

Forbes, James. *Letters from France, Written in the Years 1803 & 1804. Including a Particular Account of Verdun, and the Situation of the British Captives in that City*. 2 vols. London: Printed for J. White, 1806.

Forsyth, Joseph. *Remarks on Antiquities, Arts, and Letters during an Excursion in Italy, in the Years 1802 and 1803*. Ed. Keith Crook. Neward: University of Delaware Press, 2001.

Gell, Sir William. *Pompeiana*. London, 1817-19.

Gibbon, Edward. *The Miscellaneous Works of Edward Gibbon, Esq. with Memoirs of his Life and Writings*. Ed. John, Lord Sheffield. 5 vols. London: John Murray, 1814.

—. *The Decline and Fall of the Roman Empire*. 3 vols. New York: The Modern Library, [n.d].

Gilpin, William. *Three Essays*. London: Printed for R. Blamire, 1792.

—. *Remarks on Forest Scenery and Other Woodland Views (Relative Chiefly to Picturesque Beauty) Illustrated by the Scenes of the New-Forest in Hampshire*. 2 vols. London: Printed for R. Blamire, 1791.

Hakewill, James. *A Picturesque Tour of Italy, from Drawings Made in 1816-17*. London: John Murray, 1820.

Hall, Basil. *Forty Etchings, from Sketches Made with the Camera Lucida, in North America, in 1827 and 1828*. Edinburgh: Cadell & Co.; London: Simpkin & Marshall, 1829.

Harding, James Duffield. *Seventy-Five Views of Italy and France, Adapted to Illustrate Byron, Rogers, Eustace, and All Works on Italy and France*. London, 1834.

Hazlitt, William. *The Complete Works of William Hazlitt*. Ed. P. P. Howe. Vol. 17. London: Dent, 1933.

Hoare, Sir Richard Colt. *A Classical Tour through Italy and Sicily Tending to Illustrate Some Districts, Which Have Not Been Described by Mr. Eustace, in His Classical Tour*. London: J. Mawman, 1819.

—. *Hints to Travellers in Italy*. London: Printed by W. Bulmer and Co., 1815.

Hobhouse, John Cam. *Historical Illustrations of the Fourth Canto of Child Harold*. London: John Murray, 1818.

Holcroft, Thomas. *Travels from Hamburgh, through Westphalia, Holland, and the Netherlands, to Paris*. 2 vols. London: Printed for Richard Phillips, 1804.

Hookham, Thomas. *A Walk through Switzerland, in September 1816*. London: Printed for T. Hookham, and Baldwin, Craddock and Joy, 1818.

Hope, Thomas. *Anastasius: or, Memoirs of a Greek; Written at the Close of the Eighteenth Century*. 3 vols. London: John Murray, 1819.

Jameson, Anna. *Diary of an Ennuyée*. New edn. London: Henry Colburn, 1826.

Jerdan, William. *Six Weeks in Paris; or, A Cure for the Gallomania*. 2nd edn. London: J. Jonston, 1818.

Jones, Frederick L., ed. *Maria Gisborne & Edward E. Williams, Shelley's Friends: Their Journals and Letters*. Norman: University of Oklahoma Press, 1951.

Kelsall, Charles. *Classical Excursion from Rome to Arpino*. Geneva, 1820.

Kotzebue, August Friedrich Ferdinand von. *Travels through Italy in the Years 1804 and 1805*. 4 vols. London: Printed for Richard Phillips, 1806.

Knight, Richard Payne. *An Analytic Inquiry into the Principles of Taste*. London: Printed for T. Payne and J. White, 1805.

Laurent, Peter Edmund. *Recollections of a Classical Tour through Various Parts of Greece, Turkey and Italy Made in the Years 1818 & 1819*. London: G. and W. B. Whittaker, 1821.

Lemprière, John. *Lemprière's Classical Dictionary of Proper Names Mentioned in Ancient Authors Writ Large, with a Chronological Table*. 3rd edn. London: Routledge & Kegan Paul, 1984.

The Life and Remains of the Rev. Edward Daniel Clarke, LL.D. Professor of Mineralogy in the University of Cambridge. London, 1824.

Malthus, Thomas. *An Essay on the Principle of Population and A Summary View of the Principle of Population*. Ed. Antony Flew. London: Penguin, 1970.

Manners, John Henry, and Elizabeth Manners. *Journal of a Trip to Paris by the Duke and Duchess of Rutland, July 1814*. London, [1814?].

Matthews, Henry. *The Diary of an Invalid Being the Journal of a Tour in Pursuit of Health in Portugal Italy Switzerland and France in the Years 1817 1818 and 1818*. 2nd edn. London: John Murray, 1820.

Monson, W. J. *Extracts from a Journal*. London: Rodwell and Martin, 1820.

Moore, John. *A Journal During a Residence in France, from the Beginning of August, to the Middle of December, 1792*. 2 vols. London: Printed for G. G. J. and J. Robinson, 1793.

Morgan, Sidney Owenson, Lady. *France*. 2 vols. London: Printed for Henry Colburn, 1817.

—. *Italy*. 2 vols. London: Henry Colburn and Co., 1821.

Moritz, Karl Philipp. *Travels, Chiefly on Foot, through Several Parts of England in 1782*. London: Printed for G. G. and J. Robinson, 1795.

Nicholson, Francis. *The Practice of Drawing and Painting Landscape from Nature, in Water Colours*. London: Printed for the Author by J. Booth, 1820.

Peacock, Thomas Love. *The Letters of Thomas Love Peacock*. Ed. Nicholas A. Joukovsky. 2 vols. Oxford: Clarendon Press, 2001.

—. *The Halliford Edition of the Works of Thomas Love Peacock*. Eds H. F. B. Brett-Smith and C. E. Jones. 10 vols. London: Constable and Co.; New York: Gabriel Wells, 1924-34.

Pinkerton, John, ed. *A General Collection of the Best and Most Interesting Voyages and Travels in All Parts of the World*. 17 vols. London: Longman & Co., 1808-14.

Piozzi, Hester Lynch. *Observations Made in the Course of a Journey through France, Italy, and Germany [1789]*. Ed. Herbert Barrows. Ann Arbor: University of Michigan Press, 1967.

Playfair, William. *France As It Is: Not Lady Morgan's France*. 2 vols. London: Printed by W. McDowall, 1819.

Plumptre, James. *The Lakers, 1798*. Oxford and New York: Woodstock Books, 1990.

Pope, Alexander. *The Twickenham Edition of the Poems of Alexander Pope*. Vol. 2. Ed. Geoffrey Tillotsen. London: Methuen & Co., Ltd; New Haven: Yale University Press, 1966.

Prout, Samuel. *One Hundred and Four Views of Switzerland and Italy, Adapted to Illustrate Byron, Rogers, Eustace, and Other Works on Italy*. London, 1833.

Reinagle, R. R. *An Explanation of the View of Rome, Taken from the Tower of the Capitol. Now Exhibiting at the Panorama, near the New Church, in the Strand*. Smithfield: Printed by J. Adlard, [n.d.].

Review of *History of a Six Weeks' Tour*, [by Mary Shelley and Percy Bysshe Shelley], and *A Walk through Switzerland*, [by Thomas Hookham, Jun.]. *The Eclectic Review*, ser. 2, vol. 9 (May 1818), pp. 473-4.

Review of *History of a Six Weeks' Tour*, [by Mary Shelley and Percy Bysshe Shelley], and *A Walk through Switzerland*, [by Thomas Hookham, Jun.]. *Monthly Review*, 88 (Jan. 1819), pp. 97-9.

Review of *A Tour through the Southern Provinces of the Kingdom of Naples*, by the Hon. Richard Keppel Craven. *Edinburgh Review*, 36 (Oct. 1821), pp. 153-73.

Review of *France*, by Lady Morgan. *Quarterly Review*, vol. 17, no. 33 (Apr. 1817), pp. 260-86.

Review of *Travels from Berlin through Switzerland to Paris in the Year 1804*, by August Von Kotzebue. *Edinburgh Review*, 5 (Oct. 1804), pp. 78-91.

Review of *Travels through Sweden, Finland, and Lapland, to the Northern Cape*, by Joseph Acerbi. *Edinburgh Review*, 1 (Oct. 1802), pp. 163-72.

Rogers, Samuel. *The Italian Journal of Samuel Rogers*. Ed. J. R. Hale. London: Faber and Faber, 1956.

Rousseau, Jean-Jacques. *Basic Political Writings*. Trans. and ed. Donald A. Cress. Indianapolis: Hackett Publishing Company, 1987.

—. *The Confessions*. Trans. J. M. Cohen. London: Penguin, 1953.

Ruskin, John. *Praeterita*. Oxford: Oxford University Press, 1989.

Saussure, Horace Bénedict de. *An Account of the Attempts that Have Been Made to Attain the Summit of Mont Blanc*. In Pinkerton, John, ed. *A General Collection*. Vol. 4.

Schlegel, A. W. *A Course of Lectures on Dramatic Art and Literature*. Trans. John Black. 2 vols. London: Printed for Baldwin, Craddock, and Joy, 1815.

Scott, John. *Sketches of Manners, Scenery, & c. in the French Provinces, Switzerland, and Italy*. 2nd edn. London: Printed for Longman, Hurst, Rees, Orme, and Brown, 1821.

—. *A Visit to Paris in 1814; Being a Review of the Moral, Political, Intellectual, and Social Condition of the French Capital. By John Scott, Editor of the Champion, a Weekly Political and Literary Journal*. 2nd edn, corr., with a New Preface Referring to Late Events. London: Printed for Longman, Hurst Rees, Orme, and Brown, Paternoster-Row, 1815.

—. 'General Reflections Suggested by Italy, Seen in the Years 1818 and 1819'. *London Magazine*, 1 (Jan. 1820), pp. 3-7.

—. Review of *The Diary of an Invalid: Being the Journal of a Tour in Pursuit of Health; in Portugal, Italy, Switzerland, and France*, by Henry Matthews. *London Magazine*, (July 1820), pp. 59-65.

Shelley, Mary Wollstonecraft. *The Novels and Selected Works of Mary Shelley*. Ed. Nora Crook, with Pamela Clemit. London: William Pickering, 1996.

—. *The Letters of Mary Wollstonecraft Shelley*. 3 vols. Ed. Betty T. Bennett. Baltimore and London: Johns Hopkins University Press, 1980-88.

—. *The Journals of Mary Shelley*. Eds Paula R. Feldman and Diana Scott-Kilvert. Baltimore and London: Johns Hopkins University Press, 1987.

—. *Collected Tales and Stories*. Ed. Charles E. Robinson. Baltimore: Johns Hopkins University Press, 1976.

Shelley, Mary Wollstonecraft, and Percy Bysshe Shelley. *History of a Six Weeks' Tour through a Part of France, Switzerland, Germany, and Holland: with Letters Descriptive of a Sail round the Lake of Geneva, and of the Glaciers of Chamouni*. London: Published by T. Hookham, Jun., and C. and J. Ollier, 1817.

Shelley, Percy Bysshe. *Shelley's Poetry and Prose*. 2nd edn. Ed. Donald H. Reiman and Neil Fraistat. New York: W. W. Norton & Co., 2002.

—. *The Poems of Shelley*. Vol. 1: 1804-1817. Eds Geoffrey Matthews and Kelvin Everest; Vol. 2: 1817-1819. Eds Kelvin Everest and Geoffrey Matthews; Contributing eds Jack Donovan, Ralph Pite, and Michael Rossington. London: Longman, 1989-2000.

—. *The Prose Works of Percy Bysshe Shelley.* Ed. E. B. Murray. Vol. 1. Oxford: Clarendon Press, 1993.
—. *Shelley's Prose or the Trumpet of a Prophecy.* Ed. David Lee Clark. London: Fourth Estate, 1988.
—. *Bodleian MS. Shelley e. 4: A Facsimile Edition with Full Transcription and Textual Notes.* Ed. P. M. S. Dawson. New York & London: Garland Publishing, 1987.
—. *Shelley and His Circle 1773-1822.* Eds K. N. Cameron, vols 1-4; D. H. Reiman, vols 5-8. Cambridge, MA: Harvard University Press, 1961-86.
—. *Shelley: Poetical Works.* Ed. Thomas Hutchinson. Corr. G. M. Matthews. Oxford: Oxford University Press, 1970.
—. *The Letters of Percy Bysshe Shelley.* Ed. Frederick L. Jones. 2 vols. Oxford: Clarendon Press, 1964.
—. *Essays, Letters from Abroad, Translations and Fragments.* Ed. Mary Shelley. 2 vols. London: Edward Moxon, 1840 [i.e. 1839].
Sheppard, John. *Letters, Descriptive of a Tour through Some Parts of France, Italy, Switzerland, and Germany, in 1816.* Edinburgh: Printed for Oliphant, Waugh and Innes, 1817.
Smith, John. *Select Views in Italy, with Topographical and Historical Descriptions in English and French.* 2 vols. London, 1792-96.
Smollett, Tobias. *Travels through France and Italy [1765].* Ed. Frank Felsenstein. Oxford: Oxford University Press, 1979.
Southey, Robert. *Metrical Tales and Other Poems.* London: Printed for Longman, Hurst, Rees, and Orme, 1805.
Spencer, Aubrey George. *The Coliseum; of A Letter from Rome.* Norwich, 1818.
Staël-Holstein, Anna Louise Germaine de. *Corinne, or Italy.* Trans. and ed. Sylvia Raphael. Oxford and New York: Oxford University Press, 1998.
Volney, Constantine F. *The Ruins, or, A Survey of the Revolutions of Empires.* Trans. [James Marshall]. 5th edn. London, 1807.
Wilkins, William. *The Antiquities of Magna Graecia.* Cambridge, 1807.
Williams, Helen Maria. *Letters Written in France, 1790.* Oxford: Woodstock Books, 1989.
—. *Letters Written in France in 1790, 1793, and 1794, to a Friend in England, Containing Anecdotes Relative to the French Revolution; Concerning Important Events, Particularly Relating to the Campaign of 1792; A Sketch of the Politics of France during 1793-4, and Scenes in the Prisons of Paris.* 7 vols in 3. London, 1793-96.
—. *New Travels in Switzerland, Containing a Picture of the Country, the Manners and the Actual Government.* 2 vols. London, 1796.
—. *A Tour in Switzerland; or, A View of the Present State of the Governments and Manners of those Cantons: with Comparative Sketches of the Present State of Paris.* 2 vols. London: G. G. and J. Robinson, 1798.
Winckelmann, Johann Joachim. *Thoughts on the Imitation of the Painting and Sculpture of the Greeks.* Trans. H. B. Nisbet. In *German Aesthetic and Literary Criticism.* Ed. H. B. Nisbet. Cambridge: Cambridge University Press, 1985.
Wollstonecraft, Mary. *An Historical and Moral View of the Origin and Progress of the French Revolution and the Effect It Has Produced in Europe.* 2nd edn. [1795]. Delmar, NY: Scholars' Facsimiles and Reprints, 1975.
—. *Letters Written during a Short Residence in Sweden, Norway, and Denmark.* London: Printed for J. Johnson, 1796.
Wordsworth, William. *Lyrical Ballads, and Other Poems, 1797-1900.* Ed. James Butler and Karen Green. Ithaca, NY: Cornell University Press, 1992.
—. *Poems in Two Volumes, and Other Poems, 1800-1807.* Ed. Jared Curtis. Ithaca, NY: Cornell University Press, 1983.

—. *The Prelude, 1799, 1805, 1850*. Eds Jonathan Wordsworth, M. H. Abrams, and Stephen Gill. New York: Norton, 1979.
—. *The Prose Works of William Wordsworth*. Eds W. J. B. Owen and Jane Worthington Smyser. 3 vols. Oxford: Clarendon Press, 1974.
—. *The Excursion, Being a Portion of The Recluse, a Poem*. London: Printed for Longman, Hurst, Rees, Orme, and Brown, 1814.
Young, Arthur. *Travels during the Years 1787, 1788, and 1789 . . . with a View of Ascertaining the Cultivation, Wealth, Resources, and National Prosperity of the Kingdom of France* (1792). In Pinkerton, John, ed. *General Collection*. Vol. 4.

Secondary Sources

Altick, Richard. *The Shows of London*. Cambridge, MA: Harvard University Press, 1978.
Andrews, Malcolm. *The Search for the Picturesque: Landscape Aesthetics and Tourism in Britain, 1760-1800*. Stanford: Stanford University Press, 1989.
Angeli, Helen Rossetti. *Shelley and His Friends in Italy*. London, 1911.
Angelomatis-Tsougarakis, Helen. *The Eve of the Greek Revival: British Travellers' Perceptions of Early Nineteenth-Century Greece*. London and New York: Routledge, 1990.
Aveling, Edward, and Eleanor Marx Aveling. *Shelley's Socialism*. Repr. 1888 edn. London: The Journeyman Press, 1975.
Avery, Harold. 'John Bell's Last Tour'. *Medical History*, 8 (1964), pp. 69-77.
Barrell, John. *The Idea of Landscape and the Sense of Place, 1730-1840*. Cambridge: Cambridge University Press, 1972.
Barrows, Herbert. 'Convention and Novelty in the Romantic Generation's Experience of Italy'. *Bulletin of the New York Public Library*, 67 (June 1963), pp. 360-75.
Batten, Charles L. *Pleasurable Instruction: Form and Convention in Eighteenth-Century Travel Literature*. Berkeley: University of California Press, 1978.
Baudrillard, Jean. *The Mirror of Production*. Trans. Mark Poster. St Louis: Telos Press, 1975.
Behrendt, Stephen C. *Shelley and His Audiences*. Lincoln and London: University of Nebraska Press, 1989.
Bennett, Betty T., and Stuart Curran, eds. S*helley: Poet and Legislator of the World*. Baltimore and London: Johns Hopkins University Press, 1996.
Bermingham, Ann. *Landscape and Ideology: The English Rustic Tradition, 1740-1860*. Berkeley: University of California Press, 1986.
Bhabha, Homi. 'Signs Taken for Wonders: Questions of Ambivalence and Authority under a Tree Outside Delhi, May 1817'. In *Europe and Its Others*. Ed. Francis Barker, et al. 2 vols. Colchester: University of Essex, 1985.
Binfield, Kevin. '"May they be divided never": Ethics, History, and the Rhetorical Imagination in Shelley's "The Coliseum"'. *Keats-Shelley Journal*, 46 (1997), pp. 125-47.
Birns, Nicholas. 'Secrets of the Birth of Time: The Rhetoric of Cultural Origins in *Alastor* and "Mont Blanc"'. *Studies in Romanticism*, 32 (Fall 1993), pp. 339-65.
Black, Jeremy. *The British Abroad: The Grand Tour in the Eighteenth Century*. London: Sandpiper Books, 1999.
—. *The British and the Grand Tour*. London: Croom Helm, 1985.
Blunden, Edmund. *Shelley: A Life Story*. London: Collins, 1946.
Bohls, Elizabeth A. *Women Travel Writers and the Language of Aesthetics, 1716-1818*. Cambridge: Cambridge University Press, 1995.

Brand, C. P. *Italy and the English Romantics: The Italianate Fashion in Early Nineteenth-Century England*. Cambridge: Cambridge University Press, 1957.

Brinkley, Robert. 'Documenting Revision: Shelley's Lake Geneva Diary and the Dialogue with Byron in *History of a Six Weeks' Tour*'. *Keats-Shelley Journal*, 39 (1990), pp. 66-82.

—. 'On the Composition of "Mont Blanc": Staging a Wordsworthian Scene'. *English Language Notes*, 24.2 (Dec. 1986), pp. 45-57.

Brinkley, Robert, and Keith Hanley, eds. *Romantic Revisions*. Cambridge: Cambridge University Press, 1992.

Butler, Marilyn. *Romantics, Rebels and Reactionaries: English Literature and Its Background, 1760-1830*. Oxford: Oxford University Press, 1981.

—. *Peacock Displayed: A Satirist in His Context*. London: Routledge & Kegan Paul, 1979.

Buzard, James. *The Beaten Track: European Tourism, Literature, and the Ways to Culture, 1800-1918*. Oxford: Clarendon Press, 1993.

Cameron, Kenneth Neill. 'A Major Source of *The Revolt of Islam*'. *PMLA*, 56 (1941), pp. 175-206.

Campbell, Mary. *Lady Morgan: The Life and Times of Sydney Owenson*. London: Pandora, 1988.

Carothers, Yvonne. 'Alastor: Shelley Corrects Wordsworth'. *Modern Language Quarterly*, 42 (1981), pp. 21-47.

Chandler, James. *England in 1819: The Politics of Literary Culture and the Case of Romantic Historicism*. Chicago and London: University of Chicago Press, 1998.

Chard, Chloe. *Pleasure and Guilt on the Grand Tour: Travel Writing and Imaginative Geography 1600-1830*. Manchester: Manchester University Press, 1999.

Chernaik, Judith, and Timothy Burnett. 'The Byron and Shelley Notebooks in the Scrope Davies Find'. *Research in English Studies*, n.s., 29 (Feb. 1978), pp. 36-49.

Churchill, Kenneth. *Italy and English Literature, 1764-1930*. London: Macmillan, 1980.

Clark, Roger. 'Threading the Maze: Nineteenth-Century Guides for British Travellers to Paris'. *Parisian Fields*. Ed. Michael Sheringham. London: Reaktion Books, 1996. pp. 8-29.

Clark, Timothy. 'Shelley's "The Coliseum" and the Sublime'. *Durham University Journal*, 85 (July 1993), pp. 225-35.

Clay, Edith. 'Introduction'. *Sir William Gell in Italy: Letters to the Society of Dilettanti, 1831-1835*. Ed. Edith Clay in collaboration with Martin Frederiksen. London: Hamish Hamilton, 1976.

Colbert, Benjamin. 'Aesthetics of Enclosure: Agricultural Tourism and the Place of the Picturesque'. *European Romantic Review*, 13.1 (Mar. 2002), pp. 23-34.

—. 'New Pictures of Paris: British Travellers' Views of the French Metropolis, 1814-1816'. *Seuils & Traverses: Enjeux de l'écriture du voyage*. Eds Jean-Yves Le Disez and Jan Borm. 2 vols. Brest: Centre de Recherche Bretonne et Celtique, Université de Bretagne Occidentale, 2002. Vol. 1, pp. 45-54.

—. 'Contemporary Notice of the Shelleys' *History of a Six Weeks' Tour*: Two New Early Reviews'. *Keats-Shelley Journal*, 48 (1999), pp. 22-9.

Colwell, Frederick S. 'Figures in a Promethean Landscape'. *Keats-Shelley Journal*, 45 (1996), pp. 118-31.

—. 'Shelley and Italian Painting'. *Keats-Shelley Journal*, 29 (1980), pp. 43-66.

—. 'Shelley on Sculpture: The Uffizi Notes'. *Keats-Shelley Journal*, 28 (1979), pp. 59-77.

Copley, Stephen, and Peter Garside, eds. *The Politics of the Picturesque: Literature, Landscape and Aesthetics Since 1770*. Cambridge: Cambridge University Press, 1994.

Cox, Jeffrey N. *Poetry and Politics in the Cockney School: Keats, Shelley, Hunt and Their Circle*. Cambridge: Cambridge University Press, 1998.

Crary, Jonathan. *Techniques of the Observer: On Vision and Modernity in the Nineteenth Century*. Cambridge, MA: MIT Press, 2001.

Crook, J. Mordaunt. *The Dilemma of Style: Architectural Ideas from the Picturesque to the Post-Modern*. London: John Murray, 1989.

—. *The Greek Revival: Neo-Classical Attitudes in British Architecture, 1760-1870*. London: John Murray, 1972.

Crook, Nora, and Derek Guiton. *Shelley's Venomed Melody*. Cambridge: Cambridge University Press, 1986.

Curran, Stuart. *Shelley's Annus Mirabilis*. San Marino, CA: Huntington Library, 1975.

Dabundo, Laura. 'The Extrospective Vision: The Excursion as Transitional in Wordsworth's Poetry and Age'. *Wordsworth Circle*, 19.1 (Winter 1988), pp. 8-14.

De Beer, Gavin. 'An "Atheist" in the Alps'. *Keats-Shelley Memorial Bulletin*, 9 (1958), pp. 1-15.

De la Croix, Horst, Richard G. Tansey, and Diane Kirkpatrick. *Gardner's Art through the Ages*. 9th edn. Vol. 2. Fort Worth, TX: Harcourt Brace Jovanovich, 1991.

Dolan, Brian. *Ladies of the Grand Tour*. London: Flamingo, 2001.

—. *Exploring European Frontiers: British Travellers in the Age of Enlightenment*. London: Macmillan, 2000.

Dowden, Edward. *The Life of Percy Bysshe Shelley*. London: Routledge & Kegan Paul, 1969.

Duffy, Edward. *Rousseau in England: The Context for Shelley's Critique of the Enlightenment*. Berkeley: University of California Press, 1979.

Eisner, Robert. *Travelers to an Antique Land: The History and Literature of Travel to Greece*. Ann Arbor: University of Michigan Press, 1993.

Elton, Charles I. *An Account of Shelley's Visits to France, Switzerland, and Savoy, in the Years 1814 and 1816*. London: Bliss, Sands, and Foster, 1894.

Fabian, Johannes. *Time and the Other: How Anthropology Makes Its Object*. New York: Columbia University Press, 1983.

Favret, Mary. *Romantic Correspondence: Women, Politics & the Fiction of Letters*. Cambridge: Cambridge University Press, 1992.

Ferguson, Frances. 'Shelley's Mont Blanc: What the Mountain Said'. In *Romanticism and Language*. Ed. Arden Reed. London: Methuen, 1984. pp. 202-14.

Ferris, David. *Silent Urns: Romanticism, Hellenism, Modernity*. Stanford: Stanford University Press, 2000.

Fischman, Susan. '"Like the Sound of His own Voice": Gender, Audition, and Echo in *Alastor*'. *Keats-Shelley Journal*, 43 (1994), pp. 141-69.

Fitzroy, Sir Almeric. *History of the Travellers' Club*. [London]: George Allen & Unwin, 1927.

Foster, Shirley. *Across New Worlds: Nineteenth-Century Women Travellers and Their Writings*. London: Harvester Wheatsheaf, 1990.

Freistat, Neil. 'Poetic Quests and Questionings in Shelley's Alastor Collection'. *Keats-Shelley Journal*, 33 (1984), pp. 161-81.

Gerbod, Paul. 'Voyageurs et Résidents Britanniques en France au XIXe Siècle: Une Approche Statistique', *Acta Geographica*, 4.76 (1988), pp. 19-35.

Gikandi, Simon. 'Englishness, Travel, and Theory: Writing the West Indies in the Nineteenth Century'. *Nineteenth-Century Contexts*, 18.1 (1994), pp. 49-70.

Gilroy, Amanda, ed. *Romantic Geographies: Discourses of Travel, 1775-1844*. Manchester: Manchester University Press, 2000.

Glendening, John. *The High Road: Romantic Tourism, Scotland and Literature, 1720-1820*. Basingstoke: Macmillan, 1997.

Goslee, Nancy Moore. 'Shelley at Play: A Study of Sketch and Text in His Prometheus Notebooks'. *Huntington Library Quarterly*, 48.3 (Summer 1985), pp. 211-55.

—. *Uriel's Eye: Miltonic Stationing and Statuary in Blake, Keats, and Shelley*. University of Alabama Press, 1985.

—. 'Shelley's "Notes on Sculpture": Romantic Classicism in *Prometheus Unbound*'. *The Comparatist*, 4 (1980), pp. 11-22.

Hale, J. R. 'Account of Rogers' Life and of Travel in Italy in 1814-1821'. *The Italian Journal of Samuel Rogers*. Ed. J. R. Hale. London: Faber and Faber, 1956.

Hall, Jean. *The Transforming Image: A Study of Shelley's Major Poetry*. Urbana: University of Illinois Press, 1980.

Hammond, John H., and Jill Austin. *The Camera Lucida in Art and Science*. Bristol: Adam Hilger, 1987.

Hayden, John O. *The Romantic Reviewers*. Chicago: University of Chicago Press, 1968.

Hayter, Alethea. *A Voyage in Vain: Coleridge's Journey to Malta in 1804*. London: Robin Clark, 1993.

Heppner, Christopher. 'Alastor: The Poet and the Narrator Reconsidered'. *Keats-Shelley Journal*, 37 (1988), pp. 91-109.

Hogle, Jerrold. *Shelley's Process: Radical Transference and the Development of His Major Works*. Oxford: Oxford University Press, 1988.

Holmes, Richard. *Shelley: The Pursuit*. London: Quartet Books, 1976.

Howcroft, Francis W. *Travels in Italy, 1776-1783, Based on the Memoirs of Thomas Jones*. Manchester: Whitworth Art Gallery, 1988.

Husenbeth, Frederick Charles. *The Life of the Right Rev. John Milner*. Dublin, 1862.

Huscher, Herbert. 'Alexander Mavrocordato, Friend of the Shelleys'. *Keats-Shelley Memorial Bulletin*, 16 (1965), pp. 29-38.

Hyde, Ralph. *Panoramania!: The Art and Entertainment of the 'All-Embracing' View*. London: Trefoil Publications, 1988.

Ingpen, Roger. *Shelley in England: New Facts and Letters from the Shelley-Whitton Papers*. London: Kegan Paul, Trench, Trubner and Co. Ltd, 1917.

Jarvis, Robin. *Romantic Writing and Pedestrian Travel*. Basingstoke: Macmillan, 1997.

Johnson, Paul. *The Birth of the Modern: World Society, 1815-1830*. London: Weidenfeld and Nicolson, 1991.

Johnston, William M. *In Search of Italy: Foreign Writers in Northern Italy Since 1800*. University Park and London: Pennsylvania State University Press, 1987.

Jordan, Frank, ed. *The English Romantic Poets: A Review of Research and Criticism*. New York: The Modern Language Association of America, 1985.

Keach, William. 'Obstinate Questionings: The Immortality Ode and *Alastor*'. *Wordsworth Circle*, 12 (Winter 1981), pp. 36-44.

Kessel, Marcel. 'An Early Review of the Shelleys' Six Weeks' Tour'. *Modern Language Notes*, 58 (Dec. 1943), p. 623.

Kipperman, Mark. 'Macropolitics of Utopia: Shelley's *Hellas* in Context'. In *Macropolitics of Nineteenth-Century Literature: Nationalism, Exoticism, Imperialism*. Eds Jonathan Arac and Harriet Ritvo. Philadelphia: University of Pennsylvania Press, 1991.

Kroeber, Karl. 'Experience as History: Shelley's Venice, Turner's Carthage'. *English Literary History*, 41 (1974), pp. 321-39.

Leask, Nigel. *Curiosity and the Aesthetics of Travel Writing 1770-1840*. Oxford: Oxford University Press, 2002.

—. *British Romantic Writers and the East: Anxieties of Empire*. Cambridge: Cambridge University Press, 1992.

Leighton, Angela. *Shelley and the Sublime: An Interpretation of the Major Poems*. Cambridge: Cambridge University Press, 1984.

Levinson, Marjorie. *Wordsworth's Great Period Poems: Four Essays*. Cambridge: Cambridge University Press, 1986.
—, et al. *Rethinking Historicism: Critical Readings in Romantic History*. Oxford: Basil Blackwell, 1989.
Literature of Travel and Exploration: An Encyclopedia. Ed. Jennifer Speake. 3 vols. New York and London: Fitzroy Dearborn, 2003.
Liu, Alan. *Wordsworth: The Sense of History*. Stanford: Stanford University Press, 1989.
Lynam, Edward, ed. *Richard Hakluyt & His Successors*. London: The Hakluyt Society, 1946.
MacCannell, Dean. *The Tourist: A New Theory of the Leisure Class*. Berkeley: University of California Press, 1999.
McGann, Jerome J. *The Romantic Ideology: A Critical Investigation*. Chicago and London: University of Chicago Press, 1983.
Mackenzie, John. 'Edward Said and the Historians'. *Nineteenth-Century Contexts*, 18.1 (1994), pp. 9-25.
McNiece, Gerald. *Shelley and the Revolutionary Idea*. Cambridge, MA: Harvard University Press, 1969.
Marshall, Roderick. *Italy in English Literature, 1755-1815: Origins of the English Romantic Interest in Italy*. New York: Columbia University Press, 1934.
Matthews, Geoffrey. 'A Volcano's Voice in Shelley'. *English Literary History*, 24. 3 (Sep. 1957), pp. 191-228.
Mead, Edward. *The Grand Tour in the Eighteenth Century*. Boston and New York: Houghton Mifflin, 1914.
Medwin, Thomas. *The Life of Percy Bysshe Shelley*. 2 vols. London: Thomas Cautley Newby, 1847.
Michasiw, Kim Ian. 'Nine Revisionist Theses on the Picturesque'. *Representations*, 38 (Spring 1992), pp. 76-100.
Mueschke, Paul, and Earl L. Griggs. 'Wordsworth as the Prototype of the Poet in Shelley's *Alastor*'. *PMLA*, 49 (1934), pp. 229-30.
Murray, E. B. 'Shelley's *Notes on Sculptures*: The Provenance and Authority of the Text'. *Keats-Shelley Journal*, 32 (1983), pp. 150-71.
Newey, Vincent. 'Shelley's "Dream of Youth": *Alastor*, "Selving" and the Psychic Realm'. *Percy Bysshe Shelley: Bicentenary Essays*. Cambridge: D. S. Brewer, 1992.
Parslow, C. C. *Discovering Antiquity: Karl Weber and the Excavation at Herculaneum, Pompeii, and Stabiae*. Cambridge: Cambridge University Press, 1995.
Paulson, Ronald. *Representations of Revolution (1789-1820)*. New Haven and London: Yale University Press, 1983.
Pulos, C. E. *The Deep Truth: A Study of Shelley's Scepticism*. Lincoln: University of Nebraska Press, 1962.
Oettermann, Stephan. *The Panorama: History of a Mass Medium*. Trans. Deborah Lucas Schneider. New York: Zone Books, 1997.
Raban, Joseph. 'Coleridge as the Prototype of the Poet in Shelley's *Alastor*'. *Review of English Studies*, n.s., 17 (1966), pp. 278-92.
Redford, Bruce. *Venice & the Grand Tour*. New Haven and London: Yale University Press, 1996.
Redpath, Theodore. *The Young Romantics and Critical Opinion, 1807-1824* London: Harrap, 1973.
Reynolds, Graham. *Turner*. London: Thames and Hudson, 1969.
Reiman, Donald H. 'Shelley as Agrarian Reactionary'. *Keats-Shelley Memorial Bulletin*, 30 (1979), pp. 5-15.

—. 'Roman Scenes in *Prometheus Unbound* III.iv'. *Philological Quarterly*, 46 (1 Jan. 1967), pp. 69-78.
—. 'Structure, Symbol, and Theme in "Lines Written Among the Euganean Hills"', *PMLA*, 77 (1962), pp. 404-13.
Richardson, Donna. 'An Anatomy of Solitude: Shelley's Response to Radical Scepticism in *Alastor*'. *Studies in Romanticism*, 31 (Summer 1992), pp. 171-95.
Robinson, Charles E. 'Percy Bysshe Shelley, Charles Ollier, and William Blackwood: the Contexts of Early Nineteenth-Century Publishing'. *Shelley Revalued: Essays from the Gregynog Conference*. Ed. Kelvin Everest. Leicester University Press, 1983. pp. 183-226.
—. *Shelley and Byron: The Snake and Eagle Wreathed in Fight*. Baltimore: Johns Hopkins University Press, 1976.
Rosenblum, Robert. *Transformations in Late Eighteenth Century Art*. Princeton: Princeton University Press, 1967.
Rossington, Michael. 'Shelley and the Orient'. *Keats-Shelley Review*, 6 (Autumn 1991), pp. 18-36.
Rutherford, Andrew. 'The Influence of Hobhouse on *Childe Harold's Pilgrimage*, Canto IV'. *Review of English Studies*, n.s., 12 (1961), pp. 391-7.
Schor, Esther H. 'Mary Shelley in Transit'. In *The Other Mary Shelley: Beyond Frankenstein*, eds Audrey A. Fish, Anne K. Mellor, and Esther H. Schor. New York and Oxford: Oxford University Press, 1993. pp. 235-57.
Scott, Grant. 'The Fragile Image: Felicia Hemans and Romantic Ekphrasis'. In *Felicia Hemans: Reimagining Poetry in the Nineteenth Century*. Eds Nanora Sweet and Julie Melnyk. London: Palgrave, 2001.
Scott, Winifred. *Jefferson Hogg*. London: Jonathan Cape, 1951.
Sha, Richard. *The Visual and Verbal Sketch in British Romanticism*. Philadelphia: University of Pennsylvania Press, 1998.
Shaw, Philip. *Waterloo and the Romantic Imagination*. London: Palgrave, 2002.
Strickland, Edward. 'Transfigured Night: The Visionary Inversions of *Alastor*'. *Keats-Shelley Journal*, 33 (1984), pp. 148-60.
Swinglehurst, Edmund. *Cook's Tours: The Story of Popular Travel*. Poole: Blandford Press, 1982.
Tetreault, Ronald. *The Poetry of Life: Shelley and Literary Form*. Toronto: University of Toronto Press, 1987.
Tomalin, Claire. *The Life and Death of Mary Wollstonecraft*. New York: New American Library, 1974.
Towner, John. *An Historical Geography of Recreation and Tourism in the Western World, 1540-1940*. Chichester: John Wiley & Sons, 1996.
Turner, Katherine. *British Travel Writers in Europe, 1750-1800: Authorship, Gender and National Identity*. Aldershot: Ashgate, 2001.
Turner, Louis, and John Ash. *The Golden Hordes: International Tourism and the Pleasure Periphery*. London: Constable, 1975.
Ulmer, William. *Shelleyan Eros: The Rhetoric of Romantic Love*. Princeton: Princeton University Press, 1990.
Vaughan, John Edmund. *The English Guide Book, c.1780-1870; An Illustrated History*. Newton Abbot; North Pomfret, VT: David & Charles, 1974.
Viswanathan, Gauri. *Masks of Conquest: Literary Study and British Rule in India*. New York: Columbia University Press, 1989.
Von Martels, Zweder, ed. *Travel Fact and Travel Fiction: Studies on Fiction, Literary Tradition, Scholarly Discovery and Observation in Travel Writing*. Leiden: E. J. Brill, 1994.

Walker, Carol Kyros. *Walking North with Keats*. New Haven and London: Yale University Press, 1992.
Wallace, Anne D. *Walking, Literature, and English Culture: The Origins and the Uses of Peripatetic in the Nineteenth Century*. Oxford: Clarendon Press, 1993.
Wallace, Jennifer. *Shelley and Greece: Rethinking Romantic Hellenism*. Basingstoke: Macmillan Press, 1997.
Wasserman, Earl R. *Shelley: A Critical Reading*. Baltimore and London: Johns Hopkins University Press, 1971.
Watkin, David. *Thomas Hope 1769-1831 and the Neo-Classical Idea*. London: John Murray, 1968.
Webb, Timothy. 'The Unascended Heaven: Negatives in "Prometheus Unbound"'. In *Shelley Revalued: Essays from the Gregynog Conference*. Ed. Kelvin Everest. Leicester University Press, 1983. pp. 37-62.
—. *The Violet in the Crucible: Shelley and Translation*. Oxford: Clarendon Press, 1976.
Weinberg, Alan M. *Shelley's Italian Experience*. London: MacMillan, 1991.
Weiskel, Thomas. *The Romantic Sublime: Studies in the Structure and Psychology of Transcendence*. Baltimore: Johns Hopkins University Press, 1976.
White, Newman Ivey. *Shelley*. 2 vols. London: Secker and Warburg, 1947.
Whitfield, J. H. 'Mr. Eustace and Lady Morgan'. In *Italian Studies Presented to E. R. Vincent on His Retirement from the Chair of Italian at Cambridge*. Ed. C. P. Brand, K. Foster, and U. Limentani. Cambridge: W. Heffer and Sons, 1962. pp. 166-89.
Wilkes, Joanne. *Lord Byron and Madame de Staël: Born for Opposition*. Aldershot: Ashgate, 1999.
Williams, Raymond. *Culture & Society: 1780-1950*. New York: Columbia University Press, 1983.
Wilson, Milton. 'Travellers' Venice: Some Images for Byron and Shelley'. *University of Toronto Quarterly*, 43 (1973-74), pp. 93-120.
Wilton, Andrew, and Ilaria Bignamini, eds. *Grand Tour: The Lure of Italy in the Eighteenth Century*. London: Tate Gallery Publishing, 1996.
Wood, Gillen D'Arcy. *The Shock of the Real: Romanticism and Visual Culture, 1760-1860*. New York: Palgrave, 2001.
Wordsworth, Jonathan. 'Introduction'. In Mary Shelley and Percy Bysshe Shelley. *History of a Six Weeks' Tour 1817*. Otley: Woodstock Books, 2002.
Wu, Duncan. *Wordsworth's Reading, 1770-1799*. Cambridge: Cambridge University Press, 1993.
Young, Robert. *White Mythologies: Writing History and the West*. London: Routledge, 1990.

Index

accuracy
  faithfulness, compared 122, 165, 169
  feeling of, Hall on 170-71
  in representation 122, 125 n.28, 166, 169, 181, 183, 219
  scientific 95 n.37
  visual 181
Addison, Joseph, *Remarks on Several Parts of Italy* 127, 161
aesthetic
  appropriation 49, 94, 99, 100, 128, 208, 236
  idealisation 40, 51, 63, 72, 77, 103, 197, 221
  vision 10, 50, 104, 117, 123, 138, 140, 145, 149, 157, 160, 163, 164, 165, 171, 179, 182, 184, 212, 236
aesthetics
  categories 98
    beautiful 17, 193
    picturesque 234 n 59
    sublime 17, 98, 99 n.47, 103-4, 109 n.75, 197
  as discourse 182, 183
  'eye of taste' 7, 55, 57, 59, 64, 65, 116, 123, 178
  and ideology 103
agriculture, and culture 212
Alison, Archibald 7
Allason, Thomas 126
Alps, Shelley on 86, 94
America
  Birkbeck on 205, 206 n.3, 208-9, 212-13
  Gibbon on 24, 213

  Niagara Falls 165
  revolutionary promise of 206
  Shelley on 210 n.17, 213, 233, 234
  wilderness 66, 70, 236
Amiens, Peace of (1802) 11, 13, 31, 126, 131
art, Shelley on 193-4
authenticity
  and perception 8, 179
  and travel 160, 176

Baillie, Marianne, *First Impressions...Italy* 123
Barker, Henry A. 124-5, 172
Barrell, John 37 n.88
Barrows, Herbert 6
Barthélemy, Jean-Jacques
  A Discourse... 133
  Voyage...en Grèce 133
Batten, Charles L. 14, 15, 85
Batty, Elisabeth 126
Baudrillard, Jean 211
beautiful *see under* aesthetics
Beckford, William 83, 87
Behrendt, Stephen C., *Shelley and His Audiences* 7 n.26
Bell, John, Dr 119
Bermingham, Ann 36, 103
Bhabha, Homi 46
Binfield, Kevin 181, 182
Birkbeck, Morris
  on America 205, 206 n.3, 212-13
  Notes on a Journey in America 205, 206-9, 212-13
  Notes on a Journey Through France 35
Birns, Nicholas 53, 74

Black, Jeremy 13
Blackwood's Edinburgh Magazine 84, 87, 96, 173
Blagdon, William, *Paris As It Was and As It Is* 15 n.18
Blunden, Edmund, *Shelley: A Life Story* 5 n.18
Bohls, Elizabeth 164
Bologna, Shelley's visit 159-60, 192
Bonaparte, Napoleon 13, 15, 32, 42, 125, 135, 153, 155
Bostetter, Edward E. 66
Bowles, William Lisle 165
Brinkley, Robert 82, 107
The British Critic 139
Bruce, James 169
Bruen, Matthias, Rev 165
Brydone, Patrick, *Tour through Sicily and Malta* 85, 86
Burke, Edmund
    on Europe 23-4, 28
    Reflections on the Revolution in France 18-20, 21, 22
Butler, Marilyn 23, 25
Buzard, James 127
Byron, Lord 141-2
    on the Coliseum 178-9
    WORKS
        Childe Harold 92, 93, 107, 125, 137-8, 142, 152-3, 159
            Greek Canto 217-18
            Italian Canto 165
            Peacock on 143-4
        Don Juan 227
        Manfred 178-9

Cambridge Hellenists 132
camera lucida 169, 173
    illustration 170
    use by Hakewill 170
    use by Hall 170-71
camera obscura 169, 173
Cameron, Kenneth Neill 25 n.50
Capitol *see under* Rome
Carothers, Yvonne 48
Carr, John, Sir 85

Stranger in France 42
Cascata delle Marmore
    illustrations 167-8
    Shelley's visit 161-72
Castlereagh, Lord 13
Chard, Chloe 134
Chios, Edward D. Clarke on 220-21
chivalry 19, 20, 23, 24, 27
Churchill, Kenneth 185
civilisation
    European 23
    Greek 216, 228, 235
    and imagination 22 n.42
    imperial imperative 90-91
    Italian 133
    and sensibility 115
Clairmont, Claire 5, 45, 52, 147, 172, 223
    Letters from Italy 119
Clark, Timothy 182
Clarke, Edward D. 142
    on Chios 220-21
    Travels 132, 218-20
Clubbe, William, *Three Days Tour into France* 42
Cobbett, William 210
Coleridge, Samuel Taylor 4, 45, 107, 113, 190, 210
    on the imagination 22
    travels 13-14
    WORKS
        Biographia Literaria 22
        'Hymn Before Sunrise' 88
Coliseum *see under* Rome
colonialism 18 n.26, 213-14
Colston, Marianne 126
Colwell, Frederick 6, 189-90
Copenhagen 55
Copley, Stephen 62
Coryate, Thomas 49 n.20
Coulson, Walter 5
Coxe, William, *Sketches of...Switzerland* 85
Crary, Jonathan 7, 169
Crook, J. Mordaunt 7, 134
Crook, Nora 116 n.1, 119 n.9

culture
   and agriculture 212
   classical 8, 128, 203
   definition 17
   European 15 n.18, 35, 53, 55, 91, 213
   Greek 132, 196, 225
   leisure class 23, 27
   and manners 23
   mass 3, 5, 10
   metropolitan 35, 63
   and nature 19 n.29, 41, 57, 79, 113, 195
   nature, resistant to 40
   Prometheus, as representative of 202
   Roman 156
   Romantic 164
   roturier 13
   Scandinavian 55
   and 'strategies of containment' 38, 39
   transmission 160
   travel 4, 119, 236
   visual 4, 5
   Western 204
   see also manners
Cunningham, J.W., *Cautions to Continental Travellers* 3-4
curiosity, and travel 3, 16, 121, 122
Curran, Stuart 46

Dabundo, Laura 64
Dante 193, 200
deism 45
discourse
   aesthetics as 182, 183
   gender 126, 164
   Leask on 'discourse of curiosity' 122
   of manners 27, 31
   travel 3, 8, 10, 17, 47, 147, 159
Dolan, Brian 2, 47, 132
Duffy, Edward 85
Duppa, Richard 15 n.18

Eaton, Charlotte, *Rome in the Nineteenth Century* 127, 174, 176
The Eclectic Review 84
Edinburgh Review 102, 103, 138, 212, 219, 234
Eisner, Robert 218 n.32
Elgin marbles, and Shelley 191
Elton, Charles 6 n.21
Englishness, 17 n.25, 64
   see also identity
ethnology, travel as 63, 64, 65
Europe
   Burke on 23-4, 28
   Gibbon on 24-5
Eustace, John C.
   A Classical Tour Through Italy 6, 123, 126, 127, 129, 130, 132-3, 134, 152, 176
   on Padua 155-6
   reviews 138, 139, 140
   on Rome 156-7
   use by Shelley 130-32, 135-7, 141-2, 148
   background 130-31
   on the French 127-8
   on the Italians 135, 152
Everest, Kelvin 148
eye
   as figure 7, 8
   reflexive 8 n.32
   'Shelley's eye' 8, 122, 145, 178
'eye of taste' *see under* aesthetics

Fabian, Johann 17 n.24
Favret, Mary 123
Ferguson, Frances 99 n.47, 113 n.78
Ferris, David 191 n.18
Florence, Uffizi Gallery 119
Forbes, James, *Letters from France* 14 n.12
foreign, concept 122
foreignness, and alienation 122
Forsyth, Joseph, *Remarks on Antiquities...* 126, 166, 169

reviews 138
Forum *see under* Rome
Foster, Shirley, *Across New Worlds* 12 n.4
France
   Restoration 92
   travel accounts 3, 13, 14 n.12, 15, 30, 32, 34-5, 42, 90, 124
Freistat, Neil 62, 72
French Revolution 2, 11, 13, 15, 18, 19, 20, 24, 28, 29, 30, 32, 35-6, 41, 42
   and travel 11, 13, 28-9
   travel writing 30-31

Gell, William, Sir 132
   Pompeiana 126
gender
   as discourse 123, 126, 164
   and subjectivity 10
genius
   Byron as 144, 159
   'genius of the place' 180
   'malady of genius' 56, 61
   and river metaphor 113
   Rousseau as 40-41, 111, 113
Gerbod, Paul 124 n.24
Gibbon, Edward
   on America 24, 213
   Decline and Fall... 23-4, 25, 109
   on Europe 24-5
Gikandi, Simon 17
Gilpin, William 2, 14, 37, 38, 47, 98, 164, 209
   'On Picturesque Travel' 99-100
Gisborne, Maria 142
Gisborne, Maria & Thomas 119-20
Godwin, William, *Political Justice* 29
Goslee, Nancy Moore 8 n.30, 190 n.12-13, 15
Graham, Maria, *Three Months...* 127
Grand Tour 1-2, 5, 13, 14, 64-5
   as cultural metaphor 10
   Italian cities 3

Greece
   Greek Revival 127, 134, 135, 180
   philhellenism 132
   revolution in 216, 217, 224, 235
   see also Magna Graecia
Griggs, Earl L. 45, 66, 73

Hakewill, James 126
   A Picturesque Tour of Italy... 130, 166, 170
   use of *camera lucida* 170
Hale, J.R. 85 n.12, 124 n.24
Hall, Basil
   on feeling of accuracy 170-71
   use of *camera lucida* 170-71
Hazlitt, William 43, 190
   Notes of a Journey... 42, 165
   'Travelling Abroad' 42
Heppner, Christopher 45
historiography
   of manners 27, 28, 42, 43, 54
   in travel writing 42, 43, 54, 55, 56
Hoare, Richard C. 3
   A Classical Tour... 129-30
   Hints to Travellers in Italy 1
Hobhouse, John Cam 138-9
   Historical Illustrations 138, 139
Hogg, Thomas Jefferson 5, 161
Hogle, Jerrold 45
Holcroft, Thomas, *Travels from Hamburg...to Paris* 31
Holman, James, *Narrative...* 126
Holmes, Richard, *Shelley: The Pursuit* 209 n.15
Hookham, Thomas, *A Walk Through Switzerland...* 84, 87, 88, 101
Hope, Thomas 132
   Anastasius... 226-7, 228
Hoppner, Richard B. 119
Hunt, Leigh 216
Huscher, Herbert 224 n.44, 225 n.47, 49, 227 n.54

identity
   'citizen of the world' 43, 47, 48, 64
   cultural 18

English 64
European 18
instability 100
international 17
literary 99
national 2, 51, 72, 100, 128
observation as self-identity 145
personal 43
ideology, and aesthetics 103
imagination
    Coleridge on 22
    colonial 73, 78, 208, 213
    Romantic 8, 22
    theory of 183
Ingpen, Roger, *Shelley in England* 5 n.18, 118 n.4
intertextuality 6, 158
Italians
    Eustace on 135, 152
    Shelley on 120, 143, 180, 185, 193
Italy
    Shelley's visit 6, 117-84
    travel books 124-30

Jameson, Anna 165
    Diary of an Ennuyée 140
Jarvis, Robin 2
Jerdan, William, *Six Weeks in Paris...* 4
Johnson, Paul 3
Joukovsky, Nicholas A. 118 n.3-4

Kames, Lord, *Elements of Criticism* 121-2
Kelsall, Charles 132
Kessel, Marcel 84
Kipperman, Mark 215, 229 n.57
Knight, Richard Payne 8, 58, 96 n.40, 109
    An Analytic Inquiry... 102
Kotzebue, Augustus von, *Travels through Italy* 161
Kroeber, Karl 200

Lake District
    guidebooks 64-5

tourism 2, 64
landscape
    description 3, 14, 15, 16, 36, 41, 71, 75 n.65, 83, 96, 103, 187
    Shelley on 187-8
language, of travellers 10, 80, 88, 96, 97
Leask, Nigel 121, 164, 169
    British Romantic Writers... 7, 46
    on 'discourse of curiosity' 122
Leighton, Angela 7 n.25, 97, 104 n.61
leisure 20, 27, 49, 164, 183, 209
    Shelley on 211
Levinson, Marjorie 37
Liu, Alan 58 n.35, 63 n.47, 73
London Magazine 140
Louis XVI 26, 30
Lucan, *Pharsalia* 149 n.102, 104

MacCannell, Dean 145 n.94, 146
Macdonald, Thomas, *Thoughts...* 47-8
McNiece, Gerald 33, 34
Magna Graecia 196, 216, 217
Malthus, Thomas 154
manners
    and culture 23
    definition 19-20, 21
    discourse 27, 31
    historiography of 27, 28, 42, 43, 54
Matthews, Geoffrey 148, 199
Matthews, Henry, *Diary of an Invalid* 121, 126, 140
Mavrocordatos, Alexander, Prince 224-5, 227-8
Mawman, Joseph 130
Medwin, Thomas 5 n.18, 131, 223, 224
memory 99, 106, 112, 163, 182, 221
    Mary Shelley on 107 n.68
    and oblivion 180
Michasiw, Kim I. 98
Michelangelo, Shelley on 193
Milner, John 131

Monson, W.J. 140
Mont Blanc, vision, Shelley 8, 97-9, 112
Monthly Review 83, 84, 87-8, 140
Moore, John, *A Journal...in France* 30-31
Moore, Thomas 125
Morgan, Lady 12, 16
   France 32-3, 35
   Italy 139-40, 141, 162
The Morning Post 13
Mueschke, Paul 45, 66, 73

Naples
   Lake Avernus 188
   Baia 117, 189 n.9
   Elysian Fields 188
   Grotto of the Sibyl 203
   La Scuolo di Virgilio 188
   Lazzaroni 135
   Shelley's visit 188
nationalism 214
   aesthetic 63
nature, and culture, 19 n.29, 41, 57, 79, 113, 195
Newey, Vincent 66 n.52
Nicholson, Francis, *The Practice of Drawing...* 163

oblivion, and memory 180

Padua
   Eustace on 155-6
   Shelley on 153-5
Paestum 117, 134, 161, 196, 197, 216
Paine, Tom, *Rights of Man* 29
painting 79, 164, 201
   picturesque 187
   and Shelley 6, 117, 136, 159, 186, 189, 190, 191, 192, 194, 200 n.26, 205
'panorama'
   Pompeii 173
   Rome 172-3
      illustration 175

Paris 11, 15, 26, 28, 31, 34, 55, 125 n.28
Peacock, Thomas Love 5
   on *Childe Harold* 143-4
   Shelley, correspondence 92, 94-5, 117-18, 143-4, 186-7
   WORKS
      Headlong Hall 102
      Nightmare Abbey 143, 144, 159, 190
Petrarch 35, 39, 144, 145, 146, 156
picturesque *see under* aesthetics
Pinkerton, John, *A General Collection...Voyages and Travels* 37 n.86, 86 n.18, 104 n.63
Piozzi, Hester Lynch 20 n.32
Playfair, William 42
   France as It Is 32
Plumptre, James, *The Lakers* 95-6
Pompeii 117
'panorama' 173
   Shelley on 189 n.9, 195
Pope, Alexander, *Eloisa to Abelard* 76
Price, Uvedale 58
primitivism 52, 236
   cultural 62, 71, 73
Prometheus, as representative of culture 202
Pulos, C.E. 70 n.58

Quarterly Review 85

Radcliffe, Ann, *Journey...* 85-6
Raffles, Thomas, *Letters during a Tour* 88
Raphael, *Cecilia* 117, 192
Redford, Bruce 141
Reiman, Donald 82, 83, 87, 199, 209-10
Reinagle,R.R., *An Explanation of the View of Rome* 178
Reynolds, Joshua, Sir, *Discourses on Art* 193
Richardson, Donna 45

Robinson, Charles 107
Rogers, Samuel, *Italian Journal* 85
    n.12, 124 n.24
Rome
    Baths of Caracalla 117, 119, 177,
        179 n.180, 184, 196, 199, 200
        n.26, 203, 222
    Borghese Gardens 119
    Capitol 4, 125, 172, 174, 176,
        199
    Coliseum 117, 128, 172, 180,
        183, 184, 203
        Byron on 178-9
        Shelley on 177-8, 181, 182
    Egeria fountain 190
    Eustace on 156-7
    Forum 2, 117, 172, 176, 177, 180
    Palatine 121, 137, 172
    'panoramas' 172-3
        illustration 175
    Pantheon 117, 172, 196, 197,
        199, 216
    Quirinal fountain 176
    St Peter's 117, 172, 174, 196,
        197, 198
    Shelley's visit 172-84
    Temple of Concord 180, 184
Rossington, Michael 46
Rousseau, Jean Jacques
    Shelley, influence on 108, 110-
        14
    on travel 62
WORKS
    Discourse on Inequality 62
    Julie... 84-5, 107, 111
Ruskin, John 176

Said, Edward 46
Saussure, Horace Bénedict de,
    Voyage dans les Alpes 86
Schlegel, A.W., *Lectures* 190, 191
Scott, John 3, 121, 159, 171
    on travel writing 122
Scott, Winifred, *Jefferson Hogg* 5
    n.19
sensibility, and civilisation 115

Sha, Richard, *Visual and Verbal*
    Sketch 164
Shaw, Philip 3
Shelley, Mary 5, 48-9, 50, 52
    on memory 107 n.68
WORKS
    Essays, Letters from Abroad 118,
        171-2
    Journals 91 n.31, 205
    'The English in Italy' 124
    'Valerius' 184
Shelley, Mary (co-author)
    History of a Six Weeks' Tour 5, 12,
        34, 42-3, 51, 52, 81-2, 87, 183
    aesthetics 104-15
    language 108
    reviews 83-8
Shelley, Percy Bysshe
    aesthetics, studies 7
    on the Alps 86, 94
    on America 210 n.17, 213, 233,
        234
    on art 193-4
    Bologna visit 159-60, 192
    at Cascata delle Marmore 161-72
    on the Coliseum 177-8, 181, 182
    and Elgin marbles 191
    France, travels in 20, 29, 34, 42,
        50
    Greece, plans to visit 5, 215,
        223-4
    health 116
    on the Italians 120, 143, 180,
        185, 193
    Italy, travels in 6, 117-84
    on landscape 187-8
    on leisure 211
    on Michelangelo 193
    Mont Blanc, vision 8, 97-9, 112
    Naples, visit 188
    on Padua 153-5
    and painting 6, 117, 136, 159,
        186, 189, 190, 191, 192, 194,
        200 n.26, 205
    Peacock, correspondence 92, 94-
        5, 117-18, 143-4, 186-7

on Pompeii 189 n.9, 195
Rhine voyage 49, 51, 52, 54, 85, 106
Rome, visit 172-84
Rousseau, influence of 108, 110-14
on ruins 195-6, 221-2
Switzerland, visit 8, 48, 89
on tourism 89-90
on travel 91-3, 120, 122-3
travel observer 8
travel reading 29-30, 31-4
travel sketches 8
on travel writing 120-21
travel writings 5, 42, 236
language 96-7
travels 5-6, 28-9
on Venice 149-53
on Vesuvius 187, 188-9, 199
Wordsworth, criticism of 45-6
WORKS
   Alastor 43, 45-80, 207, 208
     aesthetics 72-80
     influence of Wollstonecraft's *Short Residence* 53-63
     influence of Wordsworth's *The Excursion* 66-72
     Narrator in 72-80
     and Six Weeks' Tour 48-53
   The Cenci 118, 120 n.13, 131
   'The Coliseum' 118, 123-4, 179-82
   Defence of Poetry 22-3, 27, 34, 110, 171, 183
   A Discourse...Ancient Greeks 216, 217, 223, 228, 235
   Epipsychidion 220, 223, 224, 229
   Essay on Christianity 61
   The Excursion 49 n.19
   Hellas 109, 214, 225, 229-36
   Julian and Maddalo 118, 186, 222-3
     illustration 9
   Laon and Cythna... 8 n.32, 32, 33, 34, 106 n.67, 231 n.58
   'Letters from Italy' 118
   Lines Written...Euganean Hills 118, 123, 142-60
     language 147-9
   'Listen, listen, Mary mine' 147
   'Mont Blanc' 79, 81-115, 194-5
     reviews 87
   'Ode to Naples' 149 n.104, 189 n.9
   'On the Medusa of Leonardo da Vinci' 194 n.21
   'Ozymandias' 58, 156 n.118
   A Philosophical View... 25, 157, 206, 207, 209-10, 213, 215-16, 218, 222
   Prometheus Unbound 109, 116-17, 118, 198-204, 205-6, 207, 210-12, 214, 228
   Queen Mab 25, 30, 62, 89, 211
   A Refutation of Deism 45
   The Revolt of Islam 30, 34, 101, 109
   Rosalind and Helen... 145
   Symposium (Plato), translation 216, 217
   'To Wordsworth' 45, 230
   on Venice 149-50
Shelley, Percy Bysshe (co-author)
   History of a Six Weeks' Tour 5, 12, 34, 42-3, 51, 52, 81-2, 87, 183
     aesthetics 104-15
     language 108
     reviews 83-8
Shelley, Timothy 5, 118
Sheppard, John
   on tourism 90-91
WORKS
   Letters... 90
   'To Mont Blanc' 91
Smith, John, *Select Views in Italy...* 165-6
Smollett, Tobias 161
Society of Dilettanti 13
Southey, Robert 14
WORKS
   'God's Judgment on a Bishop' 49 n.20

Thalaba 51
spectator 8, 22, 173, 174, 177, 192, 193-4, 236
Staël, Madame de
  Corinne, or Italy 134-5, 185, 186
  on travel 122
Starke, Mariana, *Information and Directions for Travellers...* 127
Strickland, Edward 52
subjectivity, and gender 10
sublime *see under* aesthetics
Switzerland
  Shelley's visit 8, 48, 80
  travel books 83 n.6, 84, 101

Terni, Cascade *see* Cascata delle Marmore
Tetreault, Ronald 7
Thomas Cook 12
Tomalin, Claire 27
tourism
  agricultural 17 n.22
  classical 127, 138, 144, 188, 201
  commodification 164-5
  domestic 3
  geological 60
  John Sheppard on 90-91
  mass 10, 165, 170, 236
  pedestrian 2
  picturesque 2
  Shelley on 89-90
  statistics 124 n.24
  virtual 10, 173
Towner, John 1 n.3, 90 n.29, 124 n.24
travel
  and authenticity 160, 176
  culture 4, 119, 236
  and curiosity 3, 16, 121, 122
  discourse 3, 8, 10, 17, 47, 147, 159
  as ethnology 63, 64, 65
  and the French Revolution 11, 13, 28-9
  Madame de Staël on 122
  Rousseau on 62

Shelley on 91-3, 120, 122-3
travel books
  France 124
  Italy 124-7, 124-30
  Switzerland 83 n.6, 84, 101
travel writing 14-18
  French Revolution 30-31
  guidebooks 12
  historiography in 42, 43, 54, 55, 56
  John Scott on 122
  observer 7-8
  Shelley on 120-21
travellers
  language of 10, 80, 88, 96, 97
  women 12, 127
Traveller's Club 2, 13
Turner, J.M.W. 169, 170
Turner, Katherine 2, 47, 85

Ulmer, William, *Shelleyan Eros...* 7

Venice, Shelley on 149-53
Vesuvius 117
  Shelley on 187, 188-9, 199
Virgil, *Aeneid* 165, 166
Volney, C.F., *The Ruins* 25-6

Waldie, Jane, *Sketches Descriptive of Italy...* 127
Walker, Carol Kyros 205 n.2
Wallace, Ann 2
Wallace, Jennifer 133
  Shelley and Greece... 7
Wasserman, Earl 6
  Shelley 45
Waterloo, tourism 1, 3, 14
Webb, Timothy 216
Weinberg, Alan, *Shelley's Italian Experience* 6, 199, 201
West, Thomas 2, 47
  A Guide to the Lakes 65
Whale, John 37, 73
Wilkins, William 132
  The Antiquities of Magna Graecia 133-4

Williams, Helen Maria 12
  A Tour in Switzerland 16, 101
  Letters Written in France 29
Williams, Raymond 17
Winckelmann, Johann Joachim 190, 191, 193
Wollaston, William H. 169
Wollstonecraft, Mary 12, 20
WORKS
  An Historical and Moral View... 26-8, 29, 54
  Short Residence 105, 106, 147, 157
    influence on Shelley's *Alastor* 53-63
women, travellers 12, 127
Wood, Gillen D'Arcy, *The Shock of the Real...* 4
Woodring, Carl 228

Wordsworth, William
  Guide to the Lakes 64
  'I travelled among Unknown Men' 93
  'Ode' (Intimations Ode) 45
  'Preface' (to *Lyrical Ballads*) 40 n.94
  The Recluse 73
  The Excursion 46, 47, 48, 52, 54, 55, 64, 65, 73, 208
  influence on Shelley's *Alastor* 66-72
  The Prelude 28
  'Tintern Abbey' 100

Young, Arthur 20, 32
  on enclosure 36
  on landscape 39-40, 41, 50
  Travels in France 34-42
Young, Robert 46, 47